BRIT GUIDE

NEW YORK

2014

Amanda Statham

D0544008

foulsham
LONDON • NEW YORK • TORONTO • SYDNEY

foulsham

Capital Point, 33 Bath Road, Slough, Berkshire,
SL1 3UF, England

Foulsham books can be found in all good bookshops and
direct from www.foulsham.com

ISBN: 978-0-572-04418-3

Series, format and layout design © 2014 W. Foulsham & Co. Ltd

Cover photographs © 2014 Getty Images

Maps by PC Graphics (UK) Limited

A CIP record for this book is available from the British Library

The moral right of the author has been asserted

While every effort has been made to ensure the accuracy of all the information
contained within this book, neither the author nor the publisher can be liable for any
errors. In particular, since prices, times and any hotel, holiday or venue details tend to
change frequently, it is vital that each individual checks relevant information for him or
herself.

Look out for the latest editions in this series:
Brit Guide to Orlando and Walt Disney World, Simon and Susan Veness
Brit Guide to Disneyland Resort Paris, Simon and Susan Veness
Brit Guide to Las Vegas, Brit Guide Research Team

Typeset in Great Britain by Chris Brewer Origination
Printed in Dubai

Contents

Introduction

Welcome to the 2014 edition of the *Brit Guide to New York*, the guidebook that aims to be your very own personal tour guide to this amazing city.

We hope the guide will inspire you to want to visit the Big Apple again and again, for this is a city that really does capture the heart. Very few people only visit once and never return, simply because they're always left with the feeling that there's so much more to see and do.

As I write this, I've just returned from another great break, researching all the new things (and some of the old) happening in Manhattan for the Brit Guide. I enjoyed all my old favourites again, such as taking the Staten Island ferry past the Statue of Liberty (it's free!), taking in the Museum of Modern Art and strolling through Central Park in the early morning and being overtaken by joggers and yummy mummys with their prams. There are plenty of exciting new restaurants, bars and clubs (information about which you'll find in these pages) but don't forget that the classic New York experiences, such as going to the top of the Empire State Building, are fun whether you've done them once or ten times. Of course, once you've seen the sights, then it's time to start investigating the cosmopolitan neighbourhoods of the likes of SoHo, Greenwich Village and Chelsea and, in each new place you venture into, you'll discover a veritable treasure of shops, cafés, hotels and bars and witness the 'zoo' of residents going about their daily business.

53 million visitors from around the world visited the city in 2012 (figures for 2013 not available as we went to press), beating New York City's Mayor Bloomberg's goal of attracting 50 million tourists by 2015. Of the visitors, over 10 million hailed from overseas, with the UK as the Big Apple's biggest market. So what is it that makes us love this city so much?

One of the reasons is that we see it so often on television programmes and films, that it already feels familiar to us. When you consider that there are around 40,000 location shoots per year in the city, including 100-plus TV shows and more than 250 feature films, it's little wonder that we feel an affinity with New York.

Another reason for its magnetism is that it is a relatively new city that is in a constant process of renewal, regeneration and regrowth. Quite simply, there's always something new to see and do. This year there is set to be a dizzying array of new hotel rooms, global cuisine, blockbuster Broadway shows, exceptional exhibitions and incomparable shopping. The record number of visitors flocking to the city proves that the insatiable demand for all things New York continues to climb, despite the recent and ongoing recession.

BRITTIP
If you want to pay your respects at the 9/11 Memorial, this is also an ideal place from which to visit Wall Street and the Statue of Liberty, so give yourself time to explore Lower Manhattan.

Financial hardships and even terrorist activity doesn't hold New York back for long; foreign visitors from all over the world continue to pour into the Big Apple, trade is booming and it's brimming with life and excitement whichever neighbourhood you venture into.

THE NEW YORK STATE OF MIND
While New York is undoubtedly a melting pot of cultures and religions (Italians, Chinese, Jews, Africans, Irish and French to name but a few) there is one thing that unites everyone living in this cosmopolitan city: attitude. Resident New Yorkers are a breed unto themselves, unlike other American states where you're constantly instructed to 'have a nice day', they're not prone to saccharine

Broadway, New York

sweetness. Here's how to spot a genuine New Yorker: on face value, they tend to have a sort of totally cheesed-off-with-the-world, don't-mess-with-me look. They also speak incredibly quickly as if they were eating their own words, so it can sometimes be hard to understand them.

Scratch the surface, though, and you just have your ordinary, everyday kind of person with the same kind of worries, fears and doubts as the rest of us. We've discovered two things that work a treat: firstly, smiling like mad and being genuinely polite; secondly, the British accent. You can see them looking at you askance when you smile (smile? Who on earth does that in New York?), but then deciding that you must be one of those British eccentrics they've heard about. It does the trick, though, because more often than not they'll respond in a helpful way. In fact during my most recent visit, I was struck by how helpful people were, from assisting me at a Metro station steps with my luggage, to holding my place in a 'line' at a deli while I got some more olives, New York strangers couldn't have been friendlier.

And don't go thinking that all New Yorkers will tell you to f*** off if you ask for directions. Many are happy to help and we've even had people stop to help us work out where we're going when they've spotted us studying a map. This heady mix of rudeness and helpfulness is no better demonstrated than in the following anecdote from New York author Douglas Kennedy:

'On a crosstown bus I noticed two visitors from Japan having difficulty with the exact change for the fare,' he recounts. 'The driver, an overweight guy with a scowl, started giving them a hard time. "Like can't you read English or what?" he said loudly. "It says a buck-fifty. Surely they teach you how to count in Japan."

'The Japanese looked as if they wanted to commit hara-kiri on the spot until an elegantly dressed woman in her late sixties seated opposite the door came to their defence. Out of nowhere she turned to the driver and said: "Hey asshole, be polite."'

PLANNING YOUR HOLIDAY

One of New York's greatest charms is its cosmopolitan nature, its hugely diverse ethnic mix. In this city you will find any type of cuisine, often available at any time of the day or night. Where music is concerned, everything from jazz and R&B to techno and rap is out there on any night of the week and the many nightclubs are among the hottest and most stylish of any in the world.

BRITTIP

If you really want to get an insight into how a New Yorker thinks, log on to The New York Times website www.nytimes.com, and read the Metropolitan Diaries, stories of city life supplied by the locals.

The drawback is that it may seem a bit overwhelming and it doesn't help that everyone gives the impression of being in the biggest hurry. But beneath their ice-cool veneer, you'll find people willing to answer questions or offer help.

In this book, we hope not only to provide all the information you need about the sights, sounds and attractions, but also to give an insight into what makes the city tick and how to get the most out of it. The book is filled with tips and insider information, but we are always happy to receive new suggestions by email at travelamanda@hotmail.com.

Once you have decided to go to New York, you need to work out what you want to do there, otherwise you could end up wasting a lot of valuable time. The city is so big and diverse and everyone's tastes are so different that each visit to New York is a unique experience. Are you a museum buff? Want to see a great Broadway show and some of the outstanding sights of the city? Your priorities will reflect not only your tastes, but also whether it is your first visit to the Big Apple, or whether you are becoming an old friend, as well as the time you have available. Whatever the case, the key to making the most of your time is in the planning.

The thing we emphasise most is the importance of location. When you fly into New York, seeing all the skyscrapers from your lofty perch makes Manhattan look pretty small, but do not be fooled by this. It is a narrow island, but it's longer than it looks from the air – 21km/13mls in fact – so don't be duped into believing it is easy to walk from Downtown to the Upper East Side. Nothing could be further from the truth.

It's also the case that the city's subway is nowhere near as fast as our much-maligned London underground, nor is it that good for getting from east to west or vice versa. That means using buses is often the better option and they, like taxis, can get stuck in heavy traffic. So, when planning your activities for the day, it is a good idea to stick to one particular area so that walking everywhere – the best way to see the city – won't be so tiring.

Most New York trips are for between

two and seven days. For the former, it's like dipping your toes in the water; for the latter it's a big commitment to getting to know the city. Regardless of how many days you have, though, you won't be able to see everything, so you'll need to be selective.

HOW TO USE YOUR GUIDEBOOK

We've tried to help you with your choices in as many ways as possible.

- The top sights and museums are listed in alphabetical order so you can go straight to the ones you will most likely want to see.
- In each case the area they are in has been specified – again to help you plan your day.
- Look out for our 'Top 5s', which are scattered throughout the chapters. They give you instant snippets of information – for example, the best restaurants with an outside garden area, or the 5 best shops for accessories – and provide you with some insider knowledge.
- The same is true for our Brit Tips – facts and advice that you probably won't find elsewhere.
- Plus, enjoy our New Yorker In The Know tips. I've asked people living and working in the city to share their favourite spots with us, which has uncovered some real gems. Look out for these as they're scattered throughout the book and if you want to feel like a true New Yorker, hunt them out while you're there.
- The self-guide walks in Chapter 4 have proved popular. If you try them, do let us know what you think and whether you'd like longer ones, plus some walking guides

into the Outer Boroughs, too.

- If you are short of time, look out for One Day in New York on page 95 – which suggests my ideas on the best choices for a 24-hour trip.
- The chapters are designed around what most tourists want to do: take in a Broadway show (p217); choose from an eclectic range of excellent restaurants from our alphabetical area guide (p157); find their way around the different neighbourhoods and get the most out of what each one offers (p33).
- Since location is so vital, we recommend choosing your hotel in the area of the city in which you plan to spend most of your time. That way you can reduce the time and money you spend on getting around. Unless, of course, the hotel is the reason you're travelling to the city; for some people the experience of staying in exclusive accommodation such as The Waldorf is worth a visit to NYC before they've even thought about sightseeing.
- The street maps that follow all have their own QR code. Scan these to download a hi-res map to your phone or tablet.

We've tried to include everything we believe the average Brit will be interested in visiting in New York, but if you come across a sight, museum, shop, gallery, coffee shop, club, hotel or restaurant not in this book that you think is worth including, email us at travelamanda@hotmail.com.

Finally, I'd just like to wish you a wonderful trip to one of the greatest cities in the world.

Manhattan from the Circle Line Ferry

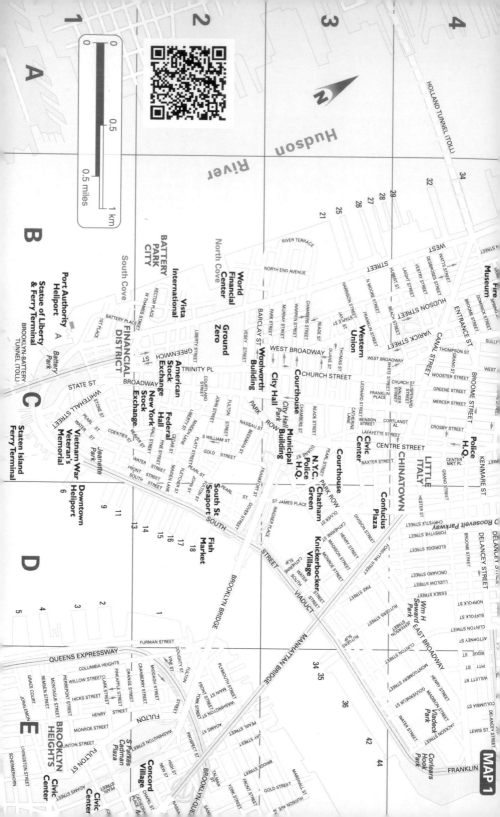

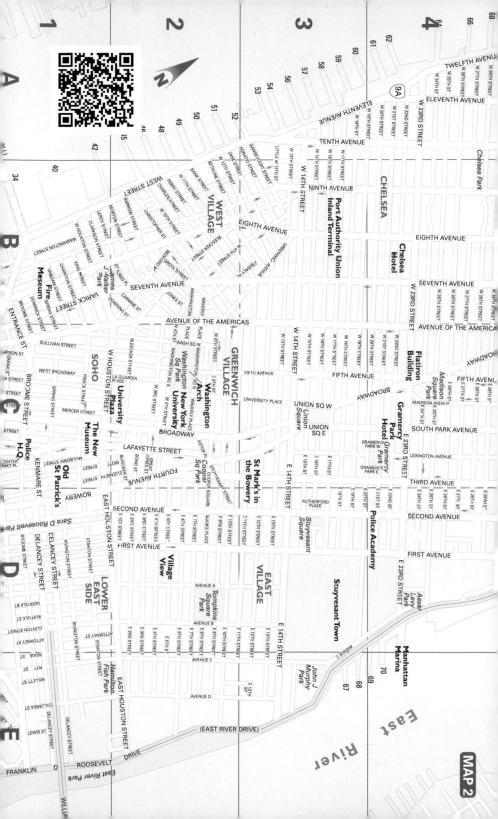

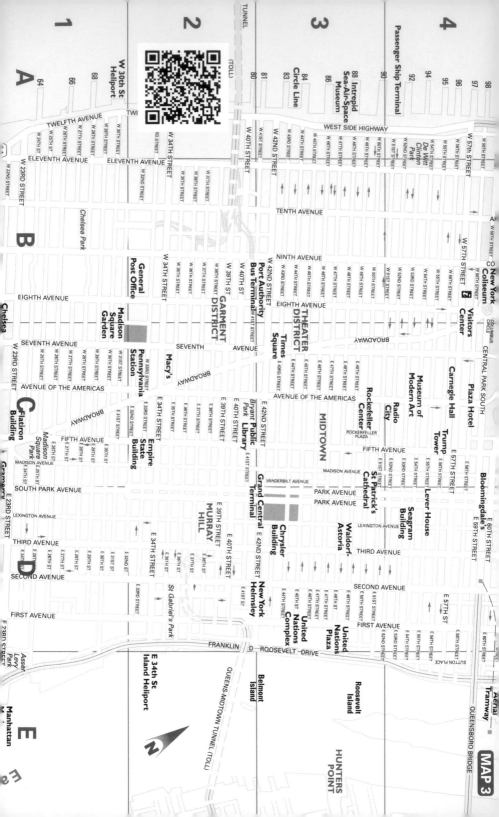

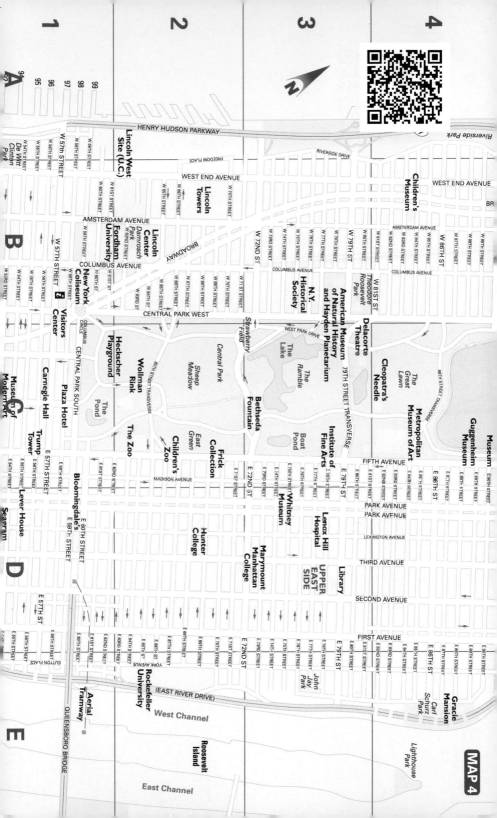

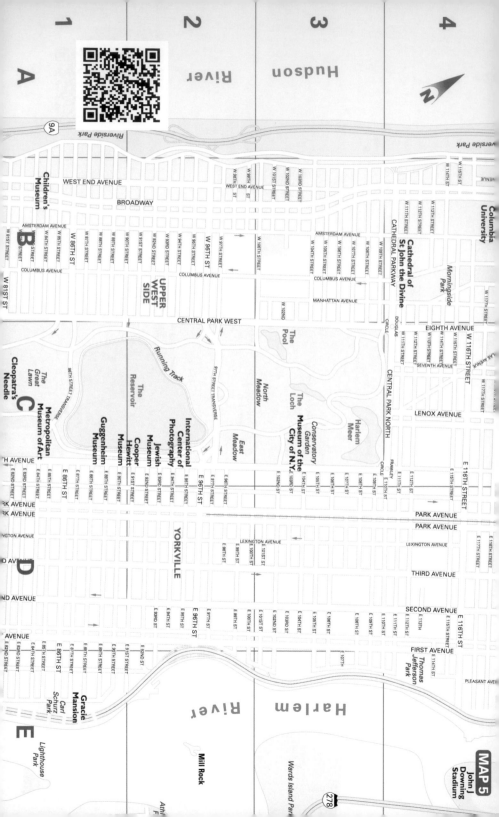

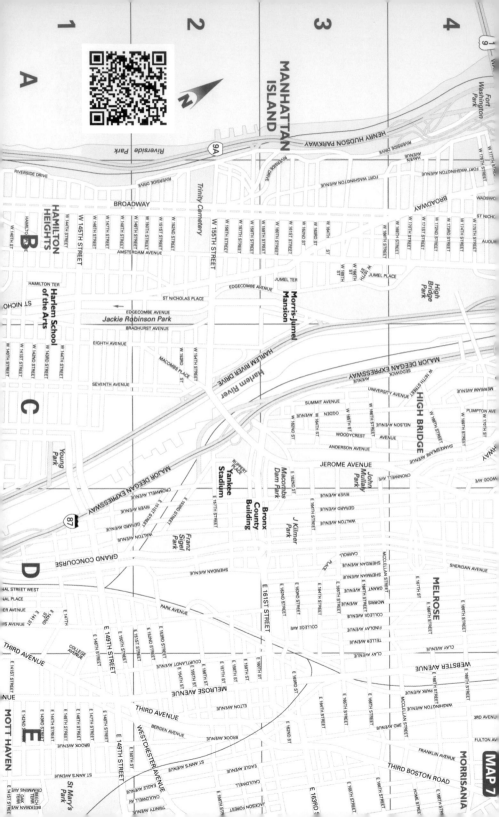

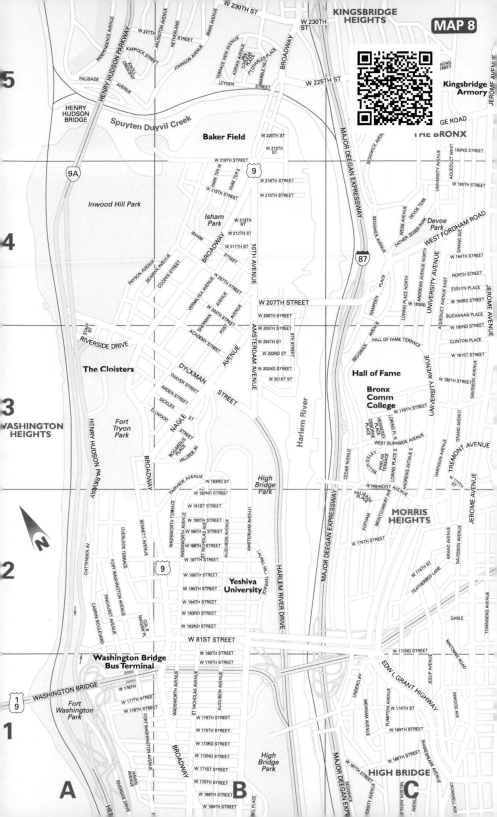

Manhattan Street Index

*Single bold number refers to map number
Alpha numerics refer to those within specified map*

STREET INDEX

Acknowledgements

With grateful thanks for all their help to Anna Catchpole at Hillsbalfour Synergy PR, which represents NYC & Co in the UK. All at NYC Visit.com, Niagara Falls Convention and Visitors Bureau and the New York State Department of Economic Development.

Thanks also to the Lower East Side Tenement Museum, the Metropolitan Museum of Art, Ellis Island Immigration Museum, the Museum of Modern Art, the Museum of Jewish Heritage, the Whitney Museum of American Art, Intrepid Sea-Air-Space Museum, the Frick Collection, the Skyscraper Museum, the National Museum of the American Indian, the Children's Museum of Manhattan, the Empire State Building, the American Museum of Natural History, the New York Stock Exchange, the Brooklyn Museum of Art, NY Waterways, the Sex And The City Tour, Harlem Spirituals, the Big Apple Greeters, David Watkins and Ponycabs, the Queens Jazz Trail, Gangland Tours, Big Onion Walking Tours, Rabbi Beryl Epstein and the Hassidic Discovery Center, former NYPD cop Gary Gorman, Gray Line, Food Tours of Greenwich, The Ritz-Carlton at Battery Park, The Warwick, The Mark, Waldorf Astoria, Le Parker Meridien, The Marriott Marquis, The Wellington, The Doral, Le Cirque, The Bull & Bear, The View at the Marriot Marquis, American Park at the Battery, Serafina Fabulous Grill, The Boathouse, Picholine, Sylvia's Restaurant, The River Café, The Water Club, World Yacht Dining Cruise, Europa Grill, The 21 Club, Tavern on the Green, Zoe's Restaurant and ONE c.p.s.

Photograph Acknowledgements

21 Club 172; 40/40 Club 216; 60 Thompson 244 top; Amy Ruth's 168; Arriba Arriba! 169 top; Art of Shaving 152; Asiate at the Mandarin Oriental 164; Audobon Center 272 bottom; Barney's 153; BB King Blues Club 212; Bongo 193; Bottino 160; Bronx Zoo 277; Brooklyn Children's Museum 105 bottom, 269; Buddy Don 149; Bull & Bear 176; Burger Joint at the Parker Meridien 173; Café Sabarsky 196; Carlton Hotel 252; Christopher Martin Hobson 1, 4, 7, 20, 24, 33, 48, 57, 72, 76 top, 77, 80, 81, 88 top, 92, 96 bottom, 97 bottom, 100, 101, 120, 140, 148, 197, 217, 220, 225 bottom, 244 bottom, 248, 256, 264, 265, 268 top, 272 top; Christopher Ong (2020chrisongblogspot.com) 245 bottom; City Club Hotel 232 bottom; Conrad Hotel 221; Cornelia Street Café 165; Crate & Barrel 144 bottom; Edison Hotel 233 top; Eventi Hotel 224 bottom; Four Seasons 177, 209; Fraunces Tavern Museum 109; Gansevoort Park Avenue 240 bottom; Ginger's 208 top; Hotel @ Times Square 233 bottom; Hotel Gansevoort 232 top; http://harlemcondolife.com 45; Ian Schrager and Nikolas Koenig (www.jenjuice8.wordpress.com) 229 top; Incentra Village House 228 top; Jay Parker 276; Jim Coyle 185 top; John Allen 56 bottom, 69, 76 bottom, 85, 96 top, 105 top, 132, 141, 257, 281; Julie Larson Maher 32; King & Grove 228 bottom; Le Bernadin 157; Lower East Side Tenement Museum 113; Macy's 260; Marcel at the Gramercy 229 bottom; Mario Burger, Burger International Inc. 280; McNulty's Tea & Coffee Co. (William Eng) 60; Midtown Comics 144 top; Molly Rigoloso 201; Murray's cheese shop 89 top; Museum of Chinese in America (Maya Lin Studio) 115; Museum of Modern Art 117; New York Transit Museum 112; NYC & Co. 168 bottom; Palm 180; Peculier Pub 204; Peter Aaron/Esto for the Jewish Museum 112; Picholine 192; Plaza 236 top; Pod Hotel 240 top; Premium Outlets Woodbury Common 156; Rao's 168 top; Red Cat 161; Richard Wilkins 5, 21, 25, 36, 49, 52, 53, 61, 73, 88 bottom, 89 bottom, 93 top, 97 top, 108, 125, 137, 212 top, 261, 268 bottom; Rickbern 93 bottom; Royalton 236 bottom; Russ & Daughters 136; Saks 5th Avenue 128; Salon de Ning 212 bottom; Shoreham 237 bottom; SoHo Grand 245 top; SPQR 169 bottom; Steve Brickles 145, 168, 184, 185 bottom, 205; Strip House 189; Townhouse 208 bottom; Tribeca Grand 249; Tribeca Grand 68; Tribeca Grill 188; W Hotel 54 top; Waldorf-Astoria 241 top; Warwick 237 top; www.centralparknyc.org 257; www.his-america.com 181; www.hostelworld.com 241 bottom; www.kidcityny.com 273; www.leatherboundbook.wordpress.com 200; www.localecologist.blogspot.co.uk 41; www.newyork-isnis.blogspot.com 44; www.somethingcleveraboutnothing.com 225 top

CHAPTER 1

Getting to Know New York

S o what is New York all about? Due to the vast number of films set in different periods of the city's history, many of the key people, sights and areas are familiar to us Brits, though you may be a little hazy as to their whereabouts or true influence. From unusual slang words and the best spots to get married to a brief history of how the city got its name and top visitor centre advice, this chapter is devoted to getting you in the mood to meet Manhattan.

A BRIEF HISTORY OF NEW YORK

The story of New York started in 1524 when Florentine Giovanni da Verrazano arrived on the island now known as Manhattan. It was a mixture of marshes, woodland, rivers and meadows, and was home to the Algonquin and Iroquois tribes of Native Americans.

No one settled on the island, though, until British explorer Henry Hudson arrived in 1609. Working for the Dutch West India Company, he discovered Native Americans were happy to trade in furs, skins, birds and fruit. By 1624 the Dutch West India Company was governing the area and Dutch settlers had arrived.

Manhattan was named New Amsterdam and governor Peter Minuit bought the island for $24-worth of trinkets and blankets. Peaceful relations were disturbed by the settlers' insistence on taking over the land,

and a costly and bloody 2½-year war ensued. Finally, Peter Stuyvesant, an experienced colonialist, came in to restore peace.

Stuyvesant went about establishing a strong community with a proper infrastructure. One of the first things he did was to order the building of a defensive wall and ditch along what we know today as Wall Street. The new settlement prospered and even doubled in size, but Governor Stuyvesant was not well liked. He introduced new taxes, persecuted Jews and Quakers, and even limited the amount of alcohol people could drink. The locals became less and less inclined to obey him. By the time 4 British warships sailed into the harbour in late 1664, he surrendered to Colonel Richard Nichols without a shot being fired. The colony was immediately renamed New York in honour of the Duke of York, brother to the English king, and remained in the hands of the British until the American Revolution.

By 1700, the population had reached 20,000 and it was already the rich melting-pot of cultures and religions that it remains today. In 1764, following the Seven Years War between the British and French, the Brits passed a number of laws, including the Stamp Act, allowing them to raise taxes in the colony. In response, Americans nationwide revolted and rescinded Britain's right to collect taxes. In 1774, the Americans set up the Continental Congress, made up of representatives from each of the colonies,

The Metlife Building

WHAT'S IN A NAME?

The Big Apple has become synonymous with New York City, but was popularised during the 1920s by horse-racing writer John Fitzgerald. On assignment in New Orleans for *The Morning Telegraph*, he overheard stablehands refer to New York City racing tracks as The Big Apple and decided to call his column on New York's racing scene 'Around the Big Apple'.

A decade later, jazz musicians adopted the term to refer to New York City. The story goes that when the musicians from Small's Big Apple jazz club in Harlem went on tour around America they'd say to each other: 'I'll see you in the Big Apple'. But the term was still relatively unknown until it was adopted by the New York Convention and Visitors' Bureau in 1971, when they launched The Big Apple campaign.

Many New Yorkers also like to call the city Gotham – taken from the Batman stories that are based in Gotham City and believed by many to be a thinly veiled reference to New York. The name Manhattan is derived from Mannahatta, or 'land of many hills', the name given to the island by its first inhabitants, the Algonquin.

who urged all Americans to stop paying taxes. Two years later, the Declaration of Independence was drawn up, largely by Thomas Jefferson.

During the War of Independence that inevitably followed, New York was considered strategically vital, as it connected the New England colonies with the southern colonies. In 1776, British commander Lord Howe sailed 500 ships into the harbour and occupied the city. George Washington's army was defeated and forced to leave. The peace process began in 1779 and led to a treaty in 1783. The Brits, who had remained in New York since the end of the war, left just before George Washington returned to claim victory.

New York then became the country's first capital and George Washington its first president, taking his oath of office in 1789. The city was capital for just 1 year, but business boomed. The New York Stock Exchange, established under a tree on Wall Street by Alexander Hamilton in 1792, positively buzzed with activity as new companies were set up, bought and sold.

As the city grew, it became clear that a proper infrastructure and sanitation system was needed, so the governors introduced a grid system throughout the entire island. North of 14th Street, it abandoned all the existing roads except for Broadway, which followed an old Native American trail, and set up wide avenues that ran south to north and streets that ran between the rivers.

TOP 5 BOOKS SET IN NEW YORK: TRY BEFORE YOU FLY!

Truman Capote: *Breakfast at Tiffany's*

J.D Salinger: *The Catcher in the Rye*

Edith Wharton: *The Age of Innocence*

Mario Puzo: *The Godfather*

Candace Bushnell: *Sex and the City*

THE RICH GET RICHER...

By 1818, reliable shipping services between New York and other American cities and Europe were well established and trade was booming. It was boosted further by the opening of the Erie Canal in 1825, which, together with the new railroads, opened trade routes to the Midwest. With so much spare cash to play with, businessmen started to build large summer estates and mansions along 5th Avenue up to Madison Square. At the same time, many charities and philanthropic institutions were set up and great libraries were built, as education was seen as being very important.

But the divide between rich and poor was getting wider. While water supplies, indoor plumbing and central heating were being installed in 5th Avenue mansions, thousands of immigrant families – particularly from Ireland – were living in the appalling tenements erected on the Lower East Side of Manhattan.

The impending Civil War over the question of slavery became a major issue for the poor of New York, who couldn't afford to buy their way out of conscription. Uppermost in their minds was the concern that freed slaves would be going after their jobs. The fear reached fever pitch and led to America's worst-ever riot, a four-day-long affair in which over 100 people died and thousands, mostly blacks, were injured. By 1865, however, the abolitionists won the war, finally freeing 4 million black people from the plight of slavery.

At the same time, New York and Boston were being hit by great tidal waves of immigrants. In the 1840s and 1850s it was the Irish fleeing famine; in the 1860s it was the Germans fleeing persecution; and in the 1870s it was the Chinese, brought into America specifically to build the railroads. In the 1880s it was the turn of the Russians, along with 1.5 million Eastern European

Jews. Over 8 million immigrants went through Castle Clinton in Battery Park between 1855 and 1890. The Ellis Island centre was built in 1892 and handled double that number. Between 1880 and 1910, 17 million immigrants arrived, and by 1900 the population had reached 3.4 million.

Most of the new arrivals ended up in the crowded Lower East Side tenements. Finally, in 1879, after the terrible conditions were brought to light, the city passed housing laws requiring landlords to increase water supplies and toilets, install fire escapes and build air shafts between buildings to let in air and light. The introduction of streetcars and elevated railways helped to alleviate the transport problem.

THE GILDED AGE

Meanwhile, the wealthy were enjoying the Gilded Age, as Mark Twain dubbed it. Central Park opened in 1858 and mansions were built on 5th Avenue for the likes of the Whitneys, Vanderbilts and Astors. Row houses were also built on the Upper West Side for wealthy European immigrants. Henry Frick, who made his fortune in steel and the railroads, built a mansion (now a museum) on the east side of the park at 70th Street, 10 blocks from the new Metropolitan Museum of Art. Luxury hotels such as the original Waldorf Astoria and the Plaza opened, as did the original

BEAT IT

The 1950s Beat Movement was a partly social, partly literary phenomenon centred on Greenwich Village, New York, the North Beach in San Francisco, and Venice West in Los Angeles. Socially, the movement was all about rejecting middle-class values and commercialism and embracing poverty, individualism and release through jazz, sexual experience and drugs. The term 'beat' conveys not only the American connotations of being exhausted, but also suggests 'beatitude'. The chief spokesmen were Allen Ginsberg, Jack Kerouac, whose most famous novel is *On The Road* (which became a film in 2012), Gregory Corso, William S. Burroughs, Lawrence Ferlinghetti and Gary Snyder.

Metropolitan Opera House. The Statue of Liberty, St Patrick's Cathedral, the Brooklyn Bridge and Carnegie Hall were all built during this time.

The names of people we associate with New York were from this time: like Cornelius Vanderbilt, a shipping and railroad magnate; Andrew Carnegie, a steel and railroad baron; and John D. Rockefeller, who made his millions in oil. The names of many of these millionaires live on in gifts given to the city: they provided concert halls, libraries and art museums, and donated entire collections

USEFUL WEBSITES

www.askanewyorker.com Your questions answered by real life New Yorkers.

www.cityguideny.com The online site of the weekly *City Guide* that is provided to hotels, with all the latest events, activities, etc.

www.newyork.citysearch.com Packed with information on New York, events and what's happening.

www.clubplanet.com Complete list of what's cool, where and why; the final word on nightlife.

www.manhattanusersguide.com The insider's guide to what's going on where.

www.downtownny.com Directory of places to visit in Downtown.

www.nyc.gov Comprehensive information about the city's services.

www.nyctourist.com An official tourism site for the city.

www.nycgo.com The New York Convention and Visitors' Bureau's comprehensive listing includes suggested itineraries for where to stay and shop and what to do.

www.nymag.com The latest information on city news, politics, restaurants, bars, clubs and entertainment.

www.nytab.com The New York Travel Advisory Bureau's site is helpful for trip planning and gives information on major savings.

www.newyorkology.com Everything from arrivology to technology!

www.newyork.com Just-launched website with up-to-date listings aimed at both locals and tourists.

www.nytimes.com The *New York Times* website.

www.villagevoice.com The *Village Voice* website.

to put in them. Carnegie built and donated Carnegie Hall to the city, Rockefeller was a major backer of the Museum of Modern Art, and the Whitneys created a museum containing their own collection of modern American works of art.

The turn of the century also saw the birth of another phenomenon: the skyscraper. First to be built was the Flatiron Building in 1902, which was constructed using the new technology for the mass production of cast iron. Frank Woolworth's Gothic structure followed in 1913. The beautiful Chrysler Building went up in 1929 and the Empire State Building was completed in 1931.

PROHIBITION ARRIVES

The Volstead Act of 1919 banned the sale of alcohol at the start of the Roaring Twenties. Fuelled by lively speakeasies, illegal booze, gangsters, the Charleston and jazz, this was the heyday of famous venues like Harlem's Cotton Club and the Apollo Theater. The fun and frolics came to an abrupt end with the collapse of the Wall Street stock market in 1929. It destroyed small investors and led to unemployment and poverty across the whole of America. Things started to improve only after President Franklin D. Roosevelt introduced the New Deal, employing people to build new roads, houses and parks.

In New York, Fiorello LaGuardia (pronounced La-gwar-dia), was elected mayor and set up his austerity programme to enable the city to claw its way back to financial security. During his 12 years in office, LaGuardia worked hard at fighting corruption and organised crime, and introduced a massive public housing project.

BRITTIP

One of the most famous speakeasies during Prohibition was Jack & Charlies 21. You can visit it today as the rather more respectable 21 Club at 21 West 52nd Street (212-582 7200, www.21club.com).

These were also the days of a great literary and artistic scene in the city. Giants of the spoken and written word, including Dorothy Parker and George Kaufman, would meet at the famous Round Table of the Algonquin Hotel, where they were joined by stage and screen legends Tallulah Bankhead, Douglas Fairbanks and the Marx Brothers.

The Second World War was another watershed for New York, as people fled war-ravaged Europe and headed for the metropolis. Both during and after the war, huge new waves of immigrants arrived, fleeing first the Nazis and then the Communists. New York was as affected by McCarthy's hunt for 'reds' among the cultural and intellectual elite as was the rest of the country, but it bounced back when a new building boom followed the election of President Harry S. Truman, whose policies were aimed at helping the poor.

The Port Authority Bus Terminal was finished in 1950, the mammoth United Nations Headquarters was completed in 1953, and in 1959 work started on the huge Lincoln Center complex – built on the slums

The Supreme Court

Macy's

of the San Juan district that were the setting for *West Side Story*.

By the 1950s, a new period of affluence had started for the middle classes of New York. The descendants of the earlier Irish, Italian and Jewish immigrants moved out to the new towns outside Manhattan, leaving space for a new wave of immigrants from Puerto Rico and the southern US. The Beat generation evolved into the 1960s hippy culture and Greenwich Village became the centre of a new wave of artists extolling the virtues of equality.

By the 1970s, however, this laissez-faire attitude, coupled with New York's position as a major gateway for illegal drug importation and the general demoralisation of the working classes and ethnic groups, led to an escalation in crime. Muggings and murder were rampant, and the city was brought to the brink of bankruptcy.

Chaos was averted only by the introduction of austerity measures, which mainly affected the poor. New mayor Ed Koch implemented major tax incentives to rejuvenate the business community. A boom followed, reflected in the erection of a series of mammoth skyscrapers, including the World Trade Center and Trump Tower.

In the 1990s, Mayor Giuliani's clean-up operation was unpopular with liberal New Yorkers, but many believe it was his policies that turned New York into a city fit for the new millennium.

Most recently, the city has been known around the world for the dark day of 11 September 2001, when terrorists in two hijacked planes destroyed the twin towers of the World Trade Center and killed nearly 3,000 people. It's typical of the spirit of this vibrant city that it has come back even stronger than before. After all, from the time of the earliest immigrants, New York has represented a gateway to a new life: the American dream offered a future filled with happiness and success. And nowadays New York still draws in people in their millions. After all, as the Sinatra song goes, 'If you can make it there, you'll make it anywhere'.

THE BEST TIMES TO GO

Jan to Mar, and July and Aug are best for accommodation and good for flights. Just bear in mind that July and Aug are the hottest months, though it is not as bad as you might expect because all the shops and cabs have air-conditioning and you get blasts of cool air from the shops as you pass.

BRITTIP
Get a 4-day prediction from www.weather.gov to make sure you've got the right clothes.

SEASONAL WEATHER

Month	Temperature	Rainfall
Jan	-3–3°C/27–38°F	8cm/3in
Feb	-3–5°C/27–40°F	8cm/3in
Mar	1–9°C/34–49°F	11cm/4¼in
Apr	7–16°C/44–61°F	10cm/4in
May	12–22°C/53–72°F	10cm/4in
June	17–27°C/63–80°F	8cm/3in
July	20–29°C/68–85°F	10cm/4in
Aug	19–29°C/67–85°F	10cm/4in
Sep	16–25°C/60–77°F	9cm/3½in
Oct	10–19°C/50–66°F	9cm/3½in
Nov	5–12°C/41–54°F	11cm/4¼in
Dec	-1–6°C/31–42°F	10cm/4in

AT-A-GLANCE HISTORY

1524	Giovanni da Verrazano arrives on Manhattan
1613	Trading post is set up at Fort Nassau
1624	Dutch West India Company establishes rule of New Amsterdam
1626	Peter Minuit buys Manhattan for trinkets worth $24
1664	Dutch surrender to the British and New Amsterdam is renamed New York
1776	War of Independence and battle for New York begins
1785	New York becomes the nation's capital
1792	New York Stock Exchange is founded
1811	Grid plan for Manhattan is introduced
1827	Slavery is officially abolished in New York
1858	Work on Central Park begins
1883	Brooklyn Bridge opens
1886	Statue of Liberty is built
1892	Ellis Island opens
1902	The Fuller (Flatiron) Building becomes the world's first skyscraper
1904	New York's first subway line opens
1919	Prohibition Act sees alcohol sales banned in New York
1923	Yankee Stadium opens
1929	New York stock market crashes
1931	Empire State Building opens
1950	United Nations building completed
1970	First New York City Marathon
1993	A terrorist bomb in the World Trade Center kills six and injures 1,000
1994	Rudy Giuliani appointed mayor and brings crime to an all-time low
2001	World Trade Center Twin Towers attacked by terrorists, killing nearly 3,000 people

WHAT TO PACK

Layers are the key to comfortable clothes in New York, whatever time of year you go.

In summer the air-con in buildings can get pretty cold, while outside it is stiflingly hot. A lightweight, rainproof jacket is a good option.

BRITTIP

To inspire kids of 8–12, get a copy of *Melanie in Manhattan* by Carol Weston (www.melaniemartin. com), a novel about a girl and her family travelling in the Big Apple. Or buy a copy of Disney's *Eloise at the Plaza* DVD.

Natural fibres, like silk or cotton, in light shades are good for humidity and, of course, sunscreen is essential.

In winter it is the other way round – warm buildings and cold streets – so it's best to have a warm but not too heavy coat; or

TOP 5 ATTRACTIONS FOR KIDS

Circle Line Sightseeing Cruise (p86)

Statue of Liberty (p71)

Empire State Building (p73)

Times Square (p52)

Central Park (p261)

warmer if you're planning to be out of doors a lot. Make sure you have a hat, scarf and gloves in your bag just in case. At any time of the year, the skyscrapers of the city act as a kind of wind tunnel and unless you're in the sun it can get nippy pretty quickly – another reason to make sure you have a cardigan or lightweight jacket in the summer.

NEW YORK FOR FAMILIES

New York is a great place to take the family. Towering skyscrapers, mammoth bridges, vast parks, circuses and shows, bright lights and rows of shops packed with enticing kid-friendly products are enough on their own to keep children entertained. But there are plenty of other attractions to hunt out that can make a stay in NYC for the under-16s even more exciting. Central Park, for example, has a wealth of entertainment year-round, while some of the museums offer some real hands-on, fun activities. A word of warning: visiting any of the incredible children's stores with a real-life child in tow is likely to lead to credit card meltdown!

DISABLED TRAVELLERS

New York is one of the easier destinations to tackle for disabled travellers – and certainly puts Britain to shame. Most of the road corners, for instance, have kerbs that dip to the ground, making it a lot easier to wheel yourself about the city. Again, for the wheelchair-bound, bus platforms can be lowered to the same level as the pavement to allow easy access and, where possible, some of the subway stations have lifts. To make your life as easy as possible, here are the main organisations that deal with different aspects of travel for the disabled.

Note: TDD or TTY = Telecommunications devices for the deaf.

Able-Ride: This is a shared-ride kerb-to-kerb bus service for disabled visitors in New York State (516-228 4000, www.nicebus.com/ Accessibility).

Access-A-Ride: AAR is a 24-hour door-to-door shared ride service for people who are unable to use the subway or bus; proof of disability is needed. (877-337 2017 toll free or 718-393 4999/4259 (TTY) 7am–5pm for information and to reserve a trip, www.mta.info).

Accessible NYC: A coalition of New York City businesses that work together to cater to travellers with disabilities. (1-718 507 0500, www.accessiblenyc.org).

Big Apple Greeter Access Coordinator: Has been running a disability Access Programme since 1993. Will provide a free tour guide for anyone with a disability. Reserve 3–4 weeks ahead (online or by post), 212-669 8159, www.bigapplegreeter.org).

Hands On: Provides accessibility to arts and cultural events for the hard of hearing through sign-interpreted performances and a monthly cultural calendar of accessible events (212-740 3087/TTY use relay 711, https://handson.org).

Hospital Audiences Inc (HAI): Has an online access-for-all database that provides comprehensive information on venue access, toilet facilities and water fountains at a whole range of cultural centres from theatres to museums. Its audio description service, Describe, for people who are blind or visually impaired includes programme notes that describe all aspects of a show and staging on a CD you can listen to before the performance. Also, during a pause in the dialogue it transmits a live audio description to audience members who have a small receiver. Reservations for both the tickets, which have to be bought either through HAI or the theatre, and receivers, which are provided free of charge, must be made through HAI (212-575 7676, http://hainyc.org).

Lighthouse International: Help and advice for blind people living in or visiting the city

NEW YORK TALK

Of course, in addition to the differences between American and Brit-speak, the locals have a dialect and phraseology all of their own, or *slanguage* as it's known, and often talk so quickly that words run into each other. Here are just a few examples:

8th Wonder of the World: Brooklyn Bridge
Big one: A $1,000 bill
Bloomies: Bloomingdale's
Brownstone: Terraced city house (usually brown!)
Capeesh: Pronunciation of capisce, Italian for 'understand'
Cattle call: A theatre casting call
Dead soldier: Empty beer can or bottle
Do me a solid: Do me a favour
Don't jerk my chain: Don't fool with me
DPh: Damned fool, based on transposing PhD
Enough already: Stop it, that's enough!
Finger: Pickpocket (also mechanic, dip, cannon, goniff or moll buzzer)
Fuggedaboduid: No way
Go to Jersey: An insult
Guppies: Gay yuppies
How awe ya? Typical greeting
In line: Stand in a queue
JAPs: Jewish American princesses
Jocks: Sporty types, after their straps
Mazuma: Slang for money
Meet me between the lions: A favourite meeting place: the lion statues at the New York Public Library
Met: The Metropolitan Opera House or the Metropolitan Museum
No problem: You're welcome
Nudnik or nudge: A persistently dull and boring person
On account: Because
Out in left field: Weird, unorthodox
Ozone: Very fresh, pure air
Shoot the works: Gamble or risk everything
Stoop: Steps leading up to a house, usually a brownstone
Straphanger: Subway commuter
Suit: Businessman
Yard: Back garden

(212-821 9200 (voice) or 212-821 9713 (TTY), www.lighthouse.org).

MTA: To find out which 59 stations are accessible to wheelchair passengers, check www.mta.info/accessibility. For up-to-date information on the accessibility status of lifts and escalators, call 718-596 8585/8273 (TTY) daily 6am–10pm. Recent initiatives have included a reduced-fare MetroCard for the disabled – apply online – and induction loops at stations for the hard of hearing.

New York Society for the Deaf: Provides advice and information on facilities for the deaf (212-366 8400, 212-524 1789 (TTY), www.fegs.org).

ScootAround: You can rent a wheelchair on arrival with this 7-day, 24-hour service (888-441 7575, www.scootaround.com).

Society for Accessible Travel and Hospitality: Has been a leader in this field for decades, raising awareness of the needs of disabled travellers (212-447 7284, www.sath.org).

The Theater Access Program: TAP is specifically for Broadway shows and is run by the Theater Development Fund (TDF). There's an accessibility programme to make theatre going easier for those hard of hearing, with low vision or who are blind, who cannot climb stairs or who require aisle seating or wheelchair locations (212-912 9770, www.tdf.org).

Vega Transportation: Vega offers the luxury of a chauffeur-driven car for those in a wheelchair (888-507 0500, www.vegatransportation.com).

COMMUNICATIONS

Toll-free calls for booking lines or attractions when in New York save on costs and are mentioned when available. These start with the codes 800, 888, 866 and 877.

PHONES

To call New York from abroad: Dial 001 and the prefix – for instance, the main prefix for Manhattan is 212 – then dial the 7-digit number. The codes for Brooklyn, Queens, The Bronx and Staten Island are 718 and 347. Mobile phones usually use the 917 prefix.

BRITTIP

Make sure your mobile phone has tri-band and that you've told your phone operator, otherwise it may not operate in the US. Also, make sure your mobile call plan covers calls and texts from foreign countries, or you'll be charged a fortune!

To call abroad from New York: Dial 011 + country code + area code (dropping the first 0) + local number. The code for Britain is 44.
To call any number in New York from New York: Dial 1 + the area code + the number.
Useful numbers
Operator: 0

Directory enquiries: 411 (free from payphones)
Long-distance directory enquiries: 1 + area code + 555 1212
Free numbers directory: 1 + 800 + 555 1212 (no charge)

POST

You can buy stamps (first class stamps are 46c each) in shops – the Duane Reade chain of chemists has machines – but there is a mark-up. If you don't want to pay over the odds, go to one of the many post offices dotted around the city (800-275 8777, www.usps.com).

The main post office on 8th Avenue at West 33rd Street is a huge and beautiful Beaux Arts building. If the queues are long, you can buy stamps from the vending machines.

Post boxes are square, dark blue metal boxes about 1.2m/4ft tall with a rounded top that has a pull-down handle. They have a sign saying US Mail and a striking big American eagle logo on the side and can be found on street corners.

THE INTERNET

The internet revolution now means you can use your smart phone, laptop or BlackBerry all over the city, plus have access online in cafés, libraries and even bars. In fact, there are now thousands of wi-fi spots in Manhattan including 178 in cafés, so you're going to be able to surf whenever you like! Here are a few trusted places you can stop off for a surf.

Wi-fi cafés:
Abingdon Guest House/Brewbar Coffee: 327 West 11th Street between Greenwich and Washington Streets, 212-675-7365, www.abingdonguesthouse.com/brewbar.shtml.
Ace Bar: 531 East 5th Street between Avenue A and Avenue B, 212-979 8476, www.acebar.com.
Gorilla Coffee: 97 5th Avenue Brooklyn, 718-230 3244, www.gorillacoffee.com.
Housing Works Used Book Cafe: 126 Crosby Street between Houston and Prince Streets, 212-334 3324, www.housingworks.org/bookstore/cafe-menu.
Starbucks: 450 7th Avenue, 212-279 1122, www.starbucks.com.

Libraries/shops with free internet access:
Apple Store: 767 5th Avenue, 212-336 1440, www.apple.com. Free wi-fi, workshops and demos.
Mid-Manhattan Library: 455 5th Avenue at 40th Street, 212-340 0863, www.nypl.org.
NY Public Library: 40 Lincoln Center Plaza, 212-870 1630, www.lincolncenter.org.

Internet cafés:
Cybercafé: 250 West 49th Street between Broadway and 8th Avenue, 212-333 4109, www.cyber-cafe.com. Open 8am–11pm Mon–Fri and 11am–11pm Sat–Sun and costs $6.40 for half an hour on the internet.

🇬🇧 BRITTIP

If you want to surf the web and get a snack at the same time, Cybercafe (cyber-cafe.com) has some great packages, such as Surf & Dine for $5.75, which includes 15-minute computer usage, tea or coffee and a pastry.

AMERICAN-SPEAK

It has often been said that the Brits and Americans are two races divided by a common language, and when you make an unexpected faux pas you'll certainly learn how true this is. So to help you on your way, here is a guide to American-speak.

General

English	American
Air hostess	Flight attendant
Anti-clockwise	Counterclockwise
At weekends	On weekends
Autumn	Fall
Behind	In back of
Camp bed	Cot
Cinema	Movie theatre
City/town centre	Downtown (not Lower Manhattan)
Coach	Bus
Cot	Crib
Diary (appointments)	Calendar
Diary (records)	Journal
Football	Soccer
From... to...	Through
Lift	Elevator
Long-distance call	Trunk call
Nappy	Diaper
Ordinary	Regular, normal
Paddling pool	Wading pool
Plaster	Band Aid
Post, postbox	Mail, mailbox
Pram, pushchair	Stroller
Receptionist	Desk clerk
Tap	Faucet
Toilet	Restroom (public) or bathroom (private)

Money

English	American
Banknote	Bill
Bill	Check or tab
Cash machine	ATM
Cheque	Check
1 dollar	Single
25 cents	Quarter
10 cents	Dime
5 cents	Nickel
1 cent	Penny

🇬🇧 BRITTIP

There are no ground floors in America; what we call the ground floor, they call the first floor. It may seem a silly point, but it can cause confusion!

Food and drink

If you opt for a fried breakfast, you need to sort out your terminology before you go! Order eggs 'sunny-side up' and you'll end up with what seems like a half-cooked egg! The Americans don't flick fat over the top of the egg when frying it, but turn it over to cook on both sides, so for eggs cooked on both sides but soft, order eggs 'over easy' and if you like yours well done, then ask for eggs 'over hard'.

There are plenty of other differences, such as a British 'biscuit' is a cookie, whereas an American 'biscuit' is a corn scone. You'll find food terms specific to New York on p178.

English	American
Aubergine	Eggplant
Biscuit (savoury)	Cracker
Biscuit (sweet)	Cookie
Chick pea	Garbanzo bean
Chips	(French) fries
Choux bun	Cream puff
Clingfilm	Plastic wrap
Cornflour	Cornstarch
Courgette	Zucchini
Crayfish	Crawfish
Crisps	Chips
Crystallised	Candied
Cutlery	Silverware or place-setting
Demerara sugar	Light-brown sugar
Desiccated coconut	Shredded coconut
Digestive biscuit	Graham cracker
Double cream	Heavy cream
Essence (e.g. vanilla)	Extract or flavouring
Filled baguette	Sub or hero
Fillet (of meat/fish)	Filet
Fizzy drink	Soda
Golden syrup	Corn syrup
Grated, fried potatoes	Hash browns
Grilled	Broiled
Icing sugar	Powdered/confectioners' sugar
Jam	Jelly/conserve
Jelly	Jello
Ketchup	Catsup

TIPS ON TIPPING

You need to get used to the fact that you tip for everything in the US – from a meal to a door being opened for you. Just remember, at a posh restaurant the tip alone can come to more than the price of a decent meal!

Bartender: $1–2 a round.

Hotel doormen: $1–5 for hailing a cab/bringing bags in.

Maid service: Around $3–5 per day when you leave your accommodation.

Porters: $2–5 per bag.

Taxi drivers: 15%, and if you travel by private car or limousine they'll automatically add 20%.

Waiters: 15–20%. The best way to work it out is to double the sales tax, which will come to 17%, and add a little more if you are very impressed.

Just remember, at a posh restaurant the tip alone can come to more than the price of a decent meal!

King prawn	Shrimp
Main course	Entrée
Measure	Shot
Mince	Ground meat
Off-licence	Liquor store
Pastry case	Pie shell
Pips	Seeds (in fruit)
Plain/dark chocolate	Semi-sweet or unsweetened chocolate
Pumpkin	Squash
Scone	Biscuit
Shortcrust pastry	Pie dough
Single cream	Light cream
Soda water	Seltzer
Sorbet	Sherbet
Soya	Soy
Spirits	Liquor
Sponge fingers	Lady fingers
Spring onion	Scallion
Starter	Appetiser
Stoned (cherries, etc.)	Pitted
Sultanas	Golden raisins
Sweet shop	Candy store
Takeaway	To go
Tomato purée	Tomato paste
Water biscuit	Cracker

Shopping

English	American
Braces	Suspenders
Bumbag	Fanny pack
Chemist	Drug store
Flip-flops	Thongs
Ground floor	First floor
Handbag	Purse
High street	Main street
Jumper	Sweater
Knickers	Panties
Muslin	Cheesecloth
Queue	Line, line up
Suspenders	Garters
Tights	Pantyhose
Till	Check-out
Trainers	Sneakers
Trousers	Pants
Underpants	Shorts, underwear
Vest	Undershirt
Waistcoat	Vest

Travelling around

English	American
Aerial	Antenna
Articulated truck	Semi
Bonnet	Hood
Boot	Trunk
Caravan	House trailer
Car park	Parking lot
Carriage (on a train)	Car
Crossroads/junction	Intersection
Dipswitch	Dimmer
Dual carriageway	Four-lane (or divided) highway
Flyover	Overpass
Give way	Yield
Jump lead	Jumper cables
Layby	Pull-off
Lorry	Truck
Manual transmission	Stickshift
Motorway	Highway, freeway, expressway
Pavement	Sidewalk
Request stop	Flag stop
Ring road	Beltway
Roundabout	Traffic circle
Slip road	Ramp
Subway	Pedestrian underpass
Turning	Turnoff
Underground	Subway
Walk	Hike
Wheel clamp	Denver boot
Windscreen	Windshield
Wing	Fender
Zebra crossing	Cross walk

BRITTIP

New Yorkers may consider themselves broad-minded, but it's not the done thing to ask where the toilet is. Ask for the restroom in a public place and the bathroom if you're in someone's house!

TOURIST INFORMATION

NYC & COMPANY CONVENTION & VISITORS' BUREAU

www.nycgo.com

London: 020 7367 0900 (line open Mon–Fri 9.30am–5.30pm). New York City's official tourism agency – call to discuss any queries you have with the information officers or ask them to send you a *Visitors' Guide*, also downloadable online.

New York: 3rd Floor, 810 7th Avenue between 52nd and 53rd Streets, 212-484 1222. Mon–Fri 8.30am–6pm; Sat and Sun 9am–5pm. Subway N, R, Q to 49th Street, B, D, E to 7th Avenue/53rd Street or 1 to 50th Street/Rockefeller Center. Email enquiries can be sent to: visitorinfo@nycgo.com.

BRITTIP
While you're at the NYC visitor centre, pick up a copy of the *NYC Guide*. It has up-to-date listings of Broadway shows, plus money-off coupons.

This state-of-the-art visitors' information centre in Midtown has touchscreen kiosks that provide up-to-date information on the city's attractions and events accompanied by a detailed map. There is also a cashpoint and a souvenir shop, plus an incredible range of brochures covering hotels, shops, museums, sights, tours and Broadway shows. There are also visitors' centres in Downtown, Chinatown, Harlem and the Financial District.

BRITTIP
Sign up for the NYC&Co newsletter, which is packed with great deals, recommendations and the latest events and is sent straight to your email inbox.

LOST YOUR PASSPORT?

If you lose your passport or have any big problems, call the emergency number at the New York British Consulate on 212-745 0200 option 2, www.ukinusa.fco.gov.uk/en.

CURRENCY

The world is slowly emerging out of the global recession, which thankfully means the pound is getting stronger against the dollar (at the time of going to press) so we'll get a little more for our money. The exchange rate for the US dollar at the time of writing is around $1/£0.66, but this is fluctuating constantly (check www.xe.com for exchange rates before

you go). UK banks' and travel agencies' rates vary, so shop around to find the best. Also check the commission – some will charge for both selling and buying back, but many will only charge once, so you can return unused dollars you bought from them free of charge. Travel agencies tend to compete with each other on rates and don't charge commission. The Post Office and Marks & Spencer, among others, do not charge commission.

BRITTIP
For a quick currency converter go online to www.xe.com/ucc/, which also offers the latest exchange rates.

Some people still use travellers' cheques, but it is often a real palaver to cash them, especially at banks in New York. Many banks simply won't take them, and if they do they'll need photo ID so you'll have to carry your passport around. Chase Bank, Manhattan has more than 400 branches and doesn't charge a fee for exchanging currencies. Visit www.chase.com to find a branch with full contact details, including phone numbers.

The alternative is to exchange a reasonable amount of cash in one hit to use for tips, buses and in cafés, then use your credit card as much as possible (the exchange rate is generally reasonable). If you need extra cash, make sure you know your PIN number for your credit card and you'll be able to use any of the many cashpoints (ATMs), for which there is usually a fee.

BRITTIP
You must have plenty of change and singles ($1 notes) as you'll be tipping everyone for everything, and you'll also need change for buses.

DISCOUNT DIVAS

NYC & Co (www.nycvisit.com) in its Deals

TOP 5 PLACES TO PROPOSE

Just in case you haven't got down on one knee yet, here are some of the most idyllic spots to ask for her (or his) hand:

- Top of the Empire State Building
- By the boating lake in Central Park
- In a helicopter flying over the city
- The penthouse suite of the Four Seasons
- A $10,000 Martini at the Algonquin Hotel – it's a mix of vodka, vermouth, olive and ice, except that the ice is a sparkling diamond from the hotel's jeweller!

section runs various money-off campaigns that cover restaurants, hotels, theatres and sightseeing tours and things to do that 'don't cost a dime' under its Free section.

Each year, the popular Summer Restaurant Week takes place for 2 weeks from mid-July when you can get 3-course meals at more than 150 of the city's top restaurants for around $25 (excluding tip, tax and drinks). There's also a Winter Restaurant Week, which usually runs from mid-Jan to early Feb. Many restaurants also continue serving their prix-fixe lunches to the end of Aug. Establishments include Nobu, Union Square Café, Spice Market, 66, Blue Water Grill and Vento. For further information and to sign up for alerts, visit www.nycvisit.com/restaurantweek or phone either 1-800 NYC VISIT (toll-free within America) or 212-484 1222.

> **BRITTIP**
> Smoking is banned in most indoor places, and in taxis, buses and subways. There's a list of smoker-friendly restaurants, clubs and bars on http://newyork.citysearch.com.

TYING THE KNOT IN NEW YORK

If you're thinking about getting married in the city, then you've picked a top spot, because the Big Apple is one of the most popular places for Brits to marry abroad.

NYC Marriage Bureau: It's best to get it all booked before you go, so for all the legal aspects of a wedding in New York, such as the minimum age, documentation and costs (City Clerk of New York in Manhattan), 141 Worth Street, NY 10013, dial 311 in New York or 212-NEW YORK, www.cityclerk.nyc.gov).

There's no shortage of exceptional places to marry in New York, but here are just a few ideas for locations.

Central Park: The obvious place for an outdoor ceremony is not difficult to organise. The Central Park Conservancy grants the permits for wedding ceremonies and photography in venues throughout the park, including the lovely Conservatory Garden and Shakespeare Garden (212-360 2766, www.centralparknyc.org).

> **BRITTIP**
> To get a better grasp of all the great NYC wedding venues check out the Great Places Directory, www.greatplacesdirectory.com, for ceremony and reception locations.

Gotham Hall: A historic landmark in Midtown Manhattan that is a great venue for occasions such as weddings, holding from 25 to over 1,000 guests (1356 Broadway at 36th Street, 212-244 4300, www.gothamhallevents.com).

Hotels: Most upmarket hotels will accommodate weddings, so be sure to contact the ones we've listed in our accommodation section (Chapter 9) for some of the best in town.

New York Aquarium: For an unusual venue (610 Surf Avenue at West 8th Street, Coney Island, Brooklyn, 718-265 FISH, www.nyaquarium.com).

The Lighthouse and Pier Sixty at Chelsea Piers: For an intimate affair to remember (23rd Street at 12th Avenue, 212-336 6144, www.piersixty.com).

If you're gay and planning a wedding, you'll be pleased to know that New York's Marriage Equality Act was signed recently, allowing same-sex couples to marry legally in the city. Log on to www.cityclerk.nyc.gov/html/marriage/same_sex_couples_faq.shtml for more details.

New York Aquarium

CHAPTER 2
New York Neighbourhoods

Each neighbourhood of Manhattan has a distinct flavour and is filled with its own unique sights and sounds. From the historic Downtown area of the Financial District to the charming cobbled streets of Greenwich Village and the vibrancy of Times Square, every one is well worth visiting.

Here's an outline of what you'll find in each neighbourhood, what makes them so special and how to make the most of your time there. They are placed in alphabetical order for ease of reference and each one has an at-a-glance table to co-ordinate your planning, plus a QR code which links to a high-res downloadable map.

34TH STREET

34th Street at a glance: Empire State Building and shopping

Nightlife:	Live music	212
Parks:	Herald Square	34
Shopping:	Department stores	141
Sights:	Empire State Building	73
	Madison Square Garden	76
	Penn Station	34

Subways to get there:
B, D, F, N, Q, R, V, W to 34th Street/Herald Square and 1, 2, 3, 9 to 34th Street–Penn Station

You'll have two major reasons for coming to this part of New York (Map 3) – the divine **Empire State Building** (p73) and the shopping. **Macy's** is here (p141), as well as a range of chains and a lot of retail outlets for the nearby Garment District. This was once a pretty seedy area, but thanks to the efforts of the 34th Street Business Improvement District Partnership (BID), it has been transformed.

Throughout this chapter, scan the QR code to download a hi-res map of the neighbourhood to your smartphone or tablet.

Now the streets are constantly maintained, clean and lined with pretty flower tubs and green benches. The BID has even installed some smart green telephones with a semi-enclosure to block out some of the street noise.

If you plan to do the Empire State Building, make it your first port of call before the crowds and queues build up. Take the B, D,

View from the Empire State Building

F, N, Q, R, V, W to 34th Street and walk one block east to 5th Avenue where you'll find the beautiful Art Deco entrance.

Once you've come back down to earth, take a cheap coffee break at the **365 Express** at the little-known Graduate Center (www.gc.cuny.edu) at 365 5th Avenue on the corner of 34th Street, diagonally opposite the Empire State Building. You'll need photo ID to sign in as a visitor, but you can can buy filtered coffee or a luscious latte with a croissant and sit in relative peace at any time of the day before 4pm, which is when the graduates start pouring in. The building used to be a department store, which is why there are ribbons and ties sculpted into the exterior columns. Now it is used as a research centre for students and holds free concerts.

HERALD SQUARE

Named after the now defunct newspaper, Herald Square is home to the famous **Macy's** (www.macys.com), one of the world's largest retail outlets Prior to Macy's opening in 1901, the area was down-at-heel, with lots of bordellos and seedy clubs. The opening of the store was a fashion moment and improved the entire district.

For the grown-ups there is the wonderful **Cucina & Co.** (p144) in the basement. A combination of buffet foods to eat in and take away, a grill restaurant and a coffee shop, it also has a sandwich station, pasta station and take-aways at incredible prices. Bearing in mind the average New Yorker spends $10 for a sandwich-style lunch and drink, Cucina's lunches are amazing value, as are their meal specials.

But don't expect it to look cheap; this is a wonderful space filled with fabulously fresh food in an indoor-market setting. Adjacent to it is **Macy's Cellar Bar & Grill**, where you can order a delicious Angus beef Cellar Burger and fries for $16.

LITTLE KOREA

This tiny neighbourhood is expanding rapidly and is a great place to visit for lunch or dinner, thanks to the many excellent restaurants packed into West 31st and West 32nd Streets.

Situated in the Herald Square area, next to the Garment District and Chelsea in the west, Little Korea is part of the melting pot of nationalities that have made New York their home. In the 1980s more than a million immigrants, a large percentage from Asia, took over various corners of the city, such as this one. Bordered by some of New York's major landmarks, this small area lies in the shadow of the Empire State Building, only a couple of blocks away from Macy's on 6th Avenue, and near Penn Station.

As well as the great restaurants, such as **Gam Mee OK** at 43 West 32nd Street and **Han Bat** at 53 West 35th Street (open 24 hours Mon–Sun), there are also Korean bookshops, beauty salons and a great supermarket selling all sorts of exotic produce until 2am.

SHOPPERS' PARADISE

Between 5th and 8th Avenues on 34th Street is a shopper's paradise. Read all about it in Chapter 6 (p125).

BRITTIP

The main taxi ranks for Penn Station are on 7th Avenue opposite the Pennsylvania Hotel and on 8th Avenue opposite the Beaux Arts General Post Office. If you want a taxi from here, it's best to walk a block north as the queues can get quite long, or use the A, C, E, 1, 2, 3, 9 subways at 34th Street–Penn Station.

PENN STATION

One block south on 33rd Street and 7th Avenue is the entrance to **Penn Station**, short for Pennsylvania Station. Before you enter you'll see a **Lindy's** pastry shop.

BRITTIP

The original Lindy's in the theatre area was famous for its cheesecake. The Lindy's here and the branch in Times Square trade off the name, but they're pricey and not unique.

As you enter Penn Station, you'll see a handy **Duane Reade** (think Boots the chemist) on the left. Walk down to the round area under the **Madison Square Garden** building and on your left you'll see the information booth for the **34th Street BID Partnership**. All around are coffee shops, bakeries and a sit-down restaurant called **Kabooz** – an okay joint for a quick American bite and a beer (it also has clean toilets, much better than the ones in the station, so nip in here if you're desperate!).

CHELSEA

Chelsea at a glance: Art galleries, clubbing and gay NY

Accommodation:	224
Gay:	206
Museums and galleries:	

Subways to get there:
A, C, E line to 14th Street

Scan QR code for hi-res map of Chelsea

Only likely to be on your list of places to see if you like art galleries, clubbing or if you're gay, Chelsea is worth a visit to see an up-and-coming area. Originally farmland in 1750, by the late 1800s it was a commercial area filled with slaughterhouses, warehouses and the working classes. The mixture of sought-after brownstone townhouses and warehouses have made it a perfect target for artists priced out of SoHo, and although it's still rough around the edges, many of the quaint streets and buildings have been restored.

It is bounded by 6th Avenue (Avenue of the Americas) in the east, the Hudson river in the west, 16th Street in the south and 29th Street in the north. If you get off the subway at 14th Street and walk north on **8th Avenue**, you'll see the main drag of restaurants, shops, bars and gyms. Along the way you'll notice an abundance of Chippendale-type male bodies – the neighbourhood's gay boys, who love to flaunt their pecs in the local nightclubs.

At the corner of 19th stands the **Joyce Theater** (www.joyce.org), famous for dance and its Art Deco building. A little further north and you're not only in the **Chelsea Historic District** – the blocks around 9th and 10th Avenues at 20th, 21st and 22nd Streets – but also at the heart of the new gallery community between 10th and 12th Avenues.

First port of call should be the **Dia Art Foundation** (www.diacenter.org), a 4-storey, 3,700m^2/40,000ft^2 warehouse, which opened in 1987 and still plays a pivotal role in the art world. Other great galleries nearby include **LFL/Zach Feuer, Leslie Tonkonow, Meulensteen, 303 Gallery** and the **D'Amelio Terras Gallery**. Two blocks north on 24th Street is the 1,950m^2/21,000ft^2 **Gagosian Gallery, Matthew Marks, Barbara Gladstone Gallery** and the **Andrea Rosen Gallery**. Photographer **Annie Leibovitz**'s studio is on 26th.

CHELSEA HOTEL

One of the most infamous of New York's hotels, the Chelsea Hotel (or Hotel Chelsea as it is officially known, www.hotelchelsea.com) is not only still going strong, but is also in the midst of a great revival. Before Sex Pistols front man Sid Vicious moved in with his girlfriend Nancy Spungen and allegedly killed her, back in the 1970s, famous inhabitants included Mark Twain, Dylan Thomas, William S. Burroughs, Arthur Miller and Arthur C. Clarke.

Built in 1883 and named a historic landmark in 1966, its lobby walls are covered with plaques commemorating venerated guests and their artworks, while the Spanish El Quijote restaurant is famous for its lobster. Unfortunately it's currently closed for refurbishment (there's no information on when it will reopen its doors), so keep checking the website for details.

CHINATOWN AND FIVE POINTS

Chinatown and Five Points at a glance:
Chinese restaurants and markets

Subways to get there:
A, C, E, J, M, N, Q, R, W, Z, 6 to Canal Street

Scan QR code for hi-res map of Chinatown

The sprawling mass that is Chinatown (Map 1) has spread its wings north into the remnants of Little Italy, east into the Lower

East Side and south in the Civic Center area. It is also home to the infamous Five Points, once the most dangerous part of New York. Its name is derived from the 5 streets that intersect next to Columbus Park. Originally called Orange, Mulberry, Anthony, Little Water and Cross Streets, they are now known as Bayard, Park, Worth, Mulberry and Baxter.

In the 1820s, a pond graced a lovely area where the rich had their country homes, but they started sub-letting to tanners, who polluted the lake. Attempts to get rid of the dreadful smells by building a canal down Canal Street failed, and in the end only the poorest came to live in the area, including freed slaves and immigrant blacks.

> **BRITTIP**
> Have a game plan when visiting Chinatown – it's easy to feel daunted by all the bustle.

Irish immigrants arrived in the 1850s, then Italians and Eastern Europeans in the 1880s. Poverty was rife, and gangs flourished. The streets were not safe for the police to patrol, and at least one person was killed each night. For almost 100 years, Five Points was considered the worst slum in the world and even shocked Charles Dickens. During that time the gangs were schools for criminals and politicians such as Johnny Torrio, Charles 'Lucky' Luciano, Al Capone and Frankie Yale. Paul Kelly set up boxing gyms to teach them how to be gangsters, use guns and extort money. Amazingly, the gangs even produced flyers with their 'services': $100 for the big job (murder), $50 for a slash on the face or $15 for an ear chewed off.

Chinatown

> **BRITTIP**
> Take advantage of Big Onion's (www.bigonion.com) Chinatown walking tour, which takes in the Church of Transfiguration, outdoor markets and Confucius statue (p93).

The appalling violence and corruption of this era has been brought to life by Martin Scorsese's movie *Gangs of New York*, starring Leonardo DiCaprio and Daniel Day-Lewis. Fortunately, Chinatown is now a very different place. Many of the overcrowded tenements were pulled down at the turn of the 20th century to build a park. Since then, the Criminal Court Building has also been built nearby, retaining a contact with the area's violent past!

The original Chinese immigrants in the 1850s huddled around Pell Street. Sadly, it was not long before the Tongs, with their extortion rackets, illegal gambling and opium dens, gave the area a new reputation for violence. As a result, the US Government passed the Exclusion Act in 1882, which banned Chinese from entering America.

That all changed in 1965 with the new Immigration Act and a new wave of Chinese immigrants arrived. Very quickly, the women in particular were snapped up for poorly paid work in the garment industry, which gradually moved from its old Garment District above 34th Street into Chinatown. More recently, a new wave of immigrants from the Fujian province of China has once again changed the face of the area. Now many of the well-off Cantonese have moved to Queens and the Mandarin-speaking Fujinese have the upper hand.

> **BRITTIP**
> You'll have a hard time getting a taxi on Canal Street – they don't often make it into Chinatown. Head toward The Bowery and try to hail a taxi as it comes off the Manhattan Bridge, or use the subway stations at Canal and Broadway.

At 277 Canal Street at Broadway and up some rickety stairs you will find Pearl River Mart, Chinatown's department store, stocking everything from crockery to Buddhas, paper umbrellas, clothes, shoes and slippers.

Back on the street again, you could be forgiven for feeling a little overwhelmed by the licensed and unlicensed street traders, who sell anything from fake watches to handbags. It's often impossible to walk on the pavements, but dangerous to step too far into the incredibly busy Canal Street!

Further down the road, you can get another insight into the local lifestyle by visiting the **Kam Man** grocery store at 200 Canal Street. It offers a wide range from plucked ducks to squid. Try a bag of Konja, which is filled with deliciously refreshing bite-sized pots of lychee jelly.

Mott Street is the main thoroughfare of Chinatown. Here, along with Canal, Pell, Bayard, Doyers and The Bowery, is a host of restaurants plus tea and rice shops.

South towards Doyers Street you'll find the **Church of the Transfiguration** (www. transfigurationnyc.org) – 1 of 2 in New York – which portrays the changing nature of the immigrant population here. The oldest Catholic church building in New York, it was built in the early 19th century and Padre Felix Varela Morales, a Cuban priest who helped form the Ancient Hibernian Order, preached here. But between 1881 and 1943, no Chinese were allowed into it, apart from some wealthy merchants. It was first used by the Irish immigrants, then the Italians, but is now, finally, used by the Chinese and has services in Chinese. Also worth checking is the Wall of Democracy on Bayard Street, which is festooned with posters and cuttings documenting the changing situation in China.

◀╬▶ BRITTIP

It's pointless arriving at Chinatown before 10am as only the local McDonald's will be open.

Mei Li Wah Bakery at 64 Bayard Street serves some of the freshest steam buns in the city. The classic pork bun included in Chinese dim sum is delicious and at 80c you can afford to indulge! Dim sum, incidentally, means the 'little delicacy that will lighten up your heart' – and it certainly does when it's good! On nearby Pell Street is the **Vegetarian Food Center** where you can buy enough ingredients to make your own picnic to eat sitting in the nearby **Confucius Plaza**.

You should try to visit the beautiful **Bowery Savings Bank** on Bowery Street at Grand. When it was built in the 1890s, people liked to save locally and so the bankers tried to create the feeling that their building was a safe place for people to leave their money by making banks stunningly beautiful inside. The Neo-Classical exterior is an incongruous sight in Chinatown but it's worth having a peek.

DOWNTOWN

Scan QR code for hi-res map of Downtown

This is where the history of New York started and some of the most important financial sites in the world were founded. The Downtown area covers the whole of the Financial District and the Civic Center, stretching from river to river and north to the Brooklyn Bridge/Chambers Street (Map 1).

Today, the winding, narrow streets of the true Downtown – an area of 2.6km²/1ml² south of Chambers Street from City Hall to the Battery – are a dizzying juxtaposition of colonial-era buildings and towering temples of capitalism. They were the location of some of the most important events in American history. This is where the Bill of Rights was signed, where George Washington was inaugurated as the first president and where millions arrived to search for the American Dream.

This neighbourhood was the home of the World Trade Center and has completely transformed in the years following the tragic 9/11 attacks that killed 2,752 people and destroyed 1.3 million m²/14 million ft² of office space, displaced residents and closed hundreds of restaurants and shops bringing the neighbourhood abruptly, unthinkably, to its knees. The recently opened 9/11 Memorial is New York's newest attraction, and expected 3 to 4 million visitors in its first year.

With an investment of $30 billion in its resurgence, Downtown has fought back, with 1 World Trade Center and 4 World Trade Center climbing towards the skyline and due to open in 2016 and a Performing Arts Center in a few years' time. It now has 18 hotels – 3 times the number that existed on 10 September 2001 – and is a hot new place for New Yorkers to live. Residents have more than doubled in the last decade and are expected to reach 60,000 by 2013.

BRITTIP

To find out what's new, what to see and do and info on free events in Downtown New York, log on to www.downtownny.com before you go. You can download a Downtown NYC app to find restaurants, hotels and more.

THE WALL STREET SHUFFLE

The Dutch were the first to arrive and it was Peter Stuyvesant, New York's first governor, who ordered the building of a wooden wall at the northern edge of what was then New Amsterdam to protect the colonialists from possible attacks from Indians and the British – hence **Wall Street**. This aspect of New York's history is presented in an exhibition in the Ionic-looking **Federal Hall National**

Memorial (26 Wall Street, 212-825 6990, www.nps.gov/feha/), built on the site of New York's original City Hall. Cross the road into Broad Street and you're at the Neo-Classical entrance to the **New York Stock Exchange** (p78).

Other fascinating landmarks include the **Federal Reserve Bank** in Liberty Street at Maiden Lane, which stores one-quarter of the world's gold bullion, and the Neo-Gothic **Trinity Church**, where Alexander Hamilton, the country's first secretary of the treasury, was buried after losing a duel. There has been a church on this site since the end of the 17th century and, for the first 50 years after it was built, Trinity was actually the tallest structure in New York.

BRITTIP

The Bowling Green end of Broadway is lined with coffee shops, cafés and pizza parlours. A freshly cooked slice eaten in or taken to go makes a perfect pit stop.

Just off Wall Street at 25 Broadway is probably one of the poshest post office buildings in the world. Known as the old **Cunard Building**, it was once home to the booking offices of the steamship company and the interior walls of the building are still lined with marble. There are other signs of its former use, with murals of ships and nautical mythology around the ceiling.

It seems only fitting that the former headquarters of John D. Rockefeller's Standard Oil Company at 28 Broadway should now be the home of New York's only independent public museum, the **Museum of American Finance** (p115).

Wall Street today is still one of the world's most prestigious addresses and with the renaissance of this area, creative industries are among the new companies moving in.

BOWLING GREEN

Blink and you'll miss this oval of greenery at the end of Broadway. You'll know you're there by the presence of the Greek revival-style US Customs House, which now houses the **National Museum of the American Indian** (p119), which has the world's largest collection devoted to North, Central and South American Indian cultures. Bowling Green was the site of the infamous deal between the Dutch colony of New Amsterdam and the Indians, who were conned into selling Manhattan for a bucket of trinkets.

In the 18th century, the tiny turfed area was used for the game of bowls by colonial

Brits on a lease of 'one peppercorn per year'. The original iron fence that encloses it was built in 1771, though, ironically, the once-proud statue of King George III was melted into musket balls for the American Revolution.

Here you'll also find the 3,175kg/7,000lb life-sized **bronze bull**. A symbol of the Financial District's stock market, it appeared overnight outside the New York Stock Exchange in 1989. Now it is a tradition to rub his testicles for good luck!

BATTERY PARK AND CASTLE CLINTON

Thanks to hundreds of years of landfill, the Downtown area is quite different to how it once was. Years ago, State Street houses looked over Upper New York Bay, and Water and Pearl Streets were at or near the water's edge. The excavation works to build the deep foundations for the World Trade Center in the 1960s, destroyed by terrorists on 11 September 2001, created enough granite blocks of earth to form 9ha/23 acres of new land, which then became home to Battery Park City and the World Financial Center.

Castle Clinton originally stood on an island. Built in 1811 as one of several forts that defended New York harbour, it is now part of Manhattan. It has been an opera house, an aquarium and was the original immigration sorting office, dealing with 8 million immigrants before the opening of Ellis Island. It is now used as the ferry ticket office.

The opening of a plethora of new shops and cafés and the remodelling of Battery Park's public spaces has given the area a new lease of life.

BATTERY PARK CITY

North-west of Battery Park, you'll find a relatively new area known as **Battery Park City**, which is actually created by landfill. It's still pretty much a quiet district, though there has been plenty of development. This is home to 2 of New York's newer museums. The **Museum of Jewish Heritage** (p116) has been so successful, it already has plans for an extension.

🇬🇧 **BRITTIP**
For fantastic views of Dame Liberty and the harbour, sit and gaze at the harbour from the public roof deck in the Robert F. Wagner Junior Park on Battery Park City's southern tip.

At 39 Battery Place is the **Skyscraper Museum** (p122), which tells the fascinating

story of the creation of those famous buildings. On the southern tip of the 'City' is the landscaped **Robert F Wagner Junior Park** with a restaurant, WCs and street vendors selling food and drink.

To the north is the **World Financial Center**, which has 4 tower blocks and a calendar of fairs and festivals. It's worth coming here for the Winter Garden (p81), a huge, glass-ceilinged public plaza decorated by massive palm trees. From here you can see the private boats docked in North Cove.

🇬🇧 **BRITTIP**
For more fantastic views of Dame Liberty and the harbour, treat yourself to a drink at Loopy Doopy Rooftop Bar which has an outside terrace with amazing views at the Conrad Hotel (p223).

EAST OF BATTERY PARK

To see what life was like in 18th-century Manhattan, head for the **Fraunces Tavern Block Historic District**, which has 11 early 19th-century buildings that escaped the fire of 1835. The three storey Georgian brick house that is home to the **Fraunces Tavern Museum** (p109) on the corner of Pearl and Broad Streets was built in 1904 and houses an exhibition on the site's history.

A little further north-east along Water Street to the Old Slip, you'll see the tiny **First Precinct Police Station**, which was modelled on an Italian mansion and which has been used for exterior shots for both the IV series *Kojak* and the film *The French Connection*. Fittingly, this is now the permanent home of the **New York City Police Museum** (p120).

Just off Water Street at 70 Pine Street is the incredibly beautiful Art Deco wedding-cake-shaped **American International Building**. It has one of the most beautiful Art Deco-designed lobbies in New York and visitors are welcome to have a look.

A little further north at pier 17, you find yourself at **South Street Seaport** (p79), where you can savour Häagen-Daz ice-cream while taking in river views and browsing art galleries and shops. At night, there's a restaurant complex and a chance to sip on Guinness at **MacMenamin's** Irish pub.

CITY HALL PARK AND THE CIVIC CENTER

City Hall Park is opposite the entrance to Brooklyn Bridge and is also the dividing point between the Financial District and Chinatown. From here you can stroll across the **Brooklyn Bridge** or visit the Neo-Gothic

Woolworth Building (p82) on Broadway at Barclay Street. Check out the lobby's vaulted ceilings and its magnificent mosaics and mail boxes. When it was first built it was the tallest structure in New York and Mr Woolworth paid cash for it!

Back in the 1930s, when Prosecutor Dewey decided to target organised crime, he made the Woolworth Building his base. He locked up 15 prostitutes in the building for 4 months before he worked out that the prostitutes were controlled by 'Lucky' Luciano and successfully prosecuted him for white slavery. 'Lucky' got 32 years in prison, but lived up to his name by serving just 10 before he was pardoned for his patriotic efforts during the Second World War. Just north of City Hall Park are the **Police Plaza, US Courthouse, New York County Courthouse** and **Criminal Court Building**.

There's a Lower Manhattan information kiosk at the southern tip of City Hall Park where you can find information on attractions and upcoming events plus maps and directions.

EAST VILLAGE

East Village at a glance: Bohemian cafés and shops

Gay:	207
Museums and galleries:	
Merchant's House Museum	113
Nightlife:	
Bars, lounges and pubs	198–99
Nightclubs	215
Restaurants:	162–63
Shopping:	131–32
Tours: Rock 'n' Roll Walking Tour	91

Subways to get there:
L, N, Q, R, W, 4, 5, 6 to 14th Street/Union Square and L to 3rd Avenue and 1st Avenue

Scan QR code for hi-res map of East Village

Forget the picturesque cobbled streets of Greenwich and the West Villages. Once you cross The Bowery (otherwise known as Skid Row) and head up to St Mark's Place you're in the heart of East Village (Map 2). It's an area more reminiscent of the Lower East Side than a village and currently in vogue as one of the coolest neighbourhoods. The stereotypical East Villager has long hair and more metal in their face than a jewellery shop window display! You'll also know you've entered the neighbourhood by the many tattoo studios, along with **boutiques** selling punk and leather outfits.

Where Greenwich Village has become upper middle class, East Village retains its roots as a Bohemian enclave of free-thinkers and non-conformists, though the tramps are gradually being replaced by a more genteel set attracted by newly built apartment blocks and the comparatively reasonable, though not low, rents.

This was once the home of Beat Generation writer Allen Ginsberg (on East 7th Street) and was frequented by Jack Kerouac and other radical thinkers of the 1950s. One of the area's oldest clubs, **CBGB** (Country, BlueGrass and Blues) on The Bowery closed in 2006 after more than 30 years. The legendary club is famous for hosting the likes of Blondie, the Ramones, Talking Heads and the Police. Patti Smith played the final gig before it shut down, but enthusiasts will be pleased to know there's now a CBGB Music & Film Festival, which takes place in October and at various venues across Manhattan and Brooklyn.

Now the area is most well known for its second-hand shops, which can be found all along 7th Street and 2nd and 3rd Avenues. There's a tiny **Little India** on 6th Street, where you'll find a row of curry houses, but the most famous eating outlet is the **Yaffa Café** (p163) on St Mark's Place heading towards Tompkins Square Park.

Tucked away on East 7th Street (you'll spot the green barrels first) is home to what is claimed to be New York's oldest pub, **McSorley's Old Ale** House (www.mcsorleysnewyork.com), which dates back to 1854 and still serves its own beer, while a line of Harley Davidson's on 3rd Street between 1st and 2nd Avenues is evidence of the base of the New York chapter of the Hell's Angels.

Alphabet City, which lies between Avenues A to D towards the East River, is also part of East Village. Once considered a no-go area for tourists, it was predominantly filled with a working class Latino community and had a reputation as the drug-dealing area of the city. These days, the drug problems are largely a thing of the past, and an influx of young professionals has given the area a lift. Its major historical attractions are two churches, **San Isidero y San Leandro** and **Iglesia Pentecostal Camino Damasco**, built in an elaborate Spanish-colonial style.

GARMENT DISTRICT

Garment District at a glance: Sample sales and designers
Nightlife:

Bars, lounges and pubs	199
Live music	213

Subways to get there: A, C, E or 1, 2, 3 to 34th Street–Penn Station or 42nd Street

From 34th Street to 42nd Street between 6th and 8th Avenues, you'll find the Garment District of New York (Map 3). Having shrunk a little in the past to only a square mile – a lot of work disappeared overseas or moved to the cheap labour available in Chinatown – the area is once again up-and-coming, as designers are now choosing to have their clothes manufactured in New York. If you wander around this area – and you may well if you're in search of sample sales – you'll see racks of clothes being pushed around the streets. Some are going to showrooms and warehouses, but as no one manufacturer makes an entire piece of clothing, many of the garments are being shunted from company to company to have different bits sewn on at each place!

Scan QR code for hi-res map of the Garment District and Gramercy Park

GRAMERCY PARK

Gramercy Park at a glance: Beautiful architecture

Accommodation:	229
Restaurants:	164–66
Shopping:	133

Subways to get there: 6 to 23rd Street

Two blocks south and 2 blocks east of the Flatiron Building on East 20th and 21st at Irving Place (Map 3) is one of the prettiest squares in New York City. The park itself was once a swamp, but has now been beautifully laid out, though you won't be able to go in unless you are staying with a resident of the surrounding square or at the Gramercy Park Hotel (p229).

The most famous building in the neighbourhood is **The Players** (www.theplayersnyc.org) at 16 Gramercy Park, a private club created for actors and theatrical types by actor Edwin Booth when Gramercy Park was the centre of the theatre scene. Booth was the greatest actor in America in the 1870s and 1880s and opened the Gothic revival-style house as a club in 1888 so that actors and literary types could meet in private to interact. One tragic event overshadowed the end of Booth's life – his brother John Wilkes Booth assassinated Abraham Lincoln.

BRITTIP

Check out the sales section of New York's *Time Out* magazine or online at www.timeout.com/newyork for up-to-date information on designer sample sales here.

GREENWICH VILLAGE

Greenwich Village at a glance: Brownstone houses, restaurants and boutiques

Accommodation:	230
Gay:	207
Museums and galleries:	
Forbes Galleries	109
Nightlife:	
Bars, lounges and pubs	199
Hotel bars	209
Live music	213
Nightclubs	215
Restaurants:	166–68
Shopping:	133–36
Tours: Foods of New York	89

Subways to get there:
For Washington Square A, B, C, E, F or V to West 4th Street and Washington Square
For Bleecker Street 6 to Bleecker Street or B, D, F, V to Broadway/Lafayette Street

This is one of the most picturesque parts of New York (it feels a little like you're wandering around a film set) and, although

Washington Square Park

the radical free-thinkers have gone, its quaint cobbled and tree-lined streets, shops and Federal and Greek-style buildings are well worth a visit.

Scan QR code for hi-res map of Greenwich Village

Greenwich Village proper (Map 2) is bounded in the north by 14th Street, in the south by Houston (pronounced 'Howston'), in the east by Broadway and in the west by 7th, where it becomes the West Village, which stretches west to the Hudson River.

When the Dutch first arrived in Manhattan, 'the Village' as it is known, was mostly woodland, but was turned into a tobacco plantation by the Dutch West India Company. Then in the early 1800s people came here fleeing from a series of cholera and yellow fever epidemics in the unhygienic Downtown.

When the wealthy moved into their 5th Avenue mansions at the end of the 19th century, rents came down and a whole new breed of artists, radicals and intellectual rebels moved in, creating a kind of Parisian Left Bank feel to the neighbourhood. It has been home to such literary lions as Mark Twain, Edgar Allen Poe, Dylan Thomas, Eugene O'Neill and Jack Kerouac.

Now writers and artists have largely been forced out by soaring rents – a tiny two-bed apartment costs at least $2,500 a month and a shoebox of a studio is at least $275,000 to buy – and in their place have come upper middle-class Americans for whom making money is the abiding principle. Movie star Sarah Jessica Parker sold her five-bedroom house here recently for a cool $25 million! Yet there is still the sense of a community spirit, many restaurants cater mostly to locals rather than tourists (in New York, only Village restaurants seem filled with people who are in no particular rush) and a great variety of off-Broadway shows and other cultural events can be seen in this neighbourhood.

WASHINGTON SQUARE PARK

Many people consider this to be the heart of the Village – and one of the very few genuine squares in Manhattan. The first thing you'll notice is the Stanford White-designed marble square **Triumphal Arch** at the bottom of 5th Avenue, built in 1892 to commemorate

GREAT TOURS OF THE VILLAGE

If eating's your thing, then you'll love the **Foods of New York** tour (p89) of Greenwich Village and West Village, which not only shows you the sights, food shops, restaurants and architectural secrets, but will also give you a chance to taste the unique local foods.

Other great tours are the **Literary Pub Crawl** (p94), which takes you to the watering holes once frequented by literary giants, and **Rock 'n' Roll Walking Tour** (p91), which is a fun tour around legendary nightspots in East Village.

George Washington's inauguration as the first US president.

You may become aware of how dingy it all looks, but this area is considered 'alternative' rather than dodgy. It's full of locals skating, playing chess and just hanging out, plus students from the nearby university. It used to be a place where a lot of people took drugs, but that problem is largely in the past.

A little-known fact is that the park was once used by City officials to conduct public hangings until they were moved to Sing Sing penitentiary. Apart from the arch and the people, the other main point of interest in the park is the **Dog Run**. A uniquely New York phenomenon, the idea is that instead of taking your dog for a walk along the roads, you bring them to dog runs where they can literally run around off the lead. It's rather like a parent taking their child to the swings – hilarious and has to be seen to be believed!

North from the park on 6th Avenue between Waverly Place and 9th Street is **Bigelow's Pharmacy**, the oldest traditional chemist in America. Opposite is the beautiful Jefferson Market Courthouse, now used as a library, and just off 10th Street is one of the most famous rows of mews houses in the Village, **Patchin Place**, which has been home not only to many a writer, including e e cummings and John Reed, but also to Marlon Brando. Also of note on the square is the **Forbes Galleries** (p109), a museum filled with antique toys as well as a signed copy of Lincoln's Gettysburg Address, while the **Church of the Ascension** is an English Gothic Revival church built in 1840 with a mural of the Ascension above the altar by John La Farge.

BLEECKER STREET

Effectively the main drag of the Village, this is one of the best places to be in New York, filled as it is with sidewalk cafés, shops, restaurants and clubs. The corner of Cornelia and Bleecker

Streets gives you access to some of the finest food shops and restaurants in Manhattan.

At 254 Bleecker Street is **Murray's Cheese Shop** (p134), New York's oldest, with more than 350 cheeses from around the world. Nothing is pre-cut and they have great names such as Wabash Cannonball, Crocodile Tears, Mutton Buttons and Cardinal Sin, a British cows'-milk cheese. They also have 15 types of olives and sell tuna, chorizo, pâtés and breads. Opposite at 260 Bleecker is **Faicco's Pork Store** (p134), a landmark shop that has been here since 1900. Its famous range of sausages is made every morning and sold not only to local residents but also to many of the local restaurants. It also sells home-cooked, ready-made meals and offers a huge deli selection.

Around the corner is Cornelia Street, home to four of the best restaurants in the Village. **The Cornelia Street Café** (p166 and 210) hosts jazz, readings and other events (from $8 to $25), while **Home Restaurant** specialises in American comfort food, **Le Gigot** is a traditional country French restaurant and **Little Havana** offers great Cuban food.

Bleecker Street has two more incredible bakeries with their own seating areas. **Pasticceria Bruno** (on cross street LaGuardia Place) is run by popular chef Biagio Settepani and his son Sal. They produce an amazing range of tarts, mousses and pastries for $2 to $3. Best sellers include opera, favori, chocolate peanut butter and hazelnut pastries. The café itself has a lot of atmosphere and old world charm. Next door is **Pasticceria Rocco** (p135), run by Rocco, who used to be a head pastry chef at Bruno's until 1972 when he opened his own place. An entire Italian cheesecake made of ricotta cheese costs just $10. The interior is much more modern, with steel-framed chairs, mirrors and more seats than Bruno's.

HARLEM

Harlem at a glance: Jazz and African-American culture
Museums and galleries:

Subways to get there: For the Schomberg Center 2, 3 to 135th Street

Scan QR code for hi-res map of Harlem

Harlem is a huge area that covers a substantial part of the northern reaches of Manhattan above Central Park, though it has various subsections. What we refer to when we use the name Harlem is actually the African-American area, which stretches from 8th Avenue in the west to 5th Avenue in the east and goes north to the East River (Map 6). The area from East 96th Street east of 5th Avenue going up to the East River is Spanish Harlem, known as **El Barrio** and populated largely by Puerto Ricans.

◄🇬🇧► BRITTIP

If you want to try some authentic soul food, visit popular Sylvia's Restaurant at 318 Lenox Avenue, run by Queen of Soulfood Sylvia Woods (www.sylviasrestaurant.com). The Gospel Soulfood Menu is particularly good (hot cakes and southern fried chicken breast, anyone?) but book as it's popular.

Named after the Dutch town of Haarlem, the area received its first Dutch settlers in the mid-19th century, when it was used as farmland and as an escape from the dust and traffic of Midtown. Better-off immigrant families started moving here following the arrival of the railroad link and the building of attractive brownstone townhouses. Property speculators, eager to take advantage of the new subway heading for Harlem, started building good-quality homes for the upper middle classes in the early 1900s. But they'd got a little ahead of themselves. A couple of mini depressions and Harlem's distance from Midtown Manhattan put the dampers on hopes of a middle-class move into the area.

African-American estate agents spotted a golden opportunity, bought up a batch of empty homes cheaply and rented them out to blacks eager to escape the gang warfare of the West 40s and 50s in Hell's Kitchen and Clinton. This was the beginning of Harlem as the capital of the black world and when African-Americans started migrating from America's southern states, they headed straight here.

Apollo Theater, Harlem

And it's no wonder really. Brits are frequently shocked to discover that the blacks may have been freed from slavery by the end of the 19th century, but there was still segregation until the 1960s. Black people were not allowed to sit on the same benches as whites, they had to drink at different water fountains and in church they were forced to wait until after the whites for Communion. When great black musicians such as Duke Ellington and Louis Armstrong went on tour, they had to stay at black-only hotels and eat at black-only restaurants.

BRITTIP

Less well-known than Sylvia's Restaurant, but definitely as tasty, is Billies Black on West 119th between St Nicolas Ave and Frederick Douglass Blvd for a traditional southern meal to the background sounds of great soul and jazz singers.

Back in Harlem, at least, there was some semblance of belonging and thanks to the influx of political activists, professionals and artists to the area following the opening of the subway lines between 1904 and 1906, many African-American organisations had sprung up by the early 1920s. They included the National Urban League, which helped people who were moving into the area to get training for jobs, and the White Rose Mission, which helped African-American female migrants coming to New York from the South. They were followed by the political Universal Negro Improvement Association

and the Union Brotherhood of Sleeping Porters, whose leader Phillip Randolph was at one time considered by the government to be the most dangerous black person in America.

BRITTIP

To experience the life and times of Harlem, take a look at a copy of *Harlem's Culture: A Guide to Great Events*, at cultural centres such as the Schomburg.

THE GLORY DAYS OF HARLEM

The 1920s and 1930s were a great time for the neighbourhood, filled as it was with poets, writers, artists, actors and political activists. The combination of prohibition and great jazz musicians such as Count Basie, Duke Ellington and Cab Calloway made famous nightspots like the Cotton Club attractive to the upper middle classes who came in their droves to enjoy Harlem's speakeasies.

But all this was hardly doing anything for the lot of the average African-American who lived in the area. The speakeasies were strictly for whites only and even W. C. Handy, who co-wrote a song with Duke Ellington, was not allowed into the Cotton Club to hear it being played for the first time. Then there was the matter of the racism on 125th Street – Harlem's very centre, which runs from Frederick Douglas Boulevard to Malcolm X Boulevard. The white-owned shops and hotels here, which were used by the African-Americans, were staffed by whites and it was impossible for blacks to get anything but the most menial jobs.

In 1934, Adam Clayton Powell Junior,

preacher at the Abyssinian Baptist Church, organised a boycott of these businesses, entitled 'Don't Buy Where You Can't Work'. The campaign was successful and the shops started hiring blacks. You can still see the remnants of those businesses along 125th.

You can start your experience of Harlem with a tour round the **Apollo Theater** on 125th (p93), which was the focal point for African-American entertainment between the 1930s and 1970s. Known for its legendary Amateur Night, now broadcast on TV, it launched the careers of Ella Fitzgerald, Marvin Gaye, James Brown and The Jackson Five.

At the corner of 7th Avenue stands the former **Theresa Hotel**, now an office block, but which was once considered to be the Waldorf of Harlem. Back in the days of segregation Josephine Baker stayed in the penthouse with its vaulted ceiling and views of both rivers. Malcolm X's Unity organisation was based here in the 1950s and 1960s and, in a show of support for African-Americans, Fidel Castro moved his entire entourage to the Theresa when he came to New York in 1960 for a United Nations conference.

BRITTIP

For soul food, try Miss Maude's Spoonbread Too, Malcolm X Boulevard (Lenox Avenue) at 137th Street or visit Manna's Too at 134th Street (or Manna's at 8th Avenue and West 125th) for a great selection of well-priced fresh food and drinks.

A little further down the street is **Blumsteins**, once the largest department store in Harlem, and the historic place Martin Luther King was stabbed in an assassination attempt in 1958. With its dilapidated frontage and peeling paintwork, it's hard to imagine this was once the Macy's of the area.

Another major location is on 135th to 137th Streets between Powell Boulevard and Malcolm X Boulevard. You can either walk from 125th Street or take the 2, 3 subway to 135th Street. Once there you'll find yourself right outside the **Schomburg Center**, which chronicles the history of black people in North and South America and the Caribbean. Opposite is the **Harlem Hospital Center** where Martin Luther King was operated on after being shot. It was the first hospital in New York to be integrated.

A couple of blocks north and you'll find the famous **Abyssinian Baptist Church** at 132 West 138th Street. It was founded in 1808, and as the blacks moved from the Lower East Side to Greenwich Village, then up to the West 50s and 60s before finding a home in Harlem, the church moved with them. It was built in 1923 and, with Adam Clayton Powell Junior as its preacher for many years before he became a senator, it was a centre of political activity, particularly in the 1920s.

BRITTIP

To experience a gospel choir, go to the Abyssinian Baptist Church on 138th Street on Sunday, but arrive early because it gets packed (there are sometimes queues on the street!). Another great place is the Second Canaan Baptist Church on 110th Street and Lenox Avenue.

One block west on 138th and 139th Streets between Powell and Frederick Douglas Boulevards are the four rows of Stanford White houses built in 1891 known as **Striver's Row** because this is where the middle and upper classes strove to live. The houses were filled by doctors, lawyers, nurses from Harlem Hospital, jazz musicians and politicians such as Malcolm X. Boxer Harry Wills, known as the Brown Panther, also lived here. He was paid $50,000 not to fight Jack Dempsey. The mayor banned the fight because he thought a black boxer fighting a white man would lead to riots.

BRITTIP

A terrific variety of tours of Harlem are available from Harlem Heritage Tours (212-280 7888, www.harlemheritagetours.com).

The alleys at the back of these buildings were originally created for parking horses and carriages. Houses were usually built back to back so the alleys are a rarity, but a boon for

Abyssinian Baptist Church

the current occupants to park their BMWs. You can still see the signs that say 'Walk your horses' or 'Park your carriages'.

DECLINE AND FALL

Sadly, the good times didn't last long and, from the 1940s to the 1960s, Harlem declined into an urban no-man's land as a result of a lack of government support and racial conflict.

Eventually City Hall and certain businesses started investing in the area. In 1976 the city began reclaiming properties abandoned by landlords who couldn't afford to pay their taxes. Fortunately, many have already been refurbished and, with the influx of banks and even a Starbucks, improvements continue.

For some time, the brownstones of Hamilton Heights and other local neighbourhoods have been targeted by those trying to escape the substantial rents elsewhere in Manhattan. There have been other developments, too. Former president Bill Clinton has his offices on 125th Street between Lenox and 5th. He's always been a favourite with African-Americans because he did a lot for racial equality and he was invited to move his offices to Harlem from Carnegie Hall. Former baseball star Magic Johnson has also been doing much to encourage a sense of community pride.

◀🇬🇧▶ BRITTIP
Find all kinds of information about what goes on in Harlem at www.harlemcondolife.com. Designed primarily for locals, it's still worth a look.

RENAISSANCE

Fast-rising house prices in other parts of the city forced the upwardly mobile to flock to the neighbourhood. Toned white women now jog down the streets and students stroll out of Starbucks. Old nightspots once frequented exclusively by African-Americans have also been bought up and are being earmarked for renovation, including the **Renaissance Ballroom**, once a neighbourhood institution but demolished in 2010 to make way for condos. Everyone would watch the Harlem Rens basketball team early in the evening here, then clean up to hit the nightclub. It was shut in the 1940s, but is now owned by the Abyssinian Church.

Another major venue was **Small's Big Apple jazz club**. Its sister establishment, Small's Paradise, was a restaurant in the 1930s and 1940s. It was so popular and the dance floor so small that it was said people had to dance on a dime here. It enjoyed a revival from the 1960s and was where Professor du Bois, who once ran the National Association for Advancement of Coloured People, held a birthday party in the 1980s. It closed in the same decade, but is now owned by the Abyssinian Church and there's a chance it may reopen as a tourist centre.

Harlem is now a hot and happening neighbourhood. Buoyed by the influx of downtowners and a strong creative spirit, it's now chocka with new upmarket shops, restaurants, music halls, lounges and the **Aloft Harlem**, a new trendy hotel.

HAMILTON HEIGHTS

The Hamilton Heights neighbourhood (Map 6) is up on the high ground north of Morningside Heights and is effectively the middle-class enclave of Harlem. It takes its name from **Alexander Hamilton**, the first secretary of the treasury to the newly formed United States of America. He lived here from 1802 until he was killed in a duel in 1804.

The area is now the home of **City College**, one of the senior colleges in the New York university system. It was founded in the 19th century to educate the children of the working classes and immigrants and used to be known as the poor man's Columbia. It used to be free, but it is still a lot cheaper than private universities in America.

Further north on West 145th Street off Amsterdam is the area known as **Sugar Hill**, which was made famous by the Duke Ellington song 'Take the A Train (to Sugar Hill)'. Now a conservation area, it is filled with beautiful brownstone townhouses, and was dubbed Sugar Hill because life here was considered to be so sweet.

LITTLE ITALY

Little Italy at a glance: Mediterranean food
Museums and galleries:
Children's Museum of the Arts 106
Nightlife: Bars, lounges and pubs 200
Restaurants: 169–70
Shopping: 136
Subways to get there: N, R, Q, W, 6 to Canal and then walk east to Mulberry, or 6 to Spring and walk south.

Scan QR code for hi-res map of Little Italy

With its strong ties to Naples and a history of Mafia connections, Little Italy is still seen as a glamorous area of the city by many. Take the subway at Spring or Canal (Map 1) then head along Grand Street towards Mott and Mulberry Streets to **Di Palo's** (p136), which marks the beginnings of what is left of Little Italy. Di Palo's shop at 210 Grand Street was founded 80 years ago and is still famous for its mozzarella, Italian sausages and salami. It has its own cheese-ageing room and gets very crowded. A little further on is **Ferrara Bakery & Café** (p170), the oldest and most popular pastry café in Little Italy.

Although much smaller now than it was in the 1970s due to a dwindling population, it is still a pleasant few blocks to wander around, particularly for foodies, as the delis, packed full of homemade breads, pastas, sausages and cheeses, are legendary. To stop it dwindling further, the Italians struck a deal with the Chinese community to retain Mulberry Street between Hester and Kenmare Streets.

BRITTIP

Ferrara's in Grand Street, near Mulberry, is a perfect spot for a coffee and pastry break, plus a real slice of the Italian lifestyle. You'll find the restrooms on the 1st floor.

It was formerly home to Italians from the Naples area of Italy and has taken St Gennaro, the patron saint of Naples, as its own saint. Every year in the 3rd week of September, Italians flock to celebrate the Feast of St Gennaro. Food carts line Mulberry Street and there is laughing, dancing and drinking until the early hours.

BRITTIP

Little Italy is at its finest at the weekend in warm weather when the restaurants put their tables outdoors. Arrive around noon or late afternoon to get a seat outside.

Little Italy's best feature is its wonderful **restaurants** with outdoor seating where you can watch the world go by while tucking into some great dishes. The restaurants have a reputation for being on the pricey side, but plenty have pasta and pizza specials for an economical $10.

Just a little bit of gruesome history for you: Da Gennaro on the corner of Mulberry and Hester Streets was the original home of **Umberto's Clam House** (which is now further south on Mulberry). This was a favoured haunt of gangster Crazy Joey Gallo and where he was murdered in 1972 while celebrating his birthday.

BRITTIP

The Lower East Side Business Improvement District (866-224 0406, www.lowereastsideny.com) offers a Podcast Tour you can download to your MP3 player. There's also a free 2-hour weekly walking tour, Sun Apr–Nov at 11am in front of Katz's Delicatessen (p170) and an art galleries tour every last Sun Apr–Oct (except Aug) at 1pm.

Further north at 247 Mulberry between Spring and Kenmare Streets is the former home of the **Ravenlight Club** and Mafia headquarters for John Gotti. He was once known as the Teflon Don because no charges could be made to stick, and this was where he made the policemen and judges on his payroll come to pay their respects. The FBI were so determined to put him away they bugged not only the Ravenlight but also all the parking meters around the streets but still they got nowhere. Then Gotti's underboss, Sammy Gravano, became a supergrass. He got away with 19 murders by doing a deal with the FBI that helped put Gotti away.

LOWER EAST SIDE

Lower East Side at a glance: Nightlife and bargain shopping

Accommodation:	230–31
Museums and galleries:	
Edwynn Houk Gallery	108
Lower East Side Tenement Museum	112
Nightlife:	
Bars, lounges and pubs	200
Gay	208
Live music	213
Nightclubs	215–16
Restaurants:	170
Shopping:	136

Subways to get there: J, M, Z, F trains to Delancey or Essex Streets.

Scan QR code for hi-res map of the Lower East Side

One of the seedier parts of town that's becoming cool again, the Lower East Side has a fascinating history but is now known for its trendy nightclubs and bargain shopping. It stretches from the East River ostensibly to Chrystie Street (though Chinatown is encroaching) and south from Canal Street to East Houston in the north, while Delancey is its main thoroughfare (Map 2). In many respects, the history of the Lower East Side is the history of America's immigration, which in turn has played a pivotal role in the country's development.

◄█► BRITTIP

The Lower East Side Business Improvement District (866-224 0406, www.lowereastsideny.com) has opened a new Visitor Center at 54 Orchard Street where staff are on hand Mon–Fri 9.30-5.30pm and Sat 9.30-4pm to offer help with shopping, sightseeing, dining and nightlife. There's also free wi-fi here.

At one time this was the most densely populated area in the world, with 1,000 inhabitants crammed into 2.6km^2/1ml^2. Almost from the word go, the Lower East Side was a settlement for new arrivals to New York because of its cheap housing and its proximity to where people disembarked. Once these immigrants had established themselves they moved on, leaving space for a new wave of arrivals. Street names such as Essex, Suffolk and Norfolk point to the origins of the first tenants. Since then streets have been named anything from a Kleine Deutschland to a Little Italy or Ireland.

Little Italy

With each new wave of immigrants came friction between new and old arrivals, which often led to violence. The Protestant English were angry, for instance, when the Roman Catholic Irish built St Mary's on Grand Street in 1828 and burned it down. That led to the formation of the Ancient Order of Hibernians in 1830 – the organisation that started the **St Patrick's Day parade**. The Hibernians rebuilt the church and put walls around the outside. It is still in existence, but now runs a kosher soup service.

Check out www.lowereastsideny.com and www.thelodownny.com for information on events and discounts.

SWEATSHOPS AND TENEMENTS

Other tenants of the early 1800s were relatively well-off Jews from Germany, who eventually moved further north. This was a pattern that was to be repeated again and again with each new wave of immigrants. But perhaps the saddest were the incredibly poor Jewish immigrants who started arriving from Eastern Europe in the 1860s and 70s. They were forced to eke out a miserly existence in sweatshops and live in tenement buildings. Whole families were crowded into 1.8m/6ft square rooms with no heating or running water and often little light. Visit the **Lower East Side Tenement Museum** (p112) in Orchard Street for their full story.

◄█► BRITTIP

The Lower East Side was once known as a mugger's paradise. It's no longer as bad, but as in any city you still need to be careful.

During this period, Hester Street was the main thoroughfare and it was filled with shops and pedlars selling their wares – meat, fruit and vegetables. The pedlars did very well, as they paid no tax and had no overheads such as rent. Often they made more than three times as much as teachers did. But the shopkeepers were unhappy with the unfair competition and by the 1930s the city had banned pedlars and created the Essex Street Market. Famous for its fresh meats, produce and other products, the market has recently been renovated at a cost of $1.5m. It is open Mon-Sat, 8am-7pm, Sun 10am-6pm.

A NEW DAWN

The main language in Hester Street between the 1880s and 1920s was Yiddish – a mixture of Hebrew, German and Slavic. The local newspaper, *Forward*, was published in Yiddish and each edition sold 200,000 copies. Now the area is very quiet. There are still many Jews left, but the new waves of immigrants include Puerto Ricans and Latinos from the Dominican Republic.

If you want to see some real action, you need to go to **Delancey** and the big shopping area around Orchard and Ludlow Streets. Here you'll find bargain basement products and cutting-edge designer fashions – many young designers have started in the Lower East Side before moving uptown. **Orchard** and **Ludlow** between Delancey and East Houston Streets are also the main drags for the new bars and clubs that have been opening in the area. The best day to experience the Lower East Side is Sun, when the market is open and the whole area is buzzing with people. A large chunk of it is still closed on Sat to mark the Jewish Sabbath, but that is gradually changing due to the arrival of the Latinos.

🇬🇧 BRITTIP

For excellently priced, clean accommodation in LES, stay at the Howard Johnson Express Inn (p230) on East Houston.

An outstanding sight on Delancey is **Ratner's Dairy Restaurant** at 138 Delancey near Essex Street. Although it's no longer a dairy restaurant, it used to be home to Lansky Lounge, a chic nightspot where mob boss Meyer Lansky used to hold court.

MADISON SQUARE

Madison Square at a glance: The Garden

Accommodation:	231
Restaurants:	170–71
Shopping: Antiques and markets	136–37
Sights: New York Life Building	right
The Little Church Around the Corner	right
Tours: Madison Square Garden	76
Subways to get there: N, R, W, 6 to 28th Street	

Scan QR code for hi-res map of Madison Square

It's a weird but true fact that the ugly **Madison Square Garden** building, constructed above Penn Station on 33rd Street (p34), is the latest (and probably least attractive) of the 4 Madison Square Gardens

Radio City

that have been built in New York. Only the first 2 were, in fact, located at Madison Square (Map 3), which is where Madison Avenue begins and is the site of the **Madison Square Park**. Facing the square is Cass Gilbert's **New York Life Building**, which was erected in 1928. In its shadow is **The Little Church Around the Corner** just off 5th Avenue at 29th Street. Its real name is the **Episcopal Church of the Transfiguration** whose stained glass windows commemorate famous actors such as Edwin Booth, who went to the church at a time when acting was not considered a very honourable profession.

MEATPACKING DISTRICT

Meatpacking District at a glance: Fashion boutiques, bars and restaurants

Accommodation:	231
Nightlife:	
Bars, lounges and pubs	200–01
Nightclubs	216
Restaurants:	171–72
Shopping:	137
Sights: High Line	50
Subways to get there: A, C, E to 14th Street	

Scan QR code for hi-res map of the Meatpacking District

The now hip and happening Meatpacking District is to be found in the north-western corner of the West Village, south of West 14th Street to West 12th Street and from

West Street to Hudson Street on the east side (Map 2). As the name suggests, the area was originally home to butchers and slaughterhouses for cattle in the 1930s. A handful of warehouses are still used for storing and cutting carcases to be distributed from wholesale markets around the city, but the majority have been abandoned over time and snapped up by eager young entrepreneurs who have used the loft-like spaces for everything from nightclubs to achingly trendy restaurants.

The big news in this area is the new **High Line** (www.thehighline.org), a fabulous park that spans from Gansevoort Street in the Meatpacking District to Chelsea and Clinton/ Hells Kitchen. Built in the 1930s, the High Line rail track was built above Manhattan allowing freight trains to rumble overhead rather than clogging the city's streets. The genius move to landscape the derelict line into an elevated public park was mooted in 2002 and gained a lot of support from residents. The 1st and 2nd sections are now open 7am–10pm daily. The third and final section is Highline At The Rail Yards (between West 30 and 34th streets and 10th and 12 Avenues to the east and west). Construction is under way and the aim is for it to open in 2014. When the whole is completed, it will be 2.4km/1.5ml long, combining concrete pathways, dramatic planting designs, fixed and movable seating, lighting and sculptures, plus lots of fun events such as talks by artists involved in the project. You can also go on organised tours.

There are some fun hang-outs around this area, such as **Hogs & Heifers** (page 201), which is frequented by a real mix of people, from motorcycle groups to celebrities and everyone in between. Many women leave their bras on the ceiling as a memento! **Tortilla Flats** in Washington Street on the corner of West 12th Street is a cool, grungy café.

Until recently the area was very edgy and still a hang-out for transvestite prostitutes – as depicted in *Sex And The City* when the man-eating Samantha moved here from the Upper East Side. Now, however, the dark, badly lit cobbled streets and alleyways have improved and lots of gentrification has taken place, so its edgy vibe is disappearing. This is also the area that Brit exports have gravitated towards. The last couple of years have seen the opening of über-cool designer shops from the Brit fashion pack, including Stella McCartney and Alexander McQueen, and the arrival of **Soho House**, the New York branch of London's coolest private members' club.

Not that this area is only about the new.

There are some historic spots to hunt out, too, including the **White Horse Tavern** on Hudson Street at 11th Street, where poet Dylan Thomas allegedly went on his last drinking binge before his death in 1953. Also, take a trip to **Chumley's** at 86 Bedford Street, an unmarked speakeasy where John Steinbeck propped up the bar during prohibition era.

MIDTOWN

Scan QR code for hi-res map of Midtown

Technically, Midtown starts at 34th Street, but for the purposes of this area guide, we're starting at the more realistic 42nd Street (Map 3). From this point up to about 59th Street are some of the most beautiful and famous shops, hotels and buildings in the world, both to the east and west and on 5th Avenue itself (p127–28). At the northern end of the area, 5th Avenue is lined with marvellous institutions such as **Saks, Bergdorf Goodman, Tiffany's** (our favourite jeweller) and **Trump Tower** (p80).

Fabulous hotels in Midtown include the media den of the **Royalton** (p236) and the famous **Algonquin** (p231). Opposite **St Patrick's Cathedral** (p79) on 5th Avenue is the main entrance into the **Rockefeller Center** complex of 19 statuesque buildings with the famous ice-skating rink in the middle of its central plaza (p78). There's so much to do here, from browsing in the shops to checking out the architecture or visiting the beautifully restored Art Deco **Radio City Music Hall** (p78). Further north on 57th Street is **Carnegie Hall** (p106) and then there's the fabulous **MoMA's New Museum of Contemporary Art** (p120).

MIDTOWN EAST

Midtown East at a glance: The Chrysler and UN buildings
Accommodation: 238–42
Museums and galleries:

Asia Society	105
Frick Collection	109
Japan Society	110
Morgan Library	115

Nightlife:

Bars, lounges and pubs	201
Gay	208
Hotel bars	210

Restaurants: 176–80
Sights:

Chrysler Building	71
Grand Central Station	75
UN Building	81

Subways to get there: 6 to 33rd Street or the 4, 5, 6, 7, S to Grand Central/42nd Street

The area between 5th Avenue and East River, Midtown East (Map 3) has its fair share of New York landmarks. No visit to the city would be complete without seeing the magnificent, marble **Grand Central Station** (p75) at 42nd Street, which has been restored to its former glory. It may be overshadowed by the **MetLife Building** from the outside, but nothing can detract from its gorgeous interior. The ceiling has been painted to show

the sky as seen by God from above.

To the east is the stunning **Chrysler Building** (p71) and down by the river is the monolithic **United Nations Building** (p81); and no visit to Park Avenue would be complete without a drink at the **Waldorf-Astoria** (p241). Out of its many cocktail bars, the lobby bar is best for people-watching.

◀▌▶ BRIT TIP

The area along East 45th Street between Vanderbilt and Lexington Avenues is packed with food carts selling everything from steak sandwiches to baked potatoes.

MURRAY HILL

It's a testimony to man's desire to tame his environment that the majority of Manhattan is flat. This is a result of the zoning plans created in the early 19th century, when the streets and avenues were laid out north of Downtown, except for the Village. At the same time, the City flattened the majority of Manhattan except for what is now Morningside Heights and Harlem, as nobody believed anyone would live up there! The only other area that has kept its contours is **Murray Hill** (Map 3), a largely residential neighbourhood for New York's gentry that lies between 5th and 3rd Avenues and 32nd and 40th Streets.

The most famous resident of the area was the multi-millionaire J. P. Morgan. His son lived in a brownstone on the corner of 37th Street and Madison Avenue, which is now the headquarters of the **Lutheran Church**. J. P. Morgan lived in a house next door until he had it knocked down to make way for an expansion of his library. Now known as the **Morgan Library** (p115), it has a unique collection of manuscripts, paintings, prints and furniture, which the financier collected on his trips to Europe.

MIDTOWN WEST

Midtown West, including Times Square, Theater District and Hell's Kitchen, at a glance: Broadway
Accommodation: 242–43
Museums and galleries:

Intrepid Sea-Air-Space Museum	110
Madame Tussaud's	75

Nightlife: Gay 208

Hotel bars	211–12

Restaurants: 180–81
Sights:

Cathedral of St John the Divine	71
Riverside Church	78
Times Square	52–53

Subways to get there: 1, 2, 3, 7, 9, N, Q, R, S, W to Times Square/42nd Street

TIMES SQUARE AND THE THEATER DISTRICT

If you arrive at Times Square (Map 3) by day when all the lights and motion are less distracting, you may actually notice the lack of a square. Like Greeley and Herald Squares, Times Square is no more than a junction where Broadway crosses 7th Avenue. The Theater District starts on the boundary with the Garment District at 41st Street, goes north to 53rd Street and is bounded by 6th and 8th Avenues.

◀⊞▶ BRITTIP

Broadway isn't called The Great White Way for nothing. At night, it's at its magnificent best around Times Square, but the best way to see it is from a few blocks north, where you really can appreciate the glittering beauty of all those neon signs.

The Theater District came into being at the end of the 19th century – previously the theatres were in the Union Square area and then Chelsea – when Oscar Hammerstein I (father of the great lyricist) built his opulent but long-gone Olympia Theater on Broadway between 44th and 45th Streets. Until then, it had been an unfashionable area known as

Times Square

Long Acre Square, housing the city's stables and blacksmiths.

In 1904, when *The New York Times* set up shop in what is now 1 Times Square, the area was renamed in its honour (it's since moved offices to around the corner). That same year a massive fireworks display on New Year's Eve became the precursor to the now famous annual countdown watched by millions of people. The surrounding Theater District, home to the Ziegfeld Follies at the **New Amsterdam Theater, Minsky's** and **Gypsy Rose Lee**, blossomed in the 1920s. In fact, so many theatres burst on to the scene that even though many were converted into cinemas in the 1940s, during a clean-up of the burlesque shows by Mayor LaGuardia, 39 theatres still remain.

BAD TIMES COME

Sadly, by the 1960s, Times Square had lost its shine and the economic problems of the 1970s and 1980s compounded the situation. If you've seen Martin Scorsese's film *Taxi Driver*, you'll have some idea of the level of crime and until fairly recently it wasn't a safe place to be.

◀⊞▶ BRITTIP

For excellent dining pre- or post-show with a good chance to spot celebs, book into Angus McIndoe, 258 West 44th Street (212-221 9222, www.angusmcindoe.com).

Things started to change in the early 1990s, helped by the establishment of the **Times Square Business Improvement District**, which worked hard to clean things up and pay for security guards, and the discovery of an age-old law that prevents sex shops from operating within a certain distance of schools or churches. Since then crime in the area has dropped by 60% and many New Yorkers have even complained of its relative cleanliness. The arrival of the Disney company, which spent millions renovating the New Amsterdam Theater to put on *The Lion King* (p219), was the last nail in the coffin. Although these dirt purists shouldn't fret too much – there is still definitely an edgy vibe to the neighbourhood, while the constant stream of traffic and the grunginess of many visitors stops Times Square from being a squeaky-clean environment.

All the same, it's safe enough for the most part, attracts tenants who pay the same rents as on more elegant 5th and Madison Avenues, and has plenty to offer everyone. New hotels have sprung up and corporate companies have moved into the neighbourhood, including media giants Viacom, MTV, VH-1 studios, ABC TV's *Good Morning America*, Condé Nast Publications and Reuters news service.

There's **Nasdaq MarketSite** with its massive sign – the largest video screen in the world – and **Madame Tussaud's** (p75). In between are the Coco Chanel-style beauty emporium of **Sephora** (p140). Oh, and of course, there are the 39 theatres and around 50 cinema screens...

HELL'S KITCHEN/CLINTON

Running up the west side of Midtown from 34th Street to 57th from around 8th Avenue to the river is an area known as **Hell's Kitchen**. In the latter part of the 19th century, many poor Irish immigrants settled here, creating a ghetto. They were later joined by blacks, Italians and Latinos and inevitably gangs formed. The big employers were the docks (see *On the Waterfront* starring Marlon Brando for an insight into the lifestyle; although set in Brooklyn, it is equally true of all the dock areas), but when container ships came into play many lost their jobs. Other local industries included slaughterhouses and glue and soap factories.

BRITTIP
If you have an evening out on the World Yacht (p87), you'll find yourself walking through Hell's Kitchen/Clinton in search of a taxi. Adopt 'the New York walk' (walk quickly and confidently) and head east to 7th or 6th Avenues where it's easiest to pick up a cab.

A lot of the gangs were put out of business by the police in 1910, but it remained a scary area until fairly recently. It was renamed Clinton in 1959 to hide its violent past – which is long before Bill came on the scene, so there's no link to the former president. Now a lot of people living there work in the Theater District and it's moving up in the world. 9th and 10th Avenues are full of restaurants, the **Intrepid Sea-Air-Space Museum** (p110) is on the river and, on the whole, the area is pretty safe until 11pm.

BRITTIP
I've had trouble catching a cab in the evening in the Hell's Kitchen/Clinton area, so I'm going to let you in on my new find: www.hailocab.com/nyc. Download this app on to your smartphone and you can hail a yellow cab in one tap!

Castle Clinton

MORNINGSIDE HEIGHTS

Further north, the terrain gets hilly as you reach **Morningside Heights** (Map 6) home to the **Cathedral of St John the Divine** (p71) and **Columbia University**, one of the most exclusive universities in America where a year's tuition fees, room and board will set you back over $45,000. Even so, it has 20,000 students, of whom 4,000 are undergraduates. This is a beautiful area, which is bounded by 8th Avenue to the east and West 125th Street to the north.

BRITTIP
A great pit-stop in the Columbia University area is Tom's Restaurant on Broadway at 112th Street, www.tomsrestaurant.net (p183). If you recognise the diner's exterior, that's because it was used in *Seinfeld*.

NOHO

Noho at a glance: Boutiques, bars and restaurants
Restaurants: 182
Shopping: 144
Subways to get there: 6 to Astor Place or Bleecker Street or F, V, S to Broadway/Lafayette Street

Scan QR code for hi-res map of NoHo

Wedged between Greenwich Village and the East Village is a small section of streets now known as NoHo – North of Houston Street (Map 2). Bounded by Broadway to the west, Bowery to the east, Astor Place to the north and East Houston Street to the south, it's a tiny triangular-shaped area cut off from both of the villages, yet teeming with bars, cafés and shops. The boutiques here are a match for nearby SoHo and some are just as pricey, but for innovative and unique designs they're streets ahead of many areas, with the exception of NoLiTa.

NOLITA

NoLiTa at a glance: Cafés and boutiques
Restaurants: 182–83
Shopping: 144–45
Sights:
St Patrick's Old Cathedral 79
Subways to get there: 6 to Spring Street, F, V, S to Broadway/Lafayette Street or F, V to 2nd Avenue

Scan QR code for hi-res map of Nolita

NoLiTa stands for North of Little Italy and stretches from Kenmare Street in the south, to Houston in the north and from Crosby Street in the west to Elizabeth Street in the east (Map 2).

A fairly new part of town, it's filled with funky coffee shops, bars and restaurants. In a very short space of time Elizabeth, Mott and Mulberry Streets have seen a rapid growth in up-and-coming designers. This area was widely regarded as part of Little Italy until recent decades when it started to lose its Italian identity, following the relocation of Italian-Americans to outer boroughs.

Thanks to reasonable rents and vacant property, the latter half of the 1990s saw an influx of young urban professionals and it's now acknowledged as a neighbourhood in its own right. Due to the recent regeneration, the area is filled with cosmopolitan cafés, bars and restaurants. There's also a fashionable, edgy vibe, which is why it's become a magnet for unique boutiques selling products by up-and-coming designers.

The neighbourhood's most notable historic building is **St Patrick's Old Cathedral**, at the corner of Mott and Prince streets, which was erected in 1815 and rebuilt after a fire in 1868. It was Manhattan's main Catholic cathedral for years until a new St Patrick's was opened in 5th Avenue in Midtown in 1879. The original St Patrick's Old Cathedral is now used as a parish church and visitors are welcome to take a look around. Another landmark is the **Puck Building** on the corner of Houston and Lafayette streets. The ornate structure, built in 1885, was the headquarters of the now defunct *Puck* magazine.

SOHO

SoHo at a glance: Shopping, fashion and contemporary art
Accommodation: 243–46
Museums and galleries:
Artists' Space 105
New Museum of Contemporary Art 120
New York City Fire Museum 120
Nightlife:
Bars, lounges and pubs 202–03
Nightclubs 216
Restaurants: 183–185
Shopping: 145–52
Subways to get there: 6, C, E to Spring Street and N, R to Prince Street

Scan QR code for hi-res map of SoHo

SoHo means south of Houston, bounded by Lafayette Street at its eastern border, 6th Avenue to the west and Canal Street to the south (Map 2).

The main drag is on **West Broadway**, though Spring and Prince Streets are major shopping havens, too, and the whole area is reminiscent of Hampstead Village in London. OK, so there are no hills and the roads are wider, but it has the same picturesque, funky design-conscious element.

It's hard to imagine the totally trendy and oh-so-expensive SoHo as a slum, yet just over 30 years ago this was the case. Despite the arrival of cutting-edge artists in the 1940s, who had spotted the great potential of the massive loft spaces once used by manufacturers and wholesalers, the area was run down and shabby.

Then, in the 1960s, the artists were forced to fight for their homes when the city decided to pull down all the buildings because they were supposed to be used for light industry and not for living in. The artists argued that the architecture of the cast-iron buildings was too valuable and the whole of SoHo was declared a historic district.

◀️🇬🇧 BRITTIP

For a cheap but tasty hamburger and fries, pop into Fanelli's Café on Prince Street at Mercer Street. It's one of the oldest eateries in the neighbourhood.

In the 1970s, art galleries first started moving into the area and the art boom of the 1980s truly transformed it. In 1992, the **Guggenheim** opened a downtown site on Broadway at Prince Street. These events coincided with a kind of bubble-bursting feeling for the more cutting-edge artists, especially those who could no longer afford SoHo's sky-rocketing rents. Many have now moved on to Chelsea and TriBeCa, and SoHo has become a wealthy residential neighbourhood occupied by anyone rich enough to afford large loft spaces.

However, there are still plenty of art galleries – certainly a higher density than most areas of Manhattan – but the nature of the area has changed – and we think for the better. Designers, clothes boutiques and dedicated beauty shops have arrived en masse, though the emphasis still lies heavily on style and art in terms of presentation and decor. The Guggenheim has shut up shop to be replaced by **Prada's** stunning flagship store (p151), but a formidable sense of style remains and can be seen daily at the fashionistas' **SoHo Grand Hotel** haunt (p246). Coffee shops, bars and restaurants that normal mortals can afford are now in better supply and the beauty boutiques with their wooden flooring, high ceilings and gleaming displays are wonderful places to get cheap, expert beauty advice.

◀️🇬🇧 BRITTIP

For a well-priced, delicious lunch al fresco, head to the Gourmet Garage (www.gourmetgarage.com) on the corner of Broome and Mercer Streets. It has a wonderful deli with ready-made salads to take away.

SoHo also has several historic and architectural places of interest too. Visitors can get an art fix by hunting out **The Broken Kilometer** at 393 West Broadway, an installation by Walter De Maria that uses 500 brass rods to play tricks on the viewer's perspective.

Another notable SoHo landmark is **Hunt the Singer Building** at 561 Broadway, a beautiful building that was constructed in 1904 for the sewing machine company. The 12-storey façade is wonderfully ornate, with wrought-iron balconies and graceful arches.

You might also want to check out the **New York City Fire Museum** (p120) at 278 Spring Street, which houses a fascinating collection of Manhattan fire-fighting equipment and memorabilia from the 18th to 20th centuries.

TRIBECA

TriBeCa at a glance: Urban gentrification and film

Accommodation:	248–49
Nightlife:	
Bars, lounges and pubs	203
Hotel bars	212
Nightclubs	216
Restaurants:	186–88
Shopping:	152

Subways to get there: 1, 9 to Canal or Franklin Streets or 1, 2, 3, 9 to Chambers Street

Scan QR code for hi-res map of TriBeCa

TriBeCa (Map 1) like other acronyms is a shortening of the area's location. In this case it means the triangle below Canal Street. It is bounded by Canal to the north, Murray to the south, West Broadway to the east and the Hudson River.

TriBeCa provides a good idea of what SoHo looked like 20 years ago. With the increasing pressure to find affordable housing, the empty warehouses of TriBeCa were ripe for gentrification, following SoHo, the East Village and even the Lower East Side to an extent, and the area certainly has its fair share of pretty cast-iron buildings and quaint cobbled streets. Along **Harrison Street** is a row of well-preserved Federal-style townhouses and the area around White Street is particularly picturesque.

In the late 1970s, the former industrial buildings were targeted by estate agents for residential dwellings, but it was not really until the late 1980s that the area became a favourite with artists priced out of SoHo. Now TriBeCa is home to a variety of media and artistic businesses, such as galleries, recording

W Hotel

studios and graphic companies.

Its most famous film company, the **TriBeCa Film Center** at 375 Greenwich Street, which is part-owned by Robert De Niro, has production offices and screening rooms and is used by visiting film-makers. They, of course, frequent De Niro's extremely expensive **TriBeCa Grill** on the ground floor of the building. Visiting film-makers have also been given a boost by the opening of the triangular-shaped **TriBeCa Grand Hotel**, which has its own private screening room.

Now the area is deemed quite hip – being home to Harvey Keitel and Naomi Campbell among others – it has attracted a lot of upper middle-class families, while restaurants and nightclubs are frequented by residents from nearby Battery Park City. In the 2nd week in May it is home to the **TriBeCa Film Festival**, which showcases independent movies.

UNION SQUARE

Union Square including Flatiron District at a glance: Restaurants and the Flatiron Building

Yellow cabs

Subways to get there: L, N, Q, R, W, 4, 5, 6 to Union Square at 14th Street

Scan QR code for hi-res map of Union Square

This area was once pretty run down and overrun with drug pushers and muggers (Map 2), but now it's one of the trendiest neighbourhoods in New York. The stretch of Park Avenue South between 14th and 23rd Streets is filled with some truly 'hip' eateries and is known as **Restaurant Row**.

Along here you'll find **Tammany Hall**, the most corrupt City Hall in New York's history. It was home to Jimmy Walker, ostensibly a popular mayor, but a man who had been elected by the gangsters in the 1920s, which is effectively how organised crime was born in America. The gangsters were impossible to prosecute because they knew all the judges, cops and politicians in New York and virtually lived at Tammany Hall. Walker even had showers installed for them. Eventually, in the face of mounting financial problems in the city, Walker was forced to resign and his successor, Fiorello LaGuardia, went after the gangs.

◄▥► BRITTIP

The W Hotel Union Square on Park Avenue South at 17th Street is home to Lilium (p217), one of the newest, most stylish nightclubs in New York.

In the middle of Union Square is **Luna Park** (p265), a great casual place for a bite to eat in the summer, with outdoor seating. Further north on Broadway to Madison Square Park, you'll find **Theodore Roosevelt's birthplace** at 28 East 20th Street. It's not the original building, but it does house some great memorabilia from the former president's life (open Tues–Sat 9am–5pm; free). It was closed for renovation at the time of going to press, so check the website www.nps.gov/thrb for information before visiting. Just around the corner is the wonderful, triangular **Flatiron Building** (p74), at the end of what was once known as **Ladies Mile**, the fashionable shopping district along Broadway and 6th Avenue from 14th Street.

Scan QR code for hi-res map of the Upper East Side

One of the most conservative areas of New York, the **Upper East Side** (Map 4) stretches from Central Park South to 98th Street and is centred on 5th, Madison, Park and Lexington Avenues. It came into being after Central Park was finally completed in 1876 and the rich and famous of the Gilded Era – the Whitneys, Carnegies, Fricks, Vanderbilts and Astors – decided to build their mansions alongside. It was a time when Neo-Classicism was the favourite architectural design, but many of the houses left standing are not the originals as the grandiose properties were built and rebuilt in an ever-more opulent style or replaced with apartment blocks.

Two things have always remained the same, though. The neighbourhood is known as the Silk Stocking District because of the vast family fortunes represented in the area, and the grand old apartment houses are known as 'white glove' buildings because of the uniforms of the doormen. People still pay a fortune to live here. For instance, Jackie Onassis's former 14-room apartment at 1040 5th Avenue near East 86th Street sold some years ago for a cool $9m. The mansion on the corner of East 86th is one of 9 once owned by the Vanderbilts. Nearby residents include Michael J Fox and Bette Midler.

If you're serious about designer clothes, then you'll be visiting the designer stores that line **Madison Avenue**. If you're clever you won't buy, just gather information on what's new for when you go rummaging through the designer selections at **Daffy's** or the sample sales (p41).

This area is also full of museums, with a staggering array to choose from. They range from the world's largest and, arguably, most magnificent – the **Metropolitan Museum of Art** (p114) – to the jewel of the **Frick Collection** (p109), housed in the magnate's former mansion. Near to the Frick is the joyous **Whitney Museum of American Art** (p124), with its emphasis on contemporary art.

Further north is the beautiful-looking **Guggenheim** (p123), as well as the **Cooper-Hewitt National Design Museum** (p108), the **Jewish Museum** (p112) and the **International Center of Photography** (p110). Finally, up on the borders of East Harlem, populated by Latin Americans, are the **Museum of the City of New York** (p118) and **El Museo del Barrio** (p108)

American Museum of Natural History

Nightlife:
Bars, lounges and pubs	203
Comedy clubs	206
Live music	214
Restaurants:	191–92
Shopping:	155
Sights:	
Cathedral of St John the Divine	71
Tours:	
AOL Time Warner Center	below
Metro Bicycles	85

Subways to get there: A, B, C, D, 1, 9 to 59th Street/Columbus Circle

Scan QR code for hi-res map of the Upper West Side

Central Park divides the Upper East and West Sides not only geographically, but also in terms of attitude. If the East Side is upper crust, conservative old money, then the West Side (Map 5) is more artistic. It's a vibrant neighbourhood filled with bars, restaurants, shops, museums and the culture of the Lincoln Center.

The area is now anchored by the amazing **AOL Time Warner Center's** twin towers at Columbus Circle, which house a mixture of offices, hotel, shopping and cultural centres. The $1.7bn complex includes the **Mandarin Oriental Hotel and Spa**, the new home of jazz at the **Lincoln Center** (p214), broadcast facilities for live transmission of CNN, apartments and **The Palladium**, a massive space for shops, restaurants and entertainment venues and The Shops at Columbus Circle. As you navigate the traffic lights to cross the roads at Columbus Circle, you can ponder on the fact that this is where Joe Colombo, the boss of 1 of the 5 Mafia families of New York, was shot.

BRITTIP

Take a break at Whole Foods, a huge market selling a dazzling array of prepared organic foods, on the basement level of AOL Time Warner Center. Either dine at 1 of the tables there or eat in Central Park across the street.

Up Broadway and left down West 63rd Street you'll find the **Lincoln Center**. This was once filled with the slums that housed poor Puerto Ricans (the setting for the 1961 movie *West Side Story*) until Robert Moses proposed the building of various cultural centres that include the **Metropolitan Opera House**, the **New York State Theater** and **Avery Fisher Hall**. To see more, join one of the popular backstage tours or enjoy the free lunchtime music by jazz and folk bands during the summer.

BUILT TO LAST

The Upper West Side is well known for its beautiful buildings, including the Beaux Arts **Ansonia Hotel**, now a condo development, on Broadway between 73rd and 74th Streets, home to both Babe Ruth and Igor Stravinsky in its time. Starting on the southern tip of Central Park West, which runs all the way up Central Park, is the Art Deco stunner at No 55, which was used as the setting for the film *Ghostbusters*.

BRITTIP

Once you go north across West 59th Street, 8th, 9th, 10th and 11th Avenues become Central Park West, Columbus, Amsterdam and West End Avenues.

On 67th Street near Central Park West is the **Hotel des Artistes** that was built for the artistic types who used its studios. Over the years it has been home to such celebrities as Noel Coward and Isadora Duncan. Today you can dine at the elegant **Café des Artistes** there, which reopened under new management in 2011. Back on Central Park West between 71st and 72nd Streets is the yellow façade of the Art Deco **Majestik** apartment house, which was built in 1930.

This neighbourhood is particularly favoured by stars of stage and screen who prefer the Big Apple to Hollywood. Many have apartments along Central Park West, where one of the most coveted addresses is the city's first luxury apartment building, the famous **Dakota Building**, which was the first apartment block ever to be built on the Upper West Side in 1884, and was named after the distant territory to indicate its remoteness from anything else on the West Side. Of course, since then it has had a long line of famous inhabitants, including Leonard Bernstein, Judy Garland and Boris Karloff. Its most famous resident of all, **John Lennon**, was gunned down outside the building by a crazed fan in 1980. His widow Yoko Ono still lives here – she owns several apartments – and she donated money to build the Strawberry Fields memorial to the star in

Central Park, just across the road.

A couple of blocks north between 73rd and 74th is the Neo-Renaissance style **Langham**, which was built in 1905, and between 74th and 75th is the San Remo, built in 1930, where Rita Hayworth died of Alzheimer's in 1987. Residents have included Dustin Hoffman and Paul Simon, and rumour has it that the resident committee turned down Madonna! **The Eldorado**, which Roth designed on Central Park West, has been home to Marilyn Monroe and Groucho Marx.

Several blocks north, on the corner of 81st Street and Central Park West, stands the elegant **Beresford**. Between them, these grand apartment blocks have housed a huge number of celebrities, including such names as Lauren Bacall, Dustin Hoffman, Steve Martin and Jerry Seinfeld, who bought Isaac Stern's sprawling apartment home.

MUSEUM HALF MILE

On Central Park West at 77th Street is the **New York Historical Society** (p121), which was formed in 1804 and was the only art museum in the city until the opening of the Metropolitan Museum of Art in 1872. It was founded to chronicle New York's history, but still houses the world's largest collection of Tiffany stained-glass shades and lamps and 2 million manuscripts, including letters sent by George Washington during the War of Independence.

Next door is the real big boy of museums, the **American Museum of Natural History** (p102), which was the brainchild of scientist Albert Smith Bickmore. It first opened at the New York Arsenal in Central Park in 1869, but by 1874 had moved to these bigger premises. Architect Calvert Vaux, who was also responsible for the Met Museum and largely responsible for Central Park, created the bulk of the building, which has since had a Romanesque-style façade added to its 77th Street side and a Beaux Arts-style frontage on the Central Park West side. This is a favourite museum of ours. It's crammed with well-laid-out exhibitions that really bring the world of science, scientific discovery and expeditions to life, while the **Rose Center** and **Big Bang Theater** attract major crowds to see the 13-billion-year history of the universe.

The Upper West Side's Museum Half Mile

also includes the **Children's Museum of Manhattan** (p106) on 83rd Street between Broadway and Amsterdam Avenue, where interactive exhibits keep the young ones happy.

West 106th Street, at the top end of the neighbourhood, is now known as **Duke Ellington Broadway**. This is where the great musician lived, premiered many of his songs and was buried in 1974. Over 10,000 people came to his funeral and there is a memorial to him on 5th Avenue at West 110th by Central Park's Harlem Meer.

WEST VILLAGE

West Village at a glance: Pretty streets
Nightlife:

Bars, lounges and pubs	203–04
Comedy clubs	206
Gay	208–09
Nightclubs	216–17

Tours:

Literary Pub Crawl	94

Subways to get there: 1, 9 to Christopher Street or A, C, E to 14th Street or L subway to 8th Avenue

Scan QR code for hi-res map of West Village

The West Village, on the other side of 7th Avenue, has an amazingly pretty collection of cobbled streets lined with picturesque homes and trees. These are among some of the oldest remaining houses in New York, many being built in the 1820s and 1850s, and quite a few have the one thing that is so rare in Manhattan – a back garden, albeit tiny.

FAMOUS SPEAKEASY

On the corner of Bedford Street, number 86 was one of the most famous former speakeasies in New York. Known as Chumley's, the front entrance merely had an old grille used for checking over potential customers during Prohibition. In the old days, a dumb waiter took 2 people at a time to the gambling den upstairs, and the best table in the house was right by the entrance to the cellar, where people could hide if there was raid. Unfortunately it's now closed, but there have been rumours for many years of a reopening. The latest part of the five-year saga is that 28 neighbours have objected to reopening plans – watch this space!

At the corner of **Grove Street** is the oldest wooden house in the West Village. Built in 1822, it's the most exclusive cottage in the area and costs around $6,000 a month to rent, but it does have its own little garden: what a bargain! On your left, look out for **90 Bedford**, the exterior of which was used as the apartment building in *Friends*. All around Grove Street the houses are covered in a network of vines, which blossom in May and have grown in the area for 150 years.

A MATTER OF RIGHTS

Christopher Street, the main drag of the West Village, is the heart of the gay community and a shopping paradise for antique lovers. **Sheridan Square**, one of the Village's busiest junctions, has been the scene of 2 major riots. First were the New York Draft Riots of 1863, sparked off by the requirement to join the army for the Civil War. The rich could buy their way out, but the poor had no choice and were fearful they would lose their jobs to the newly freed black slaves.

> ### BRITTIP
> Crossing Bedford is Barrow Street, where you'll find One If By Land, Two If By Sea. It's in the oldest building housing a restaurant in Manhattan, a former carriage house built in 1726. Great food, service and decor. If you're in the mood for a romantic splurge, this is the place (212-255 8649, www.oneifbyland.com).

The second riot is the more famous and is known as the Stonewall Riot. This was

sparked in 1969 by the police raiding the Stonewall gay bar and arresting its occupants – an event that frequently occurred at the many gay watering holes in the area. This time the community decided to fight back and, over a period of 3 nights, the gay community held its ground in the Stonewall as it was surrounded by police. It was the crucial first step made by gay people in standing up for their rights.

Christopher Street is still filled with bars, restaurants and bookstores that are used by gays – though not exclusively – but many members of the gay community have moved on to Chelsea.

YORKVILLE

Between Lexington Avenue and the East River from East 77th to 96th Streets is the working to middle class enclave of Yorkville (Map 5) (subway 4, 5, 6 to 86th Street), which has an interesting mix of cultures, singles and families.

> ### BRITTIP
> Stop off at The Vinegar Factory in 91st Street (p155), where you'll find an extensive selection of cheeses, meats, breads and salads, and head for the nearby Carl Schurz Park for a picnic by the river (212-987 0855, www.elizabar.com).

It was originally populated by German-Hungarians, who moved northwards from their first stopping point in the East Village's Thompkins Square with the arrival of Italian and Slavic immigrants. Now, though, you'd be hard-pressed to find the few remnants of German culture, as most left the neighbourhood during the Second World War to avoid anti-German feelings.

> ### BRITTIP
> For some of the world's finest coffees and teas, pop in to McNulty's Tea & Coffee Company (212-242 5351, www.mcnultys.com), 109 Christopher Street, between Bleecker and Hudson streets.

The most famous face in the area is the mayor, currently Michael Bloomberg, who conducts business in the official residence at Gracie Mansion (p75) overlooking the East River and the lovely Carl Schurz Park at East 89th Street.

McNulty's Tea & Coffee Company

CHAPTER 3

Getting Around

W hen most people talk about New York, they actually mean Manhattan, which is the long island in the middle of the four outer boroughs of Staten Island, Queens, the Bronx and Brooklyn. Diagrammatic maps will help you focus on the basic geography, then you'll find it easier to use the subway and bus maps on the inside front cover, and the street maps at the front of the book.

BRITTIP
Download a free NYC Map (www.nycgo.com/citymaps) app from iTunes to find your way around the 5 main boroughs. It includes information on hotels, restaurants, shopping, entertainment, bars, nightlife and daily deals.

ORIENTATION

Manhattan is 21km/13ml long and 3.2km/2ml wide and almost all of it above 14th Street is on the grid system that was introduced quite early on in New York's history. The main exceptions are Chinatown and Greenwich Village, which, like Downtown, had already established its eccentric random arrangement of streets before urban planning and refused to get on the grid system. The other exception is Broadway, which follows an old Indian trail that runs largely north to south on the west side of the island, then cuts across to the east side down towards Downtown.

Here are a few basic rules about the geography of Manhattan, which will help you get around with confidence.

▶ Manhattan is divided into 3 main areas: Downtown, south of 14th Street; Midtown, between 14th and 59th Streets; and Uptown, north of 59th Street.

▶ Roads across Manhattan east to west are streets and roads going north to south are avenues.

▶ The city is divided between east and west by 5th Avenue and all the house numbers begin there, so 2 West 57th Street is a few

steps west of 5th Avenue while 2 East 57th Street is a few steps to the east.

▶ Most streets in Manhattan are one way. With a few exceptions, traffic on even-numbered streets travels east and traffic on odd-numbered streets travels west. Traffic on major 'crosstown' streets – horizontal on the street maps – travels in both directions. From south to north, these include Canal, Houston, 14th, 23rd, 34th, 42nd, 57th, 72nd, 79th, 86th and 96th Streets.

BRITTIP
To New Yorkers, 'downtown' does not mean the city centre, but means south, while 'uptown' means north. Knowing this will help if you plan to use the subway – which is simpler to use than it looks!

▶ When travelling north to south or vice versa, remember that traffic on York Avenue goes both ways, 1st Avenue goes from south to north, 2nd Avenue goes south and 3rd goes north mostly, though there is a small two-way section. Lexington goes south, Park goes in both directions, Madison goes north and 5th Avenue goes south. Central Park West goes both ways, Columbus Avenue goes

Grand Central Terminal

south, Amsterdam Avenue north, Broadway goes in both directions until Columbus Circle, after which it continues southbound only to the tip of Manhattan. West End Avenue and Riverside Drive go in both directions.

▶ Numbered avenue addresses increase from south to north.

◀🇬🇧▶ **BRITTIP**

To calculate distances, 20 north-south blocks or 10 east-west blocks equal about 1.6km/1ml (except in the Financial District or Greenwich Village).

ENTERING THE US

All Visa Waiver Programme travellers (if you're entering the US from the UK then you are a VWP traveller) have to get official authorisation before going to America. To do this, go on to the internet-based Electronic System for Travel Authorisation (ESTA) to apply: https://esta.cbp.dhs.gov/esta/. Fill in the online application form, submit it and record your application number. Within 72 hours you can check to see if you've been approved, held or rejected (you can ask for the results to be forwarded to your email). If you're not successful, you may still be able to obtain a visa through the US embassy. Initially, VWP was free, but as of late 2011 it costs $4 to apply, which you can pay online by Mastercard, Visa or American Express. If you are approved, another $10 will be charged to your credit card.

ARRIVING BY AIR

JOHN F KENNEDY INTERNATIONAL AIRPORT (JFK)
718-244 4444
www.jfk-airport.net
JFK is in Jamaica in the borough of Queens and is the best place to enter or leave New York by air. It's 24km/15ml from Midtown Manhattan, a journey that will take you 50–60 minutes.

Taxi
New York is unusual because you can't pre-arrange a pickup by a New York taxi; you'll need a car or livery service for that. The cost of a yellow medallion taxi into Manhattan centre is a fixed rate of $52 (per taxi). Bridge and tunnel tolls are extra (around $6), as is the 15–20% tip, so think around $60.

Train
The AirTrain JFK: (212-435 7000, www. jfk-airport.net/airtrain.html) is a flat $5

AIRPORT SECURITY
US airports have notoriously high security in place, so expect longer queues and waiting times getting through immigration and baggage checks than Europe or the Far East. Remember the usual rules about not carrying sharp objects in your hand luggage, and not taking liquids – check the latest information before you fly. Be prepared to be asked to open your bags for inspection, remove your shoes and to be frisked and checked with hand-held scanner.

enter/exit fare. They run every 10 minutes 24 hours a day and takes 35 minutes to an hour via Howard Beach station from where you connect to the A subway, bus or Jamaica station on the Long Island Rail Road train to connect with, E J and Z subways and plentiful buses, to head into town.

Bus
New York Airport Express Service Bus: Westside & Eastside, 718-560 3915, www. nyairportservice.com. Catch one from the Ground Transportation Center to Grand Central Station, Port Authority and Penn Station. They run 6.05am–11pm daily every 15–30 minutes, take 1 hour and cost $15 (or $25 round trip).

◀🇬🇧▶ **BRITTIP**

A great website covering the main New York airports, www.airportinfoalerts.com, which notifies you of important information such as delays caused by weather, parking space capacity and AirTrain service charges. You can even have free alerts sent direct to your mobile phone or email account before you travel.

Private hire car and shuttle services
Go Airlink Shuttle: 212-812 9000, www.goairlinkshuttle.com offers 24/7 transport in shared vans door to door to your hotel from $12 as well as private hire.

Carmel Limo: 1-866-666 6666 or 212-666 6666, www.carmellimo.com. It costs from $40 to Manhattan.

Supersaver by Carmel: 1-800-924 9954 or 212-666 6666, carmellimo.com. To Manhattan it costs $44 5am–8pm, an additional $5-7 will be added for a pick-up between 8pm and 4am.

SuperShuttle: 800-258 3826 or 212-258 3826, www.supershuttle.com. A door-to-door minibus service from the airport to your hotel operating 24/7 as well as private hire. Look for the blue van! Costs around $19 to midtown hotels.

NEWARK LIBERTY INTERNATIONAL AIRPORT
973-961 6000
www.newarkairport.com

Taxi
The journey from Newark to central Manhattan takes around 40 minutes, but add at least 30 minutes in the rush hour. Set taxi fares range from $50 to the Battery Park area to $70 and above to 185th Street. There's a $5 extra charge for all destinations to the east side of Manhattan, plus a $5 surcharge to all points in the state of New York during weekday rush hours (6–9am and 4–9pm). For more information, contact the Newark Taxi Commission (973-733 8912, www.nyc.gov/taxi).

BRITTIP

Reader Margy Wooding sent this luggage tip: 'Neither the airports nor the train stations have left luggage facilities. I'd hoped to leave my suitcase at Grand Central Station but was told it wasn't possible. The lady at the information desk there told me the only place for left luggage in Manhattan is Schwartz Travel Services, 355 West 36th Street, between 8th and 9th Avenues near Penn Station (0800-2300) or 34 West 46th Street, between 5th and 6th Avenues near Times Square and Grand Central Station (0900-1800), 212-290-2626. I only needed it for one hour and it cost me $10 (but the nice woman there said I could have left it overnight). A bargain, I thought.'

Train
AirTrain: 1-888-397 4636, www.airtrainnewark.com. This $415m link connecting the airport terminals with Newark Liberty International Airport Train Station operates 24/7, takes from 7–11 minutes and costs $5.50; children under 11 ride free. You can get to Manhattan from the station by taking an NJ Transit or Amtrak train to New York Penn Station, and connect to the city's subways and buses with ease.
Don't chuck your AirTrain ticket! You must use your ticket twice regardless of which direction you're travelling: you're required to show the ticket to the conductor on the NJ

TRANSIT or Amtrak train, and you'll need the ticket to pass through the fare line at Newark Liberty International Airport Station.

Bus
Newark Liberty Airport Express: 877-8 NEWARK, www.coachusa.com/olympia/ss.newarkairport.asp. A convenient service to Manhattan that leaves every 15 minutes, 4am–1am, every day of the year. One-way $16, round trip $28. Three pick-up and drop-off locations in Manhattan – Port Authority Bus Terminal, Bryant Park and Grand Central Station – and terminals A, B and C at the airport.

Private hire car and Shuttle services: As from John F Kennedy International airport (p62).

LAGUARDIA AIRPORT (LGA)
718-533 3400
www.panynj.gov/airports/laguardia.html
This is the airport you'll probably arrive at if you've taken an internal domestic flight from another state. TWIA, United Airlines and Continental Airlines all operate here. It's situated about 13km/8ml from the centre of Manhattan, between Queens and the Bronx.

BRITTIP

A 7-day Pay As You Go MetroCard costs $30 and is accepted on all MTA New York City Transit trains and local buses (p66).

Taxi
You'll find a clearly marked taxi rank outside the main terminals. Unlike JFK, you pay by the meter rather than a flat rate, and you will also be charged tolls. A basic guide is $25–30 plus tolls ($4–6) and tip, and the journey should take about 20–25 minutes.

BRITTIP

Ignore offers of transport from people hanging around the terminals. If you're tired and wanting to save some cash it's tempting, but it's not safe. Also, seek out uniformed porters or airline employees if you need baggage assistance, but remember you'll need some cash for a tip.

Bus
New York Airport Express Bus: 718-875 8200, www.nyairportservice.com. A far cheaper option into town than taxi, taking around 40–50 minutes. The fare costs only $12 (or $21 round trip) and buses run daily 7.20am–11pm, leaving every 30 minutes. To

catch your ride into town, follow the Ground Transportation signs out of the terminal and wait at the M60 or Q33 bus stop sign by the curb (serving midtown hotels between 31st and 60th Streets ONLY). Midtown hotels $12 one way, round trip $27).

GETTING AROUND

The yellow cabs that you'll see in abundance are the fastest and most efficient way of getting to a destination, but they're not the cheapest. The subway in New York is easy to use and perfect for people with a limited budget, as well as being under cover when it's raining. If you'd rather see the sights, then jump on a bus, though progress can be slow in rush hour. Then there's the oldest mode of transport: your feet. Walking around Manhattan is a joyful experience and thoroughly recommended; just don't forget your comfy shoes.

TAXI

No trip to Manhattan would be complete without a ride in one of the 10,000 yellow Medallion cabs. It's the preferred means of transport for many visitors, largely because there are so many and the fares are reasonable. However, even though the fares are much cheaper than in London, the cost still mounts up pretty quickly. Fares start at $2.50 and increase 40c every 0.32km/1/5ml or 20c per minute in stopped or slow traffic, with a 50c surcharge at night (8pm–6am), $1 in peak hour (Mon–Fri 4–8pm) and 50c New York State tax. Plus you have to add the $1 tip to the hotel doorman and the 15% tip to the driver.

In any case, you will need to have a good idea of where you are going and how to get there, as most of the cab drivers in New York are the latest immigrants and have very little clue about how to get around the city, so always carry the full address of where you're going, preferably with a map reference. Fortunately it is relatively easy to master the grid system so you can give them directions!

BRITTIP
For the lowdown on prices, tips on hailing a cab and other useful hints and tips visit www. ny.com/transportation/taxis.

▶ Never expect the driver to be the chatty character you're used to. Some speak little English and most are not interested in making conversation.
▶ Make sure you get into a taxi heading in the direction that you want to be going. If

you are travelling uptown but you're on a road heading downtown, walk a block east or west so you'll be pointing in the right direction. It saves time and money, and if you don't, the taxi driver will know immediately that you're a tourist.
▶ To check if a cab is free, look at the lights on the top. If the central light is on, the driver is working and available. If all the lights are out, the driver is working but has a fare. If the outer 2 lights or all 3 lights are on, the driver is off-duty – you'll see the words.
▶ To hail a taxi, stand at the kerb and hold out your arm.

BRITTIP
I recently discovered www. hailocab.com/nyc an app you can download on to your smartphone so you can hail a yellow cab in one tap wherever you are!

▶ When you get to a toll, expect the taxi driver to turn around and demand the cash to pay for it, but you are within your rights to ask him to add it to your final fare.
▶ Beware of trying to get a cab at around 4pm. Not only is it the approach of rush hour, but it is also when most drivers change shifts, so getting a taxi is well nigh impossible as they don't want to go anywhere but home! If you really need a taxi at this time, call a car service company.

BRITTIP
In 2008, the Taxi and Limousine Commission approved a scheme to install credit and debit card payment systems in the rear of yellow Medallion cabs, so if you don't have cash with you, you can still hail a taxi if you have plastic.

▶ Cabs take cash and credit/debit cards, but if you're paying in cash it's best to have some small bills because cabbies don't usually break anything higher than $20.

BRITTIP
Remember that NYC cab drivers do not need a qualification in the city's geography like The Knowledge held by London cabbies, so have an address for your destination.

▶ In addition to the medallion on the roof, a legitimate taxi will have an automatic receipt machine mounted on the dashboard.
▶ If you find yourself below Canal Street after business hours or at the weekend, you

GETTING AROUND

might have difficulty finding a yellow cab. Your best bet is to phone one of the many companies listed under Taxicab Service in the Yellow Pages. Fares are slightly higher than for the metered cabs, but they are a safer option.

▶ There is no extra charge per person or for luggage, but a licensed taxi won't be able to take more than four people.

▶ Fasten your seatbelt once in the cab. All taxis are now required by law to provide them and passengers in the front seat have to wear them.

▶ Avoid unregulated cars at all costs. Known as gypsy cabs, these vehicles aren't registered, so are less safe, plus, unlike the UK, they usually cost more than cabs. Basically, if it's not a yellow Medallion taxi, don't get in!

BRITTIP

To get an estimate of fares, log on to www.yellowcabnyc.com/fareestimator. You key in your start and destination and time of day to calculate an average fare.

CAR SERVICE COMPANIES

When you need to be certain you have a taxi ride to the airport or some other destination, here are the companies you can phone, all of which provide a 24-hour service:

Carmel: 212-666-6666, www.carmelcarservice.com.

Dial 7: 212-777 7777/1-800-777 8888, www.dial7.com.

Tel-Aviv: 212-777 7777/1-800-222 9888, www.telavivlimo.com.

Tri-State Limousine: 516-9334759, toll-free (866) NY-LIMO2, www.tristatelimony.com.

ON THE SUBWAY

The first time you take a look at a subway map of New York, you can be forgiven for thinking you need a degree in the whole system to get anywhere. Plus the signposts – both outside and inside the stations – can easily be missed. In addition, the Metropolitan Transportation Authority (MTA) is undergoing a billion-dollar rejuvenation programme of many subway stops and has introduced new, clean trains on to the network, though New Yorkers aren't convinced that will last! On the old subway trains, the conductor would always announce stops and interchanges. These, for the large part, were unintelligible, but the new trains have pre-recorded announcements in a clear, non-New York accent.

SUBWAY MAP

There are subway maps on the inside front cover of this book. You can also get free MTA maps in most subways stations, hotel lobbies and information centres.

▶ The subway lines are all indicated on the map by a colour but, unlike the London Underground, the colours are not used in the stations and on the trains.

▶ The important bit is the number or letter. Below the name of every stop you will find the letters and numbers of lines that stop there, such as 7, S Grand Central/42nd Street.

▶ A number or letter in a diamond = rush-hour service.

▶ A number or letter in a circle it = normal service.

▶ A number of letter in a square = the end of a line.

▶ Black and white lines connecting white and black circles = a free subway transfer.

▶ White circles on coloured lines = express stops (express trains skip about 3 stops for every 1 that they make).

▶ Numbers against your destination printed in a lighter tone = peak-time only.

BRITTIP

Generally, if you're going downtown, use subway entrances on the west side of the road and if you're going uptown, use subway entrances on the east side. This way you should be heading in the right direction, but do always check before entering.

RIDING THE SUBWAY

The good news is that New York's subway system is one of the cheapest to ride in the world. Before you can start getting around on the subway you'll need to buy a MetroCard (which also works on buses, p66). You can buy these from a booth inside the entrance to the station or from a MetroCard vending machine, which you'll easily spot as they're brightly coloured. The machines accept cash, debit and credit cards. There are 2 types of ticket: pay-per-use and unlimited-ride.

BRITTIP

The subway's traditional high entrance turnstiles, known by locals as Iron Maidens, are being replaced by high entrance exit turnstiles (HEETs). HEETS only take MetroCard rather than tokens, so if you're going to be travelling a lot by subway, a MetroCard is essential.

► Don't look for obvious subway signs; look for either the discreet 'M' in blue or the signature red and green glass globes – red means the entrance is not always open and green means it's staffed 24 hours a day.

► Before going down a subway entrance, check it is going in the right direction for you – many entrances take you to either 'downtown' or 'uptown' destinations. If you swipe in to go in the wrong direction by mistake, you'll have to swipe out then back in the right direction, so you'll end up paying double. The alternative is to travel in the wrong direction until you get to one of the larger subway stations (such as 42nd Street) and then change.

BRITTIP

Changes to subway schedules often occur at the last minute, so pay attention to posters on subway station walls and any announcements you hear on the platforms.

► The same applies if you're in the outer boroughs, but instead of looking for a Downtown or Uptown sign, look for Manhattan.

► Some trains are express, so stop only at selected stations. At some stations you have to go down 2 flights to get to the platforms for express trains, while at others you don't, and it is easy to get on an express train by mistake.

► There are conflicting opinions as to whether it is worth waiting for an express – they are faster, but you may have to wait longer.

► There are many different lines going to the same destinations, but they don't all exit at the same place. For example, if you arrive at Fulton Street, the Red Line exits at Fulton and William Streets, the Brown Line exits at John and Nassau Streets, the Blue Line exits at Fulton and Nassau Streets, and the Green Line exits at Broadway and John Street – all of which are quite a long way from each other.

► The locals consider that the subway is safe to travel on until around 11pm. After that opinions vary, but be aware that the service after 11pm is generally quite slow.

► Because Manhattan is largely made up of granite, they did not have to dig as deep to find the strong foundation level, so you generally only have to go down 1 flight of steps to find the line.

► The L line runs almost the full width of Manhattan along 14th Street from 8th Avenue in the west to 1st Avenue in the

METROCARD

The flat fare to travel on the subway or bus is $2.50. For value for money, however, it's wise to buy a MetroCard. You have 2 choices when purchasing: a pay-per-ride (regular) MetroCard or an Unlimited Ride MetroCard. The former allows you to buy as many rides as you want from $5 to $89 and there's a pay-per-ride bonus of 5% added to your card if you purchase $5 or more. The second option, an Unlimited Ride MetroCard, allows you to buy an unlimited number of subway or bus rides for a fixed price. You can choose from: 7-Day Pass, $30; 30-Day, $112 or 7-Day Express Bus Plus, $55.

You can purchase the cards from subway ticket offices (cash only), vending machines in most subways, from drugstores such as Rite Aid and Hudson News or from the Times Square Visitors' Center at 1560 Broadway between 46th and 47th Streets. Some hotels also sell them at the reception desk.

For more details, contact the MTA on 1-800-638 7622 or mta.info.

As of March 2013, there's a new $1 fee for each new MetroCard you purchase, so to avoid paying these little extras keep the first card you buy and keep refilling at a MetroCard Vending Machine or station booths.

east on its way to Queens. Other stops in Manhattan include 6th Avenue, Union Square and 3rd Avenue.

► The S line should not be confused with the shuttle between Times Square and Grand Central Station. It is another good east-west train linking West and East Villages in Greenwich and runs from West 4th Street to Grand Street.

BRITTIP

If you're worried about getting lost in New York, click on to www.hopstop.com for online subway and walking directions around the city.

► In Manhattan, the new peak-time V line largely runs in conjunction with the F line and includes new stops at 5th Avenue and 53rd Street, Lexington Avenue and 53rd Street.

ON THE BUSES

Travelling by bus is always a little more nerve-wracking because you can never be sure whether you've arrived at your destination, but most people are pretty helpful if asked a direct question.

FINDING A BUS

Our Manhattan bus map inside the front cover will come in handy as often there are no route maps at the bus stops. However, as a general rule buses run north to south, south to north, east to west or west to east.

You can recognise bus stops by a yellow-painted kerb. They are usually on street corners and have a tall, round blue and white sign with a bus emblem and route number. Some stops have bus shelters and most have Guide-a-Ride information, a rectangular box attached to the bus sign pole that displays a route map and service schedule.

RIDING THE BUSES

▶ Get on the bus at the front and click in your MetroCard or feed in $2.50. Have the exact coins – no bills.
▶ If you're over 65 years old or have a disability, you're eligible for a discount if you have a proper form of ID, like your passport.
▶ Get off at the front or back.
▶ To request a stop, press the black strips that run the length of the bus between the windows or at the back along the handles.
▶ If the bus says 'Limited Stopping' it stops only at major stops, such as the cross-town streets of 14, 23, 34, 42, 50, 57, 68, 72, 79 and 86.

BRITTIP
Believe it or not, there is an app telling you where the nearest 'restroom' is: www.freepee.org.

TOURIST ROUTE

If your feet are killing you, jump on the M1 bus to continue your trawl of the Manhattan sights: 5th Avenue (Central Park), 5th Avenue/84th Street (Metropolitan Museum of Art), 5th Avenue/49th–50th Streets (Rockefeller Centre), Madison Avenue/East 43rd Street (Grand Central Terminal/Chrysler Building). There is also the M4, which covers 5th and Madison Avenues and Broadway, and the M20, which takes in the Lincoln Center and Battery Park.

BY WATER TAXI

A commuter service runs around the lower part of Manhattan, but the most useful is a hop-on/hop-off service. The 3 bright yellow catamarans with black and white check are easy to spot and there are 10 stops from DUMBO to West 44th Street, all easily accessible from the subway and bus stops. The service runs 11am–3pm on weekdays,

FINDING A WC

A public toilet is a 'restroom', and they are thin on the ground.

Barnes & Noble: The bookstore wants people to treat the stores as meeting places.

Bryant Park: Surely the city's finest – and free: neo-Grecian with pillars, giant marble urn full of flowers, real soap and uniformed attendant. No wonder it's award-winning!

Department stores: You'll need to ask where they are; they are hidden away to deter street people from using them.

Hotels: Usually on the ground floor.

Lincoln Center: There are 10 'stalls' open to the public, close to the entrance.

McDonald's and Burger King: Unisex toilets that are usually clean and modern.

Public libraries: They all have public loos.

Restaurants: Some have signs saying 'For customers only', but if you ask authoritatively enough and look okay, they'll probably let you use them.

Statue of Liberty: In the gift shop.

stopping en route at South Street Seaport, Battery Park, World Financial Center, West Village and Chelsea Piers. At weekends, it runs each hour 11.02am–7.02pm from Hunters Point, stopping at East 34th Street, Schaeffer Landing, Fulton Ferry Landing, South Street Seaport, Red Hook, Battery Park, World Financial Center, Pier 45, West 23rd Street and West 44th Street. The other direction, from West 44th Street, runs each hour 11.32am–6.32pm.

The Hop-on/Hop-off pass (212-742 1969, www.nywatertaxi.com) runs every weekend, on the hour April–Nov, 10pm–6pm taking in 10 stops at the city's top neighbourhoods and attractions, including the Statue of Liberty, the Brooklyn Bridge and Manhattan Skyline. A 1-day Hop-on/Hop-off pass costs $28 for adults, $17 for seniors and $17 for children 12 and under, and the price also includes a ride on an open-top double decker bus. If you're on a budget or here in winter, check out the commuter route and times.

BRITTIP
A new – and cheap – way to get around is by riding the new East River Ferry (www.nywaterway. com), which runs between Manhattan, Queens, Brooklyn and Governors Island (weekends) for just $4 a ride.

DRIVING IN NEW YORK

Don't even think about it. Most of the streets will be jam-packed, parking is extremely scarce and astronomically expensive at $8–10 an hour. You can park on the street, but watch out for alternate-side-of-the-street parking. This means you have to know which day of the week the cleaning truck comes past so you move the car over at the right time. Double parking is common, so it is easy to get boxed in, and frustrated drivers simply get in their cars and honk the horn until the guilty owner moves their car. As one New Yorker told us: 'People do not know how to park here. New Yorkers are not good drivers and are the wildest parkers.'

◀🇬🇧▶ BRITTIP

Unlike in Britain, overtaking is permitted on the inside and outside lanes of interstate highways, so if you're driving to Manhattan from one of the airports, be sure to use both of your wing mirrors.

If you plan to take a trip upstate and wish to do so by car, then there are some dos and don'ts about car hire. Firstly, never hire a car in Manhattan unless you want to pay around $160 a day. Take a ferry to the state of New Jersey and hire a car from there for around $85 for a medium-sized car with unlimited

Bikes at the Tribeca Grand

DRIVING TIPS

▶ Most streets in New York are one way.
▶ Drivers and front-seat passengers have to wear seatbelts by law, as do children aged 4–10 in the back.
▶ Red signs with street cleaning symbols mean you will have to move your car to allow street sweepers to pass, or be fined or towed away.
▶ Don't leave anything of value on show in your car or you're liable to have your vehicle broken into.
▶ If someone approaches your vehicle at traffic lights to ask for money or to wash your windows, it's best to ignore them and keep your doors locked.
▶ Speed limits are 30mph around town, 55mph on highways and freeways.
▶ Private parking facilities are available in the city but they cost $25–40 per day.
▶ Illegally parked cars will be towed away and there's a $150 fine plus $15 per day to be paid. Collect your car from Pier 76, West 38th Street at 12th Avenue (Midtown West). Tel 212-971 0772. It's open 24 hours a day Mon–Sat.

mileage. Secondly, don't consider hiring a car in the summer or at weekends because that's what most New Yorkers will be doing and they'll be difficult to come by. Cars are also snapped up in the autumn when New Yorkers like to go to see the autumn foliage.

CAR HIRE

If you do decide to drive, there are a number of car hire companies. Most are based at the major airports, so you can simply pick them up when you arrive. Prices vary enormously, from a one-day rental costing from $90 to a week rate of $225–300. You'll need to be over 25, and have a valid driving licence, your own insurance and some photo ID. You'll also need to have a credit card (or very large cash deposit) and most rental companies add sales tax of around 8.6%.

Car hire companies

Alamo: 1-800-462 5266, www.alamo.com.

Argus Rentals: 212-372 7266, www.argusrentals.com.

Avis: 1-800-331 1212, www.avis.com.

Dollar: 1-800-800 3665, www.dollar.com.

Hertz: 800-654 3131, www.hertz.com.

Independent (and often cheaper) car rental companies:
www.carrentalexpress.com.

CHAPTER 4

What to See and Do

There is SO much to see and do in the city that never sleeps that it can all feel a bit daunting when you first step out of your hotel, guidebook in hand. New York can induce terrible FOMO (fear of missing out!), so I've tried to pick out a mix of tourist must-sees and more quirky, in-the-know places to give you a good balance. I'd recommend making a plan of what you'd really like to see, because before you know it you'll be back on the plane heading home and wishing you'd seen much more. The major sights are often the number one priority – especially for the first-time visitor – so, to make your life a little easier, we have indicated the location of each of the iconic sights. Best to read Chapter 2 first though to get a good feel for each of the neighbourhoods. That way you can make the most of your time by planning your days to take in specific areas of the city. For instance, if you plan to see the Empire State Building, bear in mind it is deep in the heart of the 34th Street shopping district.

The section entitled Orientation (p61) will also help you make sense of the streets of New York and get to know the intricacies of the grid system and the distances involved. Having said all of that, do make sure you leave a little time in your schedule for simply wandering. Even if it's only for a couple of hours, the feeling of walking along the streets of New York like a local and discovering a charming café or cool local shop as yet unearthed by a guidebook is marvellous.

> ◀🇬🇧▶ **BRITTIP**
> Security at many sights and buildings has been tightened following the tragic events of 11 September, so allow extra time for this when planning your schedules.

PART ONE – SIGHTSEEING

This section gives you our Top 5 must-see sights, plus all the major sights in New York, including some amazing buildings. Whether you have a specific interest in architecture or not, you won't fail to appreciate just how beautiful many of the buildings in New York

69

WHAT TO SEE AND DO

Brooklyn Bridge

are. The fact that Manhattan is an island has been key to so many of the designs over the last 200 years: when space is at a premium the only way to go is up. New York gave the world skyscrapers and it's these soaring buildings that have given the city its sensational skyline. You can either visit these attractions under your own steam or take advantage of the many and varied tours available, listed in part 2.

A–Z of SIGHTSEEING

9/11 MEMORIAL
Financial District
- ✉ 1 Albany Street at Greenwich Street
- ☎ 212-266 5211
- ⌕ www.911memorial.org
- 🚇 Subway A, C, J, Z, 2, 3, 4, 5, to Fulton Street; E to World Trade Center
- ☉ Daily 10am-8pm (March-September), 10am-6pm (September to December)
- $ Admission free, but a visitor pass is required which can be booked online

Part of the World Trade Center redevelopment designed by Daniel Libeskind following the destruction of the Twin Towers by terrorists on 11 September 2001, the memorial is a tranquil place for visitors to come and pay their respects. There are two large reflection pools of cascading water, surrounded by trees, built on the site where the Twin Towers once stood - each has a bronze strip around the rim listing the names of all the victims of the attack. As you'd expect, security is pretty tight, so you'll be asked for photo ID and have your bags thoroughly checked – bags larger than 8x17in aren't allowed and there's no baggage storage area, so try to travel light on the day you choose to visit.

BRITTIP
There aren't any public toilets in the memorial, the closest public toilets are in Wagner Park or Battery Park.

A 9/11 Museum is currently under construction beneath the Memorial, which will have an exhibition that includes an entrance corridor with portrait photographs of the 3000 victims. Once inside there will be multimedia displays, archives, narratives from survivors and artefacts. It will also explore the background leading up to the events and visitors will also be able to see the remnants of the structural columns from the original Twin Towers.

9/11 TRIBUTE CENTER
Financial District
- ✉ 120 Liberty Street, between Liberty and Church Streets
- ☎ 212-422 3520
- ⌕ tributewtc.org
- 🚇 Subway A, C to Chambers Street/E to World Trade Center/R, W to Rector Street
- ☉ Mon-Sat 10am-6pm; Sun 10-5pm
- $ Gallery admission $17 adults, $12 students and seniors, $5 children (6-12)

The Tribute Center was set up by the September 11th Families' Association and is a place to discover more about what went on that day – including stories from survivors, residents, rescue workers and volunteers – and how the city recovered post-attack. I recommend taking a Walking Tour ($22 adult), which begins at the Tribute Centre and includes the memorial (two reflecting lakes) and is conducted by a guide who's a survivor, lower Manhattan resident or family member who lost a loved one on 9/11. It will really open your eyes as to what took place that day from a very personal perspective and the money you pay goes back into the center, helping those still affected.

Also consider visiting the Ground Zero Museum Workshop, a not-for-profit museum (www.groundzeromuseumworkshop.com) open Mon-Sun, advanced $25pp ticket purchase necessary. This remarkable little museum contains the dramatic photographs of Gary Marlon Susan, the only official photographer to be commissioned to take a series of images during the search and recovery after 9/11. It's incredibly moving and has been voted the eighth best museum in New York by Tripadvisor.

BROOKLYN BRIDGE
This Gothic creation was considered one of the modern engineering feats of the world when it was completed in 1883 after 16 years of construction, and at the time was both the world's largest suspension bridge and the first to be built of steel. It was also the first bridge to link the 2 separate cities of New York and Brooklyn, making it now only a 10-minute taxi ride between them.

BRITTIP
To hear the dramatic story of how the bridge was built while walking over it, take Big Onion's Brooklyn Bridge & Brooklyn Heights tour (www.bigonion.com).

The original engineer, John A Roebling, died even before the project began and his son, who took over, had to oversee the work from his Brooklyn apartment after being struck down by the bends. In all, 20 people died during the construction of the bridge. Take the A or C train to High Street station and stroll back along the walkway to see some incredible views of the Downtown skyscrapers or the 4, 5 or 6 to Brooklyn Bridge/City Hall. It's a 1.6km/1ml walk across and the most magical walk is from Brooklyn to Manhattan to watch the sun go down over the city.

CATHEDRAL OF ST JOHN THE DIVINE
Upper West Side/Morningside Heights
- ✉ 1047 Amsterdam Avenue at 112th Street and Amsterdam Avenue
- ☎ 212-316 7540 (info); tours 212-932 7347
- 🖰 www.stjohndivine.org
- 🚇 Subway 1, 9 to 110th Street
- ⏱ Mon–Sat 7.30am–6pm. Public tours Mon 11am–12pm, 2–3pm, Tues–Sat 11am–12pm, 1–2pm, select Suns 1–2pm. Vertical tours Weds 12–1pm, Sat 12–1pm and 2–3pm
- $ Entrance free. Tours $6 per person, $5 students/seniors; vertical tours $15 adult, $12 student or senior

The world's largest Gothic cathedral has one of the world's biggest rose windows with 10,000 pieces of glass. Even more amazing are the main bronze doors, which weigh 3,000 tonnes each and are opened only for an official visit by the bishop. An Episcopal church built in 1892, its grounds cover 4.9ha/12 acres of land and include a school and accommodation for the clergy. It has a capacity to seat 3,000 people, but because it holds so many art and performing art events it has chairs rather than pews. At the back of the cathedral behind the main altar are 7 different chapels, which represent different countries in Europe and are used for weddings, christenings and the services. It's well worth taking the vertical tour on a Wed or Sat, where you'll get to climb 38m/124ft up a spiral stone staircase to the top of the cathedral and get a glimpse of the nave restorations and study the grand architecture. The tour culminates on the roof with a wonderful view of the Morningside Heights area of Manhattan. Space is limited so reservations are recommended. All vertical tours meet for registration at the visitor centre inside the cathedral entrance.

One of the highlights of the cathedral's calendar is the Feast of Assisi when real animals, including an elephant and a llama, are ceremonially taken up to the altar to be blessed by the cathedral clergy. Inspired by St Francis of Assisi, whose life exemplified living in harmony with the natural world, the feast usually takes place on the first Sun in Oct. On selected Sat 10am–noon, families can join a Medieval Arts Workshop, which includes stone carving, weaving and sculpting.

BRITTIP

The Cathedral of St John the Divine is blessed with plenty of loos if you get caught short!

CENTRAL PARK
Central Park is the New Yorkers' playground and a wonderful place to spend time during your stay. For a complete description of the park and all its facilities, see p261–63.

CHRYSLER BUILDING
Midtown East
- ✉ 405 Lexington Avenue at 42nd Street
- ☎ 212-682 3070
- 🖰 www.nyc-architecture.com
- 🚇 Subway S, 4, 5, 6, 7 to Grand Central/42nd Street
- ⏱ 8am–6pm, lobby only
- $ Free

Opened in 1930, this was William van Alen's homage to the motor car. At the foot of the Art Deco skyscraper are brickwork cars with enlarged chrome hubcaps and radiator caps. Inside see its marble and chrome lobby and inlaid-wood elevators. Its needle-like spire is illuminated at night and the building vies with the Empire State for the most stunning views.

ELLIS ISLAND IMMIGRATION MUSEUM AND THE STATUE OF LIBERTY
Battery Park
- ☎ 201-604 2800 or 1 877 LADY TIX
- 🖰 www.statuecruises.com, www.ellisisland.org
- 🚇 Statue of Liberty and Ellis Island Ferry, leaves every 20–30 mins from Gangway 5 in Battery Park 9am–3.30pm, 8.30am–4.30pm summer. Subway 1 to South Ferry, 4, 5 to Bowling Green, R, W to Whitehall Street
- ⏱ 9am–5pm
- $ $17 adults, $14 seniors, $9 children (4–12), under 3s free. Credit cards accepted.

The Statue of Liberty (www.nps.gov/stli) is reached by a ferry, which also takes you to the Ellis Island Museum where you learn the immigration story of America. Ferry tickets are sold at Castle Clinton, the low, circular brownstone building in Battery Park (open 8.30am–4.30pm) but, due to the queues, it's best to buy them online (www.statuecruises. com). Luggage, including backpacks, is not permitted and the security checks can take up to an hour. The Statue of Liberty was closed in 2013, due to damage sustained during Hurricane Sandy, but it was reopened to visitors on 4th July, including limited tickets to the crown and pedestal.

BRITTIP

Leave the mainland before 1pm or there won't be enough time to visit both Liberty and Ellis Islands.

The Statue of Liberty originally came to New York in 1886 as a gift from France and celebrated its 125th birthday in 2011. You can enjoy the panoramic views from the observation deck, about 16 storeys above ground, and tour the museum in the pedestal. There's a lift at Liberty Island and if you purchase a Crown Access Ticket you have access to the statue's interior spiral staircase. However, you must be able to walk up the 354 steps to reach the crown. If you can't make the climb you can always stroll along the promenade above the star-shaped former fort on which the statue and its pedestal rise 30 storeys above the harbour. Note that although you can still access the grounds, the interior of the Statue of Liberty was closed for renovations in October 2011, but is due

to reopen in late 2012, so check the website before visiting.

The Statue of Liberty café is small and there are not enough loos. There is space to eat outside, but not much. At Ellis Island, however, you'll find plenty of WCs on all levels, a large café and a huge amount of outdoor seating that looks out over the Statue of Liberty and Lower Manhattan.

BRITTIP

Statue Cruises has started a digital audio library with information about visiting the Statue of Liberty and Ellis Island, for free, and an audio tour for $8. View them at www.statuecruises.com.

Audio tours, in lots of languages, are included free with every ticket purchase.

The Ellis Island Immigration Museum (www.ellisisland.org) is the most visited museum in New York, particularly beloved by crowds of Americans who want to see where their immigrant ancestors arrived. In use 1892–1954, it 'processed' up to 10,000 immigrants a day. Each person was interviewed to find out if they could speak English. An unfortunate 2% were turned away. Unfortunately, due to damage sustained during Hurricane Sandy, the museum was closed in 2013, but is on schedule to reopen in 2014 – keep checking the website for more details.

Ellis Island

BRITTIP

The last boat leaves from Liberty Island at 6.15pm and Ellis Island at 4.35pm in summer. It can also take up to 90 minutes to board a ferry in peak months, so it's important to factor in extra time when planning your trip.

Visitors follow the immigrants' route as they entered the baggage room and went up to the Registry and the Staircase of Separation. Poignant exhibits include photos, videos, jewellery, clothing, baggage and the stark dormitories. The Immigrant Wall of Fame lists half a million names, including those of the grandfathers of Presidents Washington and Kennedy.

BRITTIP

When leaving the Statue of Liberty to go on to Ellis Island DO NOT get on the ferry that takes you to New Jersey, which is on the left. It is clearly signposted, but it is very easy to get disorientated!

This is a great museum and well worth allocating a good portion of your day to. Films and guided tours are free. The Ranger Tours last 45 minutes and leave at regular times throughout the day (times at the information desk). At 2pm there is a re-enactment of a board of inquiry, which decides an immigrant's fate. Immigrants tell their stories in the movie Island of Hope, Island of Tears, which runs frequently in two theatres, and a new, interactive exhibit called Ellis Kids teaches children ages 12 and under about the immigration experience. Free tickets are available at the desk. Audio tours are available for $8, though do check this information before you visit in light of any changes that might have been made during the restoration work post-Hurricane Sandy.

BRITTIP

The tour, film and play on Ellis Island are free, but you need tickets for each one from the information desk (to the left on your way in). Busiest times are just after a boat has arrived, so try to be the first off the ferry and head straight for the desk.

The museum is well laid out, has lots of benches and is so big it never feels too crowded. There is a cashpoint in the corridor on the way to the café, on your right as you enter the building. The café is a little pricey but you could bring your own picnic and sit outside and enjoy the fabulous views.

EMPIRE STATE BUILDING
34th Street
- ✉ 350 5th Avenue between 33rd and 34th Street
- ☎ 212-736 3100
- 🖰 www.esbnyc.com
- 🚇 Subway B, D, F, Q, N, R, V, W to 34th Street
- ⏱ 8am–2am, last lifts go up at 1.15am, 7 days a week; be sure to bring ID
- $ $25 adults, $25 seniors, $19 children (6–12), under 5s free. Tickets can be bought online.

It is hard to believe that the Empire State, which was for almost 40 years the world's tallest building, was almost not built at all. Weeks after its building contract was signed in 1929, the Wall Street Crash brought the financial world to its knees. Fortunately, the project went ahead and was even completed 45 days ahead of schedule, rising to 443m/1,454ft in 1931. The lobby interior features Art Deco design incorporating rare marble imported from Italy, France, Belgium and Germany. It is, once again, New York's tallest building, and one of the world's most recognisable from movies, including the remake of King Kong.

BRITTIP

To avoid the pricey snack bars in the Empire State Building, get back down to ground level and visit Starbucks next door.

Empire State Building

There are two observation decks, one on the 86th floor and another on the 102nd floor, which costs an extra $42 (express) to visit but gives the most fabulous, if dizzying, views.

◄▮►BRITTIP

If you've a NY CityPass booklet, avoid the ticket queues at the Empire State. Walk straight past the crowds on the ground floor, turn right to go up one flight.

Your best bet is to arrive as early in the morning as possible to avoid long waits for tickets. Weekends, of course, get really crowded. Once you reach the glass-walled viewing deck on the 86th floor you can enjoy some fabulous views of Manhattan and the outer boroughs and really get your bearings. Those who lack the stomach for heights can catch the view live through ESB TowerCams on the concourse. One option is to hire the Observatory iView multimedia audio tour and visual guide for $10. You buy your tickets on the concourse level below the main lobby, but don't have to use them on the same day.

The New York SkyRide is on the 2nd floor and is open 7 days a week 8am–10pm. It simulates a thrilling flight around the skyscrapers and bridges of New York City. Entrance $29 adults, $19 seniors/children (12 and under). A combined SkyRide and Empire State Building ticket costs $47 adults, $37 seniors and $30 for children (212-279 9777, www.skyride.com). Save money by buying tickets online.

◄▮►BRITTIP

Just across the way from the Federal Reserve Bank is probably the poshest McDonald's in the world at 160 Broadway. It has doormen, a chandelier and a grand piano upstairs.

FEDERAL RESERVE BANK
Financial District
- ✉ 33 Liberty Street between William and Nassau Streets
- ☎ 212-720 6130
- 🖰 www.newyorkfed.org
- 🚇 Subway 2, 3, 4, 5, A, C, J, Z to Fulton Street/Broadway-Nassau Street
- ⏱ Mon–Fri 11.15am–3pm, by tour only
- $ Free

Yes, this really is the place where billions of dollars' worth of gold bars are stashed (as stolen by Jeremy Irons in *Die Hard 3*) on behalf of half the countries of the world, and

TICKET TO RIDE

The CityPass is an excellent way to avoid long queues and save money if you visit at least 3 of the participating attractions: the American Museum of Natural History, the Empire State Building and New York Skyride, the Metropolitan Museum of Art and the Cloisters, the Guggenheim Museum, the Museum of Modern Art and a harbour tour with the Circle Line or Statue of Liberty and Ellis Island. You can buy a CityPass from any of the attractions, which will save you queuing again. Prices are $106 (a $60 saving on normal admission) for adults and $79 for 6–17s. Call 208-787 4300 or buy online at www.citypass.com.

where money is printed. Security, as you can imagine, is tight, but you can still do a free 45-minute tour that takes you deep into the underground gold vaults, Mon–Fri at 11.15am, noon, 12.45pm 1.30pm, 2.15pm and 3pm and the tour can be booked as much as four months in advance – registration is online only. Passport or picture identification is essential and you can't use your camera or camera phone, for obvious reasons!

FLATIRON BUILDING
Flatiron District
- ✉ 175 5th Avenue between 22nd and 23rd Streets
- ☎ 212-477 0947
- 🖰 www.nyc-architecture.com
- 🚇 Subway F, V, N, R, 6 to 23rd Street
- ⏱ Lobby open office hours
- $ Free

The Renaissance palazzo building was the first-ever skyscraper when it was completed in 1902 and is held up by a steel skeleton covered in white terracotta. Its name refers to its unusual triangular shape. It is set at the windiest crossroads of the city where 5th Avenue crosses Broadway and in the 19th century had to be policed as local New York men hung around here to catch a glimpse up ladies' skirts as they blew up around their ears!

GRACE CHURCH
Union Square
- ✉ 802 Broadway at 10th Street
- ☎ 212-254 2000
- 🖰 www.gracechurchnyc.org
- 🚇 Subway N, R, L, 4, 5, 6 to Union Square
- ⏱ Sun services 9am, 11am, 6pm
- $ Free

A beautiful example of the Gothic Revival period that was occurring in the city when this was built by James Renwick in 1846, when he was only 23 years old! Grace Church was something of a society church and is still known for its Choir of Men and Boys established in the late 1800s. It is as pretty inside as out with Pre-Raphaelite stained-glass windows and a marvellous mosaic floor. The original wood steeple was replaced by marble in 1888, and it is a landmark on the skyline if you gaze along Broadway from Downtown. Tours run every Sun at 1pm.

GRACIE MANSION
Yorkville
- ✉ Carl Schurz Park, 88th Street at East End Avenue
- ☎ 212-570 4773
- ⌂ www.historichousetrust.org
- 🚇 Subway 4, 5, 6 to 86th Street
- ⏰ General tours from 10am–2pm (Weds)
- $ $7 adults, $4 seniors, under 12s free

Built by the shipping tycoon Archibald Gracie in 1799, this mansion is the last of the elegant country homes that once lined Manhattan's East River shore. Dinner guests here were the likes of Alexander Hamilton and Joseph Bonaparte. It later became the first home of the Museum of the City of New York and then official residence of the mayor. Now, the 'People's House', once visited by Nelson Mandela, offers 45-minute tours on Wednesdays at 10am, 11am, 1pm and 2pm by reservation only that take you through the mayor's living room, a guest suite and smaller bedrooms. The best part, though, is the view down the river.

BRITTIP — It is appropriate to tip your guide around 10–15% of the cost of the ticket, if you are happy with the service you received.

GRAND CENTRAL STATION
Midtown East
- ✉ East 42nd Street and Park Avenue
- ☎ 212-340 2345
- ⌂ www.grandcentralterminal.com
- 🚇 Subway S, 4, 5, 6, 7 to Grand Central/42nd Street
- ⏰ Daily 5.30am–2am
- $ Free

Firstly, this isn't 'just a station'. It's a truly beautiful building and I promise this huge, vaulted station, which celebrated its 100th year in 2013, is worth a visit. A $196m, 2-year renovation programme completed in the 1990s saw the ceiling once again twinkle with the stars and astrological symbols of the night skies, while the marble balusters and clerestory windows gleam in the main concourse. It's celebrating its centenary in 2013 with a year-long party!

BRITTIP — No matter what the weather, it is incredibly easy to get dehydrated. Take a small bottle of water and refill along the way.

It's also a culinary destination. The Grand Central Map, picked up from the information booth on the main concourse will lead you to a Mediterranean restaurant, Michael Jordan's The Steakhouse NYC and a cocktail lounge, Cipriani Dolci, modelled on a Florentine palazzo. The lower level dining concourse offers inexpensive meals and takeaways, while main floor shopping outlets include Banana Republic and Aveda. Between eating and shopping opportunities, take in a visit to the New York Transit Museum Shop and Gallery, with exhibitions of transit memorabilia, and to The Vanderbilt Hall, the former main waiting room, which stages entertainment. Complete your trip to this elegant edifice by tucking in at the Oyster Bar & Restaurant. There's also a popular market.

BRITTIP — Enjoy an audio tour of the terminal. MTA Metro-North Railroad has teamed up with Orpheo USA to give tourists a state-of-the-art insight into the station. The audio device and headset comes with a map of the terminal for $8 (same price adults, seniors, students and children). This tour is available seven days a week, 365 days a year at a specially marked GCT Tour window on the main concourse, from 9am to 6pm. Or, you can download the tour to your MP3 player or iPhone or smartphone, for $4.99, from www.myorpheo.com.

MADAME TUSSAUD'S
Times Square
- ✉ 234 West 42nd Street between 7th and 8th Avenues
- ☎ 212-512 9600
- ⌂ madametussauds.com/newyork
- 🚇 Subway A, C, E, S, 1, 2, 3, N, B, D, F, Q, R to Times Square/42nd Street
- ⏰ Open daily throughout the year. Mon–Sun 10am–10pm
- $ $36 adults, $29 children (4–12), under 3, free. If you book online, there's a 15% discount and tickets are valid for a year

London's famous waxworks has spread around the globe. If wax models (extremely well done) are your thing or you have the

John Travolta and Nicolas Cage at
Madame Tussaud's

kids in tow, it is worth visiting this sight
in the heart of Times Square as the celebs
portrayed reflect personalities associated
with the city, such as Woody Allen, Leonard
Bernstein, Jacqueline Kennedy Onassis, John
D. Rockefeller, Yoko Ono, Donald Trump, Andy
Warhol and former mayor Rudolph Giuliani
among others. Kids and teenagers will get to
see all their favourite stars, from Lady Gaga
and Justin Bieber to Zac Efron. Crowd-
pleasers Will and Kate arrived in 2012.

MADISON SQUARE GARDEN
34th Street
- ✉ 4 Pennsylvania Plaza at 33rd Street and
  7th Avenue
- ☎ 212-465 MSG1/6741 (information);
  212-307 7171 (Ticketmaster)
- 🖱 www.thegarden.com
- 🚇 Subway A, C, E, 1, 2, 3, 9, D, F, B, V, N, Q,
  R, W to 34th Street/Penn station

This is the round building that sits on top
of Penn station and the entrance is on 7th

Avenue at 33rd Street. It occupies the site
of the original Pennsylvania station, an
architectural masterpiece that was even
more beautiful than Grand Central Station,
but which was razed in the 1960s. (The only
good to come out of its destruction was
the creation of the Landmarks Preservation
Commission, which has helped to protect
many buildings and areas from developers.)

Madison Square Garden's arena is 10
storeys tall, covers 3.24ha/8 acres and is
famous for its circular ceiling, which is
suspended by 48 bridge-like cables. Every year
it hosts 600 events from concerts to boxing,
wrestling, basketball and hockey, bringing in 5
million people. Its most famous residents are
the New York Knickerbockers basketball team
(known as the Knicks), the New York Rangers
ice-hockey team and the New York Liberty
women's pro basketball team.

Below the arena are the theatre, exhibition
centre, box office and two club restaurants.
Incidentally, this is actually the fourth
Madison Square Garden building. The first
two were built at Madison Square on the site
of the current New York Life Building; the
third was built on 8th Avenue between 49th
and 50th Streets, where the Worldwide Plaza
stands. This building opened in 1968 with a
gala featuring Bob Hope and Bing Crosby.

Unfortunately, the All Access Tour has
been closed throughout 2010 and 2011 due
to the construction of the transformation
of Madison Square Garden. It may again
be closed for some time as although phase
1 2011–12 has been completed, phase 3 is
scheduled for 2013–14, so check the website
for details.

WHAT TO SEE AND DO

Madison Square Garden

MORRIS-JUMEL MANSION
Harlem
- ✉ Roger Morris Park, 65 Jumel Terrace at 160th Street
- ☎ 212-923 8008
- ⌂ www.morrisjumel.org
- 🚗 Subway C to 163rd Street
- ⊙ Wed–Sun 10am–4pm, closed Mon and Tues
- $ Sat tours $6 adults, $4.50 seniors, students and children, free for children under 12; group tours for 10 or more can be scheduled 7 days a week for $60

Built by British colonel Roger Morris in 1765, this is the oldest house in Manhattan. It was confiscated by George Washington in 1776 and briefly used as his war headquarters until the Brits kicked him out of New York. Charles Dickens visited it, too. Tours are offered every Sat at noon (register in advance), neighbourhood tours focussing on Harlem Renaissance residents are also offered and family programmes include free art workshops during school holiday times.

NBC TOURS
Rockefeller Center/Midtown
- ✉ Lobby level of 30 Rockefeller Plaza at 49th Street between 5th and 6th Avenues
- ☎ 212-664 3700
- ⌂ www.nbcstudiotour.com
- 🚗 Subway B, D, F, M, N, R, 1, 6 to 47th–50th Streets/Rockefeller Center
- ⊙ Mon–Thurs 8.30am–5.30pm every 15 mins, Fri and Sat 8.30am–6.30pm every 15 mins, Sun 9.15am–4.30pm every 15 mins
- $ $24 adults, $21 seniors and children (6–12), no children under 6. For a small extra fee, combine with Rockefeller Center Tour (p78)

You get a 1 hour 10 minute look behind the scenes at NBC, the major television network headquartered in New York, including a peek at some of its most famous studios such as 1A – home of the *Today Show*. You'll be shown around by an NBC Page – some of these characters have gone on to become famous entertainment personalities.

NEW YORK PUBLIC LIBRARY
Midtown
- ✉ 5th Avenue at 42nd Street
- ☎ 917-275 6975
- ⌂ www.nypl.org
- 🚗 Subway 1, 2, 3, A, C, B, D, F, M to 42nd Street, 7 to Fifth Avenue
- ⊙ Mon, Thurs–Sat 10–6pm, Tues–Wed 10–8pm, Sun 1–5pm
- $ Free

Opened in 1911, this Stephen A. Schwarzman Building is one of the best examples of Beaux Arts architecture in the city. It's the main branch of NYPL – there are four major research libraries and 87 branch libraries in the Bronx, Manhattan and Staten Island – and has a jaw-dropping 15 million items, including medieval manuscripts, ancient Japanese scrolls, not to mention contemporary novels and poetry and even comic books. It's considered one of the world's pre-eminent public resources for the study of human thought, action and experience, including volumes on anthropology, archaeology, religion, sports and world

New York Public Library

history. Take a free tour, which meets at the reception deck in Astor Hall, at 11am or 2pm Mon–Sat and 2pm Sun (except in summer) to check out the murals by Richard Haas in the Periodicals Room, the fabulous white marble Astor Hall and the cathedral-like main reading room where Leon Trotsky once read under the same brass lamps. The steps up to the library are a suntrap during the day and serve as a meeting place. Alternatively, they make a great place for a sandwich or drink stop, which you can pick up from the new kiosk in the library.

NEW YORK STOCK EXCHANGE
Financial District
- ✉ 20 Broad Street at Wall Street
- ☎ 212-656 3000
- ⌖ www.nyse.org
- 🚖 Subway 6, 4, 5 to Wall Street; J, M, Z to Broad Street
- ⏱ Not open to the public at present

Amazing fact: the stock exchange was founded by 24 brokers meeting beneath a tree; now more than 1,300 members crowd on to the building's trading floor where over 2 billion shares change hands on busy days. This Neo-Classical building that represents the heart of capitalism is an interesting place to visit, although for the foreseeable future, due to security concerns, it is closed to the public. For now, a taste of the frenetic activity within can be seen from watching the traders scurrying around the crowded pedestrian-only streets. For the inside story, such as tickertape from the morning of the big crash, head to The Museum of American Finance a few blocks away (p115).

RADIO CITY MUSIC HALL
Midtown
- ✉ 1260 6th Avenue between West 50th and West 51st Street
- ☎ 212-465 6225 information, 866 858 0008 Ticketmaster
- ⌖ www.radiocity.com
- 🚖 Subway B, D, F, V to 50th Streets/ Rockefeller Center
- ⏱ Tours daily 11am–3pm
- $ $23.70 adults, $18.75 seniors and under 12s

While you're at the Rockefeller Center you won't want to miss out on this fabulous building, which has been fully restored to its original Art Deco movie palace glory and is utterly beautiful. This is where great films such as *Gone With The Wind* were given their premieres and it has the largest screen in America. Make a point of visiting the loos – they have a different theme on each floor, from palm trees to Chinese and floral. There are even cigar-theme loos for the boys. The 1-hour Stage Door Tour takes you around the building and you meet a Rockette.

BRITTIP
Tickets for the live shows are hard to come by, but you can try for stand-by tickets by going to the 49th Street side of 30 Rockefeller Plaza. Tickets are distributed from 7am for a stand-by ticket for either an 8pm dress rehearsal or the 11.30pm taping; limited to 1 per person on a first-come, first-served basis.

RIVERSIDE CHURCH
Morningside Heights
- ✉ 490 Riverside Drive at 120th Street
- ☎ 212-870 6700
- ⌖ www.theriversidechurchny.org
- 🚖 Subway 1 to 116th Street
- ⏱ Daily 7am–10pm

Famous for having the world's largest tuned bell and its Carillon Concerts on Sun at 10.30am, 12.30pm and 3pm. After the Sunday morning service there's a free tour of the church, which includes a brief history plus visits to the Christ Chapel, Nave and Chancel, which begins at 12.15pm in the First Balcony and no advance reservations are necessary.

BRITTIP
If you're peckish on a Sun lunchtime but don't want to blow the budget you can get a bargain brunch in the dining room at the Riverside Church until 3pm.

ROCKEFELLER CENTER
Midtown
- ✉ Midtown at 5th Avenue – West 48th to West 50th Streets between 5th and 6th Avenues
- ☎ 212-698 2000
- ⌖ www.RockefellerCenter.com
- 🚖 Subway B, D, N, F, V, N, R, 1 to 47th–50th Streets/Rockefeller Center
- ⏱ Tours daily from 10am, departing from 30 Rockefeller Plaza at 50th St
- $ Tour $17 adults, $15 seniors, and children (6–12), no children under 6. Reservations are necessary on 212-664 7174

Built in Art Deco style in the 1930s, this was named after the New York benefactor whose fortune paid for its construction. As well as Radio City Music Hall, it houses opulent office space, restaurants, bars, shopping on several levels and even gardens. To help you find your way round the 19 buildings, collect a map at the lobby of the main building (30 Rockefeller Center). The central plaza, a restaurant in summer, is turned into an ice rink in winter, and a massive Christmas tree with 8km/5mls of fairy lights draws huge crowds.

BRITTIP
Buy your ticket for the Radio City Music Hall in the morning and plan your day around that. Alternatively, you can see it as part of the Rockefeller Center Tour.

You can either wander around the plaza or take the 1-hour Rockefeller Center Tour for $15. This takes in The Channel Gardens, Radio City, the ice rink, NBC and more, while giving an insight into the Center's history, architecture and more than 100 pieces of artwork that create the world's most amazing public collection of Art Deco.

BRITTIP
If you want to combine the Rockefeller Center Tour with Top of the Rock Tour, then buy an Art & Observation Tour, $35, which combines the art and architecture of the centre with the breathtaking view 70 storeys up. Call 212-698 2000, www.topoftherocknyc.com to book.

The Top of the Rock observation deck on the 70th floor at 30 Rockefeller Plaza, offers spectacular 360-degree views of the city. The observation deck, first opened in 1933, has been redeveloped into a 5,110m2/55,000ft2,multi-level complex with state-of-the-art features such as transparent safety glass panels that allow completely unobstructed views of the city's landmarks. It's open 365 days of the year 8am–midnight (last elevator 11pm) and costs $27 adults, $25 seniors, $17 children (6–12), $2.50 for a podcast, $38 for a sunrise/sunset ticket that allows you to visit twice in a day. Ticket reservations 212-698 2000 or www.topoftherocknyc.com, or take it in as part of the 1½-hour Art & Observation tour that departs every 2 hours from 10am Mon–Sun. All tours depart from the NBC Experience Store at 30 Rockefeller Plaza across from the *Today Show* studio.

BRITTIP
Lovers of the Metropolitan Museum shops can get their fix at one of its branches in the heart of the Rockefeller Center. It's just off the main plaza by the ice rink.

ST PATRICK'S CATHEDRAL
Midtown
- ✉ 5th Avenue between 50th and 51st Street
- ☎ 212-753 2261
- ⌂ www.saintpatrickscathedral.org
- 🚇 Subway 6 to 51st Street; E, V to 5th Avenue/53rd Street
- ⏰ Daily 6.30am–8.45pm
- $ Free

This cathedral is a famous landmark of New York, as the seat of New York's Roman Catholic Archdiocese, but also from its many on-screen appearances over the decades, from Robert F Kennedy's funeral to the place where *Spider-Man* Tobey Maguire swung by in the 2002 film. Construction of the magnificent building started in 1857 but the stained-glass windows weren't completed until 1930. However, the magnificent results were definitely worth the wait. Check out the Great Bronze doors, The Rose Window and the Pieta statue in the Lady Chapel. There are 7 to 10 walk-in guided tours every month, which are free, so check the website to see if one coincides with your visit.

BRITTIP
The steps leading up to St Patrick's create a perfect picnic spot for a lunch or snack stop.

SEAGRAM BUILDING
Midtown
- ✉ 375 Park Avenue between 52nd and 53rd Street
- ☎ 212-572 7000
- ⌂ www.375parkavenue.com/
- 🚇 Subway 6 to 51st Street, E, F to Lexington Avenue
- ⏰ Open weekdays 9–5pm, tours Tues 3pm

The New York City mile's only Mies Van Der Rohe building, and widely recognised as one of the finest skyscrapers in the world. It ignited a passion for plazas that you can still see in New York today. Check out the Seagram Gallery on the 4th floor and if you want to splash out, have dinner there in the much-praised The Four Seasons restaurant (www.fourseasonsrestaurant.com) designed by Philip Johnson.

SOUTH STREET SEAPORT
Financial District
- ✉ Water Street to the East River between John Street and Peck Slip
- ☎ 212-732 8257
- ⌂ www.seany.org
- 🚇 Subway A, C, J, M, Z, 2, 3, 4, 5 to Fulton Street/Broadway Nassau

Times Square

WHAT TO SEE AND DO

○ Apr–Sept Mon–Sat 10am–9pm,
   Sun 11am–9pm. Nov–Mar Fri–Mon
   10am–5pm

$ Free. Museum $10 adults, children under
   9 free

You don't have to go into the South Street
Seaport Museum (p123) to get a feeling of
the maritime history of the city – the ships
are all around you. So are the shops.

The Seaport was affected by Hurricane
Sandy and is still undergoing recovery,
however there's lots to see and do down
there, particularly in the summer months
including pop up retail containers – a multi-
storey fleet of shipping containers on Fulton
Street housing up and coming designers.
There are also weekly outdoor film nights at
the intersection of Front and Fulton streets
and Seaport Music Festival with bands
playing live every Friday night throughout
June. Plus Fulton Stall Market each Saturday
and Sunday and various art exhibitions. In
short, SSS is well worth an afternoon visit.

STATEN ISLAND FERRY
Battery Park

✉ Ferry Terminal, 1 South Street

☎ 311

🖰 www.siferry.com

🚇 Subway 4, 5 to Bowling Green; R to
   Whitehall Street, 1 to South Ferry, J, Z to
   Broad Street

$ Free

Probably the best sightseeing bargain in
the world, this free ferry between Whitehall
Street in Lower Manhattan and St George on

Staten Island transports 20 million people a
year. It passes close to the Statue of Liberty
Liberty (go straight to the right hand side of
the boat to get your viewing position early!)
and gives dramatic views of Downtown
and the bridges and skyscrapers of Lower
Manhattan. Runs regularly 24 hours a day
and takes 25 minutes for the crossing. Since
2004, 3 new ferries have been designed to
capture the feel of the old-style ferries.

🇬🇧 **BRITTIP**

Foods of New York Tours, www.
foodsofny.com, has suggestions
of mouthwatering pit stops in the 5
neighbourhoods near key sights.

TIMES SQUARE AND
THE THEATER DISTRICT

Another iconic area of New York and a must-
see place. Full details of what to see and do
are on pages 52–53.

TRUMP TOWER
Midtown

✉ 725 5th Avenue between 56th and 57th
   Streets

☎ 212-247 7000

🖰 www.trumpworldtower.com

🚇 Subway F, N, R, Q, W to 57th Street

○ Building daily 8am–10pm; shops Mon–
   Sat 10am–6pm, Sun noon–5pm

$ Free

Trump Tower

Donald Trump's monument to opulence includes an extravagant pink marbled atrium with waterfalls, cafés, restaurants and upmarket shops. The glitzy residences at the top with facilities that include a spa, swimming pool and landscaped gardens can't be visited, but a glimpse of them could be seen in Trump's reality TV show The Apprentice, filmed in the tower. This is not to be confused with Trump International Hotel and Tower at Columbus Circle.

UNITED NATIONS BUILDING
Midtown East

✉ 1st Avenue between 42nd and 48th Street
☎ 212-963 8687 for tour reservations
⌁ http://visit.un.org
🚗 Subway 4, 5, 6, 7 to Grand Central/42nd Street
🕐 Mon–Fri 9.30am–4.15pm, Sat and Sun closed
$ $16 adults, $11 seniors and students, $9 children (5–12). No children under 5

You can't miss this building; the epicentre of global peace, where world leaders meet and international issues are discussed, is heralded by a colourful array of flags from 192 member states. New security measures introduced in June 2013 prevent members of the public wandering into the building, however there are still ticket tours available online (they've got to be purchased in advance). It's not the most exciting tour in the world, but a lovely Reclining Figure by

UN Building from Circle Line

Henry Moore and the Peace Bell from Japan, among the objects on display around the building may be more tantalising. If you send a postcard from here it will be with its own stamp, being in an international zone.

WINTER GARDEN AT THE WORLD FINANCIAL CENTER
Battery Park City

✉ 200 Vesey Street at West Street
☎ 212-417 7000
⌁ brookfieldplaceny.com/
🚗 Subway E or PATH to World Trade Center, 2, 3, 4, 5, A, C, J, M, Z to Chambers Street; R, W to City Hall, 1 to Rector Street

The World Financial Center is actually the main focal point for the northern end of Battery Park City, a strip of land running down the west side of Lower Manhattan from

Winter Garden

Chambers Street to South Park. It was created by landfill from the digging work required to build the foundations for the World Trade Center. The World Financial Center has a complex of 4 office towers, but is most famous for the beautiful glass-roofed Winter Garden that looks over the boats moored in North Cove. Filled with palm trees, it houses a few upscale shops, including Ann Taylor and Banana Republic, a host of restaurants, and holds free events indoors and outdoors in summer. Check www.artsworldfinancialcenter.com for event schedules.

◀▌▶ BRITTIP

The Winter Garden is not just a pretty place to enjoy a drink or two, it also holds a series of free concerts and fairs.

WOOLWORTH BUILDING
Civic Center/Financial District
✉ 233 Broadway at Park Place
🖰 www.nyc-architecture.com
🚇 Subway 2, 3 4 to Park Place; N, R to City Hall
🕐 Weekdays 9–5pm
$ Free

There is no official tour of the city's second skyscraper, soaring 55 storeys above Broadway and now referred to as the 'Mozart of skyscrapers'. It was built in 1913 at a cost of $13.5m and it's worth sneaking a look inside the lobby of one of New York's most flamboyant interiors, with extravagant marble walls, bronze filigree and glass-tiled ceiling. The outside is pretty wild, too, with gargoyles and flying buttresses under a pyramid-shaped roof. Incidentally, one-time shop assistant F. W. Woolworth's building was derided as a 'cathedral of commerce' when it opened, but the 'five and dime' store millionaire took this as a compliment. Just to prove a point, he can be spotted as a sculpture in the lobby, counting out his money.

THE OUTER BOROUGHS

BRONX ZOO
A wonderful zoo that combines conservation and ecological awareness with Disney-style rides and a children's zoo. Further details are given on p276.

HISTORIC RICHMOND TOWN AND ST MARK'S PLACE, STATEN ISLAND
The two top historical sites on Staten Island, both give a unique insight into the New York of yesteryear. Further details are given on p282.

NEW YORK BOTANICAL GARDEN
Home to the Bronx River Gorge, it not only gives a fascinating insight into the geological history of New York, but also has acres and acres of beautiful gardens. Further details are given on p277.

PART 2 – TOUR NEW YORK

Time is a precious commodity here, so you need to make sure that any tour you take pays for itself both financially and in terms of time. Your choice will depend on whether it is your first or second visit or you are a regular. Newcomers need to get their bearings and good ways to do this are to take a boat trip and a bus tour. The boat trip goes in a semi-circle around Manhattan from Midtown on one side to Midtown on the other; the bus tour, such as Gray Line's Manhattan Experience tour, is known as New York 101 (101 being slang for a first-year university course) because it covers so much of the city in one day. An alternative is the New York Visions tour, which takes less time, is cheaper and is generally more fact filled.

Bus tours are useful when you want to visit an area such as Harlem or the Bronx, but are unsure of your personal safety, in which case the Harlem Spirituals/New York Visions tours are your best bet. Then there are helicopter tours, which will certainly give you breathtaking views, but won't show you the full ins and outs of each area.

◀▌▶ BRITTIP

If you take a tour of New York, you are likely to hear the word 'stoop'. This is taken from a Dutch word by original settlers and refers to the steps up to a townhouse, such as a brownstone – another New York term, this time for much sought-after townhouses, though they are as likely to be made out of grey stone as brown.

The reality is that the best way to see New York, get to know the city and find those interesting nooks and crannies is on foot, which possibly explains why the Big Onion Walking Tours are so popular – or it could be that they are just so darned good – and why so many people take advantage of the Big Apple Greeters, who can show you any area or sight you wish to visit. There is also a wide choice from bike tours to gangland tours and a great selection of food tours.

AIR TOURS

LIBERTY HELICOPTERS
Chelsea
- ✉ Downtown Manhattan Heliport at 6, East River Piers
- ☎ 212-967 6464 or 1-800-542 9933 toll free
- 🌐 www.libertyhelicopter.com
- 🚇 Subway A, C, E to 34th Street/Penn Station
- 🕐 Mon–Sat 9am–6.30pm, Sun 9am–5pm

This is a fantastic, if pricey, way to see New York, and perfect if you're looking for a once-in-a-lifetime experience. Choose from The Big Apple, around $150 for 15 minutes or the 20-minute New York New York for $215 that takes in the harbour. If you really want to push the boat out there's the Romance/VIP Tour that lasts for 20 minutes and costs $995 for private hire of the whole helicopter, maximum 4 people.

NEW YORK HELICOPTER
South Street
- ✉ Downtown Heliport, Pier 6 East River at South Street and Broad Street.
- ☎ 212-361 6060
- 🌐 www.newyorkhelicopter.com
- 🚇 Subway A, C, E to 34th Street/Penn Station
- 🕐 Call for times

You can choose from several tours with this company, which has been offering helicopter rides for more than 20 years. The 15 minute Liberty Tour allows you a glimpse of the Statue of Liberty, Ellis and Governors Islands, South Street Seaport, Brooklyn and Manhattan bridges and Wall Street Financial Center, $139 per person. The 19 minute NYC Central Park Tour includes The Empire State Building, Central Park and the *Intrepid* Sea-Air-Space Museum, $206 per person, and the 20–25-minute Grand Tour takes in all the above sights plus the Yankee Stadium, George Washington Bridge and Battery Park, $295 per person (there's an additional $30 heliport fee added to the listed prices).

BIKE TOURS

BIKE AND ROLL
- ☎ 212-260 0400 or 1-866-736 8224 toll free
- 🌐 www.bikeandroll.com/newyork
- $ From $85 (includes bike rental for tours and helmet rental). Half-length 3-hour tours $65

This is SUCH a fun and unique way to see the city. Don't be put off by the thought of too much traffic and crowded streets as licensed guides take you through a variety of neighbourhoods, often through quieter roads, to see both historic and hip sides of the city. The 5 main tours include The Ethnic Apple Tour through Queens, Bike and Bite Brooklyn Tour, The Sensational Park and Soul tour travelling from Central Park to Harlem, Secret Streets – from High Finance to Chinatown – and The Brooklyn Bridge and Skyline at Twilight Bike Tour. Tours can be customised to your interests and are taken at a gentle pace. When you've made your reservation you'll be sent the exact location of the meeting point for your specific tour (they operate from various bike shops in the city).

BIKE THE BIG APPLE
- ☎ 347-878 9809 or 1-877-865 0078 toll free
- 🌐 www.bikethebigapple.com
- $ $85–99 includes bike rental for tours and helmet rental. Half-length 3-hour tours $65

Licensed guides take you through a variety of neighbourhoods to see all aspects of the city. The main tours include The Ethnic Apple Tour through Queens, brews views and chocolate on The Delights of Brooklyn Tour, The Sensational Park and Soul tour travelling from Central Park to Harlem, Secret Streets – from High Finance to Chinatown, and The Brooklyn Bridge, Northern Manhattan – A Cornucopia of Unseen Delights, The Surprising Bronx Tour and Friday Night Lights. Tours can be customised to your interests and are taken at a gentle pace.

WHAT TO SEE AND DO

NYINTHEKNOW

Emma Thomas, who works for NYC & Company, gets on a bike when the sun comes out. 'Biking is a fantastic way to explore the City, and Governors Island (www.govisland.com), where free bikes are available on Fri, is a great option, especially for families. For the first time in 2012, New York Water Taxi opened a beach on Governors Island, which is now open at the weekend, too, in summer, providing an added attraction for people of all ages.'

CENTRAL PARK BIKE TOURS
Columbus Circle
- ✉ 203 West 58th Street, corner 58th Street and 7th Avenue
- ☎ 212-541 8759
- 🌐 www.centralparkbiketours.com
- 🚇 Subway A, B, C, D, 1, 2 to Columbus Circle/59th Street

The proportions have been adjusted so the map fits clearly on a page. Detailed street maps are at the back

RIVERSIDE CHURCH

CATHEDRAL OF ST JOHN THE DIVINE

HARLEM RIVER

RANDALL'S ISLAND

GRACIE MANSION

CENTRAL PARK

5th AVENUE

ROOSEVELT ISLAND

QUEENS

BROADWAY

LINCOLN CENTER
AOL TIME WARNER CENTER
CARNEGIE HALL

TRUMP TOWER
ST. PATRICK'S CATHEDRAL
ROCKEFELLER CENTER

NBC TOURS AND RADIO
CITY MUSIC HALL

HUDSON RIVER

THEATER DISTRICT
MADAME TUSSAUDS
PORT AUTHORITY
BUS TERMINAL
TIMES SQUARE

GRAND CENTRAL
STATION
CHRYSLER BUILDING
NEW YORK PUBLIC LIBRARY

UNITED NATIONS BUILDING

EMPIRE STATE BUILDING

MADISON SQUARE GARDEN
& PENN STATION

FLATIRON BUILDING

UNION SQUARE

MANHATTAN

WASHINGTON SQUARE PARK

WINTER GARDENS AND
WORLD FINANCIAL CENTER
NEW YORK MERCANTILE EXCHANGE
GROUND ZERO MEMORIAL FOUNDATIONS
NORTH COVE

WOOLWORTH BUILDING

BROOKLYN

FEDERAL RESERVE BANK

BROOKLYN BRIDGE
SOUTH STREET SEAPORT

WALL STREET
NEW YORK STOCK EXCHANGE

ROBERT WAGNER JR. PARK
BATTERY PARK
STATEN ISLAND FERRY

STATUE OF LIBERTY

ELLIS ISLAND IMMIGRATION MUSEUM

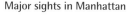

Major sights in Manhattan

- 🕐 Open Mon–Sat 9am–7pm, Sun 9am–5pm
- $ Central Park $49 adults, $40 children (15 and under) includes bike rental for tours; bike rental only is $15 for 1 hour, $20 for 2 hours and $25 for 3 hours. New York Pass holders get a free 3-hour bike rental.

🇬🇧 BRITTIP

Once you have your bike, don't feel you have to cycle everywhere you go because you can take bikes on the subway. A list of bike rental shops and cycle events can be found on www.bikenewyork.org.

There are lots of tours to choose from, I rate the 2-hour bike tour of Central Park (10am, 1pm and 4pm daily) which includes stops at the Shakespeare Garden, Strawberry Fields, Belvedere Castle and other sights, plus bike rentals for your own use. Other tours on offer include a Central Park Picnic Tour, $69, and at weekends the Movie Scenes Tour, $49, and Arts & Architecture Tour, $49.

METRO BICYCLES
Upper West Side
- ✉ 231 West 96th Street at Broadway
- ☎ 212-663 7531
- 🖱 www.metrobicycles.com
- 🚗 Subway 1, 2, 3, A, C, B to West 96th Street
- 🕐 Mon–Fri 10am–7.30pm, Sat–Sun 9.30am–6.30pm
- $ $9 hour, $45 same-day return, $55 24 hours, helmets $2.50

Pony rides in Central Park

If you want to check out Central Park and the Upper West Side along the river or the Upper East Side, rent from here. Rentals include hybrid models. Metro have 6 other in convenient locations such as Eastside Bicycles, 1311 Lexington Avenue at 88th Street (212-427 4450), Canal Street Bicycle Shop at 75 Varick Street at the corner of Watts Street and Varick Street (212-334 8000). Check the website links for hours, bikes for hire and other locations.

🇬🇧 BRITTIP

Three-person tricycles or 'pedicabs' (1 'driver' and 2 passengers) are a great way to get around the city without breaking into a sweat or breaking the bank. Try it out in good weather and don't forget to tip – drivers earn their money!

WHAT TO SEE AND DO

Central Park

PEDAL PUSHER BIKE SHOP
Central Park
- ✉ 1306 2nd Avenue at East 69th Street
- ☎ 212-288 5592 or 1-800-300 3023 toll free
- 🖱 http://pedalpusherbikeshop.com
- 🚇 Subway 6 to Hunter College/E 68th Street
- 🕐 Fri–Mon 10am–6pm, Wed 10am–7pm, Thurs 10am–8pm, closed Tues
- $ $6.99 hour, $27.96 for a day (until 6pm), helmet and lock $3.99 each

This is perhaps the cheapest bike hire in New York City and comes highly recommended by Bike The Big Apple Tours for those who want to go it alone. Just 5 blocks away from Central Park, it is handily located for a whirl around New York's backyard. Types of rentals include road, hybrid, mountain and 3-speed.

BOAT TOURS

ADIRONDACK, CLASSIC HARBOR LINE
Chelsea Pier
- ✉ Pier 62, West 22nd Street at Hudson River
- ☎ 212-627 1825
- 🖱 www.sail-nyc.com
- 🚇 Subway C, E to 8th Avenue/23rd Street
- 🕐 End April–end Oct
- $ Tickets $46–$52 for 2-hour sails, $64–$72 for Sunset Sail

A sail on this 3-mast replica of a 19th-century schooner is unforgettable. It sails from Chelsea Pier to Battery Park, allowing you the chance to catch a glimpse of Ellis Island and the Statue of Liberty, Governor's Island and Brooklyn Bridge, while sipping your complimentary glass of wine. Or, you can opt for a brunch cruise on the 80ft 1920s-style yacht *Manhattan* from Mar to end Dec. It offers sunset, city lights and dinner cruises, too and a wine tasting cruise for $95.

BATEAUX NEW YORK
Chelsea Piers
- ✉ Pier 62 at Chelsea Piers on West 23rd Street
- ☎ 1-888-957 2321 toll free
- 🖱 www.bateauxnewyork.com
- 🚇 Subway C, E, 1, 9 to 23rd Street, transfer to B23 cross-town bus heading west
- $ Brunch ticket around $64.90 without alcoholic drinks, dinner from $136.90

Another fun and unique way to see the city's magnificent skyline and getting a bite to eat – winner! Indulge in a dinner (7.30–10pm daily) or Champagne brunch (noon–2pm) while cruising around Lower Manhattan (note: boarding an hour earlier).

 BRITTIP

Special value packages combining cruises and even sights such as Top of the Rock, the Empire State Building or the 9/11 Memorial with a cruise are only available from the Circle Line Box Office at Pier 83. Check www.circleline42.com for combos and savings.

CIRCLE LINE
West Midtown
- ✉ Pier 83, West 42nd Street at Hudson River
- ☎ 212-563 3200
- 🖱 www.circleline42.com
- 🚇 Any subway to 42nd Street, then transfer to an M42 bus heading west
- $ Varies; combo packages available

Choose from a 3-hour full island cruise, $39 adults, $26 children, $34 seniors, or a 2-hour semi-circle or sunset/harbour lights cruise, $35 adults, $31 children, $24 seniors. Or take a one-hour Liberty Island cruise ($29 adults, $26 seniors and $21 children) May–Oct.

Alternatively, you can go for a spin on *The Beast* (May–Sept) a speedboat that takes you on a quick and memorable 30-minute tour. Sights fly by as you reach a speed of 64kph/45mph and stop at the Statue of Liberty for photos. May–Oct daily on the hour noon–dusk, $27 adults and seniors, $21 children. If you are lucky enough to be in the city on 4 July, then there's a special fireworks cruise, though booking way in advance is advisable.

NY WATERWAY
Financial District
- ✉ Pier 78 at 455 12th Avenue or Pier A at West St and Battery Place
- ☎ 800-533 3779
- 🖱 www.nywaterway.com
- 🚇 Any subway to 42nd Street, transfer to M42 bus heading west
- 🕐 Year-round
- $ Single ticket $4, all-day pass $12 and 10 single trips ticket $40.

 BRITTIP

The harbour cruises are very informative and give a great insight into Manhattan and beyond, but it can sometimes be hard to hear the commentary from the upper deck. Stay inside if you want to hear everything.

Hudson River Ferries serves New Jersey and New York City, including West Midtown,

Downtown and the Financial District, while the East River Ferry connects Manhattan with Brooklyn and (in summer) with Governor's Island. The ferries operate 7 days a week and are a fun and reasonably cheap way of getting to sightsee from the water. A single ticket ride on the East River Ferry, for example, is just $4.

BRITTIP

This is the city's only land and water sightseeing tour: The NYC Ducks Tour (www.taketours.com), aboard a special amphibian aquabus. The 90-minute tour, from 10am–4.30pm every 20 mins, splashes out of Times Square and gives views of the city skyline from the Hudson River. Don't worry, you won't get wet!

WORLD YACHT DINNER CRUISES
Midtown West
- ✉ Pier 81 at West 41st Street and Hudson River
- ☎ 212-630 8100 or 1-800-498 4270 toll free
- ⌂ www.worldyacht.com
- 🚌 Any subway to 42nd Street, then transfer to M42 bus heading west
- ☉ April Thurs–Sun, May–Dec daily for dinner; board at 6pm, sail 7–10pm
- $ Brunch cruise from $36–77, dinner cruise from $146–187

With 4-course menus created by a selection of New York's best chefs, linen tablecloths, live music, a dance floor and world-class videos, this is an upmarket experience you are sure to enjoy. The cruise lasts 3 hours and also provides spectacular views of the harbour. Note that the dress code is smart and that jackets are required, so make sure you allow plenty of time to put on your glad rags. The 2-hour Sunday brunch cruises (Sun April–Oct, 11.30am for noon sailing, $63.05 adults, $33.25 children) are equally glam, with drinks in the Floating Rooftop Lounge to the sound of a tinkling piano.

BUS TOURS

GRAY LINE NEW YORK SIGHTSEEING
West Midtown
- ✉ 777 8th Avenue between 47th and 48th Streets
- ☎ 212-445 0848/800-669 0051 toll free
- ⌂ www.graylinenewyork.com
- 🚌 Subway C, E to 50th Street
- ☉ Daily 7am–9.30pm
- $ Varies, see below; prices are with online booking discount

The oldest sightseeing bus company in New York, it has much to offer, although the average tour guide gives less information than the New York Visions tours. Still, if you don't want to be overwhelmed by information on your first visit, try the Classic New York Double Decker Tour ($94 adults, $70 children (5–11). A double-decker bus tour with hop-on, hop-off stops, it includes the ferry to the Statue of Liberty and Ellis Island, a ticket to the Empire State Building and a ticket to South Street Seaport Museum. It comes with the 48-hour All Loops Tour, which runs around Downtown, Midtown, uptown and Brooklyn and at night with 50 stops. You can do as few or as many as you like, so you can spend as long as you want in each area, giving you plenty of flexibility. The newest hottest tours include All Loops & Comfort Bike Rental for $93, Freestyle New York, which gives you 72 hours of hop-on, hop-off fun for $115. The Night Tour, $39, is 2-plus hours of cruising the neon-lit streets and landmarks, like Empire State, Manhattan Bridge and Times Square from the vantage point of an open-top double decker – much more fun than a cab!

A double-decker bus tour with hop-on, hop-off stops, it includes the ferry to the Statue of Liberty and Ellis Island, a ticket to the Empire State Building and a ticket to South Street Seaport Museum.

The Manhattan Experience Highlights ($44 adults, $30 children) that takes in the main sights in 4 hours is great for those tight on time. The All Loops Tour ($49 adults, $39 children) gives you 48 hours to hop on and off and as many of the 50 stops around Downtown, Midtown, Uptown and Brooklyn as you like, plus a night tour.

The Night on the Town Tour ($79/$53) is around 5 hours and includes dinner, a 1-hour cruise on a NY water taxi, glass of champagne at the Statue of Liberty, Top of the Rock entrance, a guided walk of the new Highline Park in the Meatpacking District and all the night sights such as SoHo, Battery Park and Rockefeller Center. Other tours include All Loops Tour with Top of the Rock for $71/$5 and a new NYC Tribute Tour ($99/$89), which combines the All Loops Tour with the 9/11 Memorial.

HARLEM SPIRITUALS/ NEW YORK VISIONS
Midtown
- ✉ 690 8th Avenue between West 43rd and West 44th Streets
- ☎ 212-391 0900 or 800-660 2166 toll free
- ⌂ www.harlemspirituals.com
- 🚌 Subway A, C, E, N, R,1, 2, 3, 7 to 42nd Street/Times Square

Circle Line ferry port

🕐 Mon–Sat 8am–7pm, Sun 8am–3pm
$ Varies

BRITTIP

In case you're wondering what you'll be served as soul food, this traditional African-American cuisine consists of spicy ribs, fried fish and chicken, cornbread and sides such as okra and black-eyed peas.

One of the most reputable tour companies in New York, the guides are highly qualified, great founts of knowledge and very friendly, while the buses are modern and comfortable with the all-important air-conditioning. Tours by the Harlem Spirituals include:

West 45th Street

Harlem Gospel Tour: A combined walking (though not too far!) and riding tour of Harlem (Sun), during which you attend a church service, and hear a gospel choir. Prices are $59 ($105 with brunch) adults, $45 children (5–11). Tours 9.15am–1.30pm Sunday.

Soul Food and Jazz: A chance to relive the heyday of Harlem, thanks to the return of jazz to the area. This combines a walking and riding tour through Harlem's historical sites with a soul food meal at the famous Sylvia's and the chance to see a jam session at a local jazz club. Tours are available Mon, Thurs and Sat 6.45pm–midnight and cost $155 for adults and children (5–11).

BRITTIP

The New York Visions tours around Manhattan are excellent and include an All Around Town 48h Double Decker Bus Tour, $54, which runs daily and allows you to hop-on, hop-off a double decker which takes you everywhere from Uptown to Brooklyn and includes a night tour too.

New York New York Tour: An excellent 4-hour introduction to the sights including Times Square, The Museum Mile, Rockefeller Center, Greenwich Village, SoHo, Little Italy, Chinatown, Harlem and South Street Seaport. Tours Mon, Thurs, Fri and Sat 9.30am. $59 adults, $45 children. Pay extra $74 adults/53 children and you also get tickets for the ferry to the Statue of Liberty and Ellis Island Immigration Museum (drop off at Battery Park). A 5-hour Brooklyn Tour also runs at 9am every Tues April–Dec and costs $69 adults/$55 children.

FOOD TOURS

ENTHUSIASTIC GOURMET
Chinatown
- ✉ 245 East 63rd Street
- ☎ 646-209 4724 or 1-800-838 3006 toll free
- 🖰 www.enthusiasticgourmet.com
- 🕒 10am and 2pm. Different days for different tours; check website for times and availability
- $ $50 adults, $45 child (6–12), reservations necessary

This tour company has been offering tours to foodies for over a decade now and was listed in *NYC Go's* 10 Top Tours 2011. The Chinatown Discovered Food Tour explores the neighbourhood's grocery stores, meat and fish markets and produce stands for 3 hours. If you're still hungry, head for Jing Fong Restaurant (20 Elizabeth Street, 212-964 5256, www.jingfongny.com) for some of the best dim sum in NYC. There are lots of other gourmet tours, such as the kosher NY Nosh, and a taste of Hispanic, Jewish, Chinese and Italian on the Melting Pot Food Tour. Maximum 8 people.

FOODS OF NEW YORK
Greenwich Village
- ✉ 4th Floor, 9 Barrow Street, meet near 6th and Bleecker Street
- ☎ 212-913 9964
- 🖰 www.foodsofny.com

Murray's cheese shop

- 🕒 Daily, year round 11am–2pm (but varies so check website)
- $ $49 per person

A great-value, award-winning 3-hour tour, considering the amount of food you eat, and with a friendly atmosphere as they take up to 16.

🇬🇧 BRITTIP

In the unlikely event you still feel peckish after the Foods of New York tour, head back to Fish (www.fishrestaurantnyc.com) at 280 Bleecker Street where you can have 6 oysters and a glass of wine or beer at the bar for just $8.

In Greenwich Village you'll stop to sample the wares of Rocco's pastry shop and Murray's famous cheese shop. You'll also learn about the food of New York, especially of the Italian community, you'll gain hints about architecture and properties in the Village and visit a real speakeasy. In the Explore Chinatown tour (Mon and Sat) you'll get to eat more – with 3 sit-down restaurant

Ottomanelli & Sons, Bleecker Street

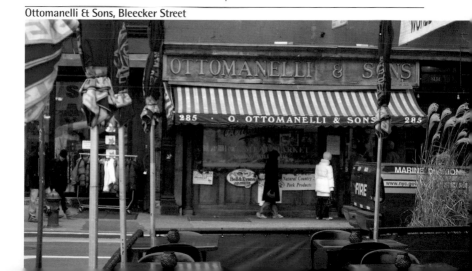

tastings. Alternatively, you can choose to go on a tour of the Chelsea Market and the Meatpacking District or Central Greenwich Village and SoHo tour (both Thurs–Mon), or Nolita/Noho (Fri, Sat, Sun).

SAVORY SOJOURNS
Chelsea
✉ 155 West 13th Street
☎ 212-209 3370
⌕ www.savorysojourns.com
$ $130–205
For a unique insight into the fine foods and culinary skills of some of New York's finest restaurants, Savory Sojourns promises to give you an insider's guide to New York's best culinary and cultural destinations followed by a great slap-up meal. Some even include a cookery lesson and can last around 4 hours. Areas covered include Upper East Side, Chinatown, SoHo and Little Italy, Lower East Side, Greenwich Village, Chelsea Market, Financial District, Hell's Kitchen, Brooklyn and Harlem, and more. They also offer a whole range of other tours from exclusive customised shopping trips with fashion industry experts to unique behind-the-scenes tours of New York's art scene and evenings of jazz and gourmet dining. If you don't like the sound of any of these, you can request your own.

URBAN OYSTER
Brooklyn
☎ 1-347 618-TOUR (8687)
⌕ www.urbanoyster.com
⌚ Sat 1–4pm
$ $55 per person
These fun foodie walking tours include: Brewed in Brooklyn (Sat noon) ($60), a great way to spend a Sat afternoon; Fermented NY – Craft Beer Crawl in the East Village on Thurs afternoons; a Food Cart Walking Tour in the Financial District (Wed and Fri afternoons) or Midtown (Fri afternoon) ($45); and Immigrant Foodways and Neighborhood Eats tours. New is a Smith and Court Street Tour in Brooklyn looking at 'moms and pops' shops – olde-worlde Italian and Middle Eastern cuisine, as well as more recent arrivals ($55 including tastings) every Sat 1–4pm as the first in a series of tours focusing on neighbourhoods' culinary treasures. Watch this space!

INSIDER TOURS

Some of the most interesting New York tours are led by residents who have unique inside perspectives that they are willing to share on everything from shopping to a haircut. Here is a fascinating selection:

KRAMER'S REALITY TOUR
West Midtown
✉ The Producer's Club Theater, 358 West 44th Street between 8th and 9th Avenues
☎ 212-268 5525 or toll free 1800 KRAMERS
⌕ www.kennykramer.com
🚇 Subway A, C, E to 42nd Street/Penn Station
⌚ Every Saturday June, July, Aug at noon; check site for winter availability
$ $37.50 plus $2 service charge
The real Kramer behind the *Seinfeld* character has come out of the woodwork and invented his own 3-hour tour based on all the *Seinfeld* spots in the city. Kenny Kramer will answer questions, share backstage gossip and the real-life incidents behind the show. Book early as this tour sells out weeks in advance. It starts from The Producers Club Theater, a short walk from Times Square.

MYSTICAL WORLD OF CHASSIDIC JEWS
Brooklyn
✉ Chassidic Discovery Welcome Center, 305 Kingston Avenue
☎ 718-953 5244
⌕ www.jewishtours.com
🚇 Subway 3 to Kingston Avenue
⌚ Sun–Fri 10am–1pm
$ $42 adults, $30 children (11 and under), $40 senior, $39 student; 3-hour tour includes a kosher deli lunch

BRITTIP
The Kingston Avenue subway stop for the Chassidic tour is just one away from Eastern Parkway, the stop for the Brooklyn Museum (p271) and the Botanic Garden (p270) – both great places to visit on a Sun afternoon.

The Lubavitcher Jews in Crown Heights, Brooklyn, are focused on sharing what they have with the outside world, providing a unique opportunity to get an insight into a Chassidic community. Guided by Rabbi Beryl Epstein, with a charming manner and great sense of humour, you'll hear the history of the Chassidic Jews; visit the synagogue to learn about some customs and traditions; watch a scribe working on a Torah scroll; and see the Rebbe's library, a Matzoh bakery and a Chassidic art gallery. A real insight into a fascinating culture.

BRITTIP
It's easy to get to the Chassidic Discovery Welcome Center by the 3 train (the red line). Allow an hour from Midtown.

ROCK 'N' ROLL WALKING TOUR
East Village
☎ 212-209 3370
🖰 www.rockjunket.com
🕐 Mon–Sun
$ Tickets $35
Die-hard rocker Bobby Pinn leads these fun 2-hour tours around East Village's legendary punk, rock and glam nightspots (Mon–Sat 1pm). Rock Junket also does tours of Union Square and Greenwich Village (Sun 11am) and artist-specific tours for the Beatles and Bob Dylan. Private and customised tours are available.

BRITTIP
If you're feeling peckish after your Rock Junket tour, www.rockjunket.com's NYC Guide has a list of cool rock 'n' roll joints serving food for $10.

ON LOCATION TOURS

CENTRAL PARK TV & MOVIE TOUR
✉ Meet at the entrance to Central Park, 59th Street between 5th and 6th Avenues
🚇 Subway N, R to 5th Avenue
🕐 Tues, Thurs–Sun
$ $22 (plus $2 ticket fee)
Take some snaps of the Boathouse Café seen in *When Harry Met Sally* and *Sex And The City*, check out Tavern in the Green that featured in *Ghostbusters* and feed pigeons in the park à la Macaulay Culkin in *Home Alone 2*. See the Bandshell from *Breakfast at Tiffany's* plus have the chance to walk where the cast of *Glee* performed. This walking tour takes two hours and, for the novelty, you could do it by bike (p83).

GOSSIP GIRL SITES
✉ Meet near the New York Palace Hotel on Madison Avenue between 50th and 51st Streets
🚇 Subway E, V to 5th Avenue/53rd Street
🕐 Fri, Sat, Sun noon
$ $42 (plus $2 ticket fee)
If you love this hit TV show, this is your chance to experience a day in the life of Manhattan's elite, visiting more than 40 locations that have appeared in the show.

This includes the Empire hotel that's home to Chuck Bass, the Constance Billard School for Girls, the lavish 5th Avenue building that Blair calls home, shop at Henri Bendel where Blair and Serena shop and the candy store where Dan helped Vanessa shop for her anniversary.

BRITTIP
Pace yourself. There's no point in trying to pack so much into your day that you arrive back at your hotel exhausted with your head spinning. Less can often be more!

ON LOCATION TOURS
Upper East Side
☎ 212-209 3370
🖰 www.screentours.com
The first and best company in New York for fun and informative bus tours around the attractions in some of the city's famous shows, plus a general TV and movie tour and a walking tour of Central Park movie sites, taking in New York's main attractions along the way.

SEX AND THE CITY HOTSPOTS
✉ Meet by the Pulitzer Fountain on 5th Avenue at 58th and 59th Street
🚇 Subway 4, 5, 6, to 59th Street/Lexington Avenue; N, R, W to 5th Avenue
🕐 Daily 11am and 3pm, Sat 11am daily
$ $46 (plus $2 ticket fee)
During this 3½-hour bus tour, which includes over 40 locations, you'll visit D&G in SoHo, where Carrie shopped for shoes, and the New York Sports Club where Miranda worked out, plus bars such as O'Neil's and Tao where Carrie, Samantha, Charlotte and Miranda did their flirting. Plus, you'll get some behind-the-scenes scoop on the show and the actors. This is a really fun experience, which gets into the spirit of the show and gives everyone plenty of browsing and chatting opportunities. You'll also get to see the famous Magnolia Bakery and even eat a cupcake on the tour (watch out – they are incredibly sweet!). By the end, you should be fluent in *Sex And The City*-speak and know your Manhattan Guy (a genetically mutant strain of single man that feeds on Zabar's and midnight shows at Angelika) from your Trysexual (someone who will try everything once). Book at least a week in advance.

SOPRANOS SITES
✉ Bus departs from the 'Button' statue on 7th Avenue at 39th Street
🚇 B, D, F, V to 42nd Street; N, Q, R, S, W, 1, 2, 3, 7, 9, S to Times Square
🕐 Sat 10am
$ $46 (plus $2 ticket fee)

The Friends' apartment building

Get the shakedown on a tour of 40 sites used in *The Sopranos* including Satriale's Pork Store, the cemetery where Livia Soprano is buried, the Bada Bing nightclub and the diner where Chris was shot. The 4-hour tour also includes a guide to New Jersey Mafia-speak, a stop for cannoli (traditional Italian pastries) and 6 other stops along the way. The tours tend to sell out quickly, so reserve your place as far in advance as possible.

TOUR NEW YORK TV & MOVIE SITES

- ✉ Bus departs from Ellen's Stardust Diner, 1650 Broadway at 51st Street
- 🚇 Subway 1, 9 to 50th Street; N, W, R to 49th Street
- 🕐 Daily at 11am
- $ $40 (plus $2 ticket fee)

Takes you to over 40 different locations from over 60 TV shows and movies such as *Friends*, *Ghostbusters*, *Will & Grace* and Woody Allen's *Manhattan* in 3½ hours. This is updated as new movies come out, so it now has sites from *Hitch*, *The Devil Wears Prada*, *The*

Dana Barrett's apartment in *Ghostbusters*

Interpreter, *The Apprentice*, *Spider-Man* and *Rescue Me*. The latest are *Glee*, *Friends With Benefits*, *How I Met Your Mother*, *Limitless* and much more.

BROOKLYN TV & MOVIE SITES TOUR

- ✉ Meet at Katz's Deli on East Houston Street at Ludlow Street
- 🚇 Subway F to 2nd Avenue; J, M, Z to Essex Street
- 🕐 Sun 11am
- $ $42 adults, $24 children (plus $2 ticket fee)

This new 4-hour bus tour launched in spring 2012 takes in over 40 TV and film sites among Brooklyn's bridges, bistros and brownstones seen in *How To Lose A Guy In Ten Days*, *French Connection*, *American Gangster*, *Moonstruck*, *Catch Me If You Can*, *Sex And The City* and *Boardwalk Empire*, with local actors to give the inside scoop and behind the scenes gossip.

WALKING TOURS

ADVENTURE ON A SHOESTRING

- ✉ 300 West 53rd Street
- ☎ 212-265 2663
- 🚇 Varies depending on area
- 🕐 Sat, Sun
- $ $10

Adventure has been going strong for nearly 45 years, offering 2-hour tours led by veteran Howard Goldberg around many Manhattan neighbourhoods, as well as outlying areas that are less familiar to tourists, such as Astoria, the Greek section of Queens, and

Hoboken, a new artists' centre in New Jersey. Among the most popular tours are Haunted Greenwich Village and Hell's Kitchen. Theme tours, such as those based on Marilyn Monroe's New York and Jacqueline Kennedy Onassis's New York, are also favourites.

ALLIANCE FOR DOWNTOWN NEW YORK
Financial District

✉ Tours start at the steps of the US Custom House, 1 Bowling Green

☎ 212-606 4064

🖐 www.downtownny.com/walkingtours

🚇 Subway 4, 5 to Bowling Green

🕐 Thurs and Sat, noon

Just turn up to take this free 90-minute Highlights of Lower Manhattan Tour exploring the birthplace of New York, from City Hall to The Battery. The Alliance has been doing much work on sprucing up the entire district and employs red-hatted security staff/ cleaners to help you find your way around. Pick up a copy of its free Downtown New York Fold-Out Map or the Lower Manhattan Shop & Dine guide to help get the best out of the area.

BRITTIP
Some Big Onion tours can get a little crowded. If so, stand as close to the guide as possible to hear their pearls of wisdom.

BIG ONION WALKING TOURS
Brooklyn

✉ 476 13th Street, Brooklyn, NY 11215

☎ 212-439 1090 or 1-888-606 WALK

🖐 www.bigonion.com

🕐 Various tours daily, most are 11am, 1pm, 2pm or 5pm. Always call after 9.30am on the morning of your tour as the time will change if the weather is bad

$ $20 adults, $15 seniors and students

'Big Onion' was the nickname given to New York in the 19th century by non-New Yorkers who believed it smelled of the immigrants' heavily spiced cooking! This award-winning company runs amazingly informative ethnic, architectural and historic 2-hour walking tours, which you can just turn up to (but reserve the multi-ethnic eating tour), led by history graduates.

Around 30 tours are offered on a rotating basis and begin in different spots. Call the main number or check the website to download the brochure or see what's on the schedule. Options include East Village, Chelsea and the High Line, DUMBO and Vinegar Hill, Gay New York, Financial District, Gramercy

US Customs House

Park and Union Square, Greenwich Village, Historic Lower Manhattan, Historic TriBeCa, Historic Harlem, the Jewish Lower East Side, Presidential New York, Revolutionary New York, Roosevelt Island, SoHo and NoLiTa and the Upper East Side. New are Historic Brooklyn Heights and Satan's Seat: New York during Prohibition.

The Original Multi-ethnic Eating Tour: Meet on the southwest corner of Essex and Delancey Streets in front of Chase Bank. Subway J, M, Z to Essex Street; F to Delancey Street.

BRITTIP
If you need to visit the loo before you start this tour, head for the McDonald's on the same side of the road as the meeting point.

Brooklyn Heights

This is one of the more popular tours, which covers the Lower East Side, Chinatown and Little Italy, and it is offered frequently. You pay a $5 supplement for nosh, which includes delicious spicy tofu, mozzarella and Italian sausage, chicken and shrimp and vegetarian dim sum, plus other food favourites of the locals, all eaten in the streets. The tour also provides a good way to get a feel for areas you may find confusing on your own. It gives a fascinating insight into the history of the area and what modern-day life is like.

You'll end the tour deep in the heart of Chinatown outside a vegetarian food centre and the Chinese Gourmet Bakery. It may be good to stop for a drink before you head off to the nearest subway stations at Canal Street, where you have the choice of the A, C, E, J, M, N, Q, R, W, 6 lines to take you just about anywhere in Manhattan.

Historic Harlem Tour: Meet at the Schomburg Center at 135th Street and Lenox Avenue. Subway 2, 3 to 135th Street. A great way to find out about Harlem, its history, politics and modern-day life through the eyes of a history graduate.

You'll hear about Martin Luther King and other African-American activists, local literary salons and gospel churches. You'll learn about the old neighbourhood joints of the Renny and Savoy, how the Apollo Theater and Cotton Clubs were only open to rich white folk looking for an 'authentic black' experience, the campaign to allow black people to work in the shops they frequented, Striver's Row, the architecture and the old black pressure groups, two of whose buildings now house beauty parlours.

The 'Official' Gangs of New York Tour: Meet on the south-east corner of Broadway and Chambers Street at City Hall Park. Subway 1, 2, 3, A, C, E to Chambers Street, R to City Hall, 4, 5, 6 to Brooklyn Bridge. This popular tour is (like the movie of the same name) inspired by Herbert Asbury's 1927 classic book The Gangs of New York, and Martin Scorsese's film, which explores every aspect of the city's brutal gang culture centred on Five Points.

Led in conjunction with Miramax Films, the tour paints a vivid picture of life for the immigrants in the 1800s and includes stops at Paradise Square, Murderer's Alley and other sites associated with Bill 'The Butcher' Poole, William Tweed and the police and draft riots. Before you get too carried away with any notions of glamour, bear in mind that the area then was so unsafe that the police refused to go near it. There was at least one murder a night and ordinary people were so scared of leaving their tenements they even buried their dead in their buildings.

JOYCE GOLD HISTORY TOURS OF NEW YORK
Chelsea
- ✉ 141 West 17th Street
- ☎ 212-242 5762
- 🖰 www.nyctours.com
- 🕐 Various starting times for 2 hours, no reservations needed
- $ $18 per person, seniors $15

Specialists in unusual, in-depth weekend forays into 30 of the city's distinctive neighbourhoods all led by Joyce herself. Fascinating tours on select dates include The Flamboyant and the Bohemian – Greenwich Village and How it became Famous, Ground Zero and its Neighbours – the First Ten Years, Historic Diversity in the East Village, and the new Northern Reaches of Central Park. Private tours are available year round.

LITERARY PUB CRAWL
West Village
- ✉ Meet at the White Horse Tavern, 567 Hudson Street at 11th Street
- ☎ 212-613 5796
- 🖰 www.literarypubcrawl.com
- 🚇 Subway 1, 9 to Christopher Street
- 🕐 Sat 2pm
- $ $20 adults, $15 students/seniors

Tour 4 pubs in the Village area that attracted writers, poets and artists, among them Dylan Thomas, Ernest Hemingway, John Steinbeck, e e cummings, Jack Kerouac, Jackson Pollock and Frank McCourt.

MUNICIPAL ART SOCIETY
Midtown
- ✉ 111 West 57th Street between 6th and 7th Avenues
- ☎ 212-935 3960
- 🖰 www.mas.org
- 🚇 Subway N, R to 57th Street
- $ Varies

Walking tours, which last around 2 hours, take in both historic and architectural sites, focusing on skyscrapers in different neighbourhoods, and are led by architects, art historians, preservationists, teachers and writers. View the website to check out the numerous upcoming tours, which in the past have included topics like What's Up Downtown: From Battery to Wall Street and Chelsea Art Galleries.

SUSANSEZ NYC WALKABOUTS
Bronx
- ☎ 917-509 3111
- 🖰 www.susansez.com
- 🚇 Subway various starting points
- $ $18–45

ONE DAY IN NEW YORK

Need to cram everything into 24 hours? I've broken down 1 day to include some of the must-see, must-do things I think New York has to offer. Obviously there are lots of wonderful experiences that I've had to leave out, but with this whirlwind tour of the city you'll at least come away with a true taste of the Big Apple!

Breakfast: Rise as early as possible (there's a lot to do today!) and, if you haven't already done so, buy a MetroCard to save money getting around (p66). The best breakfast in town is at Norma's at Le Parker Meridien Hotel, Midtown. The only difficulty is choosing from the vast selection of delights on offer, from chocolate French toast to poached eggs and corn beef hash. For something cheaper, tuck into some bagels, one of the city's signature breakfasts. There are dozens of great bagel places throughout New York. I'd recommend Ess a Bagel at 359 First Avenue (212-980 1010, www.ess-a-bagel.com). Chow down on a salmon and cheese bagel and great coffee to prepare you for your day.

Morning: It would be a shame to visit the city and not check out at least one of the incredible museums. It's hard to beat the American Museum of Natural History (p102), next to Central Park. Choose a Museum Highlights Tour, free with admission, at 10.15am. After you've had a glimpse of at least some of the museum's wonders, cross Central Park West to access Central Park for a walk, past landmarks such as the Obelisk, or Cleopatra's Needle, the oldest public monument in North America, and end at the Boathouse Restaurant Central Park (p160) at the northeast tip of the lake, the perfect place for a spot of lunch. It's busy so best to book ahead, but well worth it as this is one of the loveliest restaurants in the city. If it's summer, ask for a table on the outdoor terrace.

Afternoon: Now that you're full, it's time to walk off the calories New York style. Hop on the Metro (B, D at 72nd Street) down to SoHo (B, D to Spring Street) and wander around the unique boutiques, like Flying A (p148) and Anthropologie (p151) for clothes, and SoHo Antiques Fair (p145) for chic antiques, set amid the cobbled streets and cool buildings. If you're feeling peckish or just need to take a load off (New York speak!), pop into Fanelli's Café (p184) on Prince Street for a drink and a snack and maybe even a celeb spot; it's a former speakeasy and one of the oldest watering holes in the area.

Early evening: When it's time for a tipple after all that sightseeing, either take the Metro (V to 5th Avenue/53rd Street) or walk up 5th Avenue to the Four Seasons Hotel (p239), where The Bar offers the city's widest choice of martini and great people-watching. From here, catch a cab or Metro (N, Q, R, W to 14th Street, Union Square) to the Union Square Café (p165). Restaurants come and go but Danny Meyer's top eatery (it's always Zagat rated) continues to deliver the best American cuisine you could wish for in really beautiful surroundings – fail safe if you've only got time for one posh dinner in the city.

Night: While you're in the Union Square area, walk up Broadway (only a short distance) to Gotham Comedy Club (p205), which has some of the best line-ups in the land, including comedians who have appeared on *Saturday Night Live* and *The Tonight Show.* For late-night drinks there's so much choice it's a tough call, but for pure decadence and feeling like you're in a truly classic New York hideaway, it has to be the Campbell Apartment Bar at Grand Central Station (p74) for a whisky in a leather armchair by the massive stone fireplace.

Walking tours off the beaten track in Manhattan and the outer boroughs, the Bronx and Queens led by native New Yorker Susan Birnbaum, including curiosities such as the Knitting Crawl Walkabout, Pushcarts to Funky Swank, around the Lower East Side and the most expensive, but tempting, Downtown Chocolate/Wine Walkabout ($75).

WALK AND TALK NEW YORK

✉ Planetarium Station, PO Box 742
☎ 212-873 8534
🖱 www.walkandtalknewyork.com
$ 3-hour tour $150 for 2 people

New York resident Phyllis K takes you around the hot spots, or you can fill in a form online and let her know where you'd like to visit. Most tours are between 2 and 3 hours long and a sample tour includes Chelsea, Meatpacking district, Greenwich and West villages. I like the sound of the NYC Chocolate Walkabout, $80, but have yet to experience it!

YOUR OWN WALKING TOURS

If you don't want to join a group tour but still appreciate knowing what you are seeing as you stroll around, here are some glorious walks, none of which will take more than a

Cafés on Chambers Street

couple of hours maximum (at a very gentle pace). So don your trainers (sorry, sneakers), pack some water and enjoy!

1 LOWER MANHATTAN WALK
Little Italy
▶Start from Mulberry Street at Grand Street heading south and you'll hit the heart of this vibrant, colourful, café-filled neighbourhood, which as the name suggests is home to some 5,000 immigrant Italians. Sit and watch the world go by at one of the authentic cafés.

Woolworth Building

▶Suitably refreshed, continue your walk south, which will take you past Umberto's Clam House, the place where Mafia boss Joey Gallo was shot in the '70s.
▶When you hit Canal Street, turn left.

Chinatown
▶ You'll immediately notice the change from west to east, and if you turn first right on to Mott Street you'll be in the main thoroughfare of Chinatown.
▶ Head south and be intoxicated by the exotica aromas and noisy street vendors selling everything from fresh dim sum to fake handbags in front of the Eastern States Buddhist Temple, home to over 100 glittering Buddhas.
▶ Head right on Bayard Street until you hit Centre Street.
▶ Turn left and after about 1km/0.6mls the road turns in to Park Row; look right and you'll see City Hall Park and the Woolworth Building on Broadway.

Woolworth Building
▶ Gaze up at what was once the Big Apple's tallest building (it lost the crown in 1930) and set the standard for future skyscrapers. Named after retail tycoon Frank W. Woolworth, this Gothic-esque creation was built in 1913 and designed by architect Cass Gilbert. You'll instantly spot it thanks to the gargoyles of bats, pyramid roof and 4 towers.
▶ Carry on south down Broadway for around 7 blocks.
▶ Then turn right on to Liberty Street where you'll find the World Trade Center Memorial Visitors' Centre next to Ground Zero.

World Trade Center Memorial
▶ To see more than Ground Zero, where 2,979 people lost their lives when the World Trade Center buildings collapsed after a terrorist attack on 11 September 2001, then visit the WTC Visitor Center, which has exhibitions, programmes and even personal walking tours with survivors or the new 9/11 Memorial.
▶ When you've paid your respects, retrace your steps along Park Row, turn right at the Municipal Building on to the bridge.

Brooklyn Bridge
▶ This 1.6km/1ml gateway to Brooklyn is a Manhattan landmark. Beautiful by day and night, there's a constant flow of traffic, joggers and pedestrians and it's well worth crossing for the panoramic views of the skyline.
▶ A great way to end the day is with a meal or drink at the River Café on Water Street (p159), which lies just beneath the bridge in Brooklyn.

2 DOWNTOWN WALK
Flatiron Building
▶ Start the walk at 5th Avenue at West 23rd Street. Look up in awe at this spectacular skyscraper with an unusual triangle shape, which was once the tallest building in the world when it was completed in 1902.
▶ Head south down 5th Avenue, where if in the mood credit cards can be flexed in the designer boutiques.
▶ After 6 blocks turn right on to West 17th Street.

Rubin Museum of Art
▶ At the corner of West 17th Street at 7th Avenue is the Rubin, the first museum in the western hemisphere dedicated to the art of the Himalayas. Admire the stunning Tibetan wall hangings, bronze busts, masks and sculptures from the 2nd to the 20th centuries.
▶ Return to 5th Avenue and continue south until reaching East 14th Street.

St Mark's in the Bowery
▶ Walk along East 14th Street, past Union Square on the left, then turn right on to 4th Avenue, then after a couple of blocks turn right on to East 10th Street and see the spire of St Mark's. Built in 1799, it's one of New York City's oldest churches, where the poet W. H. Auden was a parishioner and some of the city's most prominent residents are laid to rest.

Greenwich Village
▶ Head west back along 10th Street and turn left on to University Place, where the shops and tree-lined roads of Greenwich Village emerge. This tranquil bohemian haven is a welcome break from the hustle and bustle of 5th Avenue.

Flatiron Building

▶ Walk south and see the red brick New York University buildings on the left and Washington Square Park on the right.
Washington Square Park
▶ The heart of Greenwich Village, Washington Square Park is one of the city's most vibrant open spaces. Once a magnet for artists and political activists, it's now home to some of New York's elite. Keep your eyes peeled for the magnificent marble arch on the north side of the square.

3 MIDTOWN WALK
Museum of Modern Art (MoMA)
▶ Start the walk at this inspiring modern art museum on 53rd Street between 5th and 6th Avenues, packed full of 19th and 20th-century masterpieces. If you haven't already visited, take a stroll around the world-renowned painting and sculpture galleries

Solomon R Guggenheim Museum

on the first floor and admire the renovations unveiled in 2004 (p117).

▶ Walk west until reaching Avenue of the Americas, then head south to the Rockefeller Center between 49th and 50th streets.

Rockefeller Center
▶ Home to Radio City Music Hall, this New York Art Deco landmark was built in the 1930s and named after the benefactor who paid for its construction. Take a trip to the Top of the Rock observation tower for unmissable views of the city (p78).

▶ Continue down the Avenue of the Americas, then head west down 42nd Street, the Big Apple's famous theatre district, until reaching Times Square.

Times Square
▶ Flashing neon signs and crowds of people mark an arrival at this lively spot, which is buzzing 24 hours a day. It's a great place for people watching and a magnet for New York's weird and wonderful characters, plus it's home to some of the city's top theatres.

▶ Retracing your steps, head east down 42nd Street, catching a glimpse of the Garment District on the way, before arriving at the dramatic Chrysler Building where 42nd Street meets Lexington Avenue.

Chrysler Building
▶ This iconic 77-storey skyscraper, instantly recognisable by its stainless steel Art Deco spire that resembles a car radiator grill, is one of the city's best-loved landmarks. Pop inside to marvel at the lavish marble and granite lobby with a chrome steel trim.

▶ Head west back along 42nd Street and at Grand Central Station turn left and head south down Park Avenue.

▶ Turn right on to 34th Street and see the Empire State Building on the left when reaching 5th Avenue.

Empire State Building
▶ Recognised the world over, the city's tallest skyscraper is synonymous with New York. It opened its doors to the public in 1931 and people have flocked there ever since to view the Art Deco marble lobby and to ride the lifts up to the observatories, where the views of the city are unparalleled.

◀◀⚑ **BRITTIP**
The Downtown Alliance has released a free Highlights of Lower Manhattan self-guided tour which takes you from City Hall to The Battery and offers an overview of some of the most significant sites in the city. You can download it from www.downtownny.com/walkingtours.

4 UPPER EAST SIDE WALK
Solomon R Guggenheim Museum
▶ Starting on a section of 5th Avenue nicknamed The Museum Mile, Frank Lloyd Wright's spiral masterpiece houses one of the world's best collections of modern art including 19th to 21st-century artists such as Picasso and Kandinsky. Worth returning to at night to see the rainbow lit windows which bring the building to life.

▶ Head south on 5th Avenue to reach the Metropolitan Museum of Art in 5 blocks.

Metropolitan Museum of Art
▶ Overlooking Central Park, this beautiful 1880 gothic-style building houses the western world's most comprehensive art collection, with works dating from ancient times to the 21st century, including a vast collection of American masterpieces.

▶ Take the 86th Street Transverse, the road across the Park, which starts behind the Met.

Central Park
▶ Once inside the park, it's a short stroll to East Drive, which heads south through the park taking you past Cleopatra's Needle and the Boating Lake. Stop here for a drink and bite to eat at the Boat House Restaurant, one of New York's prettiest eateries.

▶ It's easiest to exit the park at Bethseday Fountain on East 72nd Street, continue on this road, cross over 5th Avenue and head a few blocks south to reach the Frick Collection on the left.

Frick Collection
▶ This priceless art collection housed in the former mansion of steel magnate Henry Clay Frick, provides an insight into New York's gilded age. The opulent furnishings that surround the collection are equally as jaw-dropping as the old master paintings; French antique furniture, oriental rugs and rare Limoge enamels.

▶ Heading north up 5th Avenue, turn right after 5 blocks along East 57th Street to the Whitney Museum on Madison Avenue.

Whitney Museum of American Art
▶ Look up to see the grey granite cube designed by Marcel Breuer, which has an unusual cantilevered façade. Founded in 1930 by sculptor Gertrude Vanderbilt, the museum has the most comprehensive permanent collection of 20th and 21st-century American art under one roof.

5 UPPER WEST SIDE WALK
Riverside Park
▶ Start on 96th Street to catch a glimpse of the Cliff Dwellers Apartment at 243 Riverside Drive, where the façade is decorated with

ONE FREE DAY IN NEW YORK

If you're short of cash, packing in expensive sightseeing and the best restaurants and bars in town isn't an option, but there's still lots of ways to enjoy Manhattan without spending a dime.

Morning: Kick off your day in the Big Apple with a free tai chi class in Bryant Park (www.bryantpark.org, p257) 7.30-8.30am Tues and Thurs) or Birding Tour (8-9am Mon and Thurs). While there, check out the free toilets, surely the city's, if not the country's, finest; neo-Grecian with pillars, giant marble urn full of flowers, real soap and uniformed attendant! From here head down to the southernmost tip of the island to catch the Staten Island Ferry (www.siferry.com, p80), which transports around 20 million people a year to and from Staten Island. You'll see the stunning New York skyline for free plus the Statue of Liberty – sure beats a pricey harbour cruise!

Afternoon: Time for some culture, so hit the museums. Carnegie Hall and the Rose Museum (p106) and the National Museum of the American Indian (p118) are both free, and many others don't charge on a Friday evening. If you've still got time on your hands you could arrange a meet-up with a Big Apple Greeter (www.bigapplegreeter.org), a local volunteer who will show you around the city for free (they're also likely to have some good tips on bargain places to go!). Or, take a stroll through Central Park (p261–63), it doesn't cost a thing and there's lots to see and do.

Evening: If you're hungry after all that sightseeing and culture, then it's time to hit the Crocodile Lounge (p215) which, amazingly, gives out free pizza for every beer you buy. It's a really cool little bar with croc heads poking out from the ceiling and they don't fleece you with the price of the beer, it's around $3. If you're looking for entertainment visit KGB Bar (www.kgbbar.com, p199), which has poetry, book readings or live music most nights of the week without charge. There are also lots of free concerts and screenings in the parks during the summer months, check out what's on before you go at www.nycgovparks.org.

WHAT TO SEE AND DO

buffalo skulls, rattlesnakes and mountain lions. The park is a green oasis, which runs 70km/112mls along the banks of the Hudson river and was designed by Frederick Law Olmsted, who was also the brain behind Central Park.

▶ Enjoy a walk south along Riverside Drive, one of the most beautiful streets in the city, to West 79th Street and head west until hitting Central Park West, where you'll find the American Museum of Natural History. American Museum of Natural History

▶ With more than 30 million specimens and artefacts, this is one of the world's largest natural history museums spanning 4 city blocks. Previously people headed straight for the dinosaurs, but don't miss the glass Rose Center for earth and space.

▶ Carry on south down Central Park West for a couple of blocks where you'll find the New York Historical Society.

New York Historical Society

▶ New York's oldest museum, built in 1804, is notable for the world's largest collection of Tiffany lamps; plus more than 40,000 artefacts, including furniture, silver, sculptures and a research library.

▶ Enter Central Park from West 77th Street and turn south down West Park Drive.

Central Park

▶ Known as the lungs of New York, Central Park was created in 1858 on former swampland. It's green and wooded 341ha/843acres make a welcome break for tourists and residents alike. In the summer, the park is alive with children's playgrounds and the boating lake; in winter, the ice skating rink is the main attraction. Watch the cyclists, skaters and joggers whiz by and pass Strawberry Fields, a meadow memorial to John Lennon filled with flowers from all over the world.

▶ On the left heading south is Sheep Meadow, where residents and tourists can be spotted playing ball games and kite flying.

▶ Exit the park at 65th Street and continue east until reaching the Lincoln Center on Columbus Avenue.

Lincoln Center

▶ The sight of dramatic arches signifies your arrival at this centre for the arts. Take a rest by the reflecting fountain in the courtyard of this contemporary building, home to a mix of dance, music and theatre that draws audiences of around 5 million people a year. In the summer, keep a lookout for free concerts, which are held in the adjacent park.

CHAPTER 5

Museums and Galleries

New York has some of the best-known museums and galleries in the world, so it's little wonder that some tourists come to the Big Apple just to visit these major attractions. Among the names that you are most likely to be familiar with are the Metropolitan Museum of Art (the Met), the Solomon R Guggenheim Museum, Whitney Museum of Modern Art and the Museum of Modern Art (MoMA). Most of the major museums are located around a specific area of the city called the Museum Mile, which stretches along 5th Avenue on the Upper East Side from 82nd to 110th Street.

As befits a city that is famed for regenerating itself, none of the museums sits on its laurels. There is a constant wave of refurbishment and renewal, as well as cutting-edge exhibitions that inspire people to keep returning. The American Museum of Natural History spent $25m updating its Milstein Hall of Ocean Life and then more recently $37m renovating the Grand Gallery, and MoMA reopened in 2004 after a multi-million-dollar refurbishment and expansion, in a much-praised new building designed by architect Yoshio Taniguchi. The Museum of

Jewish Heritage and the Morgan Library have both reopened after extensive refurbishment, the National Museum of Design reopened its doors at the end of 2013 and the Cooper-Hewitt Museum is scheduled to reopen mid-2014 following major renovation. A raft of museums has opened in the last decade, including the American Folk Art Museum, the Annette Green Museum dedicated to the history of perfumes, the Jewish Children's Museum in Brooklyn and the National Cartoon Museum (formerly the International Museum of Cartoon Art), which opened in 2007 in the Empire State Building as the largest museum of cartoon art in the world. Also in 2007, Greek and Roman Galleries opened in an entire wing of The Metropolitan Museum of Art and the Elizabeth A Sackler Center for Feminist Art opened at The Brooklyn Museum. The National Sports Museum, the first ever museum dedicated to sports, opened in 2008.

Of course, it does mean there is a lot to choose from and, especially if you're on your first visit to New York, you'll want to ensure you don't waste any time. It should also be noted that many cultural institutions in New

Rose Center at the American Museum of Natural History

York go to great lengths to make themselves family friendly, so don't let having youngsters in tow put you off visiting.

A-Z OF MUSEUMS

9/11 MEMORIAL MUSEUM
Set beneath the 911 Memorial where the Twin Towers once stood (p70).

ALICE AUSTEN HOUSE MUSEUM & GARDEN
Staten Island
- ✉ 2 Hylan Blvd, Staten Island
- ☎ 718-816 4506
- ⌂ www.aliceausten.org
- 🚌 Staten Island Ferry from Battery Park
- 🕐 Thurs–Sun 11–5pm, March–Dec. Closed Jan–Feb
- $ Suggested donation $3 adults, under 12s free

This museum on Staten Island offers a glimpse into the world of photographer Alice Austen. Her former home, a quaint, Victorian cottage, is one of the key reasons to visit as it offers a magnificent view of New York Harbour and displays prints from the large glass negative collection of her work depicting turn-of-the-century American life. The City bought the Austen house in 1975 and restored it and the grounds in 1984–85. The Victorian garden was replanted according to Austen photographs, complete with shrubs such as weeping mulberry and flowering quince. A guide will meet you at the entrance and answer any questions you may have.

AMERICAN FOLK ART MUSEUM
Midtown
- ✉ 2 Lincoln Square, Columbus Ave at 66th Street
- ☎ 212-595 9533
- ⌂ www.folkartmuseum.org
- 🚌 Subway 1 to 66th Street/Lincoln Center
- 🕐 Tues–Sat noon–7.30pm, Sun noon–6pm, closed Mon
- $ Free

Originally called the Museum of Early American Folk Arts when it was founded in 1961, it focused on vernacular arts of 18th and 19th-century America, particularly the north-east. A name change to the more inclusive Folk Art Museum coincided with the museum's $18m new structure, designed by award-winning architects Tod Williams and Billy Tsien. A branch was opened in the Lincoln Center that a few years ago became the museum's permanent home. This museum provides an excellent opportunity to get to grips with American folk art and gives an insight into America's history and cultural heritage from the perspective of these

arts. It holds more than 5,000 permanent artworks spanning 3 centuries, from textiles to 21st-century photographs, plus has new exhibitions. Check out free music Fridays at 5.30pm for some complimentary live entertainment.

AMERICAN MUSEUM OF NATURAL HISTORY
Upper West Side
- ✉ Central Park West at 79th Street
- ☎ 212-769 5100
- ⌂ www.amnh.org
- 🚌 Subway B, C to 81st Street/Museum of Natural History; 1, 9 to 79th Street
- 🕐 10am–5.45pm daily
- $ Suggested price $19 adults, $14.50 students and seniors, $10.50 under-13s. The most comprehensive package, which includes the space shows, IMAX films and special exhibitions, is the All-Inclusive SuperSaver, which costs $33 adults, $25.50 seniors and students and $20.50 children

Like the Metropolitan, this is an epic of a museum, best seen in parts rather than attempting the whole (although you'll save money if you do!). It provides an entertaining and amazingly detailed yet comprehensive overview of life on Earth and beyond, and has undergone an enormous amount of growth and redevelopment.

◀■▶ **BRITTIP**

To avoid crowds, heat or cold, take the B or C train to 81st Street and go straight into the American Museum of Natural History from the subway. Follow the tiled signs in the mosaic wall.

One of its most famous permanent exhibitions is the **Milstein Hall of Ocean Life**, given a $25m redesign using the latest marine technology and a $15m donation by museum trustee Irma Milstein and her husband Paul. Using the hall's massive blue whale as its centrepiece, lights, video and sound effects create the breathtaking illusion of being immersed in the ocean.

Other permanent exhibits include the **Anne and Bernard Spitzer Hall of Human Origins**, which has the most amazing collection of up-to-date discoveries to chart humankind; The **Grand Gallery**, which has had a $37m renovation involving the famous castle facade on 77th Street, the museum's original entrance in the 1890s, where you can check out the Grand Canoe, the longest of its type in existence. The Fossil Halls are where you'll find more than 600 specimens, including dinosaurs. Much fun is to be had using the many interactive computer exhibits, for instance, to travel back in time to trace the roots of evolution.

In addition, there is the **Rose Center for Earth and Space** – a spectacular museum within a museum housed in glass, which incorporates the **Hayden Planetarium** as its centrepiece. This is the place to come to learn about the inner workings of Earth and the outer reaches of the universe. The Big Bang Theater gives a dramatic re-creation of the first minutes of the origins of the universe and is found inside a 26.5m/87ft wide sphere that appears to float in a glass-walled ceiling. Here you will also find the **Space Theater**, billed as the most technologically advanced in the world, which shows incredibly realistic views of outer space. There's a spectacular new film, *Journey to the Stars*, narrated by Whoopi Goldberg, which features images from telescopes on earth and in space and never-seen-before footage. The film is shown every half-hour from 10.30am–4.30pm.

🇬🇧 BRITTIP

If you're interested in partying with the stars (those above you and in real life), check out One Step Beyond, a party night with live bands and DJs, taking place beneath the twinkling dome of the Rose Center for Earth and Space. There are cocktails to keep the party going into the small hours. For tickets, $25, call 212-769 5200, 9am–5pm or buy online at www.amnh.org/osb.

There are also mammal halls, the incredible **Biodiversity Hall**, complete with imitation rainforest, and **Birds Halls**. The fantastic **Butterfly Conservatory**, which reopened in 2010, is like being in a Disney film as hundreds

---

BRILLIANT MUSEUMS FOR ALL THE FAMILY

New York is fantastic when it comes to providing exciting and engaging museums and museum activities for children. They not only have plenty of dedicated children's museums, but also many of the major New York museums put their wealth of resources to great use by offering fabulous events and activities that both entertain and educate children from as young as four right up to teens. Below are some of the best:

CHILDREN'S MUSEUMS:
Children's Museum of the Arts (p106)
Children's Museum of Manhattan (p106)
Jewish Children's Museum (p274)

ADULT MUSEUMS:
Intrepid Sea-Air-Space Museum (p110)
Lower East Side Tenement Museum (p112)
Museum of Comic and Cartoon Art (p116)
New York City Fire Museum (p120)
New York City Police Museum (p120)
New York Transit Museum, Brooklyn (p274)
And a brilliant site: Historic Richmond Town, Staten Island (p282)

---

of butterflies flit around ($25 adults, $14.50 children and $19 seniors/students) and IMAX films showing in the newly renovated **LeFrak Theater** (10.30am–4.30pm, every hour on the half-hour; admission prices as above). New special exhibitions include **Creatures of Light**, showing the amazing variety of bioluminescent organisms on earth, and **Beyond Planet Earth**, where you can travel to Mars – in your dreams.

Check out the website first to see which activities will be available during your visit. The museum also runs field trips, such as bird watching, bug (insect) hunts or flower inspections in the adjacent Central Park.

🇬🇧 BRITTIP

This AMNH also provides one of New York's coolest experiences for kids – sleepovers actually in the museum! The all-nighters take place on selected dates for children of 6–13, from $129 – after a tour by torchlight they get to snuggle in sleeping bags beneath a 94ft whale! These get booked up very quickly, so for availability and to book call 212-769 5200.

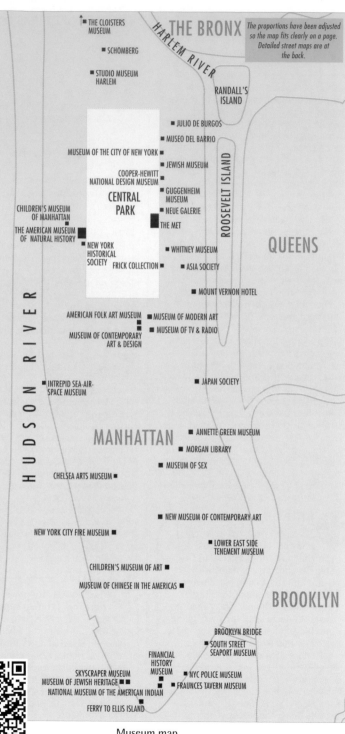

The proportions have been adjusted so the map fits clearly on a page. Detailed street maps are at the back.

THE BRONX

HARLEM RIVER

↑ THE CLOISTERS MUSEUM

■ SCHOMBERG

■ STUDIO MUSEUM HARLEM

RANDALL'S ISLAND

■ JULIO DE BURGOS

■ MUSEO DEL BARRIO

MUSEUM OF THE CITY OF NEW YORK ■

■ JEWISH MUSEUM

COOPER-HEWITT NATIONAL DESIGN MUSEUM ■

■ GUGGENHEIM MUSEUM

CENTRAL PARK

■ NEUE GALERIE

ROOSEVELT ISLAND

CHILDREN'S MUSEUM OF MANHATTAN ■

■ THE MET

THE AMERICAN MUSEUM OF NATURAL HISTORY ■

QUEENS

■ NEW YORK HISTORICAL SOCIETY

■ WHITNEY MUSEUM

FRICK COLLECTION ■

■ ASIA SOCIETY

■ MOUNT VERNON HOTEL

AMERICAN FOLK ART MUSEUM ■

■ MUSEUM OF MODERN ART

MUSEUM OF CONTEMPORARY ART & DESIGN ■

■ MUSEUM OF TV & RADIO

HUDSON RIVER

■ INTREPID SEA-AIR- SPACE MUSEUM

■ JAPAN SOCIETY

MANHATTAN

■ ANNETTE GREEN MUSEUM

■ MORGAN LIBRARY

■ MUSEUM OF SEX

CHELSEA ARTS MUSEUM ■

■ NEW MUSEUM OF CONTEMPORARY ART

NEW YORK CITY FIRE MUSEUM ■

■ LOWER EAST SIDE TENEMENT MUSEUM

CHILDREN'S MUSEUM OF ART ■

MUSEUM OF CHINESE IN THE AMERICAS ■

BROOKLYN

BROOKLYN BRIDGE

■ SOUTH STREET SEAPORT MUSEUM

FINANCIAL HISTORY MUSEUM

SKYSCRAPER MUSEUM ■

■ NYC POLICE MUSEUM

MUSEUM OF JEWISH HERITAGE ■ ■

■ FRAUNCES TAVERN MUSEUM

NATIONAL MUSEUM OF THE AMERICAN INDIAN ■

FERRY TO ELLIS ISLAND

Museum map

Carnegie Hall

AMERICAN MUSEUM OF THE MOVING IMAGE
Queens
It's only a short trip to Queens and worth a visit here if you are into films (p278).

ARTISTS' SPACE
SoHo
- ✉ 3rd Floor, 38 Greene Street
- ☎ 212-226 3970
- ⌂ www.artistsspace.org
- 🚇 Subway C, E to Spring Street
- ⊕ Mon, Tues – closed. Wed–Sun noon–6pm
- $ Free

Down a small cobblestone street in SoHo, it's hard to find but worth hunting out if you love to discover new art, as this small gallery is a launching pad for unknown artists. It's a single-floor loft space and there are friendly staff to help explain the works and contemporary styles. Well worth a visit for an hour or so.

ASIA SOCIETY
Midtown East
- ✉ 725 Park Avenue at 70th Street
- ☎ 212-288 6400
- ⌂ www.asiasociety.org
- 🚇 Subway 6 to 68th Street/Hunter College, F to 63rd Street/Lexington Avenue
- ⊕ Tues–Sun 11am–6pm, Fri 11am–9pm, closed Mon
- $ $10 adults, $7 seniors, $5 students, under 16s free; free Fri 6–9pm

Founded in 1956 by John D Rockefeller III with his collection of Asian art, it aims to build an awareness of the 30 Pan-Asian countries, which include Japan, New Zealand, Australia and the Pacific Islands. It runs films, lectures and seminars in conjunction with its exhibitions and has a regular schedule of Asian musicians who play at the museum. Daily guided tours of exhibitions are Tues–Sun 2pm, Fri also 6.30pm.

> **BRITTIP**
> Some museums offer free or half price entry late afternoon/evenings on Fri (p106).

BROOKLYN CHILDREN'S MUSEUM
New York's first children's museum, it has a great programme of events and workshops and is particularly worth the trip if you are on a family holiday (p270).

Brooklyn Children's Museum

BROOKLYN MUSEUM

One of the largest museums in the world and the oldest art museum in the country, it underwent a facelift in 2004 to become the most visitor-friendly museum in the Big Apple. It is easy to reach in Brooklyn, if you have the time to plan it into your schedule (p271). African Innovations, a collection of around 200 works from the museum's world-renowned African collection, runs until January 2013.

CARNEGIE HALL/ROSE MUSEUM
Midtown

- ✉ 2nd Floor, 154 West 57th Street
- ☎ 212-247 7800
- 🖰 www.carnegiehall.org
- 🚇 Subway A B, C, D, 1 to Columbus Circle, N, Q, R to 57th Street/7th Avenue, B, D, E to 7th Avenue, F to 6th Avenue
- 🕐 11am–6pm; closed 1 July–14 Sept; Weds and Fri tours (11.30am and 12.30pm) $10 adults, $8 seniors/students, $4 children under 12
- $ Free

Perhaps New York's most famous music venue, where all the greats have played from pop, jazz, classical and folk. for In 1991, the Rose Museum opened as part of Carnegie Hall's 100th anniversary celebrations. On the First Tier level of Carnegie Hall, the museum houses special temporary exhibitions, as well as a permanent collection of over a century's worth of photographs, letters, musical quotes and Carnegie Hall archival material, from programmes to unique memorabilia, including items from the famous names who have walked through 'the house that music built'.

CHILDREN'S MUSEUM OF THE ARTS
Little Italy

- ✉ 103 Charlton Street between Hudson and Greenwich Streets
- ☎ 212-274 0986
- 🖰 www.cmany.org
- 🚇 Subway 1 to Houston Street, B, D, F, M, A, C. E to West 4th Street, M20 bus
- 🕐 Mon, Wed, noon–5pm, Thurs, Fri noon–6pm, Sat, Sun 10am–5pm, closed Tues

GETTING IN FREE

No charge is made for admission to the following museums, so they make a great addition to your itinerary:

Carnegie Hall/Rose Museum: (left)
Edwynn Houk Gallery: (p108)
Forbes Galleries: (p109)
National Museum of the American Indian: (p119)
Schomburg Center for Research In Black Culture: (p122)

In addition to this, many museums offer times – usually on a Fri – when you can get in free or pay a voluntary donation of whatever you wish:

American Folk Art Museum: 5.30–9pm Fri (p102)
Asia Society: 6–9pm Fri (p105)
El Museo del Barrio: free on Wed (p108)
Frick Collection: after 6pm on certain Fri (p109)
International Center of Photography: 5–8pm Fri (p110)
Japan Society: Fri 6–9pm (p110)
Jewish Museum: 11am–5.45pm Sat (p112)

- $ $11 adults and children, free for infants under 1 and seniors. Pay as you wish Thurs 4–6pm

Under 7s can have an artistic ball with art computers, an art playground and a giant floor-to-ceiling chalkboard in this place, which is more like a giant playroom than a museum. There are also regular performing arts workshops led by local artists. Arts drop-in sessions designed for children aged 3–5 are on Mon, Wed, Thurs and Fri 10.45am–12pm, and cost $22 per family. A visit here is the perfect way to combine a shopping trip to SoHo for you with fun for the kids!

CHILDREN'S MUSEUM OF MANHATTAN
Upper West Side

- ✉ The Tisch Building, 212 West 83rd Street between Broadway and Amsterdam Avenue
- ☎ 212-721 1223
- 🖰 www.cmom.org
- 🚇 Subway 1 to 79th or 86th Street, B, C to 81st Street
- 🕐 Tues–Sun 10am–5pm, Saturday 10am–7pm, closed Mon; call or check the website for summer and school holiday hours
- $ $11 adults and children, infants under 1 free

The CMOM is entirely dedicated to children under the age of 10. This is a fabulous place and almost worth a visit even if you don't have kids. Its mission statement is to inspire children and their families to learn about themselves and our culturally diverse world through a unique environment of interactive exhibits and programmes. They certainly achieve it with their inspiring exhibits, such as Adventures with Dora & Diego, which includes adventures in a rainforest, with kids (aged 2-6) getting the chance to join Diego in a series of animal rescue missions and get ready for a party at Dora's house! Eat, Sleep, Play on the other hand, is an interactive exhibition for the whole family exploring how to create a healthier lifestyle together.

Weather-permitting, in the spring and summer City Splash allows all ages to play with water, from racing boats down a zigzag stream to painting a masterpiece with water.

THE CLOISTERS
Washington Heights
- ✉ 99 Margaret Corbin Drive, Fort Tyron Park
- ☎ 212-923 3700, TTY 212-570 3828
- 🖥 www.metmuseum.org
- 🚇 Subway A to 190th Street, M4 bus from Madison Avenue/83rd Street
- 🕐 Tues-Thurs, Sun 9.30am-5.30pm, Fri and Sat 9.30am-9pm, Mon closed
- $ Suggested donation $25 adults (includes free same-day admission to the Metropolitan Museum of Art (p114), $17 seniors and $12 students, under 12s free with an adult

Set in Fort Tyron Park in north Manhattan, this beautiful red-tiled Romanesque-style building was snapped up to become a branch of the Metropolitan Museum 70 years ago. Now it is purely devoted to medieval art and architecture, including 5 cloisters – hence the name – some from ruined French monasteries, dating from the 12th to the 15th centuries.

It is stunning to look at and houses some really exciting exhibits, probably the most famous being the Unicorn Tapestries, woven in Brussels in the 1500s. Staff guided tours on selected days (check the website as these change according to the time of year) are included in the price of admission and an audio guide or podcast is available. There are also gallery talks at noon and 2pm on Sat and films and medieval concerts in the wonderful 12th-century chapel from Spain.

The Cloisters has a series of free workshops for children 4–12, on the 1st and 3rd Sat of the month 1–2pm. Subjects include medieval feasts and celebrations and stories from the Middle Ages.

COOPER-HEWITT NATIONAL DESIGN MUSEUM
Upper East Side
- ✉ 2 East 91st Street at 5th Avenue
- ☎ 212-849 8400
- 🖐 www.cooperhewitt.org
- 🚗 Subway 4, 5, 6 to 86th or 96th Street
- 🕐 Tues–Fri 10am–5pm, Sat 10am–6pm, Sun 11–6pm
- $ $15 adults, $10 students and seniors, under 12s free

🔵 **BRITTIP**
If you have a student card don't forget to take it to make the most of discounted admissions to the museums.

The only American museum devoted entirely to historic and contemporary design is currently closed and undergoing major renovations. It's scheduled to reopen mid-2014, when you'll be able to view the international collection which covers everything from applied arts and industrial design to drawings, prints, textiles and wall coverings. The exterior of the building itself, was designed in a Georgian style for tycoon Andrew Carnegie and at the time was a triumph of modern engineering.

EDWYNN HOUK GALLERY
Lower East Side
- ✉ 4th Floor, 745 5th Avenue between 57th and 58th Streets
- ☎ 212-750 7070
- 🖐 www.houkgallery.com
- 🚗 Subway N, R, W to 5th Avenue/59th Street
- 🕐 Tues–Sat 11am–6pm

- $ Free admission

A delightful gallery for photography enthusiasts with both vintage and contemporary prints on display and for sale from the likes of Man Ray, Henri Cartier-Bresson and Annie Leibovitz.

EL MUSEO DEL BARRIO
Spanish Harlem
- ✉ Heckscher Building, 1230 5th Avenue at 104th Street
- ☎ 212-831 7272
- 🖐 www.elmuseo.org
- 🚗 Subway 6 to 103rd Street, 2, 3 to 110th Street/Lenox Avenue
- 🕐 Tues–Sat 11am–6pm, Sun–Mon closed
- $ Suggested donation $9 adults, $5 students and seniors, under 12s free with an adult; free on Wed

Opened in 1969 by a group of Puerto Rican parents, teachers and artists, New York's Latino museum has recently undergone $30m renovation. It houses 8,000 objects of Caribbean and Latin American art from pre-Colombian times to date. Exhibits include musical instruments, miniature houses, dolls and masks, as well as posters, paintings and sculptures. It's complemented by a film, literary and performing arts series, such as the Three Kings' Day Parade in Jan, with lively music, colourful costumes and a theatre programme. The Museum's El Cafe is open at 11am.

ELLIS ISLAND IMMIGRATION MUSEUM
Battery Park
The most visited museum in New York, this is worth dedicating a good portion of the day to, combining it with the Statue of Liberty nearby (p71).

Ellis Island Immigration Museum

FORBES GALLERIES
Greenwich Village
- ✉ 62 5th Avenue at 12th Street
- ☎ 212-206 5548
- ⌖ www.forbesgalleries.com
- 🚇 Subway A, B, C, D, E, 1, 9 from West to 14th Street, or 4, 5, 6, N, R from East to 14th Street
- ⏲ Tues–Sat 10am–4pm, except Thurs (group tours only), closed Sun and Mon
- $ Free

These Galleries in the lobby of *Forbes* magazine's headquarters showcase The Forbes Collection of home and business furnishings, decorative accessories, gifts, jewellery, books, toy boats, miniature soldiers, the Monopoly game, presidential manuscripts and fine art.

FRAUNCES TAVERN MUSEUM
Financial District
- ✉ 54 Pearl Street at Broad Street, 1st and 2nd floors
- ☎ 212-425 1778
- ⌖ www.frauncestavernmuseum.org
- 🚇 Subway R, W to Whitehall Street, J, M, Z to Broad Street; 4, 5 to Bowling Green; 1 to South Ferry
- ⏲ Daily noon–5pm
- $ $7 adults, $4 children and seniors, under 6s free

When New York was (briefly) capital of America, the Fraunces Tavern housed the Departments of Foreign Affairs, Treasury and War and was where George Washington delivered his famous farewell speech to his officers. Now, nestled among the skyscrapers of the Financial District, this 18th-century Georgian building, along with four adjacent 19th-century buildings, houses a fine museum dedicated to the study of early American history and culture. Among the collection of artefacts, paintings, drawings and documents from the revolutionary era is a lock of Washington's hair and one of his false teeth. Although well preserved, it is New York's oldest surviving building and an awful lot of restoration work has been done to keep its 1783 façade. Guided tours need to be booked in advance.

⚡ BRITTIP
Don't miss the cosy restaurant at the Fraunces Tavern Museum. It serves lovely food in a stately, if a little touristy, environment.

FRICK COLLECTION
Midtown East
- ✉ 1 East 70th Street at 5th Avenue
- ☎ 212-288 0700
- ⌖ www.frick.org
- 🚇 Subway 4, 5, 6 to 68th Street
- ⏲ Tues–Sat 10am–6pm, Sun 11am–5pm, closed Mon
- $ $18 adults, $15 seniors, $10 students; no children under 10 admitted. Pay as you wish 11am–1pm on Sun; admission includes Acoustiguide audio tour

Henry Clay Frick (1849–1919), obsessed with making money, built up a massive fortune with the Carnegie Steel Company. As his wealth grew, so did his fabulous collection of European art, which he hung in his palatial mansion on 5th Avenue. He bequeathed both the pictures and his mock 18th-century European mansion to the public when he died in 1919.

⚡ BRITTIP
The Frick Collection is well known for its Wed evening lectures, from artists to scholars, which are free and no ticket required, simply first come, first served. Check out www.frick.org to find out if there's something on while you're in town.

There are 16 galleries displaying this priceless collection of masterpieces from the 14th–19th centuries, including some of the best-known paintings by the European masters. Unusually, the pictures aren't displayed by period or style, but in the way that Frick hung them in his home, giving an insight into the lives of New York's rich in the Gilded Age. The Fragonard Room shows the large Fragonard paintings, as well as 18th-century furniture and porcelain. Paintings by Holbein, El Greco, Titian and Bellini are in the

Fraunces Tavern Museum

Living Room, while in the sky-lit West Gallery you'll find landscapes by Constable and portraits by Rembrandt, as well as a collection of rare Limoges enamels.

INTERNATIONAL CENTER OF PHOTOGRAPHY
Midtown
- ✉ 1133 Avenue of the Americas at 43rd Street
- ☎ 212-857 0000
- 🖱 www.icp.org
- 🚇 Subway B, D, F, M or 7 to 42nd Street, 1,2,3,N,Q,R,S to Times Square
- 🕐 Tues–Thurs, Sat and Sun 10am–6pm, Fri 10am–8pm, closed Mon
- $ $14 adults, $10 students and seniors, under 12s free; voluntary contribution Fri 5–8pm

The ICP is a school and a museum. It houses some excellent exhibitions, such as legendary photographer Larry Clark's work, as well as a permanent collection that consists of more than 100,000 photographs from famous photographers spanning decades. It has a large body of work by Henri Cartier-Bresson and some original prints by Weegee, who photographed crime scenes and New York nightlife in the 1930s and 1940s. Film screenings, artists' talks and lectures are on offer, as well as a store selling prints.

BRITTIP
If you're hungry, the Catherine K Café on the lower floor of the International Center of Photography is a convenient place for lunch or a snack.

INTREPID SEA–AIR–SPACE MUSEUM
Clinton
- ✉ USS Intrepid, Pier 86, west end of 46th Street at the Hudson River
- ☎ 212-245 0072
- 🖱 www.intrepidmuseum.org
- 🚇 Subway A, C, E, N, Q, R, S, W, 1, 2, 3, 7, 9 to 42nd Street, then the M42 bus to 12th Avenue
- 🕐 April–Oct: Mon–Fri 10am–5pm, Sat and Sun 10am–6pm, Nov–March: daily 10am–5pm
- $ $24 adults, $20 students and seniors, $19 youth (7–17), $12 child (3–16), children under 3 free, simulator $9 each or $24 for 3, audio tours $5 (or simulator audio combo $11), guided tours $22 adults, $16 children

A thoroughly enjoyable museum around a ship berthed on the Hudson River, which appeals to all ages and that celebrated its 30th anniversary in 2012. All the staff are very friendly and there are former members of the crew around the ship who are happy to give an insight into its history and life on board. *Intrepid* was one of 24 Second World War US aircraft carriers and, despite incidents of serious damage to these ships, none of them was ever sunk. *Intrepid*'s worst moment came on 25 Nov 1944, when two kamikaze pilots hit the ship 5 minutes apart, killing 69 and seriously injuring 85.

BRITTIP
The only way to see the submarine at *Intrepid* is on a tour and long queues build up very quickly, so get there early.

The second plane exploded on the hangar deck and the ship burned for about 6 hours, but *Intrepid* made it back to America for repairs and returned to the war. Stories of life on board are told by veterans at film screenings throughout the ship and there are also plenty of hands-on exhibits to keep kids and adults happy, from G-Force, where you get to test your flying skills, to the XD Theater where you put on 3D glasses and whiz through time and space and sensory overload with special polarised glasses at Transporter FX. The museum also exhibits the BA Concorde.

BRITTIP
Take a new New York Water Taxi to the *Intrepid* Museum and get a free pass to the 9/11 Memorial ($51.40 adults, $47.40 seniors, students, $46.40 youth (7–17), $34 child (3–6)). Be quick, though, as with only 2 departures daily, tickets are limited.

JAPAN SOCIETY
Midtown East
- ✉ 333 East 47th Street between 1st and 2nd Avenues
- ☎ 212-832 1155
- 🖱 www.japansociety.org
- 🚇 Subway E, M to Lexington Avenue/53rd Street; 6 to 51st Street
- 🕐 Tues–Thurs 11am–6pm, Friday 11am–9pm, weekends 11am–5pm
- $ $12 adults, $10 students and seniors, under 16s free, free Fri nights 6–9pm

All things Japanese, from textiles and modern photography to historical ceramics, paintings, glass and metalworks. The ideal combination of Zen and now, away from the Samurai

MUSEUMS AND GALLERIES

TOP 6 SMALL GALLERIES FOR MODERN ART

New York is a hotbed of artistic talent so if you want to pick up some original work while you are there, or just look at some, here are 6 places to head for.

Agora: Chelsea

- ✉ 530 West 25th Street
- ☎ 212-7226 4151
- ⌖ agora-gallery.com
- 🚗 Subway 23rd Street
- ⏱ Tues–Sat 11am–6pm

This high-profile gallery supports emerging and established artists. Recent exhibitions have included themes such as Pulse of Abstraction. High brow and high class.

Andrew Kreps Gallery: Chelsea

- ✉ 535 and 537 West 22nd Street
- ☎ 212-741 8849
- ⌖ www.andrewkreps.com
- 🚗 Subway 23rd Street
- ⏱ Tues–Sat 10am–6pm

An innovative band of work on display from artists including Ruth Root and Roe Ethridge.

Deitch Projects: SoHo

- ✉ 18 Wooster Street between Canal and Grand Streets
- ☎ 212-343 7300
- ⌖ www.deitch.com
- 🚗 Subway N, R, W to Prince Street; B, D, F, V to Broadway/Lafayette Street
- ⏱ Tues–Sat noon–6pm
- $ Free

Jeffrey Deitch's gallery is worth a peep if you are in SoHo – a second gallery has opened at 76 Grand Street. Focusing on large-scale installations, and sometimes live spectacles, by contemporary artists (including Yoko Ono) working in all kinds of media, it's very interesting and not as scary as it sounds.

Gagosian Gallery: Chelsea

- ✉ 555 West 24th Street between 10th and 11th Avenues
- ☎ 212-741 1111
- ⌖ www.gagosian.com
- ⏱ Tues–Sat 10am–6pm
- $ Free

An excellent, vast gallery that opened in 1999, it has featured exhibitions of work by the likes of Damien Hirst.

Maccarone Inc: Lower East Side

- ✉ 630 Greenwich Street
- ☎ 212-431 4977
- ⌖ maccarone.net
- 🚗 Subway 1, R, W to Rector Street
- ⏱ Tues–Sat 10am–6pm
- $ Free

Spread over 4 floors, this cool gallery run by Michele Maccarone features work by up-and-coming local and European artists.

Projectile Gallery: 57th Street

- ✉ 3rd floor, 37 West 57th Street between 5th and 6th Avenues
- ☎ 212-688 4673
- 🚗 Subway F to 57th Street. N, R, W to 5th Avenue/59th Street
- ⏱ Mon–Sat noon–6pm
- $ Free

A darling of the art world since it first opened in 1998, it features work by hotter than hot young artists.

Jewish Museum

swords and kimonos, its traditional Japanese garden is a Zen-like space with calming waterfall, reflecting pool and bamboo garden.

The Society, which celebrated its centenary in 2007, also puts on Japanese traditional and contemporary arts performances, films and lectures.

JEWISH CHILDREN'S MUSEUM
This specialist museum has its home in child-friendly Brooklyn (p274).

JEWISH MUSEUM
Upper East Side
- ✉ 1109 5th Avenue at 92nd Street
- ☎ 212-423 3200
- ⌂ www.thejewishmuseum.org
- 🚇 Subway 4, 5, 6 to 86th Street, 6 to 96th Street
- ⏱ Sat–Tues, Fri 11am–5.45pm and Thurs 11am–8pm, closed Wed.
- $ $12 adults, $10 seniors, $7.50 students, children under 12 free. Free on Sat

The largest Jewish museum in the Western hemisphere, the Jewish Museum, set in a château-style residence, lays on impressive annual exhibitions. The core exhibit is called Culture and Continuity: The Jewish Journey and sets out how the Jewish people have survived through the centuries and explores the essence of Jewish identity. An ongoing exhibition looks at 19th century New York poet Emma Lazarus' Jewish history and connections. Many of the objects were actually rescued from European synagogues before the Second World War. It covers 4,000 years of history with an emphasis on art and culture. Audio guides, including a family gallery guide, are free with admission. As well as talks, performances and films, there's a free drop-in arts and crafts session for children aged 3 and upwards monthly on select Sun Sept–June (check website for details).

> **BRITTIP**
> Try delicious kosher cuisine including bagels at the Jewish Museum's trendy Lox at Café Weissman (closed on Sat).

JULIA DE BURGOS LATINO CULTURAL CENTER
Spanish Harlem
- ✉ 1680 Lexington Avenue between 105th and 106th Street
- ☎ 212-831 4333
- 🚇 Subway 6 to 110th Street
- ⏱ Tues–Sat noon–6pm, Thurs 1–7pm
- $ Free

Another excellent location to see works by Latino artists, named in honour of the woman considered to have been the greatest poet in Puerto Rico. Around the museum, look out for pavement artwork by James de la Vega, a young local artist and visit the excellent workshop Taller Boricua.

LOWER EAST SIDE TENEMENT MUSEUM
Lower East Side
- ✉ 103 Orchard Street between Broome and Delancey Streets
- ☎ 212-982 8420
- ⌂ www.tenement.org
- 🚇 Subway F to Delancey Street; B, D to Grand Street; J, M, Z to Essex Street
- ⏱ Visitor Center open Mon–Sun 10am–6pm; the museum can only be visited via a tour, first tour 10.30am, last tour 5pm 7 days a week – best to book in advance
- $ $22 adults, $17 students and seniors for 1-hour tour. Under 5s free

After they had gone through Ellis Island, millions of immigrants ended up in tenements on the Lower East Side, and this museum tells their poignant stories. Tour the building and visit 4 re-created apartments in a typical, 5-storey tenement in different time periods, giving a good insight into the living conditions of the seekers of the American Dream. Meet the residents (played by actors dressed in costume) or if you have time, the Lower East Side Stories walking tour operated by the museum is an eye-opening look at how immigrants shaped this fascinating neighbourhood.

The museum consists of several tenement houses – essentially America's first public housing – predating almost every housing law in the US – accessible only via the tours. Faithfully restored and complete with furniture and clothes, it's a must-see in order to understand not only this neighbourhood,

Lower East Side Tenement Museum

which continues to function as a launching pad for fresh generations of artists and retailers, but also the American success story.

BRITTIP

Before you take one of the walking tours at the Lower East Side Tenement Museum, it is worth watching the slide show and film.

The tour **Sweatshop Workers** examines the life of the Polish Levine family, who ran a garment shop in their apartment in the early 1900s, plus the stories of other immigrants involved in the garment industry from the 1930s to the present day. The tour Hard Times focuses on 2 stories of 2 immigrant families from Germany and Sicily and how they forged new lives for themselves in America.

BRITTIP

Holiday-time tours at the Lower East Side Tenement Museum sell out quickly, so book as far in advance as possible on the internet.

The best tour for children is the 60-minute **Confino Family Tour,** which aims to bring history to life. The apartment re-creates the life of the Sephardic-Jewish Confino family from Kastoria in Greece in 1916. Teenager Victoria Confino welcomes visitors as if they were newly arrived immigrants and she were teaching them how to adapt to life in America. You can touch any items in the apartment, try on period clothing and foxtrot to music played on an authentic wind-up Victrola.

Kitchen conversations after selected tours are where participants get a chance to share thoughts and explore thoughts arising from the tours over a drink and a snack.

A new tour has been added, **Shop Life**, where visitors get to explore the immigrant businesses that were once located at 97 Orchard Street. It includes an 1870s German beer saloon, the Levine family's garment workshop and an interactive sales counter where visitors can select audio and visual media clips (tickets are slightly more, adults $25, students and seniors $20).

MERCHANT'S HOUSE MUSEUM
NoHo
- ✉ 29 East 4th Street between Lafayette and Bowery Streets
- ☎ 212-777 1089
- 🖱 www.merchantshouse.com
- 🚇 Subway 6 to Astor Place
- 🕐 Thurs–Mon 12pm–5pm, closed Tues and Wed; guided tour 2pm
- $ $10 adults, $5 students and seniors, children under 12 free

Built in 1832, this was home to prosperous merchant Seabury Tredwell and his family for over 100 years and is the city's only preserved 19th-century home, complete with original furnishings and decor, and a resident ghost! The house remains open during a structural restoration.

THE MET FOR FAMILIES

This magnificent museum uses various means to make its resources as accessible to children as possible – for free – and provides printed museum guides and hunts and a Family Map, audio guides at the Information Desk on the ground floor near the 81st Street entrance. A whole series of workshops and programmes is available for children of all ages both through the week and at weekends. For exact times and dates, check out the calendar section of the website or call 212-650 2217. Programmes include:

Drop in drawing: Children of all ages and their families are given a stimulating introduction to the Met's encyclopaedic collection through sketching its masterpieces.

Festivals: All ages can celebrate art and culture through performance, art making, storytelling and more.

Start With Art at the Met: Children 3-7 (plus an adult). Allows children to explore art at the Met through storytelling, sketching and games.

Art Workshops: Teens (11-18) can get inspired by the Met's masterpieces as they create their own.

METROPOLITAN MUSEUM OF ART
Upper East Side

- ✉ 1000 5th Avenue at 82nd Street
- ☎ 212-535 7710
- 🖱 www.metmuseum.org
- 🚇 Subway 1, 6 to 86th Street
- 🕐 Tues–Thurs, Sun 9.30am–5.30pm, Fri and Sat 9.30am–9pm, closed Mon
- $ $25 adults, $12 students and $17 seniors, under 12s free with an adult, same-day entrance to The Cloisters (p107) is included in the price

BRITTIP
Don't miss the Metropolitan's fabulous *Zagat*-rated Roof Garden Café & Martini Bar filled with sculptures on the 5th floor for stunning views of Central Park, open May–Sept or take some air in the Ming-style meditative Chinese garden in Astor Court, built with handmade tools by Chinese craftspeople.

New York is filled with fine museums, yet this really is the mother of them all and you could easily spend a day here. But with 5,000

years of art – around 2 million pieces – from all continents spread over a vast area, it's best to admit that you won't be able to see it all in one visit! If you're heading to the museum along 5th Avenue, don't be surprised to see screens, diggers and workmen – it's currently undergoing a complete reconstruction of its 4-block long plaza (one of New York's most iconic outdoor spaces) and all the entrances are open. The new gateway (which is due to be unveiled in autumn 2014) will have fountains, trees, hedges, new paving and seating and state-of-the-art lighting to illuminate the fancy façade at night.

If you can, visit the website in advance to get a good feel for the museum's layout. Think about what you really want to see and write out a list of priorities, allowing a time to absorb what each gallery has to offer. Make sure you visit the **Greek** and **Roman** Galleries, with 5,400 objects taking up an entire wing, the talk of the town.

A good place to start is with an aspect of American culture, which you will find in the **American Wing**, where there is a wonderful collection of Tiffany's along with US arts and crafts and glorious Neo-Classical sculptures in the garden court. It's one of the Met's most popular areas, with 3 floors and 25 rooms filled with more than 1,000 paintings by American artists, 600 sculptures and 2,500 drawings. The 2 real musts are the **Egyptian Art** exhibits and the **Temple of Dendur**, which was built by Egypt to thank the American people after the US helped rescue monuments threatened by the Aswan Dam. Other greats include the **Greek** and **Roman** displays, the **Japanese** and **Chinese** exhibits and the medieval art.

BRITTIP
If visiting the Met on Fri or Sat, you can chill out over cocktails to free live classical music in the Balcony Bar in the afternoon.

New galleries now house 1,000 works from the museum's department of **Islamic Art**, one of the most comprehensive collections in the world. Exhibitions here change constantly, so check the website for details.

The wonderful thing about this museum is that you can wander around by yourself, hire an audio guide for the day ($7 adults, $5 under 12s), which you can use in any order, or bag a free podcast, and take advantage of a plethora of free tours, talks and films.

The hour-long **Museum Highlights** tour leaves from the Great Hall at 2.30pm. Check the calendar on the website in advance for information on the 1-hour gallery talks or lectures, which focus on either a special exhibition or 1 of the permanent collections and films. You do not need to make reservations except for the Sat afternoon film. The highlight of the programme is **Sunday at the Met** at 3pm, a combination of lectures, film, performances and discussion.

BRITTIP

You can't take luggage, including carry-on bags and big backpacks, into the Met and they can't be checked into the museum's cloakroom either, so if necessary you'll need to leave these in the hotel or in a security locker Downtown (p63).

MORGAN LIBRARY & MUSEUM
Midtown East
- ✉ 225 Madison Avenue at 36th Street
- ☎ 212-685-0008
- ⌖ www.themorgan.org
- 🚇 Subway 6 to 33rd Street, 4, 5, 6, 7 to Grand Central
- ⊙ Tues–Thurs 10.30am–5pm, Fri 10.30am–9pm, Sat 10am–6pm, Sun 11am–6pm
- $ $18 adults, $12 students, seniors and children under 16, under 12s free. Free on Fri 7–9pm

The Morgan is based in a fabulous, renovated palazzo-style 1902 building. The glass and steel pavilions designed by Renzo Piano doubled the exhibition space for the collection which, having started as the private collection of banker Pierpont Morgan, now includes medieval and Renaissance manuscripts; drawings and prints from the 14th century including works by Rubens, Degas, Blake and Pollock; ancient Middle Eastern seals and tablets; and original handwritten music manuscripts by Bach, Beethoven, Brahms and Schubert. It also has a reading room and a central court in the style of an Italian Piazza and offers daily tours, concerts, lectures and films.

MOUNT VERNON HOTEL MUSEUM AND GARDEN
Upper East Side
- ✉ 421 East 61st Street between 1st and York Avenues
- ☎ 212-838 6878
- ⌖ www.mvhm.org
- 🚇 Subway 4, 5, 6, N, R to 59th Street/ Lexington Avenue
- ⊙ Tues–Sun 11am–4pm, arrive 3.30pm for the last tour
- $ $8 adults, $7 students and seniors, under 12s free

A must-see mansion that dates back to the colonial era, this was once the coach house of the daughter of America's second president, John Adams. Dating back to the early 18th century, it is one of the seven oldest buildings in Manhattan and has been lovingly restored by the Colonial Dames of America who will sometimes be on hand to talk about the furnishings in the house and the park.

MUSEUM OF AMERICAN FINANCE
Lower Manhattan
- ✉ 48 Wall Street, corner of William Street
- ☎ 212-908 4110
- ⌖ www.moaf.org
- 🚇 Subway 2, 3, 4, 5 to Wall Street; J to Broad Street, 1, R, W to Rector Street
- ⊙ Tues–Sat 10am–4pm
- $ $8 adults, $5 students and seniors

Founded in 1998, this museum moved into the former headquarters of the Bank of New York on Wall Street in Jan 2008, with the banking hall as its new exhibition space, and traces the growth of the world's largest financial superpower. It has the largest public museum archive of financial documents in the world and the exhibits include rare $100,000 bills.

BRITTIP

The Museum of American Finance offers some great 90-minute walking tours for $15 per person including Financial Architecture, focusing on Wall Street and the Financial District. Check www.moaf.org for list of tours and details.

MUSEUM OF ART AND DESIGN
Midtown
- ✉ 2 Columbus Circle
- ☎ 212-299 7777
- 🖰 www.madmuseum.org
- 🚇 Subway A, C, D Columbus Circle/59th Street
- ⏰ Tues, Weds, Sat, Sun 11am–6pm, Thurs-Fri 11am–9pm, closed Mon
- $ $16 adults, $12 students, $14 seniors, under 12s free; pay what you wish Thurs 6–9pm

Along with the American Folk Art Museum, this museum, formerly known as the American Craft Museum, gives an insight into American arts and crafts. It has everything from wood and metal to clay, glass and fibre. It was previously at 40 West 53rd Street but moved here after a $60m renovation of the building. The design comes complete with floor-to-ceiling windows on the ground floor and zigzagged windows on the upper floors. There are free (with admission) guided 45-minute gallery tours daily at 11.30am and 3pm and Thurs evenings at 6.30pm.

MUSEUM OF CHINESE IN AMERICA
Chinatown
- ✉ 215 Center Street between Howard and Grand Streets
- ☎ 212-619 4785
- 🖰 www.mocanyc.org
- 🚇 Subway N, R, Q, J, Z and 6 to Canal Street
- ⏰ Tues, Weds, Fri, Sat, Sun 11am–6pm, Thurs 11am–9pm
- $ $10 adults, $5 seniors, students and children, under 12s free.

Museum of Chinese in America

A fascinating little museum that was previously tucked away on the tiny 1st floor of the community centre in Mulberry Street. The new larger site contains photographs and personal belongings, and talks are given on the history of Chinese immigrants to both North and South America. Free Gallery Highlights Tour (with admission) on Sat and Sun at 2.30pm. They also run walking tours.

MUSEUM OF COMIC AND CARTOON ART
Midtown
- ✉ 594 Broadway, Suite 401
- ☎ 212-254 3511
- 🖰 www.moccany.org
- 🚇 Subway L, N, Q, R, W, 4, 5, 6 to Union Square
- ⏰ Tues–Sun noon–5pm
- $ $6 adults, under 12s free

A fun little museum that is great for kids and adult cartoon lovers alike. It represents every genre of the art, including comic books, graphic novels, cartoons, humorous illustrations, editorial doodles, caricature and computer-generated art. There are lots of events on here, so be sure to check the website to see what's on when you're in town.

MUSEUM OF JEWISH HERITAGE: A LIVING MEMORIAL TO THE HOLOCAUST
Battery Park City
- ✉ 36 Battery Place, Battery Park City
- ☎ 646-437 4202
- 🖰 www.mjhnyc.org
- 🚇 Subway 1 to South Ferry; R to Whitehall Street; 4, 5 to Bowling Green
- ⏰ Sun–Tues, Thurs 10am–5.45pm, Wed 10am–8pm, Fri 10am–5pm (Mar–Nov) 10am–3pm (Dec–mid Mar), closed Sat and Jewish holidays
- $ $12 adults, $10 seniors, $7 students, under 12s free; free for all Wed 4–8pm

◀🇬🇧▶ BRITTIP
Before entering the Museum of Jewish Heritage, take a look at the 6-sided shape of the tiered roof, a symbolic reminder of the 6 million who died in the Holocaust and of the Star of David.

Joy, tradition, tragedy and unspeakable horror are the powerful themes of this museum, which tells the moving story of 20th-century Jewish life from the perspective of those who lived it. Created as a living memorial to the Holocaust, it puts the tragedy into the larger context of modern Jewish history and includes 24 original films that feature

testimonies from Steven Spielberg's Survivors of the Shoah Visual History Foundation, as well as the museum's own video archive.

BRITTIP

It's worth renting an audio guide at the Museum of Jewish heritage, narrated by Meryl Streep and Itzhak Perlman, cost $5.

Nature sculptor Andy Goldsworthy's living memorial garden, Garden of Stones, is worth a look, too, with beautiful views of the river, and the trees, which sprout from stones. The garden was planted by Holocaust survivors and their families as well as the artist. A family guide to the museum is available, a programme of family events, concerts, lectures and performances is on offer, and there is kosher food at the Heritage Café.

MUSEUM OF MODERN ART (MoMA)
Midtown

✉ 11 West 53rd Street between 5th and 6th Avenues

☎ 212-708 9400

🖱 www.moma.org

🚇 Subway E, M to 5th Avenue/53rd Street

🕐 Sat, Sun, Mon, Wed, Thurs 10.30am–5.30pm (open until 8.30pm first Thurs of the month), Fri 10.30am–8pm, closed Tues

$ $25 adults, $18 seniors, $14 students, under 16s free with an adult; free Fri 4pm–8pm

Founded in 1929 by 3 private citizens including Abby Rockefeller, this was the first museum to devote its entire collection to the modern movement. Since then it has retained its pioneering sense of the new, and was the first museum to see architecture, design, photography and film as art forms. The museum's collection started with a gift of 8 prints and 1 drawing, and dates from the 1880s to the present day and now encompasses more than 150,000 works.

MoMA reopened in November 2004 after a much-praised redesign by Yoshio Taniguchi in time to celebrate its 75th anniversary. The new building, with a stunning atrium and high-ceilinged galleries, is a work of art itself and occupies over 58,000m²/630,000ft².

BRITTIP

For a treat, dine in The Modern, a gorgeous restaurant serving French-American cuisine, which has in the past been awarded 3 stars by The New York Times.

If you only have a day, head off with your free audio guide to the two fabulous floors of Paintings and Sculpture galleries. Many of the icons of modern art are housed here, including Van Gogh's 'The Starry Night', Monet's 'Water Lilies', Picasso's 'Les Demoiselles' and Andy Warhol's 'Gold Marilyn Monroe'. The photographic galleries are also popular, with exhibits from famous names such as Henri Cartier-Bresson and Man Ray.

Films are screened every evening in the two cinemas (cost included in the entrance fee, but you need to get a ticket to reserve your place) and afternoons and evenings at weekends. There's an annual New Directors/ New Films festival each year in March/April, that has been running for over 40 years and showcases emerging filmmakers from around the world: check the MoMa website for details. Free gallery talks Wed–Mon 11.30am and 1.30pm, plus 6.30pm Fri. If you need a breath of fresh air during your MoMA day, nip down to the Abby Aldrich Rockefeller Sculpture Garden.

⊞ BRITTIP

Pick up a copy of glossy book *MoMA Highlights*, $19.95, when you buy an admission ticket, which is not only a great guide, but also a lovely memento.

The free Family Programs introduce children 4–14 and their parents to the world of modern art through guided walks, workshops, artist talks and film screenings. Grab a free Family Activity Guide at the entrance and call 212-708 9805 or email familyprograms@moma.org for a list of activities. MoMA has dedicated websites for children to familiarise themselves with the art before coming: 5–8-year-olds can click on www.moma.org/interactives/destination and older children can visit http://redstudio.moma.org.

MUSEUM OF THE CITY OF NEW YORK
Spanish Harlem
- ✉ 1220 5th Avenue at 103rd Street
- ☎ 212-534 1672
- ⌖ www.mcny.org
- 🚇 Subway 6 to 103rd Street
- ◷ Daily 10am–6pm
- $ Suggested donation $20 families, $10 adults, $6 seniors, students and children; under 12s free

⊞ BRITTIP

At the Museum of the City of New York, groups can buy a family ticket even if they are not related.

The breadth of New York's history and those who played parts in its development are celebrated in this fascinating museum, which received The Hundred Year Association of New York's Gold Medal Award in 1982 in recognition of its outstanding contribution to the city. Prints, photographs, paintings, sculptures and even clothing and decorative household objects are used to tell the story of New York City. Particularly noted for its Broadway memorabilia, it has period rooms from famous homes such as the bedroom of philanthropist John D. Rockefeller, as well as gritty photographs showing the harsh realities of the Depression. The multimedia presentation that opened in its major renovation and extension in 2006, making the span of history accessible, is a good place to start.

MUSEUM OF SEX
Madison Square Park
- ✉ 233 5th Avenue at 27th Street
- ☎ 212-689 6337
- ⌖ www.museumofsex.com
- 🚇 Subway 1, 6, R to 28th Street
- ◷ Sun–Thurs 10am–8pm, Fri–Sat 10am–9pm
- $ $17.50 adults, $15.25 students and seniors. Minimum age 18 and ID will be checked

Times Square may have been cleaned up, but the prostitutes are back in Manhattan in force at New York's most audacious museum. Not for the fainthearted, the inaugural exhibition examined how New York City transformed sex in America by exploring the histories of prostitution, burlesque, birth control, obscenity and fetish. Exhibitions use selections such as blow-up dolls and bawdy house coins from private and public collections never shown before and if you're in doubt as to whether this is the museum for you, bear in mind that some of the material was once confiscated as obscene.

The main collections include serious works of art by contemporary artists and a massive collection of films, videos, magazines, books and artefacts acquired over 20 years by Ralph Whittington, the former curator of the Library of Congress. Clearly the entrance fee is designed to put off casual thrill-seekers and the museum strictly enforces the minimum age requirement. Despite the subject matter, it is a serious institution with an important message about past and present sexual subcultures and our modern attitudes.

BRITTIP

At the beginning of June, don't miss the wonderful Museum Mile Festival (212-606 2296, www. museummilefestival.org). For one evening (11th June in 2013) all 10 museums along 5th Avenue are free. The road is closed and the traffic is replaced by live bands, street entertainers and outdoor art activities for children.

NATIONAL ACADEMY OF DESIGN
Midtown

- ✉ 1083 5th Avenue at 89th Street
- ☎ 212-369 4880
- 🖱 www.nationalacademy.org
- 🚇 Subway 4, 5, 6 to 86th Street
- 🕐 Wed–Sun 11am–6pm, Mon–Tues closed
- $ $15 adults, $10 students and seniors, children under 12 free

The museum reopened after extensive renovations in Sept 2011. The aim was to modernise the existing galleries, which boast one of the largest collections of 19th and 20th-century American art in the country. For the first time in more than 100 years, the renovated galleries provide enough space to show the academy's collection of more than 7,000 paintings, drawings, prints and sculptures by American artists and architects. An art school studio gallery has also been added, where you can view and potentially buy (if you have a spare few thousand in your pocket!) students' work. Additional galleries present rotating thematic and single artist exhibitions of works from the 19th and 21st centuries.

BRITTIP

While you're on the Museum Mile, take a pit stop at the fabulous Café Sabarsky in the Neue Galerie, which is open every day except Tues. Catch a classical music performance (there's a grand piano in 1 corner) with Cabaret at Café Sabarsky with dinner for $110.

NATIONAL MUSEUM OF THE AMERICAN INDIAN
Bowling Green/Financial District

- ✉ The George Gustav Heye Center, Alexander Hamilton US Custom House, 1 Bowling Green between State and Whitehall Streets
- ☎ 212-514 3700
- 🖱 www.americanindian.si.edu
- 🚇 Subway 4, 5 to Bowling Green; 1 to South Ferry
- 🕐 Daily 10am–5pm, Thurs 10am–8pm
- $ Free

The first museum dedicated entirely to Native American history, art, performing art and culture housed in the US Custom House, one of America's finest Beaux Arts buildings, designed by Cass Gilbert. The collection includes fabulous leather clothing, intricately beaded headdresses, sashes, hats and shoes, explaining the white man's influence on Indian culture, as well as their own centuries-old traditions. Despite the size and grandness of the beautiful building, it has only 500 pieces on display and thus seems quite small. However, it is very well laid out and the explanations of each piece have usually been given by Native Americans. It also has a lively programme of events such as plays, music and dance performances, lectures and crafts workshops and daily film screenings on contemporary Native American life, one especially designed for families. A family guide can be downloaded from its website to help plan a visit or there are daily public tours for families and adult groups Mon–Fri at 1pm and 3pm.

BRITTIP

Small lockers are provided free of charge on the 2nd floor of the National Museum of the America Indian, so you can travel light around the various floors.

NEUE GALERIE MUSEUM FOR GERMAN AND AUSTRIAN ART
Upper East Side

- ✉ 1048 5th Avenue at 86th Street
- ☎ 212-628 6200
- 🖱 www.neuegaleric.org
- 🚇 Subway 4, 5, 6 to 86th Street at Lexington Avenue; B, C to 86th Street at Central Park West
- 🕐 Sat, Sun, Mon, Thurs, Fri 11am–6pm, closed Tues and Wed
- $ $20 adults, $10 students and seniors. Under 12s not permitted, under 16s only with an adult, free Fri 6–8pm

Founded by the late German Expressionist art dealer Serge Sabarsky and chairman of the MoMA board Ronald S Lauder, the 'New Gallery' exhibits fine and decorative arts of Germany and Austria from the first half of the 20th century, on two floors. Think Klimt, Klee and Kandinsky. A real bonus is the building itself – a Louis XIII-style Beaux Art landmark once the home of Mrs Grace Vanderbilt. Check out the Klimt painting that, when purchased in 2006 for $135m, was the most expensive painting ever sold.

National Museum of the American Indian

NEW MUSEUM OF CONTEMPORARY ART
Chelsea

- ✉ 235 The Bowery, Lower East Side
- ☎ 212-219 1222
- 🖰 www.newmuseum.org
- 🚇 Subway 6 to Spring Street, N, R to Prince Street, J, Z to Bowery
- ⏱ Thurs 11–9pm, Wed, Fri, Sat, Sun 11–6pm, Mon–Tues closed
- $ $14 adults, $12 seniors, $10 students, 18 and under free, free Thurs 7–9pm

When they say 'contemporary', they really mean it. All the works exhibited are by living artists, often looking at social issues through modern media and machinery. Designed by cutting-edge Japanese architects, SANAA, its stunning 7-storey white tower – a stack of rectangular boxes shifted off axis in different directions dressed in silvery metal and

punctuated by skylights – was named one of the top architectural projects of the year in 2003 and is the first museum constructed in Downtown Manhattan in over a century. It houses a theatre, library, learning centre and café, as well as rooftop terraces. You can download free audio guides of current exhibitions from the website.

NEW YORK CITY FIRE MUSEUM
West SoHo

- ✉ 278 Spring Street between Varick and Hudson Streets
- ☎ 212-691 1303
- 🖰 www.nycfiremuseum.org
- 🚇 Subway 1, 9 to Houston Street; C, E to Spring Street
- ⏱ Daily 10am–5pm
- $ $8 adults, $5 students, children and seniors, children under 2 free

Technically not a children's museum, though the bright shiny engines are an undoubted hit with youngsters and the young at heart. Housed in the old quarters of Engine 30, here you will find artefacts and fire engines depicting 200 years of city fire-fighting.

NEW YORK CITY POLICE MUSEUM
Bowling Green/Financial District

- ✉ 100 Old Slip between South and Water Streets
- ☎ 212-480 3100
- 🖰 www.nycpolicemuseum.org
- 🚇 Subway 4, 5 to Bowling Green; 2, 3 to Wall Street; 1 to South Ferry, R, W to Whitehall Street
- ⏱ Mon–Sat 10am–5pm, Sun noon–5pm
- $ Suggested donation $8 adults, $5 seniors and children, under 2s free

Currently closed due to damage by Hurricane Sandy, check the website for updates and information about when it will reopen. When it's accepting visitors again, you'll find this is a fascinating museum portraying the 160-year history of the NYPD in the

New York Historical Society

Downtown area is a little corker. It is now permanently housed in the former 1st Precinct building, the oldest cop shop in New York. Highlights include the Mounted Unit – one of the oldest and most prestigious within the NYPD – and the K-9 dog unit. In addition to over 10,000 items of police memorabilia – a line-up of guns, uniforms and badges – there's even the Tommy gun with its original violin case that was used to kill mobster Frankie Yale. Plus, you can have a go at playing detective yourself in the interactive crime scene area.

View the NYPD Hall of Heroes, which has a memorial to the 23 policemen and women who lost their lives in the attack on the World Trade Center in 2001 and ongoing exhibition 9/11 Remembered. There are all kinds of exhibitions, such as The Junior Officers Discover Zone, where children aged 3–10 get to learn all about the police, like a fingerprint station, detective games and finding out about sounds of the NYPD, such as police whistles and sirens.

NEW YORK HALL OF SCIENCE
Queens
A great science museum with demonstrations (p279).

NEW YORK HISTORICAL SOCIETY
Upper West Side
- ✉ 170 Central Park West at 77th Street
- ☎ 212-873 3400
- 🖰 www.nyhistory.org
- 🚇 Subway B, C to 81st Street; 1 to 79th Street
- ⏱ Tues–Thurs, Sat 10am–6pm, Fri 10am–8pm, Sun 11am–5pm, closed Mon
- $ $15 adults, $12 seniors $10 students and $5 children, under 7s free, pay as you wish Fri 6-8pm

When this jewel was formed in 1804 it was the only art museum in the city until the opening of the Metropolitan Museum of Art

in 1872. The Historical Society was founded to chronicle New York's history and is home to the world's largest collection of Tiffany stained-glass shades and lamps, 2 million manuscripts, including letters sent by George Washington during the War of Independence, a lock of his hair and his camp bed.

This museum reopened in 2011 after a 3-year restoration of its landmark building. New experiences include New York Story by Donna Lawrence, an 18-minute theatrical film about New York's rise from an outpost to a world-leading city. The DiMenna Children's History Museum is the first to bring American history to life for kids and its new restaurant, Café Storico, headed by Stephen Starr of Buddakan and Morimoto, has certainly been worth the wait.

Beautiful polished wooden floors with natural light streaming in make visiting the newly designed Robert H. and Clarice Smith New York Gallery of American History a joy. New York Rising focuses on New York's role in the founding of the US and you'll be transfixed by Here is New York, a rotating selection 6,200 photographs taken on 11 September 2001.

NEW YORK TRANSIT MUSEUM
Brooklyn Heights
A great little museum that is particularly popular with children (p274).

9/11 MEMORIAL MUSEUM
Downtown
- ✉ 20th Floor, One Liberty Plaza
- ☎ 212-226 5211
- 🖰 www.911memorial.org/museum
- 🚇 Subway A, C, J, Z, 2, 3, 4, 5 to Fulton Street; 2, 3 to Park Place, E to World Trade Center
- ⏱ Daily 10am–8pm, last entry 7pm
- $ 9/11 memorial free, but visitor time passes must be reserved

This brand-new museum is beneath the

New York Transit Museum

9/11 memorial honouring the memory of those who were killed in the attacks at the World Trade Center. While most museums house artefacts, this museum is housed in an artefact, 7 storeys underground where visitors can see the archaeological remains. It has a permanent collection of tear-jerking artefacts, stories, photos and video, personal effects, memorabilia and tributes related to that fateful day. It was scheduled to open in September 2012, a year after the memorial, but has been delayed, so check the website before visiting and to book your timed slot.

Exhibits range from the huge steel tridents or columns once part of the World Trade Center, fire trucks, steel from the point of impact of Flight 11 and the 36ft Last Column to be recovered, covered with mementos, missing posters and memorial inscriptions. The museum also has moving personal recorded stories to listen to and an interactive timeline uses images, audio and video to show what happened. Take your tissues!

THE NOGUCHI MUSEUM

The Japanese sculptor's art can be seen at this museum in Queens (p279).

P.S. 1 CONTEMPORARY ART CENTER

Long Island City, Queens
A ground-breaking modern art museum (p279).

THE PALEY CENTER FOR MEDIA

Midtown
- ✉ 25 West 52nd Street between 5th and 6th Avenues
- ☎ 212-621 6600
- ⌂ www.paleycenter.org
- 🚇 Subway E, M to 5th Avenue/53rd Street; B, D, F, M to 47th–50th Streets/ Rockefeller Center
- ⏱ Wed–Sun noon–6pm, Thurs noon–8pm, closed Mon–Tues
- $ $10 adults, $8 students and seniors, $5 under 14s

In addition to the exhibits, the museum also has a daily programme of screenings in 2 cinemas and 2 presentation rooms, as well as guided tours. Pick up a copy of the schedules in the lobby on your way in. You can also make an appointment with the library to check out the museum's collection of over 120,000 radio and TV programmes covering more than 85 years before accessing them on the custom-designed database. You won't miss the building – it looks like a giant antique radio set!

QUEENS COUNTY FARM MUSEUM

Floral Park, Queens
A fun, working historical farm with hayrides (p280).

SCHOMBURG CENTER FOR RESEARCH IN BLACK CULTURE

Harlem
- ✉ 515 Malcolm X Boulevard at 135th Street
- ☎ 212-491 2200
- ⌂ www.nypl.org/research/sc/sc.html
- 🚇 Subway 2, 3 to 135th Street
- ⏱ Tues–Thurs noon–8pm, Thurs–Fri 10am–6pm, Sat 10am–6pm, closed Mon, Sun, tours by appointment
- $ Free

Established in 1926 by Arthur Schomburg, this museum under the umbrella of the New York Public Library has more than 5 million items, including books, photographs, manuscripts, art works, films, videos and sound recordings that document the historical and cultural development of black people in the US, the Caribbean, the Americas, Africa, Europe and Asia over 400 years of migration.

BRITTIP

To see the Schomburg Center at its best, phone or check the website in advance to find information about film screenings and jazz concerts.

The research unit is open to anyone, while there are exhibitions on art dating back to the 17th century that include masks, paintings and sculptures. Incidentally, the corner of Malcolm X Boulevard, where the Schomburg sits, was once home to Harlem's Speaker's Corner where people used to come and talk about their political beliefs and organisations.

SKYSCRAPER MUSEUM

Battery Park
- ✉ 39 Battery Place
- ☎ 212-968 1961
- ⌂ www.skyscraper.org
- 🚇 Subway 4, 5 to Bowling Green; 1, R, W to South Ferry/Whitehall Street
- ⏱ Wed–Sun 12–6pm
- $ $5 adults, $2.50 seniors and students

One of New York's most apt museums, celebrating as it does the city's rich architectural heritage and examining what historic forces and which individuals shaped the different skylines of its past. Through exhibitions, programmes, publications and walking tours, the museum offers a fascinating insight into how individual buildings were created, complete with detailed information about how the contractors bid for the work, what was involved and how the building work was executed, all with comprehensive photographic illustrations. Check out the Manhattan Mini Models permanent exhibition, where you can gaze at an intricate Big Apple, and the Maps and Photographs of Lower Manhattan, to get a perspective of how the city has changed since the 60s, plus find out about the world's tallest building.

SOLOMON R GUGGENHEIM MUSEUM
Upper East Side
- ⊠ 1071 5th Avenue at 89th Street
- ☎ 212-423 3500
- ◠ www.guggenheim.org
- 🚗 Subway 4, 5, 6 to 86th Street
- ⌚ Sun–Wed, Fri 10am–5.45pm, Sat 10–7.45pm, closed Thurs
- $ $22 adults, $18 students and seniors, under 12s free, Sat 5.45pm–7.45pm by donation

The Guggenheim Museum in New York is probably best known for its beautiful spiral-shaped, space age building, designed by 'organic' architect Frank Lloyd Wright. Considered one of the greatest architectural achievements of the 20th century, it is one of the youngest buildings in the city to be designated a New York City landmark. Walk by it at night if you get the chance, to see the glass layers in its shell-like façade lit up like a rainbow. The exterior and infrastructure was under $29m restoration since 2005, but the scaffolding finally came down in spring 2009, in time for its 50th Anniversary in 2009.

🇬🇧 BRITTIP
It's best to take the elevator to the skylight at the top of The Guggenhcim and wind down the central spiral ramp that passes works by major artists from the mid-19th to the 21st century.

It houses one of the world's largest collections of Kandinsky, as well as works by Chagall, Klee, Picasso, Cézanne, Degas, Gauguin and Manet. It also has Peggy Guggenheim's entire collection of cubist, surrealist and abstract expressionist art and impressive temporary exhibitions.

Audio tours, podcasts and a Guggenheim app, which you can download on iTunes, are available, or there are free tours by the museum staff, gallery talks and screenings are included in the price of admission. Educator's Eye tours with trained staff who show you

around current exhibitions take place daily at 11am and 1pm and are free.

🇬🇧 BRITTIP
Check out the Guggenheim's sculpture gallery for some of the best views of Central Park.

SONY WONDER TECHNOLOGY LAB
- ⊠ Sony Plaza, 550 Madison Avenue at 56th Street
- ☎ 212-833 8100
- ◠ www.sonywondertechlab.com
- 🚗 Subway E, M to 5th Avenue, F to 57th Street, 4, 5, 6, N, R to 59th Street
- ⌚ Tues–Sat 9.30am–5.30pm, closed Sun and Mon
- $ Free, but book in advance as there are only a certain number of tickets allocated for walk-in visitors

A technology museum with 4 floors of interactive exhibits with robots and lots of hi-tech entertainment, adults will love playing here as much as kids. Reservations only though, so book well in advance. The 3rd and 4th floors were closed for extensive transformation in 2008, so even if you've been before it's worth popping in again to see what new technological wonders have been installed.

SOUTH STREET SEAPORT MUSEUM
Financial District
- ⊠ 12 Fulton Street between Water Street and South Street
- ☎ 212-748 8600
- ◠ www.seany.org
- 🚗 Subway 2, 3, 4, 5, A, C, J, Z, M to Fulton Street
- ⌚ Wed–Sun 10am–6pm
- $ $10 adults, children under 9 free, includes admission to the galleries and historic vessel.

The galleries at 12 Fulton Street are currently closed due to damage from Hurricane Sandy, check the website for updates about the reopening. Since 1967, the South Street Seaport Museum along the East River has presented exhibitions telling the story of life in the olden days of New York. It reopened in January 2012 under the management of the Museum of New York, with a dazzling contemporary display that interweaves the city and sea through photography, video, historical artefacts and contemporary design in its 16 galleries. Exhibitions are all temporary, so check the site for details of these and events such as artists talks, and family programmes.

This historic area was full of sailors and their ships in the 19th century and was called the 'street of sails'. A highlight is boarding the Ambrose, included in the museum fee. Since May 2012, groups can sail on the Pioneer.

STUDIO MUSEUM IN HARLEM
Harlem
- ✉ 144 West 125th Street between 7th and Lenox Avenues
- ☎ 212-864 4500
- ⌂ www.studiomuseum.org
- 🚇 Subway A, B, C, D, 2, 3, 4, 5, 6 to 125th Street
- ☉ Thurs-Fri noon-9pm, Sat 10am-6pm, Sun noon-6pm
- $ $7 adults, $3 students and seniors, under 12s free, free Sun, sponsored by Target.

Works of art by African-American artists in a beautiful space. The photographic archive gives a fascinating glimpse into Harlem history and lectures, children's programmes and a film festival combine to fulfil the museum's mission to be the major centre for African-American art.

VAN CORTLANDT HOUSE MUSEUM
The Bronx
Fascinating former family plantation estate-turned museum (p277).

WHITNEY MUSEUM OF AMERICAN ART
Upper East Side
- ✉ 945 Madison Avenue at 75th Street
- ☎ 212-570 3600
- ⌂ www.whitney.org
- 🚇 Subway 6 to 77th Street
- ☉ Wed, Thurs 11am-6pm; Fri 1-9pm; Sat, Sun 11am-6pm, closed Mon and Tues
- $ $20 adults, $16 students aged 19-25, under 18s free; Fri 6-9pm by donation, plus musical performances

The Whitney may be housed in ghastly looking buildings – a series of grey, granite cubes designed by Marcel Breuer – but it has the world's leading collection of 20th-century American art. Yet it all came about almost by accident. Gertrude Vanderbilt Whitney offered her entire collection to the Metropolitan but was turned down, so she decided to set up her own museum. As a result, in 1931, the Whitney was founded with a core group of 700 art objects.

Subsequently, the museum's holdings have been greatly enriched by other purchases and the gifts of other major collectors. It now has a permanent collection of 15,000 works including paintings, sculptures, drawings, prints, photographs and multimedia installations and is still growing.

As well as the wide range of artists in its collection, the Whitney is known for its cutting-edge exhibitions and has huge bodies of works by artists such as Alexander Calder, Edward Hopper, Georgia O'Keefe, Gaston Lachaise and Agnes Martin. To make the most of your visit, take an audio tour or join one of the free tours by museum staff.

The Museum Store in the basement, is filled with funky and colourful gifts. There's some great stuff for kids, including soap crayons that will wash off baths and tiles, and colourful soap that can be moulded into sculptures.

NYINTHEKNOW
Not to be missed! NY fave restaurateur Danny Meyer (of Union Square fame) has opened Untitled, a new café downstairs at the Whitney Museum. The idea is a contemporary take on the classic Manhattan coffee shop, with treats whipped up by executive chef Chris Bradley, formerly of Gramercy Tavern. Expect delicious soups, pancakes, burgers and divine desserts, like blue marble ice cream, Betty Bakery cakes, plus Stumptown coffees. All day menu (open from 11am-6pm Weds and Thurs, 11am-9pm Fri, 10am-6pm Sat and Sun). Guests are served on a walk-in basis, so no need to reserve.

The Whitney has worked hard to make itself accessible to children from babies to teens. Free activity guides are provided for families to introduce children and adults to selected works of art and encourage new ways of learning about art together through interactive gallery tours and hands-on activities. People, Places and Spaces is the Whitney's family audio guide to works from the Whitney's permanent collection and is included with the admission fee.

Family Fun Art Workshops 10.30am–12.30pm on selected Sat, feature gallery tours and art projects for children aged 6–10 and their families. Registration is necessary. Whitney Wees for families with children aged 4–5 are an interactive experience of looking and sharing. 10.30–11.30am select Sat. Both workshops cost $10 per family.

CHAPTER 6

Shopping and Beauty

For many people, New York is synonymous with shopping. Yes, there are jaw-dropping buildings, amazing museums and exciting nightlife, but when it comes down to it, New York City is one of the best places in the world to indulge in a spot of retail therapy. You can get a taste of fantastic American service at the fabulous and famous department stores, and shop for unique one-offs at the quirky downtown shops and vintage emporiums. Although the city does have some real American malls, like the one at the South Street Seaport, it is better known for its many boutiques.

AREAS

The distinct atmosphere of each New York neighbourhood is reflected in the type of shopping available there. The upper section of **5th Avenue** in the Midtown area is where you will find all the best department stores and other posh shops. Even posher – exclusive, actually – is Madison Avenue, which is where the top American and European designers are based, such as Prada, Valentino and Versace.

The Villages are excellent for boutique shops that tend to open late but stay open late, too. In **Greenwich Village** you'll find jazz records, rare books and vintage clothing and the **West Village**'s tree-lined streets are full of fine and funky boutiques and popular restaurants that cater to a young, trendy crowd. On the major shopping streets of Bleecker, Broadway and 8th, you'll find everything from antiques to fashion and T-shirt emporiums. There are plenty of up-and-coming designers and second-hand shops in the **East Village**. Try 9th Street for clothes and 7th for young designers.

The **Flatiron District** around 5th Avenue from 14th to 23rd Streets is full of wonderful old buildings that are brimming with one-of-a-kind shops and designer boutiques. SoHo has lots of boutiques selling avant-garde fashion and art, plus restaurants and art galleries, all housed in handsome cast-iron 1850s buildings. West Broadway is the main drag, but other important shop-lined streets include Spring, Prince, Green, Mercer and Wooster. High-profile stores include Prada and Earl Jeans.

Bloomingdale's

In **TriBeCa** you will find trendsetting boutiques such as the fantastic Issey Miyake flagship store, art galleries and restaurants in an area that combines loft living with commercial activity.

Last but not least is the **Lower East Side** (or LES as it's nicknamed), which is to bargains what Madison Avenue is to high-class acts. Many of the boutiques offer fashion by young designers – some of whom go on to open outlets in the more upmarket areas – and famous-name gear at huge discounts. This whole area reflects the immigrant roots of New York and stands out as a bargain hunter's paradise particularly when the market is open on Sun. Orchard Street from Houston to Delancey Streets is well known for leather goods, luggage, designer clothes, belts, shoes and fabrics. Ludlow Street is famous for trendy bars, and boutiques filled with clothes by flourishing new designers.

⬛▶ BRITTIP

To find out about the latest store openings and services in the Lower East Side (and for nightlife and restaurant information in LES, too) log on to www.lowereastsideny.com. You'll find free guides to the best boutiques, a detailed map and an iPhone app to download.

DEPARTMENT STORES

The big department stores in New York City are reliable places to buy good quality, brand-named merchandise at fair prices. These stores usually sell a variety of men's, women's and children's clothing, including designer label items. You can also expect to find cosmetics, small appliances, electronics and household goods. Department stores usually hold end-of-season clearance sales with significant price reductions. Most are in the Midtown area either in or near 5th Avenue. Standard opening times are Mon–Fri 10am–8pm/9pm, Sat 10am–7pm, Sun noon–6pm.

FASHION

You can find everything in New York from top designers to up-and-coming newcomers. The main shopping areas for fashion are the Upper East Side (for upmarket), SoHo (for designer), the East Village and Lower East Side (for cheap designer). Call ahead for opening times as many shops do not open until late but do stay open in the evening.

BEAUTY STORES AND SPAS

Everyone knows New York is the place to

TOP 5 SHOPPING TIPS

If you're on a really tight schedule, call ahead and book appointments with the personal shoppers at major stores. They're very helpful and their service is absolutely free. Bargain! Call Macy's on 1-800 343 0120, Bloomingdale's on 212-705 3135 (for her) 212-705 3030 (for him) and Saks on 212-940 4650.

You have a right to a **full refund** on goods you return within 20 days with a valid receipt unless the shop has signs saying otherwise. Always check, though, especially if the item is in a sale.

Call in advance for **opening hours**. Smaller shops downtown – in SoHo, the Villages, Financial District and Lower East Side – tend not to open until noon or 1pm, but are often open as late as 8pm. Many are also closed on Mon.

You can **avoid sales tax** if you arrange to have your purchases shipped outside of New York State – a facility that is available at larger stores and those that are more tourist orientated.

Don't get lured in by **'Sale' signs** on the Midtown section of 5th Avenue in the streets 30s and 40s. Here most of the shop windows are filled with signs that say 'Great Sales!', 'Going Out Of Business!' – yet they have been around for years and are still going strong. In fact, most of what is on sale there can be bought cheaper elsewhere and with a guarantee.

find fabulous fashion bargains, but not so well known are the great beauty buys to be had. In the first instance, most make-up – particularly the gorgeous American brands such as Philosophy, Hard Candy, Benefit and Laura Mercier – is cheaper in the Big Apple. The exceptions are the 'prestige' French brands such as Décleor, Christian Dior and Chanel, which are generally cheaper in the UK (they are imported to America).

Most brands have dedicated stores in Manhattan, the majority around SoHo and its environs of NoLiTa, north SoHo and West Village.

BOOKS

Books are big business in New York and book readings are a popular form of entertainment. For a real slice of the New York lifestyle, there are a number of places that specialise in readings: **The Drawing Center** (35 Wooster Street between Grand and Broome Streets, 212-694 0910, www.drawingcenter.org) a sky-lit gallery space with a bookstore and readings

TAXES AND ALLOWANCES

US taxes: Be aware that local taxes will be added to the cost of your purchases when you pay at the till, so don't get too carried away by the often seemingly very low price tags. New York sales tax is around 4.5%, though it has now been dropped on clothes and shoes costing under $110, while New York state tax is 4%.

UK allowances: Your UK duty-free allowance for items like perfume, clothes and souvenirs is £390 (or £270 if you're arriving by private plane or boat for leisure). Given the wealth of shopping opportunities, you may exceed this, but don't be tempted to change receipts to show a lesser value, because, if you are rumbled, the goods will be confiscated and you'll face a massive fine. In any case, the prices for some goods in America are so cheap that, even once you've paid the duty and VAT on top, they will still work out cheaper than buying the same item in Britain.

Duty free: Buy your booze from US liquor stores – they're better value than the airports – and the amount allowed is now 4 litres of wine and 16 litres of beer, 1 litre for spirits and liqueurs. If you're a smoker or buying for someone who is, you're allowed 200 cigarettes, 100 cigarillos or 50 cigars, the equivalent to 250g of tobacco.

Banned goods: It's worth noting that the HMRC says counterfeit goods are illegal to bring back to the UK. So, while those six fake Gucci bags you buy from a street corner may seem like a total bargain, you may be storing up trouble when you fly back. For a full list to what you can and can't bring back, see www.hmrc.gov.uk.

---

related to the exhibitions; **The Poetry Project** at St Mark's Church (131 East 10th Street, 212-674 0910, www.poetryproject.org) has 3 evening readings a week, Mon and Wed 8pm, Fri 10pm.

The **92nd Street Y** (1395 Lexington Avenue, 212-414 5500, www.92y.org) has a great series of lectures and readings, as does **The Dia Center for the Arts** (548 West 22nd Street, 212-989 5566, www.diacenter.org). Also check out **Barnes & Noble** (p152) and **192 Books** (p129) for more.

SHOPPING TOURS

Rebecca Merritt of Shop Gotham will help you get under the city's skin with shopping trips around areas like SoHo and NoLiTa, speed shop the big department stores and get huge discounts in the Garment Center. Call 212-209 3370, www.shopgotham.com. A SoHo and NoLiTa tour costs from $38, Fri–Sat 11am, Sun at noon for 2½ hours.

BRITTIP

If you don't want to go on an organised shopping tour, create your own using the Shopping Walking Tour Map at http://gonyc.about.com/library/maps/bl_shopping.htm

5th AVENUE

DEPARTMENT STORES

Bergdorf Goodman: 754 5th Avenue at 57th Street, 212-753 7300, www.bergdorfgoodman.com. Subway N, R, W to 5th Avenue/59th Street; F to 57th Street.

An air of understated elegance pervades every department – not surprising, given that it has been around for generations. This department store is not only still going strong, but it is also positively booming and has even opened a Bergdorf Goodman Men on the opposite side of the street. Well-known for its classic, high-end, high-priced fashion, homewares and accessories, the store has recently expanded its offer to include items for a younger (although still affluent!) clientele; think Stella McCartney, Antik Batik and Peter Pilotto. There are personal shoppers available for men and women if you need a helping hand, plus a great bridal department.

BRITTIP

As a mid-shopping treat, book lunch or afternoon tea at BG Restaurant (212-872 8977), Bergdorg Goodman's beautiful 7th-floor eatery with views over Central Park, polished wood floor and pretty white and pastel blue interior.

Henri Bendel: 712 5th Avenue at 55th Street., 212-247 1100, www.henribendel.com. Subway E, V to 53rd/5th Avenue.

This small, chic department store, which was originally 3 large townhouses, opened in 1895 and is a fashionista favourite, as there are lots of very cool clothes on 4 compact, easy-to-get-around floors. Bendels, as the style set call it, has Missoni, Matthew Williamson, Michael Kors and Colette Dinigan, but also Street of Shops, which is a set of exclusive in-store boutiques for the likes of Diane Von

Saks 5th Avenue

SHOPPING AND BEAUTY

Furstenberg, and Femmegems Design-Your-Own Gemstone jewellery. There are also accessories, such as hats, hosiery, casual wear lingerie and to top it all, hot stylist Frederic Fekkai, has a salon on the 4th floor.

Lord and Taylor: 424 5th Avenue at 39th Street, 212-391 3344, www.lordandtaylor.com. Subway B, D, F, V to 42nd Street; 7 to 5th Avenue.
A New York shopping institution that started in 1826, with good service and prices far cheaper than Saks, it's great for highlighting American designers. Plus, if you can't fit all your buys into your suitcase (!), it offers free shipping on purchases over $150. If you're visiting in December check out the store's famous Christmas window displays.

Saks 5th Avenue: 611 5th Avenue at 50th Street, 212-753 4000, www.saksfifthavenue.com. Subway E, V to 5th Avenue/53rd Street.
One of the finest shopping experiences in New York, it also has fabulous views of the Rockefeller Center and is right next door to St Patrick's Cathedral. Saks is a classic and has all of the big names.

BRITTIP
Saks has so many Brit customers it has revised its shipping policy and made things a whole lot easier. Duties and tax are calculated at checkout, low international shipping rates and guaranteed landing costs (plus no extra charge for delivery). If you use code UK13 when buying goods worth more than £99 online, the shipping cost is just £9.95. Happy shopping!

There's also a fabulous beauty area on the ground floor where you can have a personal consultation and makeover and also boasts an Elizabeth Arden Red Door Salon and Spa. There are lots of extras here that make for a truly A-list shopping trip, from wardrobe consultations for men and women, a complimentary package delivery to local hotels and even a taxi and limo service, not to mention the serious fashion-lovers labels like Alexander Wang and Proenza Schouler.

BRITTIP
Go for brunch, lunch or afternoon tea at Cafe SFA at Saks for impressive views of the city while you dine. Open Mon–Sat, 11am–5pm, Sun 12–5pm.

BROOKLYN

ANTIQUES AND FLEA MARKETS
Park Slope Flea Market: At PS 321, 7th Avenue between 1st and 2nd Streets, www.parkslopefleamarket.com. Open Sat and Sun 8am–6pm.
Great little market with around 50 regular stall-holders selling an eclectic mix of goodies, from fabrics and vintage fashion to bonsai trees and second-hand furniture.

FASHION
A Cheng: 152 5th Avenue, Park Slope, Brooklyn, 718-783 2826, www.achengshop.com. Subway M, R to Union St.
A mix of smart and street styles, including outerwear, dresses, accessories and shoes from this trendy designer.

E Lingerie by Enelra: 140 5th Avenue, St John's Place, 718-399 3252. Subway M, R at Union St.

Forget Victoria's Secret, this has some of the best lingerie in town, transferred to Brooklyn from the East Village, where Madonna used to visit. Worth checking out at Halloween when the window displays feature items like full-length latex devil outfits!

VINTAGE FASHION
Guvnors: 178 5th Avenue, Brooklyn, 718-230 4887, www.guvnorsnyc.com. Subway L to 1st Avenue.
Second-hand goodies at affordable prices that you can snap up to a soundtrack of rock and roll. They'll buy as well as sell, plus there's a tailoring service.

Odd Twin: 164 5th Avenue, Brooklyn, 718-633 8946, www.oddtwin.com. Subway D, N, R to Union St.
Wide array of well-chosen, good condition vintage fashion and accessories for everyone – men, women and even children.

CHELSEA

ANTIQUES AND FLEA MARKETS
The Antiques Garage: 112 West 25th Street between 6th and 7th Avenues, 212-647 0707, www.hellskitchenfleamarket.com. Subway F, V to 23rd Street. Open Sat and Sun 9am–5pm.
The Garage is exactly that: a 2-storey parking garage that transforms into another bustling venue at the weekend. There are anything from 100 to 150 vendors selling everything from paintings and prints to vintage jewellery and furniture. Well worth a nose around, even if you're not planning on purchasing.

The Showplace: 40 West 25th Street, 212-633 6063, www.nyshowplace.com. Subway F, V to 23rd Street.
Showcases more than 200 antique galleries and vendors over 4 spacious floors. Showplace on 3 is a huge antique and design emporium on the 3rd floor with more than 80 dealers selling furniture, clothes, lighting, accessories, fine art, jewellery and other collectables from a range of eras, including Art Deco, Victorian and mid-century modern.

BRITTIP
If you forget to pack something, such as your toothbrush, shampoo, sunglasses or hairbrush, don't panic. There's a branch of Duane Reade, open 24 hours, on practically every street corner of the city. It says pharmacy on the outside, but thankfully these stores offer so much more than a normal chemist, even frozen food and snacks.

BEAUTY STORES AND SPAS
Nickel: 77 8th Avenue at 14th Street, 212-242 3203, www.nickelspanyc.com. Subway A, C, E, 9 to 19th Street.
One of the only men-only spas in the city – in a chic, 2-storey haven - offering a wide range of treatments from massages (from $100) to facials and waxing. Book at least 4 weeks in advance.

Sam-C Spa and Margolin Wellness Center: 2nd Floor, 166 5th Avenue at 21st Street, 212-675 9355.
A doctor-meets-spa centre in Chelsea, owned and run by chiropractor Dr Margolin and celebrated masseur Sam-C. Famous treatments include the hydrotherapy tub in which you are immersed in a large, very hot tub of pulsating water while a therapist massages your head and applies cold compresses, and the Sam-C Massage, a unique, intensive body massage. Other treatments include chiropractic, reflexology, acupuncture, body scrubs and steam shower.

BOOKS
192 Books: 192 10th Avenue between 21st and 22nd Streets, 212 255 4022, www.192books.com. Subway C, E to 23rd Street.
A good range of art and literature titles as well as a large children's section. The atmosphere in this bright, airy shop is very comfortable, with reading tables and comfy chairs to help you relax. There are weekly readings here.

DISCOUNT STORES
Loehmann's: 101 7th Avenue between 16th and 17th Streets, 212-352 0856, www.loehmanns.com. Subway 1, 9 to 18th Street.
A 5-storey building filled with bargains – typically 30–65% off – for men and women. Go to the top floor for designer labels such as Donna Karan, Calvin Klein and Versace; other floors feature accessories, bags, clothing and shoes all at great prices.

BRITTIP
Don't be fooled by the bottles of wine you may see in food shops in New York. They are either non-alcoholic or low alcohol as it is illegal for food stores to sell wine. However, this doesn't apply to beer.

ELECTRONICS
Adorama: 42 West 18th Street near 6th Avenue, 212-741 0052, www.adorama.com. Subway 1, 9 to 18th Street.
Six floors that cover all your photographic

BEST FOR BRIDES

If you're a bride-to-be on the look-out for your dream dress, New York is a fantastic place to pick up a great gown (and is often better value for money, depending on the exchange rate), so make a beeline for **Kleinfeld** (110 West 20th Street, 646-633 4300, www.kleinfeldbridal.com). This venerable institution features the world's largest selection of wedding dresses from American and European designers, call first to make an appointment. There's also **Kleinfeld Bridesmaids Loft** (270 West 38th Street, 212-398 5255) to check out if you're travelling with friends. You'll find almost 400 samples in every style, size and fabric imaginable.

If you've got money to burn then you'll also want to make a trip to the Upper East side to visit the **Vera Wang Bridal Salon** (991 Madison Avenue, 212-628 3400, www. verawang.com). The queen of wedding gowns is world renowned for her amazing creations and boasts customers such as Sharon Stone. **Saks 5th Avenue** (p128) has an exclusive bridal salon while you'll find less pricey gowns at **RK Bridal** (318 West 39th Street between 8th and 9th Avenues, www.rkbridal.com).

needs, from disposable cameras through to $10,000 professional snappers. In addition, it offers a range of other services including creating digital prints for less than a dollar.

⚡ BRITTIP

National electronics chain Best Buy (888-237 8289, www. bestbuy.com) sells a wide variety of gadgets and gizmos from speakers to stereos plus games and computers at really competitive prices. They can be found at locations throughout the city including 60 23rd Street in Chelsea (212-366 2373) and 2 Union Square East at Union Square (212-254 0498), which is also a mobile speciality store.

FASHION

Balenciaga: 542 West 22nd Street at 11th Avenue, 212-206 0872, www.balenciaga.com. Subway C, E to 23rd Street.
The New York flagship store of this popular womenswear label often spotted on the backs of supermodels such as Kate Moss.

Barney's Co-op Store: 236 West 18th Street between 7th and 8th Avenues, 212-593

7800, www.barneys.com. Subway 1, 2 to 18th Street.
With its abundance of edgy, funky styles and accessories for men, women and kids, plus a great cosmetics area, too, this is one of the best stores in New York.

Camouflage: 139–141 8th Avenue at 17th Street, 212-691 1750. Subway A, C, E to 14th Street.
Designer menswear store that offers the highlights of the season from labels such as Michael Kors, Etro and Marc Jacobs.

Comme des Garcons: 520 West 22nd Street between 10th and 11th Avenues, 212-604 9200. Subway A, C, E to 23rd Street.
Japanese designer Rei Kawakubo's stark designs are worn by fashion's elite, and the high prices reflect that.

Keiko: 128 West 23rd Street between 6th and 7th Avenues, 212-647 7075, www. keikonewyork.com. Subway 23rd Street.
Designer swimwear for all tastes – and you may recognise the odd supermodel here.

FOOD AND DRINK

Chelsea Market: 75 9th Avenue between 15th and 16th Streets, 212-243 6005, www.chelseamarket.com. Subway A, C, E, L to 14th Street and 8th Avenue.
You'll find everything you need here for a gourmet feast, from fishmongers and bakers to wine merchants, and even florists for table decorations. Check out Buon Italia for great cheeses, sauces and all manner of Italian fodder and Amy's for breads you never dreamed of. An instant picnic!

Chelsea Wine Vault: 75 9th Avenue at Chelsea Market, 212-462 4244, www.chelseawinevault.com. Subway A, C, E to 14th Street.
More than 3,000 labels to choose from. Take advantage of the fun free tastings – mainly at weekends (see website).

HOMEWARE

Authentiques Past & Present: 255 West 18th Street at 8th Avenue, 212-675 2179, http://fab-stuff.com/ Subway 1 to 18th Street.
A must-visit for lovers of interiors from the 1950s and 60s. The long attic-style room is like a time capsule stocking fab American glass, barware, kitchen items, lamps and lots of cool kitsch items.

SPECIALITY AND GIFTS

Chelsea Merit Florist: 237 8th Avenue, 800-488 3577, www.chelseamerit.net. Subway 1, 2, 3, 7, N, Q, R, S, W to Times Square/42nd Street.
Just in case you need to grab some flowers

while you're away – a birthday or anniversary! – this is a great florist to visit with competitive prices with bouquets starting at around $50.

CHINATOWN

Asia Market: 71 Mulberry Street between Canal and Bayar Streets, 212-962 2020. Subway 6, J, M, N, Q, R, W, Z to Canal Street. The tightly packed Asia Market is loved by chefs and residents alike. There's everything here from canned curries to dried cuttlefish and dozens of varieties of noodles; every staple of Thai, Malaysian and Indonesian cuisine under 1 roof.

MUSIC

Downtown Music Gallery: 13 Monroe Street, between Catherine and Market streets. 212-473 0043, www.downtownmusicgallery. com. Subway F to East Broadway.
Jazz aficionados love this specialist shop with its wide selection of records and CDs to search through. Free, live performances take place most Sun from 6pm.

EAST VILLAGE

ANTIQUES AND FLEA MARKETS

Irreplaceable Artifacts & Demolition Depot: 216 East 125th Street between 2nd and 3rd Avenues, 212-860 1138, www.demolitiondepot.com.
An excellent selection of architectural items, from religious objects to vintage shutters.

BEAUTY STORES AND SPAS

Jin Soon Natural Hand & Foot Spa: 56 East 4th Street between Bowery and 2nd Avenue, 212-473 2047, www.jinsoon.com. Subway F, V to Lower East Side/2nd Avenue.
When in town, actress Julianne Moore books a full foot treatment with Jin Soon Choi. Expect rose petals and botanicals with the Flower Petal Float $45 pedicure – a basic manicure costs just $18. The tiny spa became such a Mecca for celebs and those wanting perfect hands and feet that a second, larger Jin Soon Spa has been established in the West Village at 23 Jones Street between Bleecker and West 4th Streets, 212-229 1070, plus a joint on the Upper East Side too, 421 East 7th

Street, 212-249 3144. Check out the 'floating room' where gorgeous orange silk hangs over a small pond.

BOOKS

Alabaster Bookshop: 122 4th Avenue at 12th Street, 212-982 3550. Subway 4, 5, 6, L, N, Q, R, W at 14th Street, Union Square.
Only 1 used bookstore remains on what was once book row. Owner Steve Crowley is still there with a great array of paperbacks that are around half the cover price, to rare photography books by the likes of Lou Reed, locked in ornate wood cabinets. There are carts to trawl through on the sidewalk, too.

St Mark's Bookshop: 31 3rd Avenue on the corner of 9th Street, 212-260 7853, www.stmarksbookshop.com. Subway 6 to Astor Place.
An excellent bookstore established in 1977 with a broad range of books. The bulletin board in the front gives details of local literary events.

DISCOUNT STORES

Gabay's Outlet: 225 1st Avenue between 13th and 14th Streets, 212-254 3180, www. gabaysoutlet.com. Subway F, V, L to Ave 1.
An East Village gem offering high-end designer fashion at seriously discounted prices. Its shoes and bags are coveted by the fashion pack and often include Manolo, Christian Louboutin and Tod's.

FASHION

Himalayan Vision: 127 2nd Avenue at 7th Street, 212-254 1952. Subway 6 to Astor Place.
Tibetan-style dresses, silk skirts, trousers, tops and hand-knit hats from around $40 can be found in this serene shop.

Jill Anderson: 331 East 9th Street at 1st Avenue, 212-253 1747, www.jillanderson. com. Subway 6 to Astor Place.
The sweeping coat-dresses and girly slips are in keeping with the bohemian vibe of the artsy East Village.

Meg: 312 9th Street at 2nd Avenue, 212-260 6329. Subway 6 to Astor Place.
Designer Megan Kinney's cool, clean lines are feminine yet functional (think tunics and jumpsuits).

Pas de Deux: 328 East 11th Street nr 2nd Avenue, 212-475 0075, http://pasdedeuxny. com. Subway L to 1st Station.
The fash world went into a bit of a frenzy when this store opened, as the duo behind it were also responsible for hugely popular menswear store Odin next door! This is like a Parisian boutique – chandeliers, chequered floor – and the offering is sublime. Check out

the Phillip Lim knit dresses, not to mention accessories like Karen Walker eyewear. A must-visit for fashionistas.

Trash and Vaudeville: 4 St Mark's Place between 2nd and 3rd Avenues, 212-982 3590, www.trashandvaudeville.com. Subway 6 to Astor Place.
Fitting out rock stars like Iggy Pop since the early 1980s, you'll get the East Village look in no time in this punk/grunge paradise: outrageous rubber dresses and shirts, black leather outfits and plenty of studded gear and footwear to match. Plus there's some fun clothing for kids, too, such as Sex Pistols baby-grows and tiny Ramones T-shirts.

FOOD AND DRINK
Astor Wines & Spirits: 399 Lafayette Street at 4th Street at the corner of Astor Place, 212-674 7500, www.astorwines.com. Subway 6 to Astor Place; R, W to 8th Street.
Stocks a wide range of wines and spirits.

MUSIC
A-1 Records: 439 East 6th Street at Avenues A, 212-473 2870. Subway F, V at Lower East Side, Second Avenue.
Geared towards those still interested in vinyl, with a focus on soul, jazz, hip-hop and an ever-changing assortment of house and dance. You can listen to records in store before you buy and A-1 has joined www.dailysession.com, so you can tune in to live broadcasts before you even visit the store!

VINTAGE FASHION
Tokio 7: 83 East 7th Street between 1st and 2nd Avenues, 212-353 8443. Subway 6 to Astor Place; N, R to 8th Street
Plenty of vintage and downtown designer gear to choose from here. Particularly good collection of Japanese designers.

Tokyo Joe: 334 East 11th Street between 1st and 2nd Avenues, 212-473 0724. Subway 6 to Astor Place.
The pre-worn designer offerings are advertised on a blackboard outside this tiny shop every day.

Village Scandal: 19 East 7th Street between 2nd and 3rd Avenues, 212-460 9358. www.thevillagescandal.com. Subway 6 to Astor Place.
A must-visit for vintage addicts as this retro store is packed full of cool hats and accessories from floppy Bianca Jagger-esque designs to trendy bucket caps. It's open until midnight.

> **BRITTIP**
> For the complete lowdown on what New York has to offer shoppers, website www.newyorkmetro.com/shopping gives comprehensive listings by neighbourhood or store type.

FINANCIAL DISTRICT

DISCOUNT STORES
Century 21: 22 Cortlandt Street between Church Street and Broadway, 212-227 9092, www.c21stores.com. Subway 1, 2, 4, 5, A, C to Fulton Street/Broadway Nassau. Excellent discounts on everything from adults' and children's clothing to goods for the home. Arrive early or mid-afternoon to avoid the lunchtime rush. An outlet has also opened on the Upper West Side at 1972 Broadway at between West 66th and West 67th streets (212-518 2121, subway 66 St – Lincoln Center).

Broadway

MUSIC

J&R Music World: 1 Park Row between Ann and Beekman Streets, 212-238 9000, www.jr.com. Subway A or C to Broadway/Nassau Street.

The weekly ads in the *New York Post* and *Village Voice* give an idea of what's on offer. They sell jazz, Latin and pop as well as loads of cheap electronic gear like cameras and iPods.

FLATIRON DISTRICT

BEAUTY STORES AND SPAS

MAC Pro: 7 West 22nd Street at 5th Avenue, 212-229 4830, www.maccosmetics.com. Subway N, Q, R, W to 23rd Street.

A haven for beauty make-up artists and pros, this huge space combines make-up products, studio, photography studio, reference materials and master classes.

DISCOUNT STORES

Burlington Coat Factory: 707 6th Avenue at 23rd Street, 212-229 1300, www.burlingtoncoatfactory.com. Subway F to 23rd Street.

A retail dream for the fashion-conscious and a proper New Yorker's secret. It's a continual designer overstock sale and it does carry more than just coats, though you have to be prepared to trawl through some less gorgeous pieces. There's lots of casual womenswear and menswear, plus formal apparel from names like Calvin Klein, Ralph Lauren, Michael by Michael Kors and DKNY. There are some golden periods, such as the arrival of AG Jeans selling for around one-third of their original price, but you won't know what's in until you hit the rails.

GRAMERCY PARK

BEAUTY

Iris Nail: 258 3rd Avenue at 21st Street. 212-228 8114. Subway 6 to 23rd Street

If you're in the area this clean, functional little place is really great value, particularly when they have a special offer on and a manicure is just $10 (it's usually $12). You don't have to book and they do eyelash extensions and pedicures, too.

FASHION

Gramercy Project: 240 3rd Avenue at East 20th Street. 212-533 4017. Subway 6 to 23rd Street.

Chic little boutique selling some lovely one-offs, particularly strong on dresses, plus accessories, too.

Apple Store

GREENWICH & WEST VILLAGE

ANTIQUES AND FLEA MARKETS

Alan Moss: 436 Lafayette Street near Astor Place, 212-473 1310, www.alanmossny.com. Subway 6 to Astor Place.

Glass gems, fine art, jewellery, vintage fashion and interesting homewares from the mid-20th century.

BEAUTY STORES AND SPAS

Aedes de Venustas: 9 Christopher Street near 6th Avenue, 212-206 8674, www.aedes.com. Subway 1, 9 to Christopher Street.

Sublime emporium where you can pick up almost impossible-to-find skincare products.

Avalon Salon & Day Spa: 112 Christopher Street between Bleecker and Hudson Streets, 212-337 1966, www.avalonsalondayspa.com. Subway 1 to Christopher Street/Sheridan Square.

A popular local hair salon that is a world away from snooty 5th Avenue. Friendly staff, lots of cutting stations and excellent products, such as Keratase and Aveda, guarantee you'll walk away happy. You can also have pedicures, manicures, massages, facials and waxing.

Fresh: 388 Bleecker Street between Perry and West 11th Streets, 917-408 1850, www.fresh.com. Subway 6 to 68th Street.

A Boston-based company specialising in beauty products made from natural ingredients such as honey, milk, soy, sugar and even Umbrian clay. Other branches can be found at 1367 3rd Avenue (212-585 3400) and 872 Broadway (212-477 1100).

Gemini 14 Salon & Spa:135 West 14th Street, 212-229 2100, www.gemini14nyc.com. Subway 1, 9 to Christopher Street.

If you have wild, untameable hair or you just want your locks to be sleeker, then book an appointment to test out this salon's patented Opti-smooth straightening treatment for yourself.

Make-Up Forever: 8 East 12th Street between 5th Avenue and University Place, 212-941 9337, www.makeupforever.com. 4, 5, 6, L, N, Q, R, W to Union Square
A French line specialising in ultra-bright colours, thanks to the triple pigment formula used in all its lipsticks and eyeshadows. This is a funky little shop decked out to look like the make-up area of a film set. The well-trained staff are happy to advise on colours and products.

BOOKS

BookBook: 266 Bleecker Street between 6th and 7th Avenues, 212-807 8655, http://bookbooknyc.com. Subway 6, Bleecker St/Lafayette St.
Independent general bookshop in the heart of Greenwich Village, features recent and backlist fiction, children's books, travel, history, drama, art and fashion, plus many more subjects. Friendly staff who'll even gift wrap a purchase if it's a present.

Partners & Crime: 44 Greenwich Avenue at the Corner of Charles Street, 212-243 0440, www.crimepays.com. Subway 1 to Christopher Street.
Anyone who loves crime and mystery books should call in here. As well as stocking a wide range of titles in the genre, some of them signed copies, there are also events such as mystery radio plays and signings.

⚑ BRITTIP
If you're looking for one-off boutiques, take the subway 1 to Christopher Street then head down Bleecker Street from St Christopher Street to Carmine Street. You'll pass lots of unique, fashion-forward womenswear stores such as Think Closet and Roni.

Shakespeare & Co: 716 Broadway at Washington Place, 212-529 1330, www.shakeandco.com. Subway N, R to 8th Street; 6 to Astor Place.
This is an excellent bookstore. Unlike many a Barnes & Noble, where the staff sometimes don't appear to have a clue about a book request, the assistants here are graduates and will be genuinely helpful. There are other branches, such as 939 Lexington Avenue, and they're all in close proximity to NYC's major universities. They also buy second-hand books.

Three Lives Bookstore: 154 West 10th Street off 7th Avenue, 212-741 2069, www.threelives.com.
A delightful shop with a charming ambience, known for attentive staff with encyclopaedic knowledge. Specialises in literary fiction, poetry and design books, as well as memoirs

FASHION

Darling: 1 Horatio Street at 8th Avenue, 212-367 3750, www.darlingnyc.com. Subway A, C, E to 14th Street.
Ann French Emonts fills this small boutique with her own designs plus choice pieces from other top-notch womenswear designers. Thurs nights are popular as the store stays open until 10pm and customers are offered champagne while they browse.

Lulu Guinness: 394 Bleecker Street between 11th and Perry Streets, 212-367 2120, www.luluguinness.com. Subway A, C, E to 14th Street; L to 8th Avenue; 1, 2 to Christopher Street.
Lulu started out in Notting Hill, West London, and has established herself in the Big Apple. Her vintage-inspired accessories include embroidered and appliquéd bags and purses, many only available in New York

Untitled: 26 West 8th Street between 5th and 6th Avenues, 212-505 9725. Subway A, C, E, F, V, S to West 4th Street.
Contemporary clothing and accessories from exclusive New York designers as well as the likes of Vivienne Westwood.

FOOD AND DRINK

Faicco's Pork Store: 260 Bleecker Street between 6th and 7th Avenues, 212-243 1974.
A landmark Italian speciality food shop established in 1900, it is known for its own sausages that are made daily (and sold to many of the neighbouring restaurants), its home-made mozzarella cheese, again made daily, plus rice balls made with three cheeses and rolled in breadcrumbs. Other specialities include prosciutto balls, potato croquettes, fried ravioli and stuffed breads.

⚑ BRITTIP
If you'd like a taste of the foods sold in some of the shops in Greenwich Village, go on the Foods of New York tour, which also introduces you to great restaurants in the area (p89).

Murray's Cheese Shop: 254 Bleecker Street between 6th and 7th Avenues, 212-243 3289, www.murrayscheese.com.
The owner travels all over the world to bring back a fascinating selection of more than 350 cheeses with amazing names such as

HOW TO FIND A REAL BARGAIN

Goods at normal prices in New York are cheaper than in the UK, but it is possible to find whatever you are looking for at an even better price.

▶ If **shopping bargains** are your main reason for visiting New York, then bear in mind that the major sales are held in March and August. The winter sales seem to start earlier and earlier and may even begin before Christmas in some stores.

▶ Visit **http://nymag.com/shopping/articles/sb/** for all the vital information on when the latest designer and sample sales are about to take place. Hot sale action is also listed on www.dailycandy.com and www.thebudgetfashionista.com.

▶ Also take a look at the **Sales and Bargains** section of *New York Magazine*, the ads in *The New York Times* and the Check Out section of *Time Out*.

▶ Get the **S&B Report** on.

▶ Bear in mind that many of the **vintage clothing outlets** are excellent for barely worn designer clothes and some even specialise in never-worn-before sample sales.

▶ As every good fashion editor knows, New York has a lot of **consignment stores** (shops selling drastically reduced last-season, end-of-line or second-hand designer pieces). Do hunt them down as you can pick up a real bargain (see Ina, p144).

▶ Download from iTunes **NYC SampleSales**, the first smartphone app that can notify shoppers of all the existing NYC sample sales using locations awareness technology – it can even notify you of all the sales including major retail sales within a mile of your current location. Genius.

Wabash Cannonball, Crocodile Tears, Mutton Buttons and Cardinal Sin, a British cow's milk cheese. They also sell olives, chorizos, pâtés and breads and you may even catch a cookery class.

Pasticceria Bruno: 506 Laguardia Place, 212 982 5854, www.pasticceriabruno.com.
An Italian-French bakery run by one of the top 10 pastry chefs in New York. It does miniature and large fruit tarts, mousses, cookies, sorbets, ice-cream cakes and home-made chocolates, and you can sit down to try any of them with a nice cup of tea or coffee.

BRITTIP

If you want a coffee stop while you're shopping in Greenwich and the West Village, head to Jacks Stir Brew café on West 10th Street, www.jacksstirbrew.com. It's tiny, but a great place to read the New York Times and sip a superb cup of coffee – owner Jack invented the stir brewer, a device that oxygenates the beans as they grind. It's a hit with local residents like Sarah Jessica Parker and Ryan Adams.

Pasticceria Rocco: 243 Bleecker Street between 6th and 7th Avenues, 212-242 6031, www.pasticceriarocco.com.
Famous for its fresh cannoli (Italian pastries filled with cream), it sells large and small sizes of everything from Italian cheesecakes to chocolate, hazelnut and lemon cakes. You can

eat in, too, with a cup of delicious coffee.

HOMEWARE
Broadway Panhandler: 65 East 8th Street, between Broadway and University, 212-966 3434, www.broadwaypanhandler.com. Subway N, R, W to 8th Street.
All things for the kitchen, from the latest gadgets to classic pieces such as Alessi toasters. There are hundreds of items to choose from and it's a must-visit for any domestic gods or goddesses who love a gizmo when in town. Famous chefs often give in-store demonstrations.

SPECIALITY AND GIFTS
Flight 001: 96 Greenwich Avenue between Jane and West 12th Streets, 212-989 0001, www.flight001.com. Subway 1, 2, 3, 9 to 14th Street.
A travel accessories shop that looks like a sleek 1960s airport lounge, it stocks fabulously cool carry-on items such as digital cameras, spray-on vitamins and WAP-activated global travel guides. It also has practical but funky luggage.

MXYPLYZYK: 125 Greenwich Avenue at West 13th Street, 212-989 4300, www.mxyplyzyk.com. Subway 1, 2, 3, 9 to 14th Street.
Kitschy-cool gifts and whatnots including Devil Ducks (with horns – glow-in-the-dark or plain red) and tractor-seat stools for when you're tired of serious shopping.

Tea and Sympathy: 110 Greenwich Avenue between 12th and 13th Streets, 212-989 9735, www.teaandsympathynewyork.com.

Russ & Daughters

Subway 1, 2, 3, 9 to 14th Street.
Filled with all things the Brit abroad loves, this is a combination of a shop and café offering sausage rolls, fish and chips and 'proper' tea. David Bowie had his 50th birthday bash here, and Kate Moss and Rupert Everett are regulars.

VINTAGE FASHION

Star Struck: 47 Greenwich Avenue, 212-691 5356, www.starstruckvintage.com. Subway 1 to Christopher Street.
Vintage couture, including pieces by Dior, from the '20s to the '80s. You'll find anything from flapper dresses to leg warmers. Well worth a look if you love vintage and original clothes.

Stella Dallas: 218 Thompson Street between Bleecker and West 3rd Streets, 212-674 0447. Subway A, C, E, F, V, S to West 4th Street.
A fabulous vintage shop full of girly chiffon dresses and other items. Doesn't open until 12.30pm.

BRITTIP

Grom Gelato (212-206 1738), an ice-cream parlour with dozens of flavours situated where Bleecker Street meets Carmins Street, is a cool (pardon the pun) place to stop for a snack in the summer. In the winter, head over the road to Molly's Cupcakes (www.mollyscupcakes.com) for a sweet treat instead.

LITTLE ITALY

FOOD AND DRINK

Di Palo's: 200 Grand Street at Mott Street, 212-226 1033, www.dipaloselects.com. Subway J, M, N, Q, R, W, Z, 6 to Canal Street.
One of the last remaining Italian speciality food stores in Little Italy, it was founded 80 years ago and is particularly famous for its mozzarella and Italian sausages and salami. It even has its own ageing room for cheeses. The antipasti and holiday sweet baskets are a great purchase if you're self-catering in the city, or ask them to make you up a basket for an upmarket picnic.

LOWER EAST SIDE

FASHION

For info on sample sales in the Lower East Side area, go to http://racked.com.

Edith Machinist: 104 Rivington Street at Ludlow Street, 212-979 9992, www.edith machinist.com. Subway F to Delancey Street.
Sara Daha used to co-own Edith and Daha, but has since struck out on her own. Lovely vintage style with endorsements from stars like Sienna Miller. One of the best of its kind in the city, where you can pick up anything from Mary Janes to a heavenly handbag.

FOOD AND DRINK

Russ & Daughters: 179 East Houston Street between Allen and Orchard Streets, 212-475 4880, www.russanddaughters.com. Subway F to 2nd Avenue.
Along with Katz's Deli (p170), this is one of the most famous outlets in the Lower East Side. Established in 1914, it sells every possible kind of fish, caviar, pickled vegetables and bagels.

MADISON SQUARE

ANTIQUES AND FLEA MARKETS

Old Print Shop: 150 Lexington Avenue between East 29th and East 30th Streets, 212-683 3950, www.oldprintshop.com. Subway 6 to 33rd Street.
The go-to shop for prints, maps, photography and art books from 1900 onwards.

FASHION

JJ Hat Center: 310 5th Avenue near 32nd Street, 212-239 4368, www.jjhatcenter.com. Subway N, R to 28th Street.
If you've even wanted a panama, fedora, pork pie or beret, New York's oldest hat store (it was established in 1911) is the place to visit.

ELECTRONICS

Datavision SuperStore: 445 5th Avenue near 39th Street, 212-689 1111, www.datavis. com. Subway 7, B, D, F, V to 42nd Street/5th Avenue.
You'll find whatever techie treat you desire, from laptops to iPod accessories, in this cramped but comprehensive store.

VINTAGE

Cheap Jacks: 303 5th Avenue at 31st Street, 212-777 9564. www.cheapjacks.com. Subway N, R to 28th Street.

This must be the largest vintage store in the city. A huge space crammed with clothes and accessories from the '20s to the '80s. Stylists, wardrobe specialists, designers and celebs all pop in for a bit of inspiration.

◀▮▶ BRITTIP

If you're shopping or sightseeing in lower Midtown around lunch time and don't want to go to a restaurant, try Calexico (www.calexicocart.com), a mobile cart selling delicious Mexican food where Broadway meets 5th Avenue opposite Madison Square Park. There are tables and chairs, or you can eat in the park if it's sunny.

MEATPACKING DISTRICT

DEPARTMENT STORES

Jeffrey: 449 West 14th Street between 9th and 10th Avenues, 212-206 1272, www.jeffreynewyork.com. Subway N, R to 5th Avenue/59th Street.

A boutique department store sounds like an oxymoron, but this little gem, on the edge of the Meatpacking District is packed full of tremendously hip clothes and accessories. It attracts A-list celebrities – note the limousines waiting at the front – and great labels like Dries Van Noten and Balenciaga. The women's shoe department is one of the best in New York.

FASHION

Alexander McQueen: 417 West 14th Street between 9th Avenue and Washington Street, 212-645 1797, www.alexandermcqueen. com. Subway A, C, E to 14th Street, L to 8th Avenue.

Despite the British fashion designer's sad death in 2010, the label continues to operate. The clothes are still way out, edgy and very expensive under the design leadership of Sarah Burton, who's more popular than ever both sides of the Atlantic following the popularity of her wedding gown for the Duchess of Cambridge. There are rumours in the fashion world that the store is trading in its Meatpacking store for a boutique in the former home of Valentino at 747 Madison Avenue. However, this isn't expected until 2014, so check the website before you visit.

An Earnest Cut & Sew: 821 Washington Street at Gansevoort Street, 212-242 3414, www.earnestsewn.com. Subway A, C, E to 8th Avenue.

High-end denim label Earnest Sewn's opened its first stand-alone store in 2005 and it has been a major hit with trendy young New Yorkers ever since. The major hook here is its customising – you can have pockets, buttons or zips tweaked and fabric added to ensure you get a genuine one-off garment. The service takes 2 hours and costs $300–350.

Diane von Furstenberg: 874 Washington Street, 646-486 4800, www.dvf.com. Subway A, C, E to 8th Avenue.

Flagship store of the queen of the classically sexy silk jersey wrap dress. The dramatic shop, with its draped changing rooms, is worth a visit in its own right.

◀▮▶ BRITTIP

If you long to wear Armani but don't have the bank balance to match, then hunt out one of five AIX Armani Exchange stores in Manhattan, which offer the label's chic, well-made clothes at a fraction of the cost of Armani – www. armaniexchange.com. Stores are at 645 and 656 5th Avenue, Time Warner Center (10 Columbus Circle), 129 5th Avenue and 568 Broadway.

MIDTOWN

ANTIQUES AND FLEA MARKETS

Hell's Kitchen Flea Market: 39th Street between 9th and 10th Avenues, 212-243 5343, www.hellskitchenfleamarket.com. Subway A, C, F or 1, 2, 3, 9 to 34th/42nd Streets.

One of America's most famous outdoor markets, where celebrities browse through

Shopping is a must in New York

FIVE TOP NEW YORK SPAS

Meatpacking District
Exhale Spa: Hotel Gansevoort (p231).
Situated on the lower level of this chic hotel, this spa has all the usual massage, facials and nail treatments on offer, but it also has a Heal section on the menu, which offers acupuncture, cupping and vibration therapy. You can also book a herbal or oriental medicine consultation to help get you back on track, plus there are some great packages, too, if you have the time.

Midtown
Caudalie Vinotherapie Spa: The Plaza, 5th Avenue at Central Park, 212-265 3182, www.theplaza.com. Subway 4, 5, 6 to 59th Street.
How to make The Plaza, Manhattan's most famous landmark hotel, even more impressive? Install a multi-million dollar spa with Caudalie, the French beauty house's only US outpost. It mixes wine and spa for the ultimate pampering experience.

La Prairie at the Ritz Carlton Spa: The Ritz Carlton Hotel, 50 Central Park South at 6th Avenue, 212-521 6135, www.ritzcarlton.com. Subway F, N, R, Q, W to 57th Street.
An extremely high-end spa beloved by celebrities. The Caviar Firming Facial is the signature treatment and rings in at around $310 a go.

Ohm Spa: 7th floor, 260 5th Avenue at 28th street, 212-481 7892, www.ohmspa.com. Subway N, R, W to 28th Street.
Aiming to be the antithesis of overly feminine spa design, owners Jonathan Ho and Kathy Yan have come up with clean lines and a gender neutral palette of blue and brown, the message being that men are welcome here, too. As you'd expect, the treatments are similarly straightforward, including massages that target certain muscle groups that give you problems and facials from Dermalogica and Plantogen. You can watch movies on flat-screen TVs while you have a manicure or pedicure.

TriBeCa
Tribeca MedSpa: 114 Hudson Street at Franklin Street, 212-925 9500, www.tribecamedspa.com. Subway 1 at Franklin Street.
Lots of therapies on the menu dedicated to getting rid of wrinkles. There are 4 treatment rooms, including one for injectables, such as Botox and Restalyne, which are only given by licensed professionals. If you want something less heavy, there are Medi-Pedis plus Titan skin-tightening and rejuvenation laser treatments. It's rumoured that Robert DeNiro is both the landlord and a customer.

vintage clothing, furniture, pottery, glassware, jewellery and art. Get there early for the best finds. Weekends only.

Lillian Nassau: 220 East 57th Street between 2nd and 3rd Avenues, 212-759 6062, www.lilliannassau.com. Subway 4, 5, 6 to 59th Street.
Come here for stunning art nouveau lamps and glassware, especially original Tiffany.

Manhattan Arts & Antiques Center: 1050 2nd Avenue between East 55th and East 56th Streets, 212-355 4400, www.the-maac.com. Subway 4, 5, 6, to 59th Street; F, N, R, W to Lexington Avenue.
A rich assortment of antiques, including tapestries, porcelain, jewellery and furniture spread over 3 floors. Pretty pricey, but it's worth a window-shop around this treasure trove.

BEAUTY STORES AND SPAS
50th Street Madison Nail: 44 East 50th Street at Madison Avenue, 212-754 2277.

Second-floor salon that isn't going to break the bank, with prices far lower than its neighbours. Look for Panini Totz Deli at street level; the sign for the nail salon is above it.

Bliss 57: 3rd floor, 12 West 57th Street between 5th and 6th Avenues, 877-862 5477, www.blissworld.com. Subway N, R to 59th Street.
Sarah Jessica Parker's favourite spa, which also sells its own skincare range, BlissLabs.

Bond No 9 New York: 897 Madison Avenue at 73rd Street, 212-794 4480, www.bondno9.com. Subway 4, 5, 6 to 59th Street.
Delicious scents with witty names like Chelsea Flowers, Gramercy Park and Madison Soirée. Or you can have your own custom blended. Branches also at 9 Bond Street (212-228 1732) and 399 Bleecker Street at 11th Street (212-633 1641).

Elizabeth Arden Red Door Salon & Spa: 663 5th Avenue between 52nd and 53rd streets, 212-546 0200, www.reddoorspas.com.

TOP MIDTOWN SHOPS FOR ACCESSORIES

Bottega Veneta: 699 5th Avenue between 54th and 55th Streets, 212-371 5511, www.bottegaveneta.com. Subway E, V to 5th Avenue/53rd Street.
Who wouldn't covet the gorgeous soft leather, logo-free handbags offered at this Italian designer store.

Jimmy Choo: Olympic Tower 645 5th Avenue at 51st Street (entrance on East 51st Street), 212-593 0800, www.jimmychoo.com. Subway E, V to 5th Avenue/53rd Street.
Originally part of Jimmy's upscale ready-to-wear stores – think London, Paris, Los Angeles and New York – the designer has sold up most of his shares and gone back to his couture clients. However, the thongs (flip-flops), slingbacks and skinny high-heeled shoes still remain the favourites of celebs like Madonna and Sarah Jessica Parker. A pair of women's shoes is upwards of $450. Men's loafers, sneakers and thongs start at around $300.

Manolo Blahnik: 31 West 54th Street between 5th and 6th Avenues, 212-582 3007, www.manoloblahnik.com. Subway E, V to 5th Avenue/53rd Street.
Anyone serious about their shoe collection wouldn't miss this Mecca for celebs. In fact, Manolo has even designed the SJP – an ankle-strapped stiletto named after Sarah Jessica Parker.

Roger Vivier: 750 Madison Avenue at 65th Street, 212-861 5371, www.rogervivier.com. Subway F at Lexington Avenue/63rd Street.
The designer who gave the world chrome-buckle, square-toe flats in the 1960s, worn by Catherine Deneuve in cult film Belle de Jour, has a fabulous store. Marlene Dietrich and our very own Queen Elizabeth have all stepped out in Vivier's creations. Pop in to marvel at the salon, even if you can't afford the shoes, as the furniture was designed to complement the footwear and handbags and the interior decoration is modelled on Vivier's luxurious home, complete with a Picasso sketch.

Subway E, V to 5th Avenue/53rd Street.
There are some great anti-ageing treatments on offer here, such as the oxygen infusion facial, which combines oxygen and collagen to boost elasticity.

Face Stockholm: Time Warner Center 10 Columbus Circle, 212-823 9415, www.facestockholm.com. Subway A, B, C, D, 1 to 59th Street/Columbus Circle
A glittery make-up emporium filled with the full range of colours and brushes, plus skin care and make up bags. You can have your make-up done here or take a lesson. Phone for an appointment or just drop in.

Green Tea Nail & Spa: 141 West 35th Street between Broadway and 7th Avenue, 212-564 6971. Subway A, C, E to 34th Street/Penn Station.
Nestled in the 34th Street district right next to Macy's is this large Japanese spa in which you are served antioxidant-rich green tea in a clean, minimalist environment. Treatments include waxing, facials, manicures, pedicures and massages.

J Sisters International: Second floor 41 West 57th Street between 5th and 6th Avenues, 212-750 2485, www.jsisters.com. Subway N, Q, R, W to 57th Street.
Family-run beauty centre famous for its extremely thorough Brazilian waxes. You can also have your make-up, nails and hair done.

Juvenex Spa: 25 West 32nd Street, 5th floor, 646-733 1330, www.juvenexspa.com. Subway N, Q, R, W, F, D, B to 34th Street.
An unusual spa with saunas, steam rooms and plunge pools, plus the Jade Igloo made from 20 tonnes of semi-precious stones! It has a big list of treatments, such as hot stone massage, $125 for 60 minutes and reflexology, $65 for 30 minutes.

NYINTHEKNOW

Francisca Ovalle, who works for NYC & Company, has a top tip for partying and preening. 'For cocktails, a favourite is the Beauty Bar (www.thebeautybar.com) on 231 East 14th Street. Transformed from a 1950s beauty parlour it offers a martini and manicure for $10 and is open until 11pm Mon–Fri.'

Ouidad Salon: 4th Floor, 37 West 57th Street between 5th and 6th Avenues, 212-888 3288, www.ouidad.com.
Named after the owner, this hair salon specialises in cutting and styling curly hair. In fact, they take curly hair so seriously you won't be allowed in without it! The dedicated team spends up to 4 hours styling and taming your locks and the salon has its own range of products. This new premises has the feel of a SoHo loft, with faux snakeskin couches to boot.

FAO Schwarz

Physical Advantage: Penthouse, 139 East 57th Street at Lexington Avenue, 212-460 1879, www.physical-knead.com. Subway 4, 5, 6 to 59th Street.
This is not the type of spa where you are going to get reiki and reflexology; it's a no-nonsense massage centre often patronised by professional athletes and dancers. The ideal place if you need a treatment without the frills.

Phyto Universe: 3rd Floor, 715 Lexington Avenue at East 58th Street, 212-308 0270, www.phytouniverse.com. Subway 4, 5, 6, N, R, Q to 59th Street.
Excellent upmarket all-purpose spa for massage, facials, skin care, hair treatments and fragrances.

Sephora: 597 5th Avenue between East 48th and 49th Streets, 212-980 6534, www.sephora.com. Subway B, D F, V to 47th–50th Streets/Rockefeller Center.
The Rockefeller Center is home to the flagship Manhattan Sephora store packed with aromatic beauty products. There are lots of other stores across the city (check the website), but this one has the excellent Anastasia Brow Studio if you want a quick shape-up.

BOOKS
Argosy: 116 East 59th between Park and Lexington Avenues, 212-753 4455, www.argosybooks.com. Subway 4, 5, 6, F, N, R to 59th Street.

The best bookshop in New York if you're looking for rare, hard-to-find books. There are 7 storeys of out-of-print publications, antiques, maps, autographs and letters to browse through. Beware, though: you can easily lose an afternoon engrossed in here.

Rizzoli: 31 West 57th Street between 5th and 6th Avenues, 212-759 2424, www.rizzoliusa.com. Subway N, R, W to 5th Avenue/59th Street; F to 57th Street.
This trendy store has a good stock of art, fashion and design publications and is popular with those in the media and with design students.

CHILDREN
The Disney Store: 1540 Broadway at Times Square, 212-626 2910, www.disneystore.com. Subway 1, 2, 3 to Times Square/42nd Street.
All singing, all dancing new interactive store with lots of extras aside from the usual Disney toys and clothing, such as a Princess castle with a talking mirror and a large Disney theatre with giant screen. In short, your kids (or possibly you) will be in heaven.

FAO Schwarz: 767 5th Avenue at 58th Street, 212-644 9400 ext. 4242, www.fao.com. Subway N, R to 5th Avenue.
The most famous children's store in the world, it's not only huge but is also an entertainment centre in its own right, with oversized displays that take your breath away (check out the massive piano!), plus every conceivable toy your child could want.

Hershey's Times Square: 48th Street and Broadway, 212-581 9100, www.hersheys.com. Subway N, R, S, 1, 2, 3, 7, 9, A, C, E to 42nd Street/Times Square.

In the heart of the rejuvenated Times Square district, this 16-storey candy (as New Yorkers would say) store is a chocoholics dream. Inside you can create your own choc thanks to the Original Automatic and Gravitational Chocolate Machine (Willy Wonka eat your heart out) and personalise your own giant Hershey's Kisses bar. Not to be missed is the chance to see your name or a message lit up in neon on the store's Times Square scrolling marquee.

Toys R Us: 1514 Broadway between 44th and 45th Streets, 212-225 8392, www.toysrus.com. Subway N, Q, R, S, W, 1, 2, 3, 7 to Times Square.

This 3-storey glass-enclosed building is home to an 18m/60ft Ferris wheel, a giant roaring dinosaur and a life-size Barbie townhouse. If you are here with kids, it's a must-see.

DEPARTMENT STORES

Macy's: Herald Square at 151 West 34th Street, 6th Avenue and Broadway, 212-695 4400, www.macys.com. Subway B, D, F, N, Q, R, V, W to 34th Street.

You can get pretty much anything you require, provided you are prepared to hunt, as this is a beast of a gigantic store, filling as it does an entire city block and soaring up 10 floors. There are lots of entrances and it's easy to get lost in here, so it's best to select a time and place to meet in the store if you're with a group. If you enter from the Herald Square side, you'll find the Visitors' Center on the mezzanine level up to your left. Here you can pick up a Welcome International Savings Card for international shoppers that entitles you to 10% off most goods for up to

30 days after issue, plus there's a cloakroom for small bags and jackets if you want to shop light. A favourite area with Brits is the jeans department and, of course, the beauty counters that throng the ground floor. Don't miss the coffee shops, restaurant and food store run by Cucina & Co (p144).

ELECTRONICS

Apple Store, 5th Avenue: 767 5th Avenue between 58th and 59th streets, 212-336 1440, www.apple.com. Subway N, Q, R to 5th Avenue/59th Street

A futuristic-looking store that's a must-visit for Apple technology lovers. It never shuts and when you've descended into the basement via a glass cube entrance above a suspended Apple, you're allowed to test-drive all the latest sleek Apple products. Check ahead on the website as the store has weekly events, such as talks from leading names in computing, film, art and music and numerous workshops.

B&H Photo & Video: 420 9th Avenue between West 33rd and West 34th Streets, 212-444 6615, www.bhphotovideo.com. Subway A, C, E to 34th Street/Penn Station. A massive 3-storey, block-long store that

Toys R Us

JEWELLERY

The 47th Street Diamond District is where the little gems are traded, cut and set. More than 2,600 independent businesses are in a single block between 5th and 6th Avenues. Many have booths in jewellery exchanges such as the World's Largest Jewellery Exchange at 55 West 47th Street (212-719 5235).

Chelsea

DVVS: 263A 19th Street near 8th Avenue, 212-366 4888, www.dvvs.com. Subway C, E to 23rd Street.
Modern, unusual jewellery from contemporary designers. Price range $1,000–2,000.

Midtown

Asprey: 853 Madison Avenue, 212-688 1811, www.asprey.com. Subway N, R to 5th Avenue.
Pricey bling beloved of stars, there are also luxury accessories to browse, including bags.
Graff: 710 Madison Avenue near 64th Street, 212-355 9292, www.graffdiamonds.com. Subway 6 to 68th Street.
Some of the best diamonds that you're ever likely to come across are here, to suit every type of price range, from tiny 1-carat to 100-carat yellow diamonds.

H Stern: 645 5th Avenue near 51st Avenue, 212-655 3910, www.hstern.net. Subway E, V to 5th Avenue. One of New York's most prestigious jewellers.

Tiffany & Co: 727 5th Avenue, 212-755 8000, www.tiffany.com. Subway N, R to 5th Avenue.
Few can resist popping in to sneak a look at the store that featured so highly in the classic film Breakfast at Tiffany's starring Audrey Hepburn. If you can't afford the $2,000-plus diamond necklaces and bracelets, you can always fork out for a $100 keyring.

SoHo

Fragments: 116 Prince Street between Greene and Wooster Streets, 212-334 9588, www.fragments.com. Subway A, C, E to Spring Street.
A hit with the fashion crowd keen to snap up the works of between 60 and 100 designers.

stocks every conceivable piece of electronic imaging, audio, video and photo equipment you've ever heard of. All the staff are professionals in their own right and really know their onions. They're helpful, too, which is why this emporium is an excellent place to go for everyone from novices to professionals.

◄█▶ BRITTIP

Remember that the voltage system is different in America, so any plug-in electrical goods will not work properly in the UK without an adaptor.

Willoughby's: 298 5th Avenue between 30th and 31st Streets, 212-564 1600, www.willoughbys.com. Subway 6 to 33rd Street.
Reputedly the world's largest collection of cameras and all things audio (film makers and would-be movie makers, you'll love it here), but the service isn't brilliant so make sure you know what you want before you go.

FASHION

Alice + Olivia: 80 West 40th Street at 6th Avenue, 212-840 0887, www.aliceandolivia.com. Subway B, D, F, V to 42nd Street.
Situated in Midtown West around Bryant Park, this is the place to stock up on the latest trends, such as shift dresses and 1960s-inspired mini-dresses. Has some cute handbags too and other stores around the city including 755 Madison Avenue (646-545 2895).

Ann Taylor: 850 3rd Avenue at East 52nd Street, 212-308 5333, www.anntaylor.com. Subway E, M, 6 to 53rd Street.
If you want to capture a little of the groomed, preppy look so many New York women sport, then shop here for mid-priced classics, such as shift dresses and well-cut blazers, ideal for posh work wear or a party. There are also accessories to covet. Lots of other stores around the city, including 5th Avenue, Madison Avenue and Sixth Avenue.

Burberry: 444 Madison Avenue, 212-707 6700, www.burberry.com. Subway N, R, W to 5th Avenue.
This great British classic has been a trendsetting force in recent years. There's something for everyone here – men, women, teenagers and even children since the introduction of the tots' clothing line.

Chanel: 15 East 57th Street between 5th and Madison Avenues, 212-385 5050, www.chanel.com. Subway E, V to 5th Avenue.
The enduring French label offers you the chance to buy all the classics from $1,000

suits to quilted handbags and, of course, the famous No 5 perfume.

Gianni Versace: 647 5th Avenue between 51st and 52nd Streets, 212-317 0224, www.versace.com. Subway E, V to 5th Avenue/53rd Street.
A beautiful shop, housed in the former Vanderbilt mansion, selling beautiful clothes for the rich and famous.

Gucci: 725 5th Avenue between East 56th and 57th Streets, 212-826 2600, www.gucci. com. Subway E, V to 5th Avenue/53rd Street.
You may not be able to afford anything on display, but it's essential to know what 'look' you are trying to achieve when you browse the copy-cat shops downtown.

Lacoste: 575 Madison Avenue near 56th Street, 212-750 8115, www.lacoste.com. Subway 6 to 51st Street. Also at 608 5th Avenue and 134 Prince Street.
The alligator-logo polo shirts are a classic item to snap up while you're in the Big Apple.

BRITTIP
Dinos Shoe Repair & Shine at Columbus Circle opposite Central Park is a NY institution. Even if you don't want your shoes polished, take a peek at the smart businessmen sitting on high stools having their shoes shined for $3 a pop and the walls adorned with the autographs of the famous faces who have frequented Dinos over the years.

Levi's: 536 Broadway, between Prince and Spring Streets. Area: SoHo, 646-613 1847, www.levi.com. Also at 750 Lexington Avenue. Area: Upper East Side.
If you've ever had trouble finding a pair of jeans that fit you perfectly, come here to be measured and have your jeans custom-made and sent to you.

New York & Company: 715 Lexington Avenue at 3rd Avenue, 212-813 1301, www.nyandcompany.com. Subway 59th Street.
Bargain prices for on-trend dresses, trousers and tops at this popular Manhattan chain store. Lots of accessories, too, from hats to shoes.

Niketown New York: 6 East 57th Street at 5th Avenue, 212-891 6453. Subway 59th Street.
Every Nike product you could wish for, from trainers to clothes and gadgets, plus you can design your own footwear. Great place for people-watching.

CLOTHES SIZES
Clothes sizes are one size smaller in the US, so a dress size 10 in the US is a size 12 in the UK, a jacket size 42 is a UK 44. But it's the opposite with shoes – an American size 10 is our size 9. For men the sizing is similar: a size 36 suit in the US is also a size 36 in the UK, while shoes are one size smaller in the UK – a US size 10 is a UK size 9. Children's sizes vary: an American size 4 is a British size 2.

TIME WARNER AT COLUMBUS CIRCLE
✉ 10 Columbus Circle
☎ 212-485 1900
🖰 www.theshopsatcolumbuscircle.com
🚇 A, B, C, D, 1 to 59th Street/Columbus Circle
🕐 Mon–Sat 10am–9pm; Sun 11am–7pm (check the website for seasonal and holiday hours).

New York is fantastic for shopping, but stores tend to be individual and spread out. If you're after more of a mall experience, with lots of choice under 1 roof, make a beeline for Time Warner at Columbus Circle, close to Central Park and a few blocks from the Lincoln Center. The shops attracting New Yorkers and tourists alike include BOSS Hugo Boss offering the complete collection Boss Vlack, Boss Selection, Boss Orange and Boss Green lines, plus accessories and fragrances. There's also A/X Armani Exchange, Godiva chocolates, H&M, JCrew (mens and womens), Stuart Weitzman and L'Occitane beauty products. See the website for a full list of stores.

BRITTIP
The wholefood market in the basement of Time Warner At Columbus Circle is a great place to pick up some bread and deli treats then head across the road to Central Park for a picnic.

Victoria's Secret: 34 East 57th Street, 212-758 5592, www.victoriassecret.com
Enormous store that you can't miss thanks to the giant pictures of gorgeous models in underwear on the outside, stocking the complete range of America's favourite lingerie line.

FOOD AND DRINK
Balducci on the Go: Hearst Tower, 301 West 56th Street at 8th Avenue, 646-350 4194, www.balduccis.com. Subway N, Q, R to 57th Street and 7th Avenue.
One of the most fabulous grocer's markets

Midtown Comics

in New York has moved from its Greenwich location to Midtown, supplying busy New Yorkers with gourmet breakfasts and lunches. Take out or eat in the café and breathe in the aroma of fresh coffee (this joint claims to make the best in the city) and gaze at the delicious soups, artisan breads, pastries and doorstep sandwiches.

Cucina & Co: In the Cellar at Macy's (p141), 151 West 34th Street, 6th Avenue and Broadway, 212-868 2388, www.patinagroup. com. Subway B, D, F, N, Q, R, V, W to 34th Street.
One of the most fabulous grocer's markets in New York, now famous for its supplies of lobster and caviar, also runs great restaurants.

Park Avenue Liquor Shop: 292 Madison Avenue between 40th and 41st Streets, 212-

Crate & Barrel

685 2442, www.parkaveliquor.com. Subway 4, 5, 6, 7 to Grand Central/42nd Street.
Family firm that specialises in Californian wines and European bottles. Discounts are given with bulk purchases.

Schumer's Wine & Liquor: 59 East 54th Street between Park and Madison Avenues, 212-355 0940, www.schumerswines.com. Subway E, F to Lexington Avenue; 6 to 51st Street.
With a great range of American and European wines, it also stocks a good selection of spirits and champagne.

HOMEWARE
Crate & Barrel: 650 Madison Avenue at 59th Street, 212-308 0011, www.crateandbarrel. com. Subway 4, 5, 6 to 59th Street.
Fashionable, funky furniture, accessories, kitchen and tableware for incredibly low prices. There's also another branch in SoHo at 611 Broadway at Houston Street.

SPECIALITY AND GIFTS
Midtown Comics: 2nd floor, 200 West 40th Street at 7th Avenue, 212-302 8192, www. midtowncomics.com. Subway 1, 2, 3, 7, N, Q, R, S, W to Times Square/42nd Street.
A 2-storey comic emporium with bags of back issues running up and down the length of the store. 500,000 volumes are available, from Japanese manga to Spider-Man.

NOHO
FASHION
Urban Outfitters: 628 Broadway between Houston and Bleecker Streets, 212-475 0009, www.urbanoutfitters.com. Subway F, V, S to Broadway/Lafayette Street; 6 to Bleecker Street.
The last word in cool, inexpensive clothes and vintage urban wear. There are quite a few stores in London now so it's not as special as it used to be, but still worth a visit for its mix of hip clothes, accessories and toys.

NOLITA
DISCOUNT STORES
INA: 21 Prince Street between Thompson and Spring Streets, 212-334 9048, www.inanyc. com. Subway C, E to Spring Street; N, R, W to Prince Street.
Women's designer resale stock that changes daily and offers discounts of 30–50% per item. You'll be able to get your hands on plenty of model cast-offs, from Manolo shoes to Prada. There's also a men's branch at 19 Prince Street, plus a men's and women's store at 15 Bleecker Street.

FASHION

Calypso Christiane Celle: 280 Mott Street between East Houston and Prince Street, 212-965 0990, www.calypsostbarth.com. Subway 6 to Spring Street.

A French boutique with a Caribbean influence, this shop is filled with designs from Christiane Celle. There's a riot of sexy silk slip dresses, tie-dye tops and cute beaded cardigans. Her newest store is at 654 Hudson Street in the Meatpacking District and there are seven others in the city – check the website for locations.

Sigerson Morrison: 28 Prince Street, 212-219 3893, www.sigersonmorrison.com. Subway B, D, F, V Broadway/Lafayette Street. Gorgeous shoes and bags designed by New York shoe connoisseurs Kari Sigerson and Miranda Morrison, who met while studying at the Fashion Institute of Technology in New York. They introduced the sister line BELLE by Sigerson Morrison, and ever since the irresistible flats, heels and boots have been snapped up by fans since, including Gisele Bundchen and Gwyneth Paltrow.

VINTAGE FASHION

Screaming Mimi: 382 Lafayette Street between 4th and Great Jones Streets, 212-677 6464, www.screamingmimis.com. Subway N, R to NYU 8th Street.

Everything from polyester dresses to denim shirts and tropical prints from the 1960s. There are also jewellery, sunglasses and other accessories, plus a home department upstairs in which to browse.

SOHO

ANTIQUES AND FLEA MARKETS

The SoHo Antiques Fair: Broadway and Grand Street, every Sat and Sun, year-round. Antiques and collectables all year round.

> **BRITTIP**
> If you're in the Big Apple on a Wed, check out the Fulton Street Plaza Flea Market at Cliff Street between Fulton and Beekham Streets near South Street Seaport. There's an outdoor market with around 25 dealers. 212-809 5000, www.keysfleamarket.com.

BEAUTY STORES AND SPAS

Acqua Beauty Bar: 7 East 14th Street between 5th Avenue and Union Square West, 212-620 4329, www.acquabeautybar.com. This hip beauty parlour in the ultra trendy Union Square area offers a full menu of nail,

body and face treatments from just $15 for a quick manicure and $75 for a Revitalist Eye Treatment (great for jet-lagged eyes).

Amore Pacific Beauty Gallery & Spa: 114 Spring Street between Mercer and Greene Streets, 212-966 0400, http://us.amorepacific-cosmetics.com.

A feng shui-influenced spa that uses Korean AP products and where you can have a massage according to your elemental disposition: wood, metal, earth, water or fire.

> **BRITTIP**
> Stores in SoHo tend to open some time between 10am and noon and stay open until 7pm Mon–Sat, while most open from noon to 6pm on Sun.

Aveda Institute: 233 Spring Street between 6th Avenue and Varick Street, 212-807 1492, www.aveda.com.

This is an appropriately tranquil setting in which to choose your favourite hair and skincare products. Aveda's holistic approach, using natural plant and flower extracts, is carried through all its products, including the make-up ranges and massage oils.

> **BRITTIP**
> The best anti-ageing facial in the Big Apple is the Intense Pulsed Light treatment at Shizuka, a Japanese day spa in Midtown East (7 West 51st Street, 6th Floor, 212-644 7400, www.shizukany.com).

Bliss Soho: 2nd Floor, 568 Broadway between Houston and Prince Streets, 212-219 8970, www.blissworld.com.

One of New York's most famous spas, this is the place where you can get it all and in the fastest possible time. You can have a manicure at the same time as your facial and even an underarm wax, too. Therein lies its

SoHo street market

TOP 5 SPAS FOR MINOR COSMETIC SURGERY

You're visiting one of the leading cities in the world for beauty treatments, including minor cosmetic surgeries such as laser eye treatment or Botox. Many tourists even combine a long weekend of shopping with a trip to a clinic so that they can return to the UK looking 10 years younger!

If you're considering a minor treatment, make sure that the spa or beauty centre is registered, book well in advance as they tend to get booked up quickly, and be sure to have a consultation prior to any treatment so that you understand exactly what you're getting. Below are 5 highly rated spas regularly used by New Yorkers, from celebrities to Upper East Side ladies who lunch.

Midtown

Smooth Synergy: 686 Lexington Avenue at East 57th Street, 212-397 0111, www.smoothsynergy.com. Subway 4, 5, 6 to 59th Street.
Laser hair and tattoo removal, microdermabrasion, Botox, vein therapy and glycolic peels are just some of the many treatments on offer at this highly regarded spa.

Upper East Side

Ajune: 1294 3rd Avenue at 74th Street, 212-628 0044, www.skinmdny.com. Subway 6 to 77th Street.
Experts in laser wrinkle reduction, collagen implants and Botox, all administered in a tranquil setting with slate floors and wooden features.

Dr Sam Rizk, director of Manhattan Facial Plastic Surgery: 1040 Park Avenue at 86th Street, 212-452 3362, www.drsamrizk.com. Subway 4, 5, 6 to Lexington Avenue.
That bump in your nose you've always wanted fixing? This is the man to call, considered one of the best in the business for rhinoplasty.

Dr Ronald Sherman/Trish McEvoy Skincare Centre: 4th Floor, 800A 5th Avenue at 61st Street, www.trishmcevoy.com, 212-758 7790. Subway N, R to 5th Avenue.
Laser hair removal, Botox and skin cancer examinations can be had at the make-up guru and top dermatologist's skincare Mecca.

Howard Sobel Skin & Spa: 960 Park Avenue at 82nd Street, 212-288 0060, www.drsobel.com. Subway 4, 5, 6 to 86th Street.
Award-winning specialists in Botox treatments.

down side, though – for some, it can seem too swift and impersonal.

Devachan: 425 Broome Street at Crosby Street, 212-274 8686, www.devachansalon.com.
Small salon where celebs come to get perfect locks and an amazing scalp massage. It also doubles as a spa.

✦ BRITTIP

Tracie Martyn is considered by many to be the best facialist in New York, using a massage technique that some – including Liv Tyler and Kate Winslet – say can leave you looking 10 years younger. 11th floor, 101 5th Avenue between East 17th and 18th Streets, 212-206 9333, www.traciemartyn.com.

Frédéric Fekkai: 394 West Broadway at Broadway, 212-888 2600, www.fekkai.com. Subway B, D, F, V to Broadway/Lafayette Streets; 6 to Spring Street.
A more relaxed vibe to the uptown hair salon, the SoHo branch is also a popular spot to get your make-up done, too. Open Tues–Sat.

Fresh: 57 Spring Street between Lafayette and Mulberry, 212-925 0099, www.fresh.com. Soaps, lotions and potions with lovely fragrances based on natural ingredients from the Boston company.

Kiehl's: 109 3rd Avenue between 13th and 14th Streets, 212-677 3171, www.kiehls.com. One of New York's most famous establishments, the crowds still flock to this emporium in the Union Square area for its luxurious moisturisers and lip balms.

MAC: 353 Mac on Bleecker Street, 212-255 0450, www.maccosmetics.com.
The wonder of this flagship store for MAC is as much in the architecture, lighting and displays as in the products. It sells all MAC products, including the MAC Pro range used by make-up artists on fashion shows and movie shoots, which are only available in a few of their outlets. During your visit you can either plump for a 45-minute makeover, complete with useful tips, or turn up with nothing but foundation on your face and let

TOP 5 FAMOUS US LABELS

SoHo

Alexander Wang: 103 Grand Street at Mercer Street, 212-977 9683, www.alexanderwang.com. Subway N, R to Prince Street.
One of the fashion world's favourite young designers, the San Fran original is also popular with the mainstream – Michelle Obama has worn him! Take a look in here for comfortable, edgy, wearable pieces that will instantly update your wardrobe, from leather jackets to baggy silk shorts, racer-back tank dresses and the perfect T-shirt. If you're not a shopper, you'll still appreciate the slabs of white marble floor, central hammock and black leather couches which, shock, you'll actually see customers (or rather their partners) using to sit and look at their phone or read a mag while the other half shops. Posh, yes, but also relaxed.

Marc Jacobs: 163 Mercer Street between Houston and Prince Streets, 212-343 1490, www.marcjacobs.com. Subway N, R to Prince Street.
The darling of supermodels and superwomen, such as movie director Sophia Coppella, Jacobs' style is minimalist and luxurious.

3.1 Phillip Lim: 115 Mercer Street, 212-334 1160, www.31philliplim.com. Subway N, R to Prince Street.
New Yorker whose drapey dresses and cool separates are spotted on the likes of Kate Bosworth, Lauren Conrad, Leighton Meester and Alexa Chung.

Upper East Side

Calvin Klein: 654 Madison Avenue at 60th Street, 212-292 9000, www.calvinkleininccom. Subway N, R to Lexington Avenue; 4, 5, 6 to 59th Street.
If you're looking for sleek, polished, understated American glamour in soothing neutrals and metallics (at high end prices), look no further.

Donna Karan: 819 Madison Avenue between East 68th and 69th Streets, 212-861 1001, www.donnakaran.com. Subway 6 to 68th Street.
A leading American designer who is best known for her elegant, simple outfits for women. The floating staircase is worth popping in for.

the artists finish off your make-up for free.

NYINTHEKNOW

Ying Chu, beauty & health director at *Marie Claire US* magazine, says, 'The new Aire Spa (88 Franklin Street nr Church Street, 212-274 3777) is a Spanish bathhouse taking up 3 floors in Tribeca. I love its many marble soaking pools (ice-cold to Jacuzzi-hot), all alight with flickering candles and lanterns. Opt for the public baths or splurge on a single or couples treatment in the private rooms.'

Mezzanine Spa at Soho Integrative Health Centre: 62 Crosby Street between Broome and Spring Streets, 212-334 8100, www.mezzaninespa.com.
Dr Laurie Polis founded this tiny spa at her office. Body treatments include volcanic mud therapy, while the Diamond Peel involves suction and microcrystals to exfoliate the face.

Prive: The Soho Grand, 310 West Broadway between Canal and Grand Streets, 212-274 8888, www.sohogrand.com.

Home of Laurent Dufourg, who looks after Gwyneth's hair when she's in town. His haircuts start at around $200.

Rose Alcido Day Spa: Suite 1005, 1133 Broadway between 25th and 26th Streets, 212-243 0432, www.rosealcido.com.
A teeny space that's become famous for Rose's signature Golden-Spoon facial. Following a full facial, 2 hot spoons are used to massage the face, giving an intense, penetrating treatment.

SCO: 5th Floor, 584 Broadway near Prince Street, 212-966 3011, www.scocare.com. Subway N, R to Prince Street.
Stands for Skin-Care Options, of which there are many. Lots of custom-blended concoctions including face products and sun blocks.

Sephora: 555 Broadway between Prince and Spring Streets, 212-625 1309, www.sephora.com.
One of many New York outlets of this pristine, clean French beauty chain, which has become a sure-fire hit, thanks to its incredibly broad range, sparkling presentations and low-key staff who can provide plenty of help and advice when requested. This is the best place to get your favourite American brands, such

as Benefit, Hard Candy, Nars and Philosophy.

SoHo Sanctuary: 3rd Floor, 119 Mercer Street at Princes Street, 212-334 4197, www.sohosanctuary.com.
Fabulous massages in this mellow favourite of the fashion pack. There are also yoga and Pilates classes, plus a steam room.

DISCOUNT STORES

Pearl River Mart: 477 Broadway between Broome and Grand Streets, 212-431 4770, www.pearlriver.com. Subway R, W at Prince Street.
Once in Chinatown, now more fashion-conscious SoHo, its Asian-inspired clothes and homewares are still at bargain prices. Pick up paper lanterns, bamboo blinds, satin slippers, chopstick and rice bowl sets and mandarin-collared jackets for low, low prices.

> ◀▚▶ **BRITTIP**
>
> Most of the department and discount stores featured also have fantastic online offers with nominal overseas package payment, so you can shop in the UK, too!

SHOPPING AND BEAUTY

FASHION

Adidas Originals Store: 136 Wooster Street near Prince Street, 212-673 0398, www.adidas.com. Subway C, E to Prince Street.
If you have a penchant for old-school trainers and sportswear, then this is the place.

Alexander Wang: (see p147, Top 5 US designers)

Bloomingdale's

Amsterdam: 454 Broadway, 212-925 0422. Subway 6, N, V, Q to Canal Street.
Cheap and cheerful fashion store that promises prices from $10 up. Worth popping in for a rummage around.

Anna Sui: 113 Greene Street between Prince and Spring Streets, 212-941 8406, www.annasui.com. Subway N, R to Prince Street.
Get the glamour-with-a-hint-of-grunge look with dresses, skirts, blouses, boots and scarves. The small collection for men includes trousers, shirts and jackets from the outrageously loud to the positively restrained.

Anne Fontaine: 677 Madison Avenue near 62nd Street, 212-421 0947, www.annefontaine.com. Subway 4, 5, 6 to 59th Street.
Just the place to snap up the perfect white shirt.

> ▚▞ **NYINTHEKNOW**
>
> Who better to give some tips on shopping in the Big Apple than Mary Slevin, fashion manager at New York PR firm Harrison & Shriftman (www.hs-pr.com). 'I like SoHo. Walking from Broadway to West Broadway on streets like Wooster and Greene you'll find some really cute stores like Alice + Olivia. I also like Flying A (www.flyinganyc.com); another good vintage shop is What Goes Around Comes Around (www.whatgoesaroundnyc.com) in SoHo. For homewares, the Conran Shop (www.conranusa.com) on East 59th Street at 1st Avenue, and for great shoes, check out Chuckies (www.chuckiesnewyork.com), 1169 Madison Avenue.'

APC: 131 Mercer Street near Prince Street, 212-966 9685, www.apc.fr. Subway N, R to Prince Street.
Men's and women's functional city clothes, such as shirt dresses, crisp shirts and jackets and trench coats, sold in a trendy loft.

Banana Republic: 550 Broadway between Spring and Prince Streets, 212-925 0308, www.bananarepublic.com. Subway N, R to Prince Street.
A classy chain, famous for classic clothing in feel-good fabrics such as cashmere, suede, velvet and soft cotton at affordable prices. The best buys are in the frequent sales.

Bloomingdale's: 504 Broadway between Spring and Broome Streets, 212-729 5900, www.bloomingdales.com. Subway N, R to Prince Street.

Shopping in SoHo

Aimed at Lower Manhattan's trendy set, this 6-level SoHo branch of the world-famous store offers something for everyone, with plenty of different designer lines.

Burberry: 131 Spring Street between Greene and Wooster Streets, 212-925 9300, www.burberry.com. Subway C, E to Spring Street. Don't miss this younger outlet of the trendy British company for rainwear, leather, trench dresses, bags, shoes and casual wear.

🇬🇧 **BRITTIP**

SoHo is the place to take a trip to if you're looking for quirky, one-off clothing that you can be sure no one back home will have. Its streets are lined with boutique designer shops and have stores from some of the world's leading designers.

Club Monaco: 520 Broadway at Spring Street, 212-941 1511, www.clubmonaco.com. Subway 6 to Spring Street.
Once a Canadian company offering high fashion at high street prices, Ralph Lauren loved it so much he bought it. Now it offers chic, preppy separates that are still very much a bargain.

Curve: 83 Mercer Street at Spring Street, 212-966 3626, www.shopcurve.com. Subway 6 to Spring Street.
This womenswear boutique is a great place to head for wardrobe classics, such as the little black dress, albeit with a designer label price

tag. Browse hip labels like Balmain, Current Eliot and Carven. There's also top quality bags, jewellery and shoes and a same-day-delivery service if you're going for a big shop and don't want to cart bags around.

Eileen Fisher: 395 West Broadway between Spring and Broome Streets, 212-431 4567, www.eileenfisher.com. Subway A, C, E to Canal Street.
Casual, maintenance-free clothing that travels anywhere. Lots to choose from, such as T-shirts, jackets, skirts and the co-ordinating colour palettes make matching up items a dream. Lots of other outlets around the city, including Upper East Side and Midtown.

Helmut Lang: 93 Mercer Street between Spring and Broome Streets, 212-242 3240, www.helmutlang.com. Subway N, R to Prince Street.
A stark, white gallery-like space that contrasts well with the designer's dark creations for men and women. It's pricey – think $500 upwards – but items like tuxedo jackets and shoes are exquisite.

J Crew: 99 Prince Street between Mercer and Greene Streets, 212-966 2739, www.jcrew.com. Subway N, R to Prince Street.
American-style men's and women's clothes plus shoes and accessories.

Kate Spade: 454 Broome Street at Mercer Street, 212-274 1991, www.katespade.com. Subway N, R to Prince Street.
This flagship store is large and light and

TOP 5 STORES FOR MENSWEAR

Ascot Chang: 110 Central Park South, 212-759 3333, www.ascotchang.com. Subway F to 57th Street.
Known as New York's finest shirt-maker, the store also makes suits and overcoats, too. It's a real investment buy as Ascot Chang items don't date and last forever – but they are pricey. If you're not feeling flush, there are off-the-rack pieces, too, from shirts to pyjamas.

Brooks Brothers: 346 Madison Avenue at 44th Street, 212-682 8800, www.brooksbrothers.com. Subway E, V at 5th Avenue.
Something for every man at this all-American flagship store. There are hundreds of outfits, plus accessories to check out and a made-to-measure service. A very famous American label known for its preppy and Ivy League type customers, it offers a great range of luxurious suits, shirts and jackets along with cashmere sweaters, polo shirts and blazers. This is the place to come if you're looking for sophisticated menswear with a unique American style.

Duncan Quinn: 8 Spring Street between Bowery and Elizabeth Streets, 212-226 7030, www.duncanquinn.com. Subway C, E to Spring Street.
For those that believe exciting clothes shopping isn't just for women, this menswear treasure is packed full of brightly patterned suits, ties and shirts all expertly crafted. There are also some excellent shoes on offer. The store is in the process of closing down and Duncan Quinn will be moving to new premises just around the corner in Kenmare Street; check the website for more details.

Sean: 199 Prince Street, 212-598 5980, www.seanstore.com. Subway 1, 9 to Houston
A superb range of menswear for work and play at low prices, from colourful shirts to wool sports jackets.

Tom Ford: 845 Madison Avenue at 70th Street, 212-359 0300. Subway 6 at 66th Street/Hunter College.
A one-stop shop for stylish men everywhere, the man who made Gucci sexy again has made this store a big hit. The ground floor stocks 3-piece suits, colognes and dress shirts in 350 colours. Upstairs, via a velvet-lined lift, there's a made-to-measure service and 3 private rooms where you can have items customised, from shirts and ties to tennis shorts and even pyjamas. Lots of lovely accessories, too, such as sunglasses and cufflinks.

filled with goodies, from brightly coloured shift dresses, to soft-as-butter handbags and purses to shoes, sunglasses and even a small selection of stationery.

NYINTHEKNOW

Ying Chu, beauty & health director at Marie Claire US magazine, says, 'I find vintage shopping in the city greatly overpriced so nothing beats finding a bargain at the Housing Works (www.housingworks.org) thrift shops. There are about a dozen locations in the city, but stick to the neighbourhoods where much of the fashion set reside – Chelsea, Gramercy Park, Upper East Side – for serious designer finds. Make sure to check out the online auctions, too.'

Le Sportsac SoHo: 176 Spring Street, 212-334 6021, www.lesportsac.com. Subway C, E to Spring Street.
US label that's a leader in the bags, luggage and accessories market. It's all high-performance, washable and hard wearing, and very cool. Japanese hipsters tend to hunt this store out, coveting lightweight nylon bags with lots of pockets, zips and a range of bright colours. Look for the one-off collectables from designers such as Stella McCartney, Diane Von Furstenberg and Gwen Stefani.

Marc Jacobs: p147.

Miss Mooz: 458 Broadway at Grand Street, 212-966 3287, www.infinityshoes.com. Subway 6, N, R, Q to Canal Street.
If you love fashionable shoes at reasonable prices, stop by Miss Mooz.

Patricia Field: 306 Bowery at East Houston Street, 212-966 4066, www.patriciafield.com. Subway A, 6 to Bleecker Street.
Once only famous for her outrageous club clobber, Patricia created much of the fashion for the *Sex And The City* girls. So if you want to emulate Carrie, Samantha or Miranda, then come here to stock up on cool bags and jewellery worn by the cast.

Philosophy Alberta Ferretti: 452 West Broadway near Prince Street, 212-460 5500,

www.philosophy.it. Subway C, E to Spring Street.
The younger, more affordable line from top designer Alberta Ferretti.

Pleats Please: 128 Wooster Street at Prince Street, 212-226 3600, www.pleatsplease.com. Subway N, R to Prince Street.
Issey Miyake's tightly pleated skirts, tops, scarves and trousers can be found here.

Prada New York Epicenter: 575 Broadway at Prince Street, 212-334 8888, www.prada.com. Subway N, R, W to Prince Street.
Art is the byword of this incredible $40m flagship store for Prada. Once the Guggenheim's SoHo museum, the 2-level space has been designed by architect Rem Koolhaas and includes a zebrawood 'wave' in the entry hall and shoe display steps that can be converted into auditorium seating. Other neat design elements include dressing rooms behind a wall that switches from translucent to transparent (be warned!) and clothes suspended from the ceiling in metal cages.

Splendid: 111 Spring Street at Mercer Street, 212-966 6600, www.splendid.com/store. Subway N, R, W to Prince Street.
New boutique selling cool preppy-looking separates for men, women and children.

Stella McCartney New York: 112 Greene Street between Prince and Broome streets, 212-255 1556, www.stellamccartney.com. Subway N, R, W to Prince Street.
The famous daughter of a Beatle moved on from shaking up fashion at Chloe to designing under her own label to great acclaim. Her NY store attracts the likes of Rihanna and Gwyneth Paltrow hen they are shopping in town.

Topshop: 478 Broadway at Broome Street, 212-966 9555, www.topshop.com. Subway N, R, W to Prince Street.
The store is as big as the flagship store in London and houses just as many exciting young designers at excellent prices. You can also have your nails done here, get a bite to eat and see a style advisor.

FOOD AND DRINK
Dean & Deluca: 560 Broadway at Prince Street, 212-226 6800, www.deandeluca.com. Subway N, R, Q, W to Prince Street.
Gourmets love the fresh bread, cheese, coffee beans and other delicious foods on sale at this SoHo secret.

HOMEWARE
Anthropologie: 375 West Broadway at Spring Street, 212-343 7070, www.anthropologie.com. Subway C, E to Spring Street.

TOP PLACES TO GET YOUR CLOTHES MADE TO MEASURE
LS Men's Clothing: 49 West 45th Street, 212-575 0933, www.lsmensclothing.com. Subway C to 50th Street.
Made-to-measure services on classic suits, sports jackets, overcoats and tuxedos.

Mary Adams: 31 East 32nd Street, 212-473 0237, www.maryadamsthedress.com. Subway F, J, M, Z at Delancey Street/Essex Street.
A fascinating shop bursting with dresses full of lace, ruffles, satin and feathers. You'll feel like you've stepped into the Moulin Rouge wardrobe and you can even get your own custom-made creation to wow your friends back home.

Ripplu: 66 Madison Avenue, 212-599 2223, www.ripplu.com. Subway S, 4, 5, 6, 7 to 42nd Street/5th Avenue.
Nip and tuck too scary and expensive? Never fear, your prayers for a better bod have been answered courtesy of Ripplu, the New York women's secret lingerie store. Their custom-made bras and pants lift and reshape those wobbly bits; they even offer free alterations.

One of my favourite shops selling gorgeous boudoir items, such as silk quilts, Venetian-style mirrors and night stands, in an airy loft-like space. There's also a collection of stylish women's clothes on sale with the same thrift-store, trendy feel. Other outlets have opened around the city, including 1 of the Upper East Side, but this was the original in NYC. Check website for details.

VINTAGE FASHION
Legacy: 109 Thompson Street, 212-966 4827, www.legacy-nyc.com. Subway C, E to Spring Street.
Choice selection of expensive vintage dresses, hats and bags. You have to ring the bell to get in, but once inside it's not intimidating, so do ring!

Second Time Around: 111 Thompson at Prince Street, 212-925 3919, www.secondtimearound.net. Subway N, R to Prince Street.
Marni, Gucci and Givenchy are all vintage finds you might find in this friendly store.
Transfer International/Rag Nation: 71 Broadway, Suite 1002, between Prince and Houston Streets, 212-941 5472, www.rag-nation.com. Subway N, R to Prince Street.
Specialises in Gucci, Prada, Chanel and Hermès – a great place to buy post-worn designer clothes and accessories. They

also carry Celine and Stella McCartney occasionally.

⚡ BRITTIP

If you're in SoHo shopping and need to take a load off (carrying all those bags can be tiring!) but don't want to fork out for a fancy restaurant or café, there's a row of permanent chairs and tables with chess boards on top beneath trees on the corner of Thompson and Spring Streets. Locals take sandwiches and a beer to sit and chat in the shade.

TRIBECA

ANTIQUES AND FLEA MARKETS

Antiqueria Tribeca: 129 Duane Street near Broadway, 212-227 7500, www.antiqueria. com. Subway 1, 2, 3, 9, A, C to Chambers Street.
Filled with French Art Deco pieces, from furniture to accessories. Often some lovely Lalique and Murano glass items to be found.

Jonathan Burden LLC: 180 Duane Street near Houston Street, 212-941 8247, www.jonathanburden.com. Subway 1, 2, 3, 9, A, C to Chambers Street.
Extremely pricey, high-end, one-of-a-kind pieces of furniture to gaze at in awe.

FASHION

Steven Alan: 103 Franklin Street between Church Street and West Broadway, 212-343 0692, www.stevenalan.com. Subway 1 to Franklin Street.
A small but perfectly formed boutique filled

The Art of Shaving

to the rafters with up to 100 up-and-coming and more established designers from ACNE to Wendy Nichol. Also A.P.C and Isabel Marant.

Tribeca Issey Miyake: 119 Hudson Street at North Moore Street, 212-226 0100, www.tribecaisseymiyake.com. Subway 1, 2 to Franklin Street.
The new Prada store got the old Guggenheim Museum space in SoHo: Issey Miyake got Frank Gehry, the architect of the amazing Guggenheim Museum in Bilbao. Now serious shoppers mingle with art buffs who come to see the titanium tornado that swirls through this 2-storey, 279m²/3,000ft² boutique, plus art by Gehry's son Alejandro. Fortunately, the purpose of the shop has not been forgotten and the entire Issey collection is here, including the Pleats Please, Haat, A/POC and fragrance lines. What's more, the staff are actually helpful. A truly wonderful experience – especially if you can afford $1,600 for a shirt. Otherwise, wait for the sales!

⚡ BRITTIP

Americans still measure in feet and inches – good news for older Brits.

VINTAGE FASHION

Geminola: 41 Perry Street near 7th Avenue, 212-675 1994, www.geminola.com. Subway 1, 9 to Christopher Street.
Owner Lorraine Kirke travels the world for vintage fabrics, then reworks and dyes them to create gorgeous and unique clothing. Skirts from $165 and accessories and belts from Afghanistan and handbags from India at around $295.

UNION SQUARE

BOOKS

Barnes & Noble: 105 5th Avenue at 18th Street, 212-675 5500, www.bnnewyork.com. Subway L, N, R, 4, 5, 6 to 14th Street/Union Square.
This is the original store of one of the largest chains of bookstores in America and offers a massive selection of books, CDs and DVDs. Barnes & Noble is responsible for putting many independent bookstores out of business, but is well worth a visit. Many branches have coffee shops and seating areas for you to browse before buying. You'll see branches everywhere.

Books of Wonder: 18 West 18th Street at 5th Avenue, 212-989 3270, www. booksofwonder.com. Subway 1 at 18th Street. Top place in New York to go for children's books, limited editions and art from children's literature. There are rare collector's editions through to picture pop-ups, and as many adults flock here as kids. There's a storytelling time for children every Sun at noon and every Fri 4–5pm.

◣◢ BRITTIP
If shopping's sapping your energy and you're feeling in need of a sugar rush, tuck into some of the delicious desserts and pastries at the Cupcake Cafe in Books of Wonder.

Strand Book Store: 828 Broadway at 12th Street, 212-473 1452, www.strandbooks.com. Subway L, N, R, Q, W, 4, 5, 6 to 14th Street/ Union Square.
This whole area used to be famous for antiquarian bookshops, but the Strand is the only one left. The store has over 2 million second-hand and new books on any subject you'd care to name – all at around half the published price.

FASHION
Joe Fresh: 110 5th Avenue at 16th Street, 212-366 0960, www.joefresh.com. Subway 4, 5, 6, L, N, R, Q to Union Square.
Great for basics, like striped Breton tops and denim shorts, for both sexes. Starting prices from just $12. Accessories, too, including shoes and bags.

◣◢ BRITTIP
For the best shave a man can have in New York, take a seat and join the queue in one of three The Art of Shaving barber shops (305-593 0667, www.theartofshaving.com) located around the city. You can get every type of shave imaginable, including a hot, straight-edged Royal Shave, at these Victorian-style outlets.

FOOD AND DRINK
Union Square Wine and Spirits: 140 Fourth Avenue at 13th Street, 212-675 8100, www.unionsquarewines.com. Subway 4, 5, 6, L, N, Q, R, W to Union Square.
More than 4,000 wines, good prices and the staff know their stock and subject. Wine tastings most Sat.

UPPER EAST SIDE

BEAUTY STORES AND SPAS
Caron: at 715 Lexington Avenue, 877-882 2766, www.parfumscaron.com. Subway 6 to 59th Street.

The complete range of glitzy, crystal-bottled French Caron fragrances, from $80 upwards in the Phyto Universe store.
Charming Nails: 212 East 87th Street at 3rd Avenue, 212-987 7239.
A beauty editor's secret, who know that you get spa-quality results for budget prices here.
L'Occitane: 1046 Madison Avenue at 80th Street, 212-639 9185, www.loccitane.com. Subway 6 to 77th Street.
Ultra-luxurious bath and beauty products from the famous French company. Also branches at 510 Madison at 52nd Street and 1288 Madison at 92nd Street.

DEPARTMENT STORES
Barneys: 660 Madison Avenue at 61st Street, 212-826 8900, www.barneys.com. Subway N, R, W to 5th Avenue; 4, 5, 6 to Lexington. Open 10am–8pm every weekday.
A truly up-to-the-minute fashion outlet, this store is filled with all the top designers and a good selection of newer ones. There isn't really a Brit equivalent; the nearest would be Harvey Nichols, but it doesn't come close. It has 8 floors of fashion where there's everything from big-name designers to more obscure, but very hip, small labels. There is a branch called Coop on 18th Street in Chelsea, and another one at the World Financial Center in Downtown, but this is the $100m megastore. Treat yourself to a trip to the Image Studio if you've got the time and money to get a whole new look before heading home. Don't miss it!

◣◢ BRITTIP
If you plan to be in New York in Aug or Mar, go to the Barneys Warehouse Sale – call ahead for locations or check www.barneys.com.

Barneys

Bloomingdale's: 1000 3rd Avenue between 59th and 60th Streets, 212-705 2000, www.bloomingdales.com. Subway 4, 5, 6 to 59th Street; N, R to Lexington Avenue. Bloomies is probably the most famous of all 5th Avenue's department stores. You can have a signature gift, collected from the state-of-the-art visitor centre if you can show a $300 or more same-day receipt, you can also have a hotel package delivery with every $250 purchase, there's currency exchange and you can even buy theatre and Metro Cards here! A truly glitzy shop filled with all the right designers, you can now also sample its delights at the SoHo branch (p148).

BRITTIP
Weekdays before lunchtime are the least crowded time to visit Bloomingdale's and the upper floors tend to be less crowded.

FASHION

agnès b: 1063 Madison Avenue, 212-570 9333, www.agnesb.com. Subway 6 at 77th Street.
Superb designs for women and children here – simple but stunning and beautifully cut. Also take a look at 50 Howard Street in SoHo.

American Apparel: 1090 3rd Avenue between 64th and 65th Streets (and 12 other outlets in New York), 212-772 7462, www.americanapparel.net. Subway N, R, W, 4, 5, 6, Lexington Av/63rd Street.
Stocks a huge selection of cool casual wear, from T-shirts to bikinis and jersey dresses. Other stores around the city, see website for details.

Billy Martin's Western Wear: 220 East 60th Street, 212-861 3100, www.billymartin.com. Subway 6 to 68th Street.
Everything for the posh cowboy.

Calvin Klein: p147.

Diesel: 770 Lexington Avenue at 60th Street, 212-308 0055, www.diesel.com. Subway N, R to Lexington Avenue 4, 5, 6 to 59th Street.
A massive store in which you'll find everything from denim to vinyl clothing, shoes and accessories.

Donna Karan: p147.

Giorgio Armani: 760 Madison Avenue at 65th Street, 212-988 9191, www.giorgioarmani.com. Subway 6 to 68th Street.
A huge boutique that sells all 3 of Armani's lines. Come here to find well-tailored classics.

Olive & Bettes: 1249 3rd Avenue between 71st and 72nd Streets, 212-206 0036, www.oliveandbettes.com. Subway 6 to 59th Street.

Pink and white striped walled emporium selling colourful jersey and floaty dresses with a small selection of choice jewellery, bags and shoes. Friendly staff and prices. There are three other outlets in the city including SoHo and Upper West Side. See website for details.

BRITTIP
Don't miss new shop Fivestory (18 East 69th Street near Madison Avenue, 212-288 1338), a townhouse converted into a small department store stocking 150 brands of clothing and accessories for women, men and kids. The brands are as high end as you'd expect in the Upper East Side, although maybe a little more fashion, such as Preen, Mark Fast and Balmain, plus some edgier, lesser-known labels. The 5 floors are connected by a marble staircase and there's a shoe garden featuring more than a dozen designers.

Ralph Lauren: 867 Madison Avenue at East 72nd Street, 212-606 2100, www.ralphlauren.com. Subway 6 to 68th Street.
The men's flagship store and worth a visit just to see the building – it's in an old Rhinelander mansion and is decorated with everything from Oriental rugs to riding whips, leather chairs and English paintings. The clothes are of excellent quality, too, and the women's flagship store is just up the road at 888 Madison Avenue.

BRITTIP
If you're looking for a cute (and cheap) gift to take home, take a look at the massive cookies near the checkout kiosks at Grace's Food Market. From Big Apples to flower and cupcake shapes, they're beautifully iced and tightly wrapped in cling film so should last a flight home (providing you don't eat them first).

FOOD AND DRINK

Grace's Market Place: 1237 3rd Avenue at 71st Street, 212-737 0600, www.gracesmarketplace.com. Subway 6 to 59th Street. This is probably the best supermarket you'll ever go in. Bursting with the best produce worldwide (I spotted jam from Tiptree in the UK in the condiments section!) it's foodie heaven, from the specialist cheeses to the tasty cakes, fish counter with clambakes and fresh lobster and fabulous meat counter, with huge roasted turkey legs, meatballs and ham hocks. The piles of giant, glistening olives are hard to resist, as is the gourmet salad bar. You can also dine on the delicious produce next door at Grace's Trattoria.

Martine's Chocolates: 400 82nd Street off 1st Avenue, 212-744 6289, www.martineschocolates.com. Subway 6 to 86th Street.
If you're not on a diet, drool over the rich Belgian choccies, which take up to 3 days to make. Chocolate heaven!

Sherry-Lehmann: 505 Park Avenue between 59th and 60th Streets, 212-838 7500, www.sherry-lehmann.com. Subway 4, 5, 6 to 59th Street.
The most famous wine shop in New York, established in 1934. A huge selection and well situated for that Central Park picnic.

The Vinegar Factory: 431 East 91st Street between York and 1st Avenues, 212-987 0885, www.elizabar.com. Subway 4, 5, 6 to 86th Street.
One of the most famous markets in the city. Here you'll find stacks of cheeses, meats, breads, salads and cakes – in fact, everything you need to create a perfect picnic.

HOMEWARE
Laytner's Linen and Home: 237 East 86th Street at 2nd Avenue, 212-996 4439, www.laytners.com. Subway 4, 5, 6 to 86th Street.
Come here to buy some luxurious high thread-count linen to take home.

SPECIALITY AND GIFTS
EAT Gifts: 1062 Madison Avenue at 80th Street, 212-861 2544, www.elizabar.com. Subway 6 to 77th Street.
You can hardly move for the shelves that are tightly packed with every conceivable gift, from gadgets to trinkets, a lot of it fun stuff for kids.

VINTAGE FASHION
BIS Designer Resale: 1134 Madison Avenue between 84th and 85th Streets on the second floor, 212-396 2760, www.bisbiz.com. Subway 4, 5, 6 to 86th Street.
For those that like a designer label but don't have the cash to splash, there is a shopping God. BIS is jammed with pieces that have only been worn once or sometimes never, from barely worn Manolos to Chanel quilted jackets. Stock is stored by items, such as shoes or skirts, but if you're after a specific label, such as Gucci, the staff will show you what's available. You may be beaten to some of the best bits by die hard fans who log on to the store's eBay site to snap up bargains. Prices are around 50% of the original value,

but while you're saving, don't forget that still means many 3-figure price tags.

Gentlemen's Resale: 322 East 81st Street between 1st and 2nd Avenues, 212-734 2739, www.gentlemensresaleclothing.com. Subway 6 to 77th Street.
Top-notch designer suits at a fraction of the original price.

ANTIQUES AND FLEA MARKETS
Green Flea Market: Columbus Avenue between West 76th and 77th Streets on Sun 10am–5.30pm and Greenwich Avenue at Charles Street between West 10th and 11th Streets on Sun 10am–5.30pm and, 212-239 3025, www.greenfleamarkets.com. Subway 1, 9 to 79th Street; B, C to 77th/81st Street.
Antiques, collectables, bric-a-brac, handmade pottery and discount clothing in this indoor and outdoor market.

BEAUTY STORES AND SPAS
Fashion 74 Nails: 303 Amsterdam Avenue at 74th Street, 212-799 5252.
Where those in the know get their nails done – even, it's rumoured, other spa owners!

FOOD AND DRINK
Acker, Merrall & Condit Wine Merchants: 160 West 72nd Street between Broadway and Columbus, 212-787 1700, www.ackerstore.com. Subway 1, 2, 3, 9 to 72nd Street.
America's oldest wine store – it opened in 1820 – is well worth a visit for its vast selection of wines from around the world that range in price from a couple of dollars to more than $20,000. In-store tastings.

> **BRITTIP**
> You can only buy wine and spirits from liquor stores, which do not sell mixers or even beer!

HOMEWARE
Avventura: 463 Amsterdam Avenue at 82nd Street, 212-769 2510, www.forthatspecialgift.com. Subway A, 9 to 79th Street.
Contemporary tableware, from cocktail and champagne glasses to Deruta dishes.

BOOKS
Left Bank Books: 17 8th Avenue at 12th Street, 212-239 3025, www.leftbankbookny.com. Subway A, C, E, L to 14th Street/8th Avenue
Specialises in first editions, particularly for fiction, poetry and drama), photography, art,

music and film; the reasonable prices and friendly staff make this a pleasant place to stop and scour the shelves for an hour.

WOODBURY COMMON PREMIUM OUTLETS

It's no exaggeration to say that shopaholics from around the world call in at this American colonial-style village that's just a 1½-hour bus ride away from Manhattan. With more than 220 discount shops, it's the equivalent of paradise. For ordinary folk, it's still a wonderful place to make useful and fun purchases. Midweek is the quietest time to visit.

WOODBURY COMMON SHOPPING

- ✉ 498 Red Apple Court, Central Valley
- ☎ 1-845 928 4000
- 🖰 www.premiumoutlets.com/woodburycommon
- 🕐 Mon–Sat 10am–9pm, Sun 10am–8pm (check the website for seasonal and holiday hours)

Upon arrival by Gray Line coach (303/394-6920, www.grayline.com), you'll be dropped off close to the tower entrance where you'll also find the information office, pushchairs (essential with a young child on a hot day), lockers, telephones, cashpoints and WCs.

Pick up a copy of the full-colour *Shopping Guide* (or download one from the website before you go) and in the centre you'll find a map with the 5 different sections in different colours. The colour coding is carried throughout the village, so as you walk around you can work out which area you are in by the colour of the apple above each shop sign.

The information tower is in the main red section, called Red Apple Court, which is largely dedicated to designer boutiques; to its south is Evergreen Court, home to many lifestyle stores; to the north of Red Apple Court is the Food Court and then Bluebird Court. To the left from the main entrance is the purple Grapevine Court.

Filled with the most upscale designer shops, Grapevine Court is serious droolsville territory and the first port of call for Japanese shoppers, who tend to be known as Goochers thanks to their love of Gucci. Here you'll find Dior, Fendi, Giorgio Armani General Store, Hugo Boss, Missoni, Off 5th – Saks 5th Avenue, La Perla, Valentino and the Thyme To Eat Restaurant. The Cosmetics Company Store here has great deals on many brands including Clinique, Estée Lauder, Bobbi Brown, MAC, Prescriptives and Origins.

Big names in Red Apple Court include A/X Armani Exchange, Burberry, Brooks Brothers, Carolina Herrera, Donna Karan/DKNY, Escada, Giorgio Armani, Gucci, Liz Claiborne, Polo Ralph Lauren, Salvatore Ferragamo and Versace.

Good shops that you should make a beeline for in the Bluebird Court are Claire's Accessories, Bombay Outlet, Puma, LeSportsac, Bebe and Nike Factory Store.

SALES TIMES

You can save even more money on your favourite labels by heading to Woodbury at sales times. Before you go, visit www.premiumoutlets.com/woodburycommon to check out the next sales date – there's usually one a month. However, the big sales times coincide with all the American holidays including 4 July, Memorial Day, President's Day, Labor Day Weekend, Columbus Day and the day after Thanksgiving (p259).

Best time of all, though, is around Christmas, when some of the biggest savings are to be had – along with the biggest crowds, so arrive early!

SHOPPING AND BEAUTY

Woodbury Common Shopping

CHAPTER 7

Restaurants

New York is a city of extremes when it comes to dining out. There are around 20,000 restaurants to choose from. At one end are the classics, such as Union Square Café, that seem to transcend fashion and continually turn out delicious cuisine to cross the Atlantic for; at the other end of the spectrum are eateries that are so hip they're practically going out of fashion before they've even served up their first plate of fusion food.

Brit Guide aims to help you to experience the must-eat-at places that have been around for years and those achingly hip joints that are as much about who you're going to spot air kissing as the food. We also include a smattering of restaurants that sit between the established and the new that are just plain good value – or unusual.

🇬🇧 BRITTIP

New Yorkers swear by the *Zagat Survey* as the best guide for foodies. It lists hundreds of top restaurants reviewed by members of the public, and you can buy it in most UK bookshops, or visit www.zagat.com.

One of the great things about New York restaurants is that they're usually excellent value for money when compared with eating out in the UK, particularly London. You can get a first class breakfast for under $10 and a slap-up dinner for less than $40. It's well worth heading off the beaten track to find some of your own delectable diners in the city's coolest neighbourhoods, but we have plenty of suggestions for you if you don't fancy chancing it. The chapter starts with a selection of our favourite restaurants for fine dining, romance and views, categories that cover the majority of enquiries we receive from Brits keen to sample the culinary delights of Manhattan in a wonderful environment.

DINING PRICE GUIDE

It's clear from the outset what price categories many Big Apple eateries fall into. Crisp white tablecloths, wine glasses the size of goldfish bowls and waiters in designer garb indicate a blow-the-budget $100-plus bill. Dark, dingy diners with Formica tabletops and a waitress with a nametag suggest that

Le Bernadin

you're going to be paying cash, and not much of it. However, there are some restaurants where the tariff doesn't match the decor or the standard of food the façade, so we have compiled a price guide to help you make your dining decisions with confidence.

$ Cheap and cheerful
$$ Good value
$$$ Posh meal out
$$$$ Blow the budget

BRITTIP

If you're a foodie, visit New York during Restaurant Week (see website for exact dates: there's more than one), when more than 100 of the city's best restaurants offer 3-course prix fixe meals for bargain prices around $24 for lunch and $35 for dinner. (212-484 1222, www.nycgo.com/restaurantweek).

A–Z AREA-BY-AREA GUIDE TO RESTAURANTS

BATTERY PARK AND BATTERY PARK CITY

2 WEST $$–$$$
Gourmet American
- ✉ 2 West Street between Battery Place and West End
- ☎ 212-344 0800
- 🖰 www.ritzcarlton.com
- 🚇 Subway 1, 9 to Rector Street

The lobby-level restaurant of the Ritz-Carlton has fabulous views of the Hudson River and Statue of Liberty, plus outdoor seating for al fresco dining in the warmer months. Menu is full of classic comfort food, such as lobster bisque, croque monsieur, organically fed salmon and oven-roasted free-range chicken. There's a vast wine list and the lunch menu also offers quick and easy Bento Boxes with Italian and Spanish themes. The Sun brunch, from 11am–2.30pm, is $39 per person but it's so big you won't need dinner.

BATTERY GARDENS $$$–$$$$
American fusion
- ✉ South-west corner of Battery Park (State Street) by the river
- ☎ 212-809 5508
- 🖰 www.batterygardens.com
- 🚇 Subway 1, 9 to South Ferry

A superb American restaurant in an elegant, glass building that shows off the spectacular views of the Hudson and East rivers and the Statue of Liberty from every table. Tuck into

tuna tartare, New England clam chowder and wood oven roast chicken. In good weather you can eat outside on the terrace. If you can't get in at night, book the excellent Sunday brunch, 11am–3pm.

GIGINO AT WAGNER PARK $$
Italian
- ✉ 20 Battery Place at Hudson River
- ☎ 212-528 2228
- 🖰 www.gigino-wagnerpark.com
- 🚇 Subway 1, 9 to South Ferry

Great little café/diner with outside dining near the Museum of Jewish Heritage in the relatively new Robert Wagner Junior Park. Great views of the harbour and Statue of Liberty while you tuck into delicious dishes like bruschetta ($10.50) or calamari fritti ($13).

BRITTIP

If you want a cheaper pit stop than Gigino while in Battery Park City, opt for items from the snack cart in Wagner Park.

NORTH END GRILL $$–$$$
American–Seafood
- ✉ 104 North End Avenue between Murray and Vesey Streets
- ☎ 646-747 1600
- 🖰 www.northendgrillnyc.com
- 🚇 Subway 6 to Bleecker Street

A 2012 opening in the Financial District that has gone down well with locals. Chef Floyd Cardoz is at the helm, packing the menu with succulent dishes like lobster omelette and poached egg floating in a sea of caviar. To watch the action, book a table at the chef's station.

BROOKLYN

BROOKLYN STAR $$–$$$
American comfort–Southern soul food
- ✉ 593 Lorimer Street near Conselyea Street
- ☎ 718-599 9899
- 🖰 http://thebrooklynstar.com
- 🚇 Subway A, C to High Street/Brooklyn Bridge

Wood floors and tables dominate this large, airy space, which manages to be fashionable yet laid back. Expect hearty fare, such as smoked marrow bones and shrimps and grits, which you can enjoy over a long, lazy lunch or late at night, as the full menu is served until 2am, 7 days a week, making this a good place to head after a night out if you're still starving – plus the bar serves some excellent cocktails.

DI FARA $-$$
Pizza
✉ 1424 Avenue J
☎ 718-258 1367
🖰 www.difara.com
🚇 Subway Q to Avenue J

Cash-only pizza joint where legend Domenico De Marco whips up Neapolitan pies in a flour-dusted apron – which he's been doing for more than 4 decades. Critics far and wide rave about these pizzas and so will you.

GRIMALDI'S $
Italian
✉ Under the Brooklyn Bridge, 1 Front Street at the Brooklyn Bridge
☎ 718-858 4300
🖰 www.grimaldis.com
🚇 Subway A, C to High Street/Brooklyn Bridge

Their pizza has been rated number 1 in the city in the Zagat Survey in the past and I can confirm that it's delicious pizza at a great price. No credit cards, no reservations!

NOODLE PUDDING $$
Italian
✉ 38 Henry Street between Cranberry and Middagh Streets
☎ 218-625 3737
🚇 Subway A, C to High Street/Brooklyn Bridge

Despite its name, this is a dedicated Italian rather than an Asian eatery, and it's very good. Traditional dishes such as osso buco (veal knuckle) and penne arrabiata ensure that it attracts an Italian-American crowd and is constantly packed. It is also praised for its fine pizza. No credit cards and the house wine is $4 a glass.

PETER LUGER STEAKHOUSE $$-$$$
American
✉ 175 Broadway
☎ 718-387 7400
🖰 www.peterluger.com
🚇 Subway J, M, Z to Marcy Avenue

Rated New York's number 1 steakhouse for 28 years in a row, this really is the best place in town to get a prime cut. Serving since 1887 (yes, really), they claim the key to their success is only choosing the finest US prime meat through a rigid selection process – members of the family shop daily in the wholesale markets for fresh sides of beef straight from the Midwest. The proof, of course, is in the eating and it is rather fabulous. There's a fairly basic menu, such as rib steak, single steak and steak for 2 or 3, plus sides of perfectly cooked fried potatoes, onion rings and baked potato with sour cream. Save room for the Luger's special Holy Cow hot fudge sundae.

RIVER CAFÉ $$$
Gourmet American
✉ 1 Water Street under the Brooklyn Bridge
☎ 718-522 5200
🖰 www.rivercafe.com
🚇 Subway A, C to High Street/Brooklyn Bridge

If a panoramic view of the Manhattan skyline makes you feel romantic, and it does the majority of us, then the River Café on Brooklyn's waterfront is for you. Even better, the food matches up to the location – in fact, it's worth leaving Manhattan for. It celebrated its 30th anniversary in 2009, and still serves up superb dishes such as Maine lobster, River Café oysters, Wagyu steak and sautéed Hudson Valley foie gras. Open for brunch, lunch and dinner.

SUPERFINE $$-$$$
Mediterranean
✉ 126 Front Street between Jay and Pearl Streets, Dumbo
☎ 718-243 9005
🚇 Subway A, C, F to High Street

Cool is moving out of Manhattan, and this hip place proves it. Serves mainly Mediterranean fare, but is best known for its themed brunches. Oh, and there's an orange felt pool table, too.

TOTONNO'S PIZZERIA NAPOLITANO $-$$
Pizza
✉ 1524 Neptune Avenue between West 15th and 16th Streets
☎ 718-372 8606
🚇 Subway 6 to 77th Street

Opened in 1924 and still serving delicious pizza to hungry locals and tourists today.

CENTRAL PARK

THE BOATHOUSE AT CENTRAL PARK $$-$$$
American–Seafood
✉ Central Park Lake, Park Drive North at East 72nd Street
☎ 212-517 2233
🖰 www.thecentralparkboathouse.com
🚇 Subway 6 to 68th Street/Hunter College

This picture-book restaurant boasts one of the most wonderfully romantic locations in New York. Set right by a lake dotted with blue rowing boats in the heart of Central Park, circled by the famous high-rise skyline, the outside terrace provides a particularly gorgeous place to bag a seat at sunset. After dark, the restaurant's sparkling lights add to the romantic atmosphere. The mainly seafood menu isn't what you'd call adventurous, but it's delicious and well cooked, and *Zagat* recommends the tasting menu. There is also a roaring open fireplace in the bar for those wintry days, when you can almost feel as if you really were deep in the countryside. Be sure to book well in advance in the summer.

BRITTIP

Bottles of water can cost $10 at some of the pricier restaurants. Save your money! New York has access to the finest and cleanest tap water, direct from the Catskill Mountains upstate.

CHELSEA

BETTER BURGER NYC $-$$
Burgers
✉ 178 8th Avenue at 19th Street
☎ 212-989 6688
🖱 www.betterburgernyc.com
🚇 Subway C, E to 23rd Street
Low-fat, health-conscience, 100% organic, antibiotic-free and hormone-free fare – ostrich, turkey, chicken, soy and vegetarian burgers (and the classic beef) plus other options. Open 11am–11pm.

BOTTINO $$
Italian
✉ 246 10th Avenue between 24th and 25th Streets
☎ 212-206 6766
🖱 www.bottinonyc.com
🚇 Subway C, E to 23rd Street
This is the place to go if you want to see the chic art dealers in recreational mode. You can tuck into the delicious Tuscan cuisine, such as roast rack of lamb with rosemary, in either the minimalist dining room or the back garden.

If you don't have time to stop and eat, grab a sarnie to take away from the next-door Bottino to Go.

BUDDAKAN $$$–$$$$
Pan-Asian
✉ 75 9th Avenue at 16th Street
☎ 212-989 6699
🖱 www.buddakannyc.com
🚇 Subway 1, 2, 3, 9 to 14th Street
A Pan-Asian import from the successful restaurant in Philadelphia. It was introduced to New York by Stephen Starr and is watched over by consultant Angelo Sosa, formerly of Yumcha. The awe factor isn't just the food (delicacies like Cantonese spring rolls and steamed pork buns in bamboo containers), but the great hall, which has oak-covered walls 2 storeys high, huge chandeliers and a banquet table to seat 30. Expect seriously beautiful people and food.

CAFETERIA $$
American diner
✉ 119 7th Avenue at 17th Street
☎ 212-414 1717
🖱 www.cafeteriagroup.com
🚇 Subway 1, 9 to 18th Street
Another diner comfort-food experience, only this time filled with the hipsters who use the 24-hour hangout before and after hitting the local clubs.

COPPELIA $$
Cuban
✉ 207 West 14th Street between 7th and 8th avenues
☎ 212-858 5001
🖱 www.ybandco.com
🚇 Subway 1, 9 to 18th Street
Great restaurant diner that's fun and casual; think sunshine yellow walls and sky blue

RESTAURANTS

Bottino

shutters, open 24 hours and a bargain menu featuring interesting bites like fried yucca and empanadas. There are late night snacks such as burgers and stuffed tortillas, but more importantly don't miss the yummy desserts, like carrot cake with dulce de leche and salted caramel flan. There's also a long marble bar with swivel stools for hogging into the small hours.

LA PROMENADE DES ANGLAIS $$$–$$$$
French–Italian
✉ 461 West 23rd Street between 9th and 10th Avenues
☎ 212-255 7400
🖰 www.lapromenadenyc.com
🚇 Subway A, C, E, L to 14th Street/8th Avenue

The chic décor of this eatery is lovely – think blue velour banquettes and booths and gleaming dark wood. The food is adventurous, such as frogs' legs and octopus, and the cocktails and desserts not to be missed. Some complaints about slow service on review sites, but I found the staff friendly and prompt.

MARKT $$
Belgian
✉ 676 6th Avenue at 21st Street
☎ 212-727 3314
🖰 www.marktrestaurant.com
🚇 A, C, E at 23rd Street

A stylish Belgian brasserie with a popular bar. Great mussels and good beer selection.

THE PARK $$$
Mediterranean
✉ 118 10th Avenue at 18th Street
☎ 212-352 3313
🖰 www.theparknyc.com
🚇 Subway C, E to 23rd Street

Once a mechanic's garage, this is one of the 'in' spots for film-industry executives. It's a huge industrial bar-cum-restaurant space with a kind of African safari camp interior serving Mediterranean food. There's a garden at the back full of Japanese maple trees and wisteria vines that seats 400 and is a great place to dine in the summer. The Penthouse, a rooftop patio, is open to the elements in the summer and enclosed and heated in the winter, with great views of the High Line at sunset all year round.

THE RED CAT $$
Mediterranean–American
✉ 227 10th Avenue between 23rd and 24th Streets
☎ 212-242 1122
🖰 www.redcatrestaurants.com
🚇 Subway C, E to 23rd Street

The Red Cat

One of the earlier arrivals in Chelsea, along with the original galleries, this is a real staple with the art pack. It serves up Mediterranean-influenced American food, such as red wine braised lamb shank or pan-roasted cod and saffron mussels, but you can just go for a cocktail.

CHINATOWN

Hundreds of tiny restaurants line the Chinatown streets, mostly serving good-value food from various regions in China. Here are our top choices to get you started.

BIG WONG KING $
Cantonese
✉ 67 Mott Street between Bayard and Canal Streets
☎ 212-964 0540
🖰 www.bigwongking.com
🚇 Subway J, M, N, Q, R, W, A, Z, 6 to Canal Street

Cheap, tasty food – particularly the duck, shrimp and chicken noodles, and congee. Don't expect much of the décor but the service is good and lots of Chinese eat here, which is always a good sign. The wonton noodle soup is a bargain.

🇬🇧 **BRITTIP**
Well-priced, steaming-hot food is the trademark of the restaurants in Chinatown. But don't expect elegance in the decor or any politeness from the waiters!

DIM SUM GO GO $$
Chinese–Vegetarian
✉ 5 East Broadway between Catherine Street and Chatham Square
☎ 212-732 0797
🖰 www.dimsumgogo.com
🚇 Subway J, M, Z, 6 to Canal Street; F to East Broadway

Zagat-rated and one of the more popular restaurants in the area, thanks to its delicious dim sum, and fantastically priced: dim sum platter, $10.95 for 10 pieces; roast chicken with fried garlic stems, $13.95; hamburger in a steamed bun with ginger sauce, $12.95.

JOE'S SHANGHAI $$
Chinese–Shanghai
✉ 9 Pell Street between Bowery and Mott Street
☎ 212-233 8888
🖰 www.joesshanghairestaurants.com
🚗 Subway J, M, N, R, Z, 6 to Canal Street
A Chinese restaurant known for creating the most fabulous soup dumplings in New York. 'Lots of food for little money' says the *Zagat Survey*. No reservations. Cash only.

NICE GREEN BO $–$$
Chinese–Shanghai
✉ 66 Bayard Street between Elizabeth and Mott Streets
☎ 212-625 2359
🖰 www.nicegreenbo.com
🚗 Subway J, M, Z, N, Q, R, W, 6 to Canal Street
Joe's Shanghai had little in the way of competition for delicious dim sum and dumplings at great prices, then along came this place, giving New Yorkers another place to rave about. The dumplings are extremely fresh, hot and succulent and their fish fillet in wine sauce is excellent.

EAST VILLAGE

There are dozens of great places to dine in the East Village. It's a very safe part of town so, if you have the time, it's well worth taking a wander around at night and having a look at all of the various options before you make your choice.

ANGELICA KITCHEN $$
Vegetarian–Vegan
✉ 300 East 12th Street between 1st and 2nd Avenues
☎ 212-228 2909
🖰 www.angelicakitchen.com
🚗 Subway L, N, Q, R, W, 4, 5, 6 to 14th Street/Union Square
A surprise for anyone who thinks veggie food is boring. This cool spot, open since 1976, serves up organic, very tasty soups, chilli

and noodle dishes like butternut squash and tempeh made from soya beans, and seasonal dishes. Macrobiotic heaven? No dairy, no eggs, no animal products and no refined sugars or preservatives. Your halo will shine if you dine here.

BENNY'S BURRITOS $$
Mexican
✉ 93 Avenue A, near 6th Street
☎ 212-254 3286
🖰 www.harrysburritos.com
This establishment looks as though it has survived from the 1960s: lava lamps, pink walls and Formica tables make up the decor. Serves super-filling burritos and enchiladas, but watch out for the lethal margaritas. (You'll find a larger and more crowded Benny's at 113 Greenwich Ave in the West Village.)

FRANK $
Italian
✉ 88 2nd Avenue between 5th and 6th Streets
☎ 212-420 0202
🖰 www.frankrestaurant.com
🚗 Subway 6 to Astor Place
A tiny Italian restaurant with a real parlour feel. No matter the hour, Frank is full of hungry hipsters looking to fill up on Grandma Carmela's slow-cooked ragu.

◀ ✚▶ BRITTIP
If you want to walk and eat rather than sit down and dine, Frank also has a great takeaway or delivery menu.

GNOCCO CUCINA & TRADIZIONE $$
Italian
✉ 337 East 10th Street between Avenues A and B
☎ 212-677 1913
🖰 www.gnocco.com
🚗 Subway 6 to Astor Place
Named after an Italian snack of crispy, puffy fried dough, you know you're in for some good Italian food at this eatery owned by Pierluigi Palazzo; think pork tenderloin sprinkled with Parmigiano shavings.

LA PALAPA $$
Mexican
✉ 77 St Mark's Place between 1st and 2nd Avenues
☎ 212-777 2537
🖰 http://lapalapa.com
🚗 Subway E, V to Lexington Avenue/53rd Street

RESTAURANTS

Superb Mexican cuisine with shrimp dishes and barbecued cod with Chile guajillo and achiote rub. Rice is flavoured with tomato, saffron and tomatillo; sauces concocted from sesame seeds, pumpkin seeds and guajillo chillies. The restaurant is dark and sultry and serves refreshing fresh fruit margaritas. Check out the calendar on the website to find out about events such as a cocktail and small bites masterclass. The cocktails here are seriously good – try the white hibiscus sangria!

MOMOFUKU NOODLE BAR $$
Noodles
✉ 171 1st Avenue, between 10th and 11th streets
☎ 212-777 7773
🖱 www.momofuku.com
🚇 Subway L to 1st Avenue

The menu changes daily at this cool noodle bar. Expect to pick up pieces of wild striped bass with pickled pearl onion or chilled somen noodles, kimchi, sesame and fried egg with your chopsticks. It's interior is quite stark, with wooden benches and chairs, but it's open noon–2am on weekends and well worth a visit if you're in the area.

BRITTIP
Sometimes the only way to get into a very popular restaurant is to go very early or very late in the evening. Ask what times are available when you book.

PANGEA $$
Mediterranean
✉ 178 2nd Avenue between 11th and 12th Streets
☎ 212-995 0900
🖱 www.pangeanyc.com

Known for its wonderful homemade pastas and Mediterranean cuisine. A-list film star siblings Jake and Maggie Gyllenhaal have been papped here and the outside tables are much in demand in summer. Go for cocktails at the large oak bar before a night out, too.

YAFFA CAFE $
Middle Eastern-American
✉ 97 St Mark's Place between 1st and Avenue A
☎ 212-677 9001
🖱 www.yaffacafe.com
🚇 Subway 6 to Astor Place

Berber chicken, daily fish special, hummous, baba ganoush, stir-frys and burgers all served

ZAGAT NEW YORK'S TOP RESTAURANTS 2012
Best food: Le Bernardin (p181)

Most popular: Le Bernardin (p181)

Best decor: Asiate (p191)

Best service: Per Se (p192)

Best burger: Burger Joint at Le Parker Meridien (p173)

Best pizza: Totonno's Pizzeria Napolitano (p159)

up in an East Village grotto with an arty vibe that's been going for years. The large garden and happy hour (2–8 Mon–Thurs, 2–7 Fri and Sat) keep it packed. Open 24 hours.

FINANCIAL DISTRICT AND SOUTH STREET SEAPORT

ADRIENNE'S PIZZA BAR $–$$
Italian
✉ 54 Stone Street near Hanover Square
☎ 212-248 3838
🖱 www.adriennespizzabar.com
🚇 Subway 2, 3 to Wall Street

If you're sightseeing Downtown and start to feel peckish, pop into this stylish place for some truly delicious thin-crust square, the restaurant's latest take on the pizza. There's also salads, antipasti and pastas to enjoy.

TOP 5 FOR FINE DINING
Considering how many thousands of eating establishments there are in New York and how many of them serve up wonderful food in delightful environments, it's difficult to narrow them down to a top 5. Yet all the restaurants listed below have earned their stripes for getting all the elements of fine dining and hospitality right: consistently excellent and innovative cuisine, attentive service and an enjoyable ambience in a wonderful setting. They obviously have prices to match, but for a once-in-a-holiday treat they won't disappoint.

Le Cirque: French–American, Midtown East (p178)

Union Square Café: Gourmet American, Gramercy Park (p165)

Le Bernardin: Seafood, Midtown West (p181)

Babbo: Italian, Greenwich (p166)

Nobu: Japanese, TriBeCa (p187)

Asiate at the Mandarin Oriental

KOODO SUSHI $–$$
Japanese
- ✉ 55 Liberty Street
- ☎ 212-425 2890
- 🖰 www.koodosushi.com
- 🚗 Subway 1, 2, 4, 5 to Wall Street

This place doesn't look like much, but it has one of the best sushi chefs in town. The fish is impeccable, but the chef really shines in his weekly specials, such as seafood hotpot for $19.95.

MARKJOSEPH STEAKHOUSE $$
Steakhouse
- ✉ 261 Water Street between Peck Slip and Dover Street
- ☎ 212-277 0020
- 🖰 www.markjosephsteakhouse.com
- 🚗 Subway 1, 2, 4, 5, A, C, J, M, Z to Fulton Street/Broadway Nassau

This restaurant has made its mark as one of the best steakhouses in the city. The porterhouse steak is so tender some people have said it 'could be eaten through a straw'. Team it with the delicious hash browns. Wearing a jacket is advisable.

GRAMERCY PARK

BAMIYAN $$
Afghan
- ✉ 358 3rd Avenue at the corner of East 26th Street
- ☎ 212-481 3232
- 🖰 www.bamiyan.com
- 🚗 Subway 6 to East 28th Street

Proof that New Yorkers are a liberal lot, an Afghan restaurant in the heart of Gramercy Park. Its ornate exterior will catch your eye, inside it's just as interesting and the food is really good, particularly the charcoal-grilled kebabs (kebobs). Lots of vegetarian options, such as dal chalow – split pea and pomegranate juice purée – and baklava is a winner for dessert.

ELEVEN MADISON PARK $$$$
French–American
- ✉ 11 Madison Avenue (the corner) at 24th Street
- ☎ 212-889 0905
- 🖰 www.elevenmadisonpark.com
- 🚗 Subway

With a soaring ceiling, marble floors and French-influenced dishes, this is one of New York's hottest restaurants. It's expensive but not snooty and the service is attentive, as seen in Sex And The City, and you would be advised to go dressy as shorts, T-shirts and trainers aren't allowed. If you want to blow the budget, the 11-course taster menu is $195.

GRAMERCY TAVERN $$$
Gourmet American
- ✉ 42 East 20th Street between Broadway and Park Avenue South
- ☎ 212-477 0777
- 🖰 www.gramercytavern.com
- 🚗 Subway N, R to 23rd Street

Another safe bet if you want an excellent supper, guaranteed. Serves tasty, traditional dishes like venison loin and sausage, always highly ranked by the *Zagat Survey*

– a first-class American restaurant with an outstanding wine list, too.

MAIALINO $$–$$$
Italian
- ✉ 2 Lexington Avenue at Gramercy Park North
- ☎ 212-201 2161
- ⌐🖰 www.gramercyparkhotel.com
- 🚇 Subway L, N, R, 4, 5, 6 to 14th Street/ Union Square

The latest offering from restaurant supremo Danny Meyer's Union Square Hospitality Group demonstrates Italian cooking at its finest. Expect the atmosphere of a traditional Rome trattoria but filled with New Yorkers. Enjoy strong coffee in the morning; wine, brushetta and olives in the afternoon, and delicious feasts of carne and antipasto (there's an antipasto station overflowing with bread, cheese and meats on one side of the room) in the evening, all eaten at simple wood tables with checked table cloths.

TAMARIND $$
Indian
- ✉ 41–43 East 22nd Street between Broadway and Park Avenue South
- ☎ 212-674 7400
- ⌐🖰 www.tamarindrestaurantsnyc.com
- 🚇 Subway N, R to 23rd Street

Lovely modern decor that defies the normal Indian dining room cliché of flock wallpaper. The cuisine is equally contemporary, with lots of fruit-infused dishes such as fritters with spinach, banana and homemade cheese. If you want a cheaper, lighter snack, try their tea room next door.

UNION SQUARE CAFE $$–$$$
American–Italian
- ✉ 21 East 16th Street between 5th Avenue and Union Square
- ☎ 212-243 4020
- ⌐🖰 www.unionsquarecafe.com
- 🚇 Subway 4, 5, 6, L, N, R to Union Square.

One of America's most popular restaurants, Danny Meyer's Union Square Cafe serves robustly flavoured, seasonal American Italian cuisine, like chicken cutlet Milanese and Vermont lamb bracciole, in a relaxed setting of casual elegance. It's worth noting that, despite the proliferation of fashionable eateries that regularly open in New York, it's this restaurant that the city's movers and shakers still flock to, to flex the company credit card. There are three dining areas: balcony seating and a cluster of tables on the lower level, both offshoots of the long mahogany bar, and an adjacent main dining room. The decor is simple but effective – think polished cherrywood floors, oversized pussy willows and colourful artwork on the walls. There's a full lunch and dinner menu with daily specials in the dining room and the bar.

> **BRITTIP**
> Restaurant mogul Danny Meyer, the brains behind the Union Square Cafe, has also opened Untitled at the Whitney Museum of American Art (212-570 3600, www. whitney.org).

Union Square Cafe is as famous for its impeccable, friendly service as it is for its

Cornelia Street Café

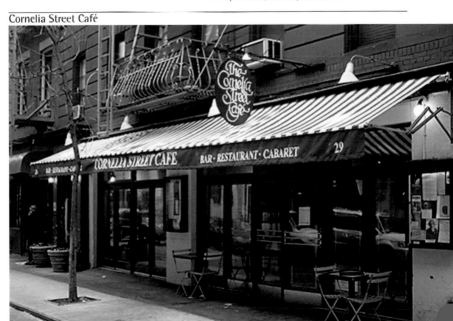

TOP 5 RESTAURANTS WITH A VIEW

2 West: Gourmet America, Battery Park (p158)

Battery Gardens: American Fusion, Battery Park (p158)

The View: Continental, Theater District (p186)

Water Club: Seafood, Midtown East (p180)

World Yacht Dinner Cruises: Gourmet American, Midtown West (p181)

unusual but fabulous food and it's now open for brunch on Sat and Sun from 11am– 2.30pm.

VERITAS $$$$
Gourmet American

- ✉ 43 East 20th Street between Broadway and Park Avenue South
- ☎ 212-353 3700
- 🖰 www.veritas-nyc.com
- 🚇 Subway N, R to 23rd Street

BRITTIP
If you're a true wine connoisseur you can download the most up-to-date list of Veritas's wine cellar before you go from www. veritas-nyc.com.

The city's largest wine list can be found here – an impressive 3,000 selections to choose from. The cuisine is equally as impressive, think roasted stone church duck and pan roasted veal chop with short rib ravioli and watercress.

GREENWICH & WEST VILLAGE

BABBO $$$$
Italian

- ✉ 110 Waverly Place between MacDougal and 6th Avenues
- ☎ 212-777 0303
- 🖰 www.babbonyc.com
- 🚇 Subway A, B, C, D, E, F, Q to Washington Square

The crown jewel of Greenwich Village restaurants is unmatched for the quality and quantity of its Italian dishes; forewarned is forearmed, so make sure you wear a skirt or trousers with an elasticated waist, because we're talking large, rich portions here. Everything in Mario Batali's restaurant is delightful, from the simple split-level dining room that seats 90 to the stunning bar area. However, it's the imaginative food that pushes this restaurant into the top 5

fine dining experiences. How about black tagliatelle with parsnips and pancetta? Or chocolate polenta cake with espresso gelato? Yum!

BRITTIP
Order one of the fabulous tasting menus at Babbo for a really great choice of dishes. The pasta-tasting menu is particularly mouth-watering, including black tagliatelle with peas and castelmagno, garganelli with funghi trifolatia and pappardelle Bolognese. It's also a cheaper option than choosing individual dishes, as the menus ring in at around $80 per person.

BOSIE TEA PARLOUR $–$$
French

- ✉ 10 Morton Street at Bleecker Street
- ☎ 212-351 9900
- 🖰 www.bosienyc.com
- 🚇 Subway 1, 9 to 79th Street

Not strictly a restaurant, this elegant café is a must-visit for anyone who loves a cuppa and appreciates a little bit of finesse; there are more than 100 hand-sourced and blended fine leaf teas. Modelled on France's tea houses, there are vintage lamps, chairs, tables and posters and you can also enjoy platters of sandwiches ($4–8), macaroons, cakes and pastries.

COMMERCE $$–$$$
New American

- ✉ 50 Commerce Street at Barrow Street
- ☎ 212-524 2301
- 🖰 http://commercerestaurant.com
- 🚇 Subway 1, 9 to Christopher Street

Commerce opened its doors in West Village at the beginning of 2008, but the original building started life as a Prohibition speakeasy and its low-lit ambiance retains a bit of that vibe. There's a massive bar beneath a massive mural or you can opt for a more intimate chestnut booth or black walnut table and dine on inventive dishes like boar ragu.

CORNELIA STREET CAFE $$
Eclectic

- ✉ 29 Cornelia Street between Bleecker and West 4th Streets
- ☎ 212-989 9319
- 🖰 www.corneliastreetcafe.com
- 🚇 Subway A, C, E, B, D, F, V to West 4th Street

A fabulous neighbourhood restaurant with good service that serves lunch and dinner 7 days a week. Specials include dishes like butternut squash risotto, sesame-crusted salmon, lobster ravioli and Thai bouillabaisse, or choose from the prix fixe menu for $25. In the summer, you can sit at a table on the pavement (great for people-watching!). Local artists' work hangs on the walls, and there is a small downstairs performance space for readings, acoustic performances and, in particular, a jazz club where doors open 5.45pm and it costs from $10 (or $15 weekends) for the whole evening plus a house drink (p210).

ELEPHANT & CASTLE $-$$$
American
- ✉ 68 Greenwich Avenue between 10th and 11th Streets
- ☎ 212-243 1400
- ⌂ www.elephantandcastle.com
- 🚇 Subway 1 to Christopher Street

You'll spot the distinctive black and white exterior of this ever-popular eatery first. Step inside and you'll be glad you did, as the menus are great, from breakfast through to dinner. Enjoy a pot of English tea and sunnyside-up eggs with hash browns first thing, or treat yourself to sliced steak and mashed potatoes with merlot ginger sauce followed by a Grand Marnier crepe for dessert come night fall. There's a sister restaurant in Dublin and you can even buy an Elephant & Castle T-shirt, if you like it that much.

FIDDLESTICKS PUB & GRILL $-$$
American–Irish
- ✉ 56 Greenwich Avenue
- ☎ 212-463 0516
- ⌂ www.fiddlesticksnyc.com
- 🚇 Subway 1 to Christopher Street

Cheap and cheerful Irish bar and restaurant, which I've included in the guide because the large number of sidewalk tables are great for people watching and always packed at lunchtime. Food is hearty, such as burgers and beef stew, but there are salads, too. This place has a great buzz about it, come on Fri or Sat night if you want to hear DJs and enjoy a bit of a party.

GARAGE RESTAURANT & CAFÉ $
American
- ✉ 99 7th Avenue South between Barrow and Grove Streets
- ☎ 212-645 0600
- ⌂ www.garagerest.com
- 🚇 Subway 1 to Christopher Street

A friendly spot for contemporary American food, including steak and seafood, in a great location; it also has live jazz.

GOTHAM BAR AND GRILL $$$
Gourmet American
- ✉ 12 East 12th Street between 5th Avenue and University Place
- ☎ 212-620 4020
- ⌂ www.gothambarandgrill.com
- 🚇 Subway L, N, R, 4, 5, 6 to Union Square/14th Street

Always highly rated (it's the only restaurant in the city to have been awarded 5 consecutive 3-star reviews by the New York Times), the excellent American cuisine – the Gotham Burger with gruyere cheese, harissa aioli, pickled vegetables and fries is unbeatable – is served up in a superb environment to a stylish crowd. It costs around $28 for the lunch prix fixe.

PHILIP MARIE $$
American
- ✉ 569 Hudson Street at West 11th Street
- ☎ 212-242 6200
- ⌂ www.philipmarie.com
- 🚇 Subway 1, 9 to Christopher Street

Hearty American fare. Try the prix fixe lunch for a bargain $10.95, which includes dishes like chargrilled steakburger with lettuce, tomato, onion and fries or grilled breaded country chicken with greens, and includes a glass of soda or iced tea.

SOTO $$$-$$$$
Japanese
- ✉ 357 6th Avenue at Washington Place
- ☎ 212-414 3088
- 🚇 Subway A, B, C, E, F, V to West 4th Street/Washington Square

Opened in May 2007 by third generation sushi chef Sotohiro Kosugi, this is a very sleek restaurant where you can savour Eastern delights such as sea urchin wrapped in squid, sweet shrimp tartare with yuzu tobiko and soy foam.

Restaurant Row

RESTAURANTS

TOMOE SUSHI $$
Japanese
- ✉ 172 Thompson Street between Bleecker and West Houston Streets
- ☎ 212-777 9346
- 🖱 http://tomoesushi.com/
- 🚗 Subway 6 to Bleecker Street

Rao's

This place doesn't look special but there is often a queue outside and not without reason. You can get some of the best sushi in New York here for about a tenth of the price it would cost you at Nobu.

> **🇬🇧 BRITTIP**
> If you need a break around 110th Street, drop in for a cuppa and delicious cupcake at Make My Cake, 121 St Nicholas Avenue at 116th Street, 212-932 0833, www.makemycake.com.

HARLEM

AMY RUTH'S HOME STYLE SOUTHERN CUISINE $$
Southern soul food
- ✉ 113 West 116th street at Lenox Avenue
- ☎ 212-280 8779
- 🖱 www.amyruthsharlem.com
- 🚗 Subway 2, 3 to 116th Street
Absolutely delicious southern-style food; BBQ spare ribs, chicken, waffles, catfish and ham hocks.

RAO'S $
Italian
- ✉ 455 East 114th Street at Pleasant Avenue
- ☎ 212-722 6709
- 🖱 www.raos.com
- 🚗 Subway 6 to 116th Street
This 10-table Italian restaurant is an institution and notoriously hard to get a reservation for, so if you fancy it, book now! Famous for its sauces, which Sinatra used to have flown to him around the world. Now the jukebox plays all the crooner's favourites.

> **🇬🇧 BRITTIP**
> If you can't get in to Rao's, you can still taste their fabulous sauces, by buying them either direct from the restaurant or from Faicco's Pork Store in Bleecker Street, Greenwich Village (p134).

SYLVIA'S $
Southern soul food
- ✉ 328 Lenox Avenue between 126th and 127th Streets
- ☎ 212-996 0660
- 🖱 www.sylviassoulfood.com
- 🚗 Subway 2, 3 to 125th Street
Southern home-style cooking – aka soul food. Sylvia's place is a New York institution and famous for its Sun gospel brunch. Book early as it's always very busy.

Arriba Arriba!

HELL'S KITCHEN

ARRIBA ARRIBA! $$
Mexico
✉ 762 9th Avenue at West 51st Street
☎ 212 489 0810
🖱 www.arribaarribawest.com
🚇 Subway C, E to 50th Street
Great value Mex food, like chilli con carne,
buffalo wings and quesadillas for $9 each,
plus killer cocktails. There are live DJs to keep
the experience even more upbeat.

⚜ **BRITTIP**
The frozen margaritas at Arriba
Arriba! are some of the city's
best and come in 3 sizes – bebe,
mama or papa.

LITTLE ITALY

Mulberry Street from Hester to Kenmare
Street and along Grand Street to Mott Street
is all that remains of a once thriving Italian
community. Thankfully, though – especially
for anyone who feels relieved to have escaped
the madness and mayhem of Chinatown –
the tiny area is incredibly vibrant and filled
with ambient pizzerias and trattorias, many
with pavement tables and some even having
gardens at the back.

Of course, the area gets packed with
tourists, but locals also eat here so the food
is 100% authentic. The restaurants all have
plenty in common – fading decor, if any, large
portions of piping hot Italian classics, friendly
service and great value for money. If you're
really on a budget, stick to the excellent fixed-
price menus, then just sit back and watch the
world go by.

BREAD $$
Italian
✉ 20 Spring Street between Elizabeth and
Mott Streets
☎ 212-334 1015
🚇 Subway 6 to Spring Street
A lovely little café serving up delicious high-
quality meats and cheese, soup, various salads
and, of course, a variety of bread, including
great fresh panini, crusty bread sandwiches
and baguettes. There's an equally good Bread
in TriBeCa (www.breadtribeca.com).

CAFE GITANE $$
French–North African
✉ 242 Mott Street at Prince Street
☎ 212-334 9552
🖱 www.cafegitanenyc.com
🚇 Subway 6 to Spring Street
Great value Moroccan-style dining; think
couscous and tajines. Tables and chairs are
put out on the sidewalk in the summer, but
they are in a hot spot so you're more likely to
end up in the noisy but nice dining room.

SPQR

BEST OF LITTLE ITALY

It's hard to go wrong with any of the restaurants in Little Italy, but here is a round-up of the best, moving northwards along Mulberry from Hester to Grand Street: **Pellegrino's** (138 Mulberry, 212-226 3177); **Angelo's** (146 Mulberry, 212-966 1277, www.angelomulberry.com); **Lombardi's** (32 Spring Street between Mulberry and Mott Streets, 212-941 7994, www.firstpizza.com); **Il Palazzo** (151 Mulberry, 212-343 7000). To get to Little Italy, take subway 6 to Spring or Bleecker Streets.

FERRARA $
Italian café
- ✉ 195 Grand Street between Mulberry and Mott Streets
- ☎ 212-226 6150
- 🖱 www.ferraracafe.com
- 🚗 Subway S to Grand Street

America's first espresso bar (it opened in 1892) in an area that was once teeming with cannoli caverns. A spacious area, it serves up delicious coffee, cakes and pastries and provides plenty of entertaining people-watching.

SAL ANTHONY'S SPQR $$-$$$
Italian
- ✉ 133 Mulberry Street between Hester and Grand Streets
- ☎ 212-925 3120
- 🖱 www.spqrnyc.com
- 🚗 Subway 6 to Spring Street

An authentic Italian that's big on fresh ingredients – the mozzarella is made twice a day on the premises to ensure it's perfect. There are lots of regional dishes such as trout with garlic and rosemary and fusilli pasta with prosciutto and tomato, all served in elegant, wood-panelled surroundings at prices far below what you'd expect to pay uptown for similar fare. There's a 'La Famiglia', family-style menu, which has extra large portions if you want to share dishes.

LOWER EAST SIDE

ALIAS $$
American
- ✉ 76 Clinton Street at Rivington Street
- ☎ 212-505 5011
- 🖱 www.aliasrestaurant.com
- 🚗 Subway F to Lower East Side/2nd Avenue

This cool bodega has subdued lighting, tablecloths and a small but serious wine list, yet remains funky with laid-back clients

and staff. The chef turns out some pretty big tastes from his mini kitchen – poached chicken breast and corn bread pudding, St Louise-style barbecue ribs – but at far less than Midtown pricing. Open for lunch, dinner and brunch on a Sat and Sun.

BEREKET $
Turkish
- ✉ 187 East Houston Street at Orchard Street
- ☎ 212-475 7700
- 🚗 Subway F to 2nd Avenue

A good place to pop into if you've got the munchies after a big night out as it's open 24/7 and the food is filling but fresh. The hummus, stuffed vine leaves and lamb shawarma sandwich are recommended.

KATZ'S DELICATESSEN $
American–Jewish
- ✉ 205 East Houston Street at Ludlow Street
- ☎ 212-254 2246
- 🖱 http://katzsdelicatessen.com
- 🚗 Subway F to 2nd Avenue

A real institution, this deli has been here since 1888. The sandwiches may sound pricey at around $15.95, but I defy you to finish one. Luckily, there are plenty of brown paper bags around to take your leftovers away with you (as everybody else does). Stick to the sandwiches though – the soups are a bit disappointing. You take a ticket on the way in, order your food at the counter and have your ticket filled out, then you pay for it all as you leave.

◆ BRITTIP
If the canteen-style seating at Katz's seems familiar to you, it's because that fake orgasm scene with Meg Ryan and Billy Crystal in *When Harry Met Sally* was filmed here.

MADISON SQUARE/FLATIRON

A VOCE $$$-$$$$
Italian
- ✉ 41 Madison Avenue near 26th Street
- ☎ 212-545 8555
- 🖱 www.avocerestaurant.com
- 🚗 Subway 6 to 26th Street

A great Italian menu: think chicken cacciatora, lamb shanks, veal chops and even wild boar and the modern decor is very calming and sophisticated. The prix fixe lunch menu is $33. There's a 100-seat outside dining piazza adorned with lemon trees, flowers and herbs.

ALDEA

$$$–$$$$

Mediterranean

- ✉ 31 West 17th Street
- ☎ 212-675 7223
- 🖰 www.aldearestaurant.com
- 🚗 Subway L, N, Q, R, W, 4, 5, 6 to 14th Street–Union Square

Opened in May 2009 by George Mendes, formerly chef de cuisine at Tocqueville and Wallse. Mendes returns to his roots with a menu of Mediterranean dishes influenced by the flavours of Spain and Portugal. Evoking a relaxed, coastal vibe, the restaurant offers a selection of petiscos, up to $13, plus a variety of seasonal appetisers and entrées, such as Spanish octopus with roasted celery root, potato and lemon-squid ink purée or duck confit. Designed by Stephanie Goto, the bi-level restaurant reflects the colour palate of azulejos, blue and white ceramic tiles common in Portugal. Open 5.30pm Mon–Sat.

MEATPACKING DISTRICT

Manhattan's Meatpacking District, between Chelsea and the West Village on the lower west side of Manhattan, used to be a no-go area for diners. In the last decade is has become a style magnet for the kind of restaurants that you want to brag to your friends about. If you don't want to splash out in the chic venues, however, there are some groovy little coffee and cake shops that will take the weight off your feet but not your wallet.

CATCH

$$$

Seafood

- ✉ 2nd Floor, 21 9th Avenue, enter on 13th Street between 9th Avenue and Washington Street
- ☎ 212-392 5978
- 🖰 www.catchnewyorkcity.com
- 🚗 Subway 1, 2, 3 to Chambers Street

A cool restaurant that's quite out of the way and hard to find through a nondescript side door, but worth the trek. There's a trendy bar to chill at pre-meal, which is a good job as it can take a while to be seated, but once you're at your table you can tuck into delicacies like stone crab claws, lobster Cantonese and stuffed calamari.

DEL POSTO

$$$

Italian

- ✉ 85 10th Avenue at 16th Street
- ☎ 212-497 8090
- 🖰 www.delposto.com
- 🚗 Subway A, C, E to 14th Street

This restaurant from Mario Batali and the Bastianich family is posh Italian nosh that has left the New York restaurant critics split. The surroundings are super-plush – think old-

TOP 5 ROMANTIC RESTAURANTS

There are many restaurants in New York that can deliver on the food front, but don't quite get it right with the ambience. The venues listed below are the top places in town if you really want to inject a bit of romance into your dining experience, from tactile furnishings and soft lighting to sensuous food, they're a must-visit for lovers who are also food lovers.

Aureole: French, Midtown (p173)

Daniel: French, Upper East Side (p190)

The View: Continental, Theater District (p186)

The Boathouse at Central Park: American-seafood, Central Park (p159)

River Café: Gourmet American, Brooklyn (p159)

style gentleman's club – with a live pianist, and the food fancy and grand tasting.

MANON

$$$

Contemporary American

- ✉ 407 West 14th Street (between 9th and 10th Avenues)
- ☎ 212-596 7255
- 🖰 www.manon-nyc.com
- 🚗 Subway A, C, E to 14th Street

Flashy new restaurant serving food as good as it looks. Currently a place to see and be seen (though that can change quickly in Manhattan), with fashionistas sipping Earl Grey-flavoured spirits at the downstairs bar and then dining beneath chandeliers upstairs on things like aged steak, crispy dorado and deconstructed chocolate cake.

OLD HOMESTEAD STEAK HOUSE $$

American

- ✉ 56 9th Avenue between 14th and 15th Streets
- ☎ 212-242 9040
- 🖰 www.theoldhomesteadsteakhouse.com
- 🚗 Subway L, A, C, E to 14th Street/8th Avenue

An original chophouse joint, complete with tacky cow sculpture outside and wood bar, that opened in 1868 and is still serving massive portions of good ol' steak and chips.

PASTIS

$$$

French

- ✉ 9 9th Avenue at Little West 12th Street
- ☎ 212-929 4844
- 🖰 www.pastisny.com
- 🚗 Subway A, C, E to 14th Street; L to 8th Avenue

One of the names that made the Meatpacking neighbourhood hip was Keith

McNally, who set up this Parisian-style brasserie. The food is good, not great, such as steak frîtes and sautéed prawns, but the atmosphere is fabulous (you feel like a local). Open for breakfast, brunch, lunch and dinner.

THE STANDARD GRILL $$$
American–Mediterranean
- ✉ 848 Washington at 13th Street
- ☎ 212-645 4100
- 🖰 http://thestandardgrill.com
- 🚗 Subway A, C, E, L to 8th Avenue/14th Street

Andre Balazc's lovely eatery is tucked away beneath the High Line. It boasts a beer garden and bar area, has a French vibe with tiled floor and long wooden bar that leads into the main dining room with red leather booths and wooden floor. The food is excellent, from breakfast (eggs any which way you please) through to dinner (Colorado lamb rack, roasted Chatham cod) and late-night drinks.

MIDTOWN

21 CLUB $$–$$$
Gourmet American
- ✉ 21 West 52nd Street between 5th and 6th Avenues
- ☎ 212-582 7200
- 🖰 www.21club.com
- 🚗 Subway F to 5th Avenue

Despite its name, this landmark restaurant has never been a club, but during Prohibition it was a speakeasy, starting life in Greenwich Village before moving to its Midtown location in 1929. West 52nd Street between 5th and 6th Avenues was known then as the 'wettest block in Manhattan' because there were at least 38 speakeasies.

One of the most discreet was the 21 Club, which purposefully remained a tiny, clandestine retreat behind the iron gate of its townhouse façade, to avoid both the gangsters and police raids. Its success depended on an employee who was assigned to spot gangsters, policemen and revenue agents through the peephole – and who was so skilful that 21 escaped most raids and troubles except for 1 in 1930. After that the owners had a new security system designed to create false stairways and walls to hide its 2,000 cases of fine wines. It involved the building of a 2-tonne door to the secret cellar, made out of the original bricks to look like a wall. The cellar is still going strong and now houses $1.5 million-worth of wine, much of which is owned by the celebrities and power brokers who call the 21 Club their own. Former US President Gerald Ford kept his bottles here, as did actress Elizabeth Taylor.

Once Prohibition ended in 1932, many of the former speakeasies went out of business, but the 21 turned itself into a fine dining establishment with several rooms and dining experiences to choose from, and it has been attracting celebrities and movers and

RESTAURANTS

21 Club

Burger Joint at Le Parker Meridien

shakers ever since. Patrons have included Joe DiMaggio, Aristotle Onassis, Franklin D. Roosevelt, Humphrey Bogart, Ernest Hemingway and Jackie Gleason and these days you could be rubbing shoulders with Brad Pitt or a Kennedy.

AQUAVIT $$$$
Scandinavian
✉ 65 East 55th Street between Madison and Park Avenues
☎ 212-307 7311
🖰 www.aquavit.org
🚄 Subway E, V to 53rd Street/5th Avenue

Swedish chef Marcus Samuelsson won the Best Chef in New York City award way back in 2003, but the menu, which has some innovative Scandinavian influences, is still as varied and imaginative today and in 2013 the restaurant was awarded a Michelin-star. Classics like Swedish meatballs and gravadlax are mouth-watering, while the tasting menus, including a vegetarian one, are a great idea and comprise 7-course Aqua Bite meals.

AUREOLE $$$$
American
✉ 1 Bryant Park, 135 West 42nd Street
☎ 212-319 1660
🖰 www.charliepalmer.com
🚄 Subway B, D, F, Q to 42nd Street

Once situated in a brownstone on the Upper East Side, now relocated in the spectacular Bank of America Tower. Celebrity chef Charlie Palmer – considered the king of New York chefs – frequently changes the menu, but

delicious concoctions have included sesame-seared Atlantic salmon with orange-miso vinaigrette and sticky rice croquettes, and foie gras with port-glazed Bing cherries and young onions. Expensive, but worth it to experience dining in one of the best restaurants in town. Closed on Sun.

BG $$$–$$$$
American nouveau
✉ 754 5th Avenue at 58th Street
☎ 212-872 0977
🖰 www.bergdorfgoodman.com
🚄 Subway N, R, W to 5th Avenue/59th Street

The restaurant at Bergdorf Goodman department store makes a posh place to stop for a long lunch during a shopping spree. Or head here for an early dinner, as the restaurant shuts at 8pm. You can also go for the afternoon tea option – which is fabulous, darling.

BURGER JOINT AT LE PARKER MERIDIEN $-$$
American
✉ 118 West 57th Street between 6th and 7th Avenues
☎ 212-245 5000
🖰 www.parkermeridien.com
🚄 Subway B, D, E to 7th Avenue

For a classic award-winning, New York-style burger, step inside Le Parker Meridien hotel, where the menu offers delicious hamburgers for $7.58, cheeseburgers for $8.04 and French fries for $3.90. A total bargain and delicious, to boot. Treat yourself to a giant milkshake while you're there.

CALVISIUS CAVIAR LOUNGE $$$-$$$$
Caviar
- ⊠ 57 East 57th Street at Park Avenue
- ☎ 212-207 8222
- ⌂ www.fourseasons.com/newyork
- 🚇 Subway 59th Street

The only lounge of its kind in the world is set in the posh Four Seasons Hotel, where you can dine on tiny dishes of two types of rare Italian roe – white sturgeon and Oscietra washed down with Champagne, some Italian bubbles or top-line vodkas in an intimate Art Deco interior.

CHINA GRILL $$$
Chinese
- ⊠ CBS Building, 60 West 53rd Street between 5th and 6th Avenues
- ☎ 212-333 7788
- ⌂ www.chinagrillmgt.com
- 🚇 Subway B, D, F, V to 47th–50th Streets/ Rockefeller Center

Classy establishment, with soaring 8m/30ft ceiling, multilevel dining platforms and limestone floor. Serves eclectic food in a fairly noisy setting and has a bar that gets pretty crowded.

db BISTRO MODERNE $$$-$$$$
French–American
- ⊠ City Club Hotel, 55 West 44th Street between 5th and 6th Avenues
- ☎ 212-391 2400
- ⌂ www.dbbistro.com/nyc
- 🚇 Subway B, D, F, V, S, 4, 5, 6, 7 to 42nd Street

The latest showcase for one of New York's superstar chefs, Daniel Boulud. It got lots of press for its $29 hamburger (now $32!) and became an instant scene. Located in the very star-chic City Club Hotel, this is one of the few really good places to eat close to the Theater District.

FORTY FOUR $$$
American
- ⊠ Royalton Hotel, 44 West 44th Street between 5th and 6th Avenues
- ☎ 212-944 8844
- ⌂ www.royaltonhotel.com
- 🚇 Subway B, D, F, Q to 42nd Street

A très trendy joint off the lobby of Philippe Starck-designed Royalton Hotel, serving American fare, like seared halibut and 44 burger with thick bacon and 44 sauce. A favourite with the media set. Recently renovated.

GORDON RAMSAY AT THE LONDON $$$$
British fusion
- ⊠ 151 West 54th Street at 7th Avenue
- ☎ 212-307 5000
- ⌂ www.thelondonnyc.com
- 🚇 Subway B, D, E to 7th Avenue

London's most notorious Michelin 3-star chef hit the Big Apple in style seven years ago at the former Righa Royal Hotel, which, after a $50 million refurbishment and name change, became the darling of the dining and bar scene. His food didn't go down too well with NY food critics initially, but we love it.

HARD ROCK CAFE $-$$
American
- ⊠ 1501 Broadway at 43rd Street
- ☎ 212-343 3355
- ⌂ www.hardrock.com
- 🚇 Subway N, Q, R, S, W, 1, 2, 3, 7, 9 to Times Square/42nd Street

Classic burger and chips 'cuisine' in a noisy environment. It's now open for breakfast every Fri–Sun, 8–10am if you fancy eating your eggs over easy while checking out rock memorabilia, such as stage costumes worn by Madonna.

INAKAYA $$-$$$
Japanese
- ⊠ 231 West 40th Street at 6th Avenue
- ☎ 212-354 2195
- ⌂ www.inakayany.com
- 🚇 Subway 1, 2, 3, 7, N, Q, R, S, W at Times Square/42nd Street

Popular Japanese eatery, with a vast menu including Japanese favourites sushi, sashimi and maki rolls that come in 18 varieties, including spicy shrimp tempura, soft-shell crab and a yummy dragon roll.

MA PÊCHE $$-$$$
French–Vietnamese
- ⊠ 15 West 56th Street between 5th and 6th Avenues
- ☎ 212-757 5878
- ⌂ www.momofuku.com/restaurants/ma-peche/
- 🚇 Subway F to 57th Street

Part of David Chang's empire, this is upscale dining courtesy of chef Tien Ho. It's all very minimalist, with blank walls and wooden tables laid out in an X formation. The food, such as pork sausage with rice noodles, is good value.

◀ BRITTIP

For the best cookies in town, pop into Momofuku Milk Bar, a takeout place at the front of Ma Pêche.

RESTAURANTS

NOBU FIFTY SEVEN $$$$
Japanese–Peruvian
- ✉ 40th West 57 Street between 5th and 6th Avenues
- ☎ 212-757 3000
- 🖰 www.noburestaurants.com
- 🚗 Subway F to 57th Street

Nobu Fifty Seven is every bit as glam as the original Nobu New York and the food every bit as delicious (the black cod with miso is heavenly), served up in must-be-seen-to-be-believed surroundings according to *Zagat*, who describe it as a 'triumph of theatrical feng shui'. It is also said to be as hot for celeb-watching as the original.

NORMA'S $-$$
American
- ✉ Le Parker Meridien Hotel, 118 West 57th Street between 6th and 7th Avenues
- ☎ 212-708 7460
- 🖰 www.parkermeridien.com
- 🚗 Subway B, D, E to 7th Avenue

This award-winning all-day breakfast joint is très chi-chi, beautifully decorated and serves some of the most inventive 'breakfast' food going! Specialities include molten chocolate French toast with pineapple chutney, caramelised onion corned beef hash with poached eggs, and a serious stack of strawberry and rhubarb pancakes. Also desserts and fruit smoothies.

OPIA $$-$$$
French
- ✉ 130 East 57th Street at Lexington Avenue
- ☎ 212-688 3939
- 🖰 www.opiarestaurant.com
- 🚗 Subway 4, 5, 6, N, R, W to 59th Street/ Lexington Avenue

Recently renovated and with a menu by chef Ted Pryor, Opia is an elegant restaurant plus lounge, bar and den too. The French-inspired cuisine is absolutely delicious. Open for breakfast as well as lunch and dinner and there's live jazz on Tues and Sat evenings from 9.30pm in the lounge.

REMI $$$
Italian
- ✉ 145 West 53rd Street between 6th and 7th Avenues
- ☎ 212-581 4242
- 🖰 www.remi.ypguides.net
- 🚗 Subway N, R to 49th Street; B, D east to 7th Avenue

To New Yorkers, this special restaurant is like a taste of Venice with its enchanting Atrium Garden that offers foreign films and live music to accompany dinner al fresco. The food, like roasted sardines or grilled octopus, is delicious and you can even get Remi takeaways.

ROCK CENTER CAFE $$
American
- ✉ Rockefeller Center, 20 West 50th Street between 5th and 6th Avenues
- ☎ 212-332 7620
- 🖰 www.patinagroup.com
- 🚗 Subway B, D, F, Q to 47th–50th Streets/ Rockefeller Plaza

A Mecca for tourists, thanks to the scenic setting on the north side of the Rockefeller's skating rink. Some original Warhol prints and open for breakfast, lunch and dinner.

THE RUSSIAN TEA ROOM $$$$
Russian
- ✉ 150 West 57th Street at 7th Avenue
- ☎ 212-581 7100
- 🖰 www.russiantearoomnyc.com
- 🚗 Subway B, D, E to 7th Avenue

The legendary tea room was shut for some time and reopened in 2008 after a group of investors stepped in to resurrect this New York institution. Opened in the 1920s, it was bought by Warner LeRoy in 1995 and he poured $30 million into it and it reopened in 1999. However, the starry clientele that adored the tea room weren't so impressed with LeRoy's theatrical furnishings and it sadly closed its doors. Thankfully, the public can now be let loose again in this over-the-top playground, which has swooping eagles on the walls, red leather banquettes and fake Picassos on the walls. As for the dining, it's caviar all the way here, the most expensive being the Iranian special reserve that costs $300 for 30g/1oz, brought to the table on silver trays. Lots of other dishes too, but not as memorable, though the pre-theatre dinner menu of 3 courses for $60 is good value.

SEAGRILL $$$$
Seafood
- ✉ Rockefeller Center, 19 West 49th Street between 5th and 6th Avenues
- ☎ 212-332 7610
- 🖰 www.theseagrillnyc.com
- 🚗 Subway B, D, F, Q to 47th–50th Streets/ Rockefeller Center

Surrounded by lush greenery, the outdoor tables topped with striped umbrellas in summer are replaced in winter by the famous skating rink. The seafood specialities include Australian barramundi with wilted arugula, poached lobster with truffled potato and herb-crusted skate. Note the dress code has changed to exclude jeans, shorts and trainers.

Bull & Bear

RESTAURANTS

TAO NEW YORK $$$–$$$$
Asian
- ✉ 42 East 58th Street
- ☎ 212-888 2288
- 🖰 www.taorestaurant.com
- 🚗 Subway 4, 5, 6, N, R to 59th Street

You'll easily spot this dramatic restaurant by its huge wooden doors and giant lantern suspended above the entrance. Step inside and the grandeur continues with an enormous 16ft tall Buddha floating above a pool with carp and Eastern artefacts scattered about. It's huge, with 300 seats, although if you're lucky or book months in advance, you could wow your partner with seats in the Skybox, which has seats overlooking the whole restaurant. The menu, laden with choice from dumplings to sushi to Peking duck, is one of the longest I've ever seen (ask a waiter to advise) and on the pricey side, not a problem for its celebrity clientele: Britney Spears, Jay-Z and Beyonce, Madonna and Tom Cruise have all been spotted here.

BRITTIP
Sunday brunch has never been more popular in the city, with lots of restaurants now offering this laid-back option for those who want to lie in at the weekend. Tao's dim sum brunch at noon is one of the more unusual options on offer.

UPSTAIRS AT 21 $$
Gourmet American
- ✉ 21 West 52nd Street between 5th and 6th Avenues
- ☎ 212-582 7200
- 🖰 www.21club.com
- 🚗 Subway F to 5th Avenue

Here you can get many of the 21 Club's classic dishes in a less formal but equally well-serviced restaurant – and see out of windows into the bargain! It has quickly become a favourite with the trendy jet set.

MIDTOWN EAST

BULL & BEAR $$$–$$$$
Steakhouse
- ✉ The Waldorf Hotel entrance on Lexington Avenue at 49th Street
- ☎ 212-872 4900
- 🖰 www.waldorfastoria.com
- 🚗 Subway 6 to 51st Street

A landmark restaurant renowned for its excellent hospitality and unashamedly masculine decor that pays homage to the stock market bull and bear symbols. This is one of the best restaurants in New York for delicious, melt-in-the-mouth, prime, aged Black Angus beef dishes, yet has plenty to offer the less carnivorously inclined. If you want something a little lighter, there are mouth-watering dishes that include yellowfin tuna mignon and shrimp Creole with

Andouille sausage and rice. For something lighter opt for one of the salads, such as lobster salad with mango, avocado and corn. Note, there's a no jeans or trainers policy here and a happy hour on drinks 5–6pm in the week.

CAVIAR RUSSE　　　　$$$$
Caviar
- ✉ 2nd floor, 538 Madison Avenue, between 54th and 55th Streets
- ☎ 212-980 5908
- 🖰 www.caviarrusse.com
- 🚇 Subway F to 5th Avenue

Posh caviar and cigar lounge where you can see how the other half lives, dining on caviar costing up to $300 for 25g. A spoon of the cheapest caviar is around $10 though and a three-course tasting menu is $65, so it's possible to indulge without going bankrupt.

CHIN CHIN　　　　$$
Chinese
- ✉ 216 East 49th Street between 2nd and 3rd Avenues
- ☎ 212-888 4555
- 🖰 www.chinchinny.com
- 🚇 Subway 6 to 51st Street

One of New York's finest Chinese restaurants, it frequently plays host to the power crowd.

DOCKS OYSTER BAR　　　　$$$
Seafood
- ✉ 633 3rd Avenue at 40th Street
- ☎ 212-986 8080
- 🖰 www.docksoysterbar.com
- 🚇 Subway 4, 5, 6, 7 to Grand Central/42nd Street

This fish and seafood speciality restaurant also has a popular bar. Main dishes, such as red snapper, from $26.

EUROPA CAFE　　　　$
Mediterranean
- ✉ 599 Lexington Avenue at 53rd Street
- ☎ 212-755 6622
- 🖰 www.europacafe.com
- 🚇 Subway E, F to Lexington/3rd Avenue

A welcoming restaurant that has been designed in natural elements of wood, stone and earth tones to create a soothing environment. There are lots of branches dotted around the city (check the website) and you can pick up breakfast, lunch and snacks here, including creating your own sandwiches, wraps and salads. This one isn't open on Sat and Sun.

FOUR SEASONS　　　　$$$$
Continental
- ✉ 99 East 52nd Street between Lexington and Park Avenues
- ☎ 212-754 9494
- 🖰 www.fourseasonsrestaurant.com
- 🚇 Subway 6 to 51st Street; E, F to Lexington/3rd Avenue

You have a choice between the Grill Room or the Pool Room at this landmark restaurant, and whichever you opt for will make you feel like one of New York's movers and shakers – this is where they come for their power lunches. The Continental dishes like beef carpaccio and filet mignon are exquisite, the setting elegant and the service impeccable. Pricey? You bet.

Four Seasons

NEW YORK FOODS AND FOOD TERMS

Arugula: The American name for rocket, used in salads.

Bagels: As opposed to bialys, these are the delicious Jewish creations, which are at their very best when filled with smoked salmon and cream cheese.

Bialy: A cousin of the bagel, it originates from Bialystock in Eastern Europe and is kosher Jewish food. The dough is not as chewy as a bagel and there is no hole in the middle, just a depression in which garlic and onions are put. Without any tasty extras such as cream cheese, this is truly boring food.

Cannoli: Tubular-shaped biscuit bells with fresh cream on the inside, these come from Italy and are truly delicious.

Cilantro: American name for the fresh leaves of coriander.

Cobbler: A fruit pie topped with a biscuit-style crust.

Grits: Corn kernels.

Halva: Sweetened, crushed sesame paste. It originates from the Mediterranean, Turkey and Arabia.

Konja: A Chinese dessert that you can buy in bags – they are individual mouth-size pots of lychee jelly.

Lox: Thinly sliced pieces of smoked salmon, generally sold with a 'schmear' of cream cheese. It tastes the same as a smoked salmon and cream cheese bagel but works out much cheaper.

Morels: Deliciously meaty mushrooms from Oregon.

Pie: Used to refer to an entire pizza. Most are much larger than the ones we eat in the UK, so people tend to buy by the slice or share a whole 'pie'.

Scallion: Spring onion.

Schmear: A spreading of cream cheese on a bagel.

Sub: An extra large, long roll, named for its submarine-like shape.

You can find a list of more general US foods and food terms on pages 17–18.

GRAND CENTRAL OYSTER BAR $$–$$$
Seafood
- ✉ Grand Central Station, lower level, between 42nd Street and Vanderbilt Avenue
- ☎ 212-490 6650
- 🖱 www.oysterbarny.com
- 🚇 Subway 4, 5, 6, 7 to Grand Central/42nd Street

It seems only appropriate to have a landmark restaurant like this in the landmark that is Grand Central Station. Its fame stems from the generations of connoisseurs who have consumed 1,000 dozen oysters every day at the counters of this atmospheric saloon since 1913. There's lots of other types of seafood available too.

LA GRENOUILLE $$$
French
- ✉ 3 East 52nd Street between 5th and Madison Avenues
- ☎ 212-752 1495
- 🖱 www.la-grenouille.com
- 🚇 Subway 6 to 51st Street

A sophisticated temple of a townhouse for Francophiles that first opened its doors in 1962, the exquisite French food is well worth its price. If money's no object, go for dinner; otherwise go for a more economical lunch.

LE CIRQUE $$$–$$$$
French–American
- ✉ One Beacon Court, The Bloomberg Building, 151 East 58th Street at Lexington Avenue
- ☎ 212-644 0202
- 🖱 www.lecirque.com
- 🚇 Subway 4, 5, 6 to 59th Street

Sirio Maccioni's family-run restaurant has been the toast of the city for 30 years. After shutting the doors on Le Cirque 2000 at the New York Palace Hotel, it took over a year for the master restaurateur to find a suitable place to reopen. One Beacon Court, as it's officially known, is a pretty impressive replacement being a soaring curve entirely covered in glass. It attracts the same regular patrons it used to, from the political, financial, music and film worlds, including Robert De Niro, Oprah Winfrey, Bill Clinton and The Rolling Stones. The 1,486m²/16,000ft² restaurant features a main dining room, separate bar area and private mezzanine for those who want to see but not be seen.

Expect lots of jaw-dropping sights such as a soaring wine tower that connects the mezzanine to the first floor, an all-glass bar and giant abstract Big Top light shade. There's a prix fixe 3-course lunch menu for $49.

NYINTHEKNOW

Michael Romei, concierge at The Waldorf Towers (www. thewaldorftowers.com), as you'd expect has a few dining secrets up his sleeve. 'Papillon (www.papillonbistro. com) is a 2-storey French Bistro which is fairly unknown; located at 22 East 54th Street between 5th and Madison Avenue. The classic French bistro fare is offered daily for lunch and dinner but what is really quite special about this restaurant is that they offer Saturday night opera. It actually has some of the best young opera stars performing continuously throughout the evening from 9pm until closing! I'd also recommend Trattoria Malatesta (www.malatestatrattoria. com) at 649 Washington Street at Christopher Street (212-741 1207). It's a charming little simple Italian restaurant owned by three young Italian guys who pull up in front in their Vespas. Bocca di Bacco (http:// boccadibacconyc.com) at 828, 9th Avenue between 55th and 54th Streets is also great. It's not listed in the Zagat, but in my opinion it's a hidden gem, offering great quality Tuscan Italian food to a young hip crowd. It offers exceptional world wines by the glass in addition to an extensive collection of Tuscan wines. The restaurant has a rustic design with a modern feel and often shows Fellini films at random on various flat screens. Moderately priced as well.'

LIPS $$
Italian
- ⊠ 227 East 56th Street between 3rd and 2nd Avenues
- ☎ 212-675 7710
- ⏏ www.lipsnyc.com

Loud and fun drag entertainment on stage while you dine on Italian dishes named after popular queens like Spanky, a lasagne; all the waitresses are in drag, too!

TOP 5 RESTAURANTS TO SPOT A CELEBRITY
Blue Water Grill: Union Square (p188)
Lucky Strike: SoHo (p185)
Nobu: TriBeCa (p187)
TriBeCa Grill: TriBeCa (p188)
Tao New York (p176)

PALM $$
Seafood–Steakhouse
- ⊠ 837 2nd Avenue between 44th and 45th Streets
- ☎ 212-687 2953
- ⏏ www.thepalm.com
- 🚇 Subway 4, 5, 6, 7 to Grand Central/42nd Street

A family-run business and now the heart of a multi-million-pound empire of Palm restaurants the length and breadth of North America. Thanks to the double steak speciality, it had earned its reputation as one of New York's greatest steakhouses by the 1930s. In the 1940s, lobster was introduced, setting the seal on the surf-and-turf trend.

Palm continues to be a Mecca for celebrities and the wheelers and dealers of Manhattan, who come not only for the giant steaks and jumbo Maine lobsters but also for the Italian classics and wide choice of dishes. Palm Too across the road (840 2nd Avenue, 212-697 5198) was opened to take the overspill and now has its own loyal customers.

SMITH & WOLLENSKY $$
American
- ⊠ 797 3rd Avenue at East 49th Street
- ☎ 212-753 1530
- ⏏ www.smithandwollensky.com
- 🚇 Subway 6 to 51st Street

Serving quality steak and chops since 1977, you'll spot this restaurant straight away by the American flags flying on the outside. There are branches in London now, but nothing beats a giant steak or ribs here.

SPRIG $$–$$$
American–Italian
- ⊠ 888 3rd Avenue in The Lipstick Building between 53rd and 54th Streets
- ☎ 212-249 4500
- ⏏ www.sprigny.com
- 🚇 Subway 4, 6 to Lexington/51st Street

It's the abundance of pavement tables with green chairs that first attracted me to Sprig (it was a hot day and I didn't want to be stuck inside for lunch!). Luckily, the seasonal food

Palm

lived up to the outside, which I'd describe as American-Euro. Think lobster and mushroom linguini, salmon salad and steak Milanese.

BRITTIP

For cheap pre-dinner drinks, take advantage of Sprig's daily happy hour, 5.30–7.30pm, when wine by the glass and cocktails are half price.

RESTAURANTS

WATER CLUB $$–$$$
Seafood
- ✉ The East River between 28th and 32nd Streets
- ☎ 212-683 3333
- 🖰 www.thewaterclub.com
- 🚗 Subway 6 to 28th Street, near Madison Square

Another delightful and special venue from the owner of the River Café (p159), this nautical restaurant, set on an East River barge, also specialises in seafood. The Crow's Nest, a seasonal outdoor patio, sits atop the main dining room and features a moderately priced menu and fun drinks mid-May–late Sept and offers fab views of the East River. Although on the pricey side, it's well worth splashing out for the fine cuisine and, if you're counting the pennies, the weekend brunch option at a prix fixe is an excellent way to sample some delicious dishes while gazing at that view.

MIDTOWN WEST

BARBETTA $$$
Italian
- ✉ 321 West 46th Street between 8th and 9th Avenues
- ☎ 212-246 9171
- 🖰 www.barbettarestaurant.com
- 🚗 Subway A, C east to 42nd Street

During the summer, the rather special Barbetta garden is one of the city's most sought-after sites for dining, with its century-old trees and the scented blooms of magnolia, wisteria, jasmine and gardenia. Having celebrated its 100th birthday in 2006, Barbetta lays claim to the oldest Italian restaurant in New York and features cuisine from Piedmont in north-west Italy. Inside it's incredibly ornate and luxurious, with drapes, candles and chandeliers.

BOMBAY PALACE $$
Indian
- ✉ 30 West 52nd Street between 5th and 6th Avenues
- ☎ 212-541 7777
- 🖰 www.bombay-palace.com
- 🚗 Subway B, D, F, V, to 47th Street.

This upmarket Indian has a regal air, thanks to the dark wood panelling and crystal chandelier. It opened in 1979 and has been feeding the city masses every since with very good dishes, primarily Punjabi, which include seekh kebab, chicken tikka and tandoori shrimp and achar gosht, a chilli lamb stew.

JEAN GEORGES $$$$
French
- ✉ Trump International Hotel, 1 Central Park West between 60th and 61st Streets
- ☎ 212-299 3900
- 🖰 www.jean-georgesrestaurant.com
- 🚗 Subway A, B, C, D, 1, 9 to 59th Street/ Columbus Circle

Celebrity chef Jean-Georges Vongerichten's exquisite French dishes are served in an elegant and visually stunning landmark restaurant that is both romantic and relaxed. 'Prepare to sit open-mouthed – when you're not eating, that is' declares a New York Metro review of this Adam Tihany-designed contemporary Art Deco-style cream and white dining room (I was paranoid about spillages). The upscale crowd also gets to enjoy superb views of Central Park, while in good weather it's possible to enjoy a table outside. An added advantage of this is the bargain $32, 2-plate, prix fixe lunches on the terrace, also served in the Nougatine Room. Dish highlights on a continually changing seasonal menu have included asparagus with rich morel mushrooms and Muscovy duck steaks with sweet and sour jus. It's an unbeatable combination, so book your table in advance.

LE BERNARDIN $$$$
Seafood

✉ 155 West 51st Street between 6th and 7th Avenues
☎ 212-554 1515
🖰 www.le-bernardin.com
🚇 Subway V, F, B, D to Rockefeller Center

This is a marvellous restaurant. It's very pricey, the prix fixe lunch alone is $75, with dinner from $130 each, but it's more than worth it if you have the money because the mouth-watering dishes are sublime. Chef Eric Ripert's cuisine is regarded by NY gourmands as very inventive. He provides an almost raw menu, which has featured delicacies such as lemon-splashed scallops with olive oil and chives. From the cooked menu, tasty treats include celeriac open ravioli with lobster and shrimp with foie gras truffle sauce, or baked snapper in spicy sour broth. The dining room itself is also a pleasure to experience, featuring crisp white linen, rich furnishings and a wood-panelled bar with smart blue-and-gold striped chairs for lounging in pre and post-dinner.

WORLD YACHT
DINNER CRUISES $$$
Gourmet American

✉ Pier 81, West 41st Street at Hudson River
☎ 212-630 8100
🖰 www.worldyacht.com
🚇 Subway A, C, East to 42nd Street

If there's one thing that you do before you leave the city, it's to book a 4-course dining experience with World Yacht. This seasonal cruise down the river and around the bay offers, without a doubt, the best views of Midtown and Lower Manhattan plus the Statue of Liberty. You can chow down on delicacies like steak and lobster skewer, filet mignon, sevruga caviar and mustard-marinated organic chicken cooked while gazing at the city spread out before you. The chefs are some of the finest in New York, yet the prix fixe meals are pretty reasonable – including a 2-hour brunch cruise with buffet and music for $69 (excluding taxes) Fri and Sat. Smart dress; jackets required.

World Yacht Dinner Cruises

HUDSON PLACE $$–$$$
American–Italian
- ✉ 538 3rd Avenue
- ☎ 212-686 6600
- 🖰 www.hudsonplacenyc.com
- 🚗 Subway 6 to 33rd Street

Murray Hill isn't home to many smart restaurants, but this lovely eatery is worth making the trip out west for. It has the vibe of a local hub rather than a tourist stop, which is appealing as is the black exterior with smart red awnings and large windows that can be pushed aside in summer. Dishes like lobster ravioli or crab cakes are delicious, but there's also a pizza menu if you want to keep things on budget. Open for brunch, lunch and dinner.

NOHO

FIVE POINTS $$
American
- ✉ 31 Great Jones Street between Lafayette Street and Bowery
- ☎ 212-253 5700
- 🖰 www.fivepointsrestaurant.com
- 🚗 Subway B, V, S to Broadway/Lafayette; 6 to Bleecker Street

Named after the once infamous gangland area, this is a popular neighbourhood restaurant with a friendly bar, so now there's no need to worry. For a good, tasty meal, try out the Maine scallop with apple cider sauce or the home-made sweet potato ravioli.

INDOCHINE $$$
Vietnamese–French
- ✉ 430 Lafayette Street between Astor Place and East 4th Street
- ☎ 212-505 5111
- 🖰 www.indochinenyc.com
- 🚗 Subway 6 to Astor Place

Attracts an upmarket crowd, including the odd celeb and serves delicious Vietnamese–French dishes, such as spring rolls and sole fish wrapped in banana leaf, in tiny portions.

BRITTIP
Indochine serves great cocktails. Try the Indochine Martini: pineapple and ginger infused Imperia vodka with fresh lime juice – delicious!

NOLITA

CAFE HABANA $
Cuban
- ✉ 17 Prince Street at Elizabeth Street
- ☎ 212-625 2001

- 🖰 www.cafehabana.com
- 🚗 Subway N, R to Prince Street; 6 to Spring Street

Cool little café where you can get your fill of burritos, chicken Diablo and side orders like Mexican-style corn and sweet plantains while rubbing shoulders with a curious mix of old-timers, hipsters and tourists.

EIGHT MILE CREEK $$$
Australian
- ✉ 240 Mulberry Street between Prince and Spring Streets
- ☎ 212-431 4635
- 🖰 www.eightmilecreek.com
- 🚗 Subway N, R to Prince Street; 6 to Spring Street

Just a few steps north of Little Italy, the laid-back Aussies have arrived serving up cuisine from Down Under. There's now an out-the-back beer garden, which is home to weekly 'You bring meat, we'll supply the barbie' parties in the summer.

HOOMOOS ASLI $–$$
Middle Eastern
- ✉ 100 Kenmare Street between Mulberry and Center Streets
- ☎ 212-966 0022
- 🚗 Subway 6 to Spring Street

This is a great find if you're on a budget, small but not a dive and offering tasty Israeli cuisine – falafel, pittas, pan-fried chicken in breadcrumbs and spices, beef with caramelised onions and rice, with prices starting at around $10.

BRITTIP
If you want refreshments but are too busy shopping or sightseeing for a lengthy stop at a restaurant, then stop off at the fantastically named Mudspot (www.onmud.com), 307 East 9th Street, where you can buy a warming espresso to perk you up. Or, get a coffee from the mobile orange Mud Truck at Astor Place between 4th Avenue and 8th Street.

ZENGO $$–$$$
Mexican–Asian
- ✉ 622 3rd Avenue at 40th Street
- ☎ 212-808 8110
- 🖰 www.richardsandoval.com
- 🚗 Subway 1, 2, 3 Grand Central Station

This 3-level restaurant includes a mezzanine with a sake lounge and the lower floor houses La Bibliotheca, which serves 400 tequilas in a library setting. The main dining room has a dark wood interior and leather

THE AMERICAN DINER

We don't have a real equivalent of an American diner in the UK, but the closest is probably a cross between a transport café and a Garfunkel's. In a nutshell, diners are relatively cheap, have a homey feel to them, but are a lot smarter than your average café. They specialise in American comfort food – pancakes, waffles, crispy bacon, eggs, grill foods, meatloaf – the kind of things that we would choose for a brunch. Go to just about any American city or town and you'll find a good smattering of diners. The one exception is Manhattan, where they are very thin on the ground. Some of the few good diners in New York include:

Midtown West
Market Diner: 572 11th Avenue at West 43rd Street, 212-244 2888, www.marketdinernyc. com. One of the most famous diners in Manhattan, this is where clubbers go to get breakfast or to fill up before the evening run.

Morningside Heights
Tom's Restaurant: 2880 Broadway at 112th Street, 212-864 6137, www.tomsrestaurant.net. It's been around since the 1940s and you may recognise the exterior if you watched Seinfeld. If you come here you'll be sharing the space with Columbia University students, who enjoy the cheap comfort food.

NoHo
Great Jones Cafe: 54 Great Jones Street between Bowery and Lafayette Streets, 212-674 9304, www.greatjones.com. Cheap and cheerful place running for 3 decades, with weekend brunch 11.30am–4pm.

Theater District
Ellen's Stardust Diner: 1650 Broadway at 51st Street, 212-956 5151, www. ellensstardustdiner.com. Tourists and children love this 1950s-style diner thanks to its kitsch-retro decor and the singing waitresses. It's great fun, but you wouldn't want to eat here too often – think burgers, chips and anything else that's greasy!

Upper West Side
EJ's Luncheonette: 1271 3rd Avenue at 73rd Street, 212-472 0600. A traditional American diner that serves a mean cup of coffee. Cash only.

(183)

RESTAURANTS

banquettes. The food is excellent and unusual, such as catfish filet with rice noodles, peanuts and black bean chilli sauce, and don't miss the desserts, such as tequila snowcones.

SOHO

SoHo is a great place to head for when eating out, day or night. Its diverse range of restaurants, at all different price points, means that you're pretty much guaranteed to find something to appeal to even the most picky of dining partners.

ANTIQUE GARAGE RESTAURANT $$-$$$
Mediterranean
- 41 Mercer Street near Grand Street
- 212-219 1019
- www.antiquegaragesoho.com
- Subway C, E to Spring Street/N, R, W, Q, J, M, Z, 6 to Canal Street

I was laden down with bags during a SoHo shopping expedition when I stumbled on the Antiques Garage and instantly fell for its charms. It's housed in a former car repair shop and has an open front in the summer, meaning it's a great place to watch SoHo while tucking into a mezze such as marinated

octopus. The decor is arty, with vintage mirrors, chandeliers and an ornate sofa at the front, plus there's live jazz several nights a week. Despite celeb fans, like Kevin Spacey, it's still low-key and local. Lovely.

AURORA $$-$$$
Modern Italian
- 510 Broome Street
- 212-334 9020
- www.auroraristorante.com
- Subway C, E to Spring Street/N, R, W, Q, J, M, Z, 6 to Canal Street

Open for brunch, lunch and dinner, this lovely Italian eatery, with exposed red brick and polished wood tables, serves up a mouth-wateringly varied and inventive menu, from primi saffron tagliatelle, rock shrimp and cherry tomato to secondi roasted Chatham Bay cod with sweet garlic and fennel emulsion.

BALTHAZAR $$
Bistro
- 80 Spring Street between Broadway and Crosby Streets
- 212-965 1414
- www.balthazarny.com
- Subway N, R to Prince Street

Blue Ribbon Brasserie

A classy French brasserie, with a genuinely French ambience, serving up good food to a trendy crowd. Great oysters and lovely old-fashioned zinc bar.

BLUE RIBBON BRASSERIE $$$
American
- ✉ 97 Sullivan Street between Prince and Spring Streets
- ☎ 212-274 0404
- 🖑 www.blueribbonrestaurants.com
- 🚇 Subway C east to Spring Street

This restaurant gets packed at any time of the day or (late) night, so don't decide to come here if you are on a tight schedule. If you're not, the eclectic seafood dishes, like fried oysters and sautéed skate, are definitely worth the wait.

DOS CAMINOS SOHO $$-$$$
Mexican
- ✉ 475 West Broadway at Houston Street
- ☎ 212-277 4300
- 🖑 www.brguestrestaurants.com
- 🚇 Subway C, E to Spring Street

Excellent margaritas here while you're gazing at the fab menu that includes salad with calamari and chorizo, red snapper scallop with spicy mango and passion fruit and lime cilantro marinated gulf shrimp.

FANELLI'S CAFE $
American
- ✉ 94 Prince Street at Mercer Street
- ☎ 212-226 9412

🚇 Subway N, R to Prince Street
Contemporary crowds pack this former speakeasy, now an old saloon-style bar and dining room serving American food. It does excellent sandwiches for lunch.

KITTICHAI $$$
Thai
- ✉ 60 Thompson Street between Spring and Broome Streets
- ☎ 212-219 2000
- 🖑 www.kittichairestaurant.com
- 🚇 Subway C, E to Spring Street

Based in trendy SoHo hotel 60 Thompson, this is a fashionable restaurant in a theatrical Bangkok-meets-New-York setting and serves up delicious Thai cuisine at pretty high prices.

L'ECOLE $$
French
- ✉ 462 Broadway
- ☎ 212-219 3300
- 🖑 www.lecolenyc.com
- 🚇 Subway 6, J, M, Z, N, Q, W to Canal Street; 6 to Spring Street.

This is the place to come if you want haute cuisine for café prices, as the chefs of this bright, airy restaurant are students of the French Culinary Institute who try out their cooking skills on willing customers. Just think, you could be eating poached sole with shrimp and mussels for just $30 from the prix fixe lunch menu made by a star chef of the future.

Fannelli's

LUCKY STRIKE $$
French
- ✉ 59 Grand Street between West Broadway and Wooster Street
- ☎ 212-941 0772
- ⌂ www.luckystrikeny.com
- 🚆 Subway A, C, E, 1, 9, N, A, 6 to Canal Street

Restaurateur Keith McNally's hot spot has become a watering hole for models, celebrities and club kids, as well as SoHo's art crowd. There are live DJs and ask for the cocktail list and marvel at the many martinis, including chocolate and espresso.

MERCER KITCHEN $$$
French–Eclectic
- ✉ Mercer Hotel, 99 Prince Street at Mercer Street
- ☎ 212-966 5454
- ⌂ www.jean-georges.com
- 🚆 Subway N, R, W to Prince Street

Jean-Georges Vongerichten (he of Jean-Georges fame) oversees the eclectic French-inspired cuisine that is served to a trendy crowd in a chic environment.

THEATER DISTRICT (BROADWAY)

From 6th Avenue in the east to 9th Avenue in the west and from West 40th Street to West 53rd Street, the Theater District is, as you'd expect, a good place to head for a wallet-friendly pre-theatre meal.

BLUE FIN $$
Seafood
- ✉ W Hotel Times Square, 1567 Broadway at 47th Street
- ☎ 212-918 1400
- ⌂ www.bluefinnyc.com
- 🚆 Subway N, R, W to 49th Street

A true treasure, where fresh fish is served to the sounds of live music in a sleek setting. Sushi is available on the 1st floor.

CAFE UN-DEUX-TROIS $$
French
- ✉ 123 44th Street between 6th and 7th Streets
- ☎ 212-354 4148
- ⌂ www.cafeundeuxtrois.com
- 🚆 Subway all lines to 42nd Street

A tip from a *Brit Guide* reader, this beautiful bistro serves up mouth-watering favourites like steak frites and poulet cordon bleu in a lovely space, complete with long wooden bar, chandeliers, black and white pictures on the wall and leather and wood seating. A little bit of Paris in NYC.

BRITTIP
The main drag for eating in the Theater District is between 8th and 9th Avenues on West 46th Street and is known as Restaurant Row.

FIREBIRD $$$–$$$$
Caviar–Russian
- ✉ 365 West 46th Street between 8th and 9th Avenues
- ☎ 212-586 0244
- ⌂ www.firebirdrestaurant.com
- 🚆 Subway A, C east to 42nd Street

The opulent Russian decor creates a fabulous setting for tucking into the caviar and blinis.

Lucky Strike

The prix fixe pre-theatre dinner is pretty good value at $45, but prices have crept up. The vodka list, as you'd expect, is lengthy.

FRANKIE & JOHNNIE'S STEAKHOUSE $$
Steakhouse
- ✉ 269 West 45th Street between Broadway and 8th Avenue
- ☎ 212-997 9494
- ⌖ www.frankieandjohnnies.com
- 🚇 Subway A, C, E, N, R to 42nd Street

This is considered to be one of the longest-running shows on Broadway, having first opened as a speakeasy in 1926. Now it still retains its intimate hideaway aura and archetypal New York reputation as a classic steakhouse that has become renowned for its generous portions.

◀💂 BRITTIP
Due to a law banning smoking in all indoor public spaces, it's not possible to smoke even at a restaurant's bar. Some restaurants with outdoor seating are able to set aside tables for smoking, though.

PALM NEW YORK WEST SIDE $$-$$$
Seafood–Steakhouse
- ✉ 250 West 50th Street between Broadway and 8th Avenue
- ☎ 212-333 7256
- ⌖ www.thepalm.com/palm-west
- 🚇 Subway 1, 9 to 50th Street

A sister restaurant to the incredibly successful Palm restaurant (p179), this has very quickly become a hot spot for theatre-goers and tourists. Decent food at a decent price.

PETROSSIAN $$$
Caviar–Russian
- ✉ 182 West 58th Street at 7th Avenue
- ☎ 212-245 2214
- ⌖ www.petrossian.com
- 🚇 Subway N, R to 57th Street

Caviar, foie gras and smoked salmon served in the historic and ornate Alwyn Court Building. Brunch, lunch and dinner can be enjoyed in the Art-Deco-style mirrored bar or the dining room, with Lalique wall sconces and Limoges china.

PLANET HOLLYWOOD $
American
- ✉ 1540 Broadway at West 45th Street
- ☎ 212-333 7827
- ⌖ www.planethollywood.com
- 🚇 Subway N, Q, R, S, W, 1, 2, 3, 7 to Times Square

Hollywood memorabilia with the standard American burger fare.

RUBY FOO'S $$
Asian
- ✉ 1626 Broadway at 49th Street
- ☎ 212-489 5600
- ⌖ www.rubyfoos.com
- 🚇 Subway A, C, E, 1, N R to Times Square

Asian décor, such as dozens of hanging lanterns and bronze Buddha statues combine beautifully with delicious Asian food. Dim sum is a speciality of the house.

THE VIEW $$$-$$$$
Continental
- ✉ Top floor, Marriott Marquis Hotel, 1535 Broadway at 45th Street
- ☎ 212-398 1900
- ⌖ www.nymarriottmarquis.com
- 🚇 Subway N, R, S, 1, 2, 3, 7, 9 to Times Square/42nd Street

New York's recently spruced-up revolving restaurant attracts lovebirds and tourists in droves, and serves up a high standard of Continental cuisine. As expected, the views over Manhattan are spectacular, particularly at sunset.

TRIBECA

ACAPPELLA $$$-$$$$
Italian
- ✉ 1 Hudson Street at Chambers Street
- ☎ 212-240 0163
- ⌖
- 🚇 Subway 1, 9 to Franklin Street

You can chow down on wild boar, quail and venison at this lovely restaurant specialising in northern Italian cuisine. The decor is as impressive as the menu, with 5m/16ft high, beamed ceilings and Italian tapestries on the walls, plus huge windows offering views over TriBeCa. Closed Sun.

◀💂 BRITTIP
Don't be too put off by the prices of landmark restaurants – many offer fixed price menus and the cheapest is for lunch, when it's also easier to get a table. Go on, treat yourself!

BOULEY $$$-$$$$
New French
- ✉ 163 Duane Street
- ☎ 212-964 2525
- ⌖ www.davidbouley.com
- 🚇 Subway A, C, 1, 2, 3, 9 to Chambers Street

Spearheaded by chef David Bouley, offering incredibly intricate dishes like Maine day boat

RESTAURANTS

lobster, rhubarb, peas and parsnip cloud, in a fabulous setting of red, vaulted ceilings. Has gone down a storm with critics and locals alike.

BRUSHSTROKE $$$-$$$$
Japanese
- ✉ 30 Hudson Street at Duane Street
- ☎ 212-791 3771
- 🖰 www.davidbouley.com
- 🚌 Subway A, C, 1, 2, 3, 9 to Chambers Street

Another eatery from creative chef David Bouley, this fabulous Japanese restaurant has ambient, low lighting, slick staff and lots of polished wood. The menu is knockout and, at the time of going to print, tasting menus were around $85 per person, and included such delicacies as crab and black truffle sauce and chunks of lightly seasoned tuna served on dashi steamed rice.

THE HARRISON $$-$$$
Continental
- ✉ 355 Greenwich Street at Harrison Street
- ☎ 212-274 9310
- 🖰 www.theharrison.com
- 🚌 Subway 1, 2 to Franklin Street

Created by the owners of the hip Red Cat in Chelsea (p161), this chic restaurant serves up rustic Continental cuisine in an elegant setting – white tablecloths and candles in the evening, or grab an outside wood table in the day.

LOCANDA VERDE $$-$$$
Italian
- ✉ 377 Greenwich Street, at Moore Street
- ☎ 212-941 8900
- 🖰 www.locandaverdenyc.com
- 🚌 Subway 1, 9 to Franklin Street

Located in Robert De Niro's hip Greenwich Hotel, this bustling restaurant offers exceptionally good traditional Italian dishes in a real home-from-home environment, with shelves of wine and books, wood tables and comfortable banquettes. There's outdoor seating on Greenwich Street's sidewalk, plus inside diners can view the wood-burning stove and open kitchen.

NYINTHEKNOW
Native New Yorker Gwyneth Paltrow shares her favourite spots to dine on her lifestyle blog www.goop.com. Her favourites include Babbo (p166), Balthazar (p183), Angelica Kitchen (p162) and Momofuku Noodle Bar (p163).

NOBU $$$$
Japanese-Peruvian
- ✉ 105 Hudson Street at Franklin Street
- ☎ 212-219 0500
- 🖰 www.noburestaurants.com
- 🚌 Subway 1, 9 to Hudson Street

It's been around for 14 years now (ancient for a fashionable New York restaurant), but this TriBeCa Mecca is still without a doubt the best Japanese restaurant in the US, serving excellent fresh cuisine that will find 'tastebuds you never knew you had' according to critics. The decor, by architect David Rockwell, is east meets west, with birch trees, wood floors, seaweed mats and subdued lighting. The multi-award-winning menu includes lots of cooked and raw delicacies, the black cod with miso continues to be a favourite and the new-style sashimi lightly cooked with garlic is also amazing.

BRITTIP
If you can't get into the celeb-jammed Nobu, try Nobu Next Door (212-334 4445), which only takes walk-ins and is, unsurprisingly, located next door to the main restaurant. It is a more reasonably priced outlet for mere mortals who would rather wait for an hour than a month to sample some of the food everyone is raving about.

ODEON $$
American–French
- ✉ 145 West Broadway between Duane and Thomas Streets
- ☎ 212-233 0507
- 🖰 www.theodeonrestaurant.com
- 🚌 Subway 1, 9 to Chambers Street

A très hip hangout that attracts celebrities, thanks to its cool atmosphere and American–French cuisine. You'll need to book ahead. A great late-night stop as it stays open until 2am or for brunch the next day.

SUPER LINDA $$
South American
- ✉ 109 West Broadway at Reade Street
- ☎ 212-227 8998
- 🖰 http://superlindanyc.com
- 🚌 Subway 1, 2, 3, A, C to Chambers Street

Opened in 2012 and offers lip-smacking South American specials like ceviche, flat iron steak and chicken with sweet potato and piquillo peppers for brunch, lunch and dinner. Takeout service is available, too.

TERROIR TRIBECA $-$$
American
- ✉ 24 Harrison Street
- ☎ 212-625 9463
- 🖱 www.wineisterroir.com
- 🚗 Subway A, B, C to Franklin Street

Technically a wine bar, but the fodder here is so good and reasonable we're putting it in the restaurant section. You can order lots of dishes or a large main, like funky meatballs, sage leaves with lamb sausage or beet gorgonzola risotto balls, all $7 each. Simple, tasty and with a great selection of wines, too. There are several more Terroirs around the city, including Terroir T E ViL at 413 East 12th Street and Terroir Murray Hill at 439 3rd Avenue.

TRIBECA GRILL $$$
American
- ✉ 375 Greenwich Street at Franklin Street
- ☎ 212-941 3900
- 🖱 www.myriadrestaurantgroup.com
- 🚗 Subway 1, 9 to Franklin Street

Popular American restaurant which opened in 1990 and is one of the main reasons why TriBeCa has become such a hip hangout in recent years. It's located on the first 2 floors of the TriBeCa Film Center where De Niro has his film production company, so it's a good place to try to spot a celeb or two. Dishes like braised short ribs are rich and filling. The lunch menu attracts major crowds, with dishes like rare seared tuna and red wine braised octopus.

UNION SQUARE

BLUE WATER GRILL $$$$
Seafood
- ✉ 31 Union Square West at 16th Street
- ☎ 212-675 9500
- 🖱 www.brguestrestaurants.com
- 🚗 Subway L, N, Q, R, W, 4, 5, 6 to Union Square

Rated highly by *Zagat*, this place is not only brilliant for people-watching and celeb-watching, it is also a Mecca for all those who love their seafood. Dishes include delicacies like almond-crusted mahi mahi and blackened swordfish. It also has an oyster bar and a 150-seat jazz club for nightly entertainment and dining.

CHAT 'N' CHEW $
American diner
- ✉ 10 East 16th Street between 5th Avenue and Union Square West
- ☎ 212-243 1616
- 🖱 www.chatnchewnewyorkcity.com
- 🚗 Subway L, N, R, 4, 5, 6 to Union Square/14th Street

Classic 1950s diner with huge servings of meatloaf and other favourites. Regulars know to order the crispy-topped macaroni and cheese, with chicken or bacon added.

MESA GRILL $$
South-western
- ✉ 102 5th Avenue between 15th and 16th Streets near Union Square
- ☎ 212-807 7400

RESTAURANTS

Tribeca Grill

Strip House

www.mesagrill.com

Subway L, N, R, 4, 5, 6 to Union
Square/14th Street

Delicious and inventive south-western
cuisine, such as roasted sweet potato soup
and Mexican spice-rubbed pork tenderloin,
from chef Bobby Flay. A real winner, so give it
a try if you are in the area.

REPUBLIC $

Asian

✉ 37 Union Square West between 16th and
17th Streets

☎ 212-627 7172

www.thinknoodles.com

Subway L, N, R, 4, 5, 6 to Union
Square/14th Street

Specialists in excellent, quick, noodle-
based pan-Asian dishes in a canteen-style
environment that seats 150. There is also a
branch in Upper West Side.

STRIP HOUSE $$

American

✉ 13 East 12th Street between 5th Avenue
and University Place

☎ 212-328 0000

www.striphouse.com

Subway L, N, Q, R, W, 4, 5, 6 to 14th
Street/Union Square

You can eat succulent beef here, especially,
of course, the New York 'strip'. Lots of other
cuts are available as well as some fish, all
served in the glorious surroundings of leather
banquettes and velvet. Open for lunch and
dinner.

UPPER EAST SIDE

ATLANTIC GRILL $$–$$$

Seafood

✉ 1341 3rd Avenue between 76th and 77th
Streets

☎ 212-988 9200

www.atlanticgrill.com

Subway 77th Street

A long-standing popular restaurant with
the well-to-do Upper East Side set. It's all
very chic, from the polished wood floors and
artwork to the well-prepared, very fresh fish.
There's also an excellent wine list.

CAFE SABARSKY $$

Bistro

✉ 1048 5th Avenue at 86th Street

☎ 212-288 0665

www.cafesabarsky.com

Subway 4, 5, 6 to 86th Street

This is not just in a fabulous location – all
but opposite the Metropolitan Museum of
Art, yet quietly tucked away in the new Neue
Galerie Museum for German and Austrian
Art (p119) – but is a wonderful pit stop for
light breakfasts, lunches and afternoon tea;
crêpes with smoked trout and scallops with
asparagus. You'll also love its elegant Viennese
café decor of wood panelled walls and marble
fire place to match the Austrian-German art
theme of the museum itself.

CANDLE 79 $–$$

Vegan

✉ 154 East 79th Street at Lexington Street

189

RESTAURANTS

☎ 212-437 7179
🖰 www.candle79.com
🚇 Subway 6 to 77th Street
An unusual place in this swish neighbourhood as it's veggie – though undoubtedly upscale. It's an award-winner, and you can see why when you glance at the menu, which is well thought out and attracts plenty of meat-eaters because it's so tasty. There's organic wine on offer, along with fresh juices and smoothies.

NYINTHEKNOW

'I favour Abe & Arthur's (409 West 14th Street, http://abeandarthurs.com, 646-289 3930). It has an American menu that speaks to everyone's palate, you are sure to find a new favourite dish. Afterward, head out for drinks in the Meatpacking district – you have plenty of options and atmospheres to choose from. I also recommend Freeman's (191 Chrystie Street, http://freemansrestaurant.com, 212-420 0012). I love, love, love the whole ambience, from the alleyway to the small bar area to the taxidermy on the walls. Their menu is excellent and features out-of-the-norm American specialties from trout to a perfectly savoury cured pork loin. You don't have to be a total foodie to appreciate their awesome flavours.' Jocelyn Ojeda, Eventi hotel's concierge.

CARLYLE $$$
French
✉ Carlyle Hotel, 35 East 76th Street at Madison Avenue
☎ 212-744 1600
🖰 www.thecarlyle.com
🚇 Subway 6 to 77th Street
An old establishment that attracts a more mature clientele. If you want to see how NY socialites mix, try the divine French cuisine for breakfast or brunch.

DANIEL $$$$
French
✉ 60 East 65th Street between Park and Madison Avenues
☎ 212-288 0033
🖰 www.danielnyc.com
🚇 Subway 6 to 68th Street; F to Lexington Avenue/63rd Street
This is the place to 'dazzle a date' according to hip website www.gonyc.about.com. It's a

grand, elegant place with soaring ceilings, gilded columns, plush wall hangings and upholstery, plus fine art and mosaics. Daniel Boulud's haute cuisine is sumptuous, the best of which are the amazing, award-winning desserts; the chocolate bombe is indeed the bomb. It's fine dining with excellent service that will transport you as close to heaven as a mortal can get! A jacket is required to start the journey.

BRITTIP
Café Boulud at 20 East 76th Street (212-772 2600) also offers the Daniel's creativity at more accessible prices in a casual setting.

ITHAKA $$
Greek
✉ 308 East 86th Street between 1st and 2nd Avenues
☎ 212-628 9100
🖰 www.ithakarestaurant.com
🚇 Subway 4, 5, 6 to 86th Street
A superb Greek restaurant with Mediterranean-style decor of exposed brick walls painted white, stone floor and recessed lighting filtered through white fabric. It's known for its large portions, a real locals' favourite with the added benefit of a guitar player Wed–Sat.

ROSA MEXICANO $$
Mexican
✉ 1063 1st Avenue at 58th Street
☎ 212-753 7407
🖰 www.rosamexicano.com
🚇 Subway 4, 5, 6 to 59th Street
Extremely popular Mexican eatery, known as much for its margaritas as for its delicious food. Its signature dish is its guacamole mashed

SERAFINA ALWAYS $$
Italian
✉ 33 East 61st Street at Madison Avenue
☎ 212-702 9898
🖰 www.serafinarestaurant.com
🚇 Subway 4, 5, 6 to 59th Street
Famous for thin-crust pizzas that have been voted the best in the world by gourmets. Toppings include Al Porcini with porcini mushrooms, fontina cheese, and mozzarella and Al Caviar with salmon caviar, potatoes and crème fraîche. The signature focaccias – 2 layers of stuffed dough with delicious fillings – range from a delicious Scottish smoked salmon, asparagus and Italian robiola cheese, to truffle oil and robiola.

RESTAURANTS

ASIATE $$$–$$$$
French Japanese fusion
- ✉ 80 Columbus Circle at 60th Street
- ☎ 212-805 8800
- 🖰 www.mandarinoriental.com
- 🚇 Subway A, B, C, D, 9 to 59th Street/ Columbus Circle

On the top floors of the AOL Time Warner Center on the north-west arc of Columbus Circle lies the super posh Mandarin Oriental Hotel (p243), with spectacular views of the Manhattan skyline. Even if you can't afford to stay here, it's worth coming for drinks at trendy MO bar, followed by dinner in Asiate on the 35th floor, which offers a fusion of delicious French and Japanese cuisine – think wagyu beef with smoked potato purée and braised short rib. Also marvel at the glittering tree branch sculpture, representing Central Park, and dramatic wine wall.

BRITTIP
Brit Guide to New York reader Gina Higgs highly recommends Good Enough to Eat, 483 Amsterdam Ave at 83rd. 'Vast and inventive brunch menu and exceptional service. Absolutely worth the 10-minute wait'.

BENOIT $$
French Bistro
- ✉ 60 West 55th Street between 5th and 6th Avenues
- ☎ 646 943 7373
- 🖰 www.benoitny.com
- 🚇 Subway N, Q, R, W to 57th Street

This upscale casual French Bistro from Alain Ducasse opened in 2008 to great acclaim. Booking is wise.

EL MALECON II $
Dominican Caribbean
- ✉ 764 Amsterdam Avenue between 97th and 98th Streets
- ☎ 212-864 5648
- 🖰 www.maleconrestaurants.com
- 🚇 Subway 1, 9 to 66th Street

Great value for money. Locals pop in for the fried chicken, plantain, rice, peas and steak. The dining room is pretty mediocre, but who cares when the food is this tasty and $6 for the best roasted chicken outside the Caribbean. You can eat in or take out.

FATTY CRAB $$
Malaysian
- ✉ 2170 Broadway at 77th Street
- ☎ 212-496 2722
- 🖰 www.fattycrab.com
- 🚇 Subway 1, 2, 3 to 72nd Street

US celeb chef Zak Pecaccio's *Zagat*-rated place has a really eclectic menu just perfect for foodies who like to try something new, like Malay fish fry, quail egg shooters and chilli crab. There's also a branch in West Village.

BRITTIP
The Fatty Crab has introduced a brunch menu, so pop in here if you're feeling peckish and you've missed your hotel brekkie!

GABRIEL'S $$$
North Italian
- ✉ 11 West 60th Street
- ☎ 212-956 4600
- 🖰 www.gabrielsbarandrest.com
- 🚇 Subway A, B, C, D, 1 West 59th Street/ Time Warner Center

Recommended to us by a reader, this is a classy little joint with crisp, white tablecloths, wooden chairs and leather banquettes. It's where people from the entertainment industry like to congregate and sip blueberry bellinis and dine on delicious dishes like tortelloni filled with lamb and sea scallops sautéed with tarragon aioli and roast potatoes.

NYINTHEKNOW
'For a great outdoor venue – and one of our best kept secrets – try the Boat Basin (212-496 5542, www.boatbasincafe.com) under the West Side Highway at West 79th Street. It's hard to find even for New Yorkers but the views of the Hudson perched above the water's edge are amazing. Don't expect gourmet, it's fun food (burgers, hot dogs, nachos) and drinks – basically beer and coke,' says Mike Ricci, director of communications Hilton Hotels Corp north-east US and Canada.

OUEST $$–$$$
French–American
- ✉ 2315 Broadway between 83rd and 84th Streets
- ☎ 212-580 8700
- 🖰 www.ouestny.com
- 🚇 Subway 1, 2 to 86th Street

Award-winning restaurant, with chef and owner Tom Valenti at the helm. The menu is rich and bold, such as roast rabbit with garlic cappellini, and the decor pleasing, with wood walls and round red-leather booths.

191

RESTAURANTS

PASHA
$$
Turkish
- ✉ 70 West 71st Street between Columbus Avenue and Central Park West
- ☎ 212-579 8751
- 🖱 www.pashanewyork.com
- 🚇 Subway 1, 2 to 86th Street

A delightfully sumptuous restaurant; think deep reds and yellows, luxurious fabrics and tapestries hanging on the walls. You can order Turkish delights, from stuffed vine leaves to kebabs and there are some outside tables too.

PER SE
$$$$
American nouveau/French
- ✉ 10 Columbus Circle, 4th floor, at 60th Street
- ☎ 212-823 9335
- 🖱 www.perseny.com
- 🚇 Subway A, B, C, D, 9 to 59th Street/ Columbus Circle

The Manhattan restaurant that critics consistently adore, from its food to its service. The main dining room, which looks out across Central Park, is grand and spacious, with a grey and brown decor and towering arrangements of lilies at either end, plus a working fireplace, which is fabulous in winter. There food is just as elegant, with a menu that changes daily – try the 9-course chef's tasting menu for a memorable evening, with dishes such as oysters and pearls, snails and boeuff grillée.

PICHOLINE
$$$
Mediterranean
- ✉ 35 West 64th Street between Broadway and Central Park West
- ☎ 212-724 8585
- 🖱 www.picholinenyc.com

Picholine

- 🚇 Subway 1, 9 to 66th Street/Lincoln Center

A beautiful restaurant serving exquisite Mediterranean dishes in a refined and elegant setting. Opt to make it one of your 'special' treats while in the city so you can sample the amazing cheese trolley – yes trolley, not board. Each day more than 50 different cheeses, out of a total of 70 varieties, are on offer and, if you don't know which to choose, all the waiter (Maître d'Fromage!) is well versed in what cheeses go well with what wines and for what kind of palates. Take advantage of their considerable knowledge. A tradition to be savoured.

PIER 72
$-$$
American
- ✉ 270 West 72nd Street at West End Avenue
- ☎ 212-799 1019
- 🚇 Subway 1, 2, 3 to West 72nd Street

Great spot for some breakfast or fuel stop mid-sightseeing if you're in the area. There's a counter you can sit at and order giant slabs of watermelon, fresh pastries and coffee. Or pull up a chair at one of the diner-style tables for a hearty lunch of American fare, such as burger and fries. A bottle of Heinz tomato ketchup sits on every table.

PIZZERIA UNO
$
Italian
- ✉ 432 Columbus Avenue at 81st Street
- ☎ 212-595 4700
- 🖱 www.unos.com
- 🚇 Subway B, C to 81st Street

OK, so this is a chain restaurant, but it actually provides good-quality food for those wanting a simple, but tasty, meal at a very good price. This one is a great little neighbourhood joint offering an excellent range of family-friendly dishes just around the corner from the American Museum of Natural History (p102). There is an excellently priced children's menu, plus crayons. What more could you ask after tramping round dinosaur exhibits?

WEST VILLAGE

BOBO
$$-$$$
French
- ✉ 181 West 10th Street on corner of 7th Avenue
- ☎ 212-488 2626
- 🖱 www.bobonyc.com
- 🚇 Subway 1 to Christopher Street

I was strolling past and just had to go and investigate what was inside this pretty townhouse with a blue façade and colourful flower boxes – it turned out to be equally as enchanting inside. The menu is a treat, from

RESTAURANTS

asparagus salad and steak tartare starters to slow-cooked Arctic char and bouillabaisse for mains and each month, the chef creates cuisine inspired by a different region of France's cuisine, offered each Sunday for $35.

BONGO WEST VILLAGE $$$–$$$$
Seafood
- ✉ 395 West Street, corner of 10th Street and the Westside Highway
- ☎ 212-675 6555
- 🖰 www.bongonyc.com
- 🚗 Subway C, E to 23rd Street; 1, 9 to 28th Street

A swish oyster bar where you can sip Champagne and slip down half a dozen oysters for $18. If you're not a fan, there are other delicacies, including smoked trout salad, lobster roll and cod cakes. There are 3 rooms to choose from – Bar, Living Room and the Den, which retro furniture lovers will adore as they're all filled with cool mid-century pieces, from Eames to Miller.

CHARLEMAGNE $$–$$$
American
- ✉ 679 Greenwich Street at Christopher Street
- ☎ 646-558 5623
- 🖰 www.charlemagnenyc.com
- 🚗 Subway 1 to Christopher Street

This new brasserie has a laid-back neighbourhood vibe, serving excellent comfort food like roast chicken and leg of lamb with finesse – menu highlights include the raw bar with oysters and lobster. Serves brunch Sat and Sun.

COWGIRL $$
American
- ✉ 519 Hudson Street at West 10th Street
- ☎ 212-633 1133
- 🖰 www.cowgirlnyc.com
- 🚗 Subway C, E to 23rd Street; 1, 9 to 28th Street

This isn't just great for men and women who feel at home surrounded by cowgirl memorabilia, it's also frequented by families. Now in its 25th year of serving bargain American food – fried onion loaf, huge spare ribs and chicken-fried steak – and is also known for its margaritas. The people-watching outside the restaurant in summer is a treat.

DIABLO ROYALE $$
Mexican
- ✉ 189 West 10th Street at West 4th Street
- ☎ 212-620 0223
- 🖰 http://west.diabloroyale.com
- 🚗 Subway 1 to Christopher Street

Known for its tacos and tequilas. It's a fun, very popular place, which stays open late and has floor-to-ceiling windows that fold back, making it a favourite spot in summer. This isn't the restaurant for a romantic celebration, it is somewhere to head for cheap eats and cocktails in a buzzy, fun atmosphere.

GARAGE RESTAURANT $$–$$$
American
- ✉ 99 7th Avenue South at Christopher Street
- ☎ 212-645 0600
- 🖰 www.garagerest.com

Serves traditional American cuisine including steaks and a raw bar, with live jazz nightly and a friendly crowd.

LA RIPAILLE $$
French
- ✉ 605 Hudson Street at West 12th Street
- ☎ 212-255 4406
- 🖰 www.laripailleny.com

Authentic French country dining since 1980. A small, cosy and romantic restaurant with excellent bistro food.

MELIBEA $$–$$$
Contemporary Mediterranean
- ✉ 2 Bank Street at Greenwich Avenue
- ☎ 212-463 0090
- 🖰 www.melibeanyc.com
- 🚗 Subway A, C, E, L to 14th Street

Just-opened hot spot with a menu and interior drawing inspiration from Spain, Italy, Greece, Israel and Morocco. In layman's terms this means a beautiful tiled floor, wood tables and red velvet banquettes and dishes like hummus with beets, stuffed mozzarella with tomato confit, chicken marinated in Syrian spices and lamb tagine. I highly recommend.

SACRED CHOW $–$$
Vegan
- ✉ 227 Sullivan Street between Bleecker and West 3rd Streets
- ☎ 212-337 0863
- 🖰 www.sacredchow.com

Healthy bohemian vegan food shop and café.

Bongo

Restaurant reference guide

Name	Area	Style	Price range	Page
2 West	Battery Park	Gourmet American	$$–$$$	158
21 Club	Midtown	Gourmet American	$–$$$	172
A Voce	Madison Square/Flatiron	Italian	$$$–$$$$	170
Abe & Arthur's	Meatpacking	American	$$$	190
Acappella	TriBeCa	Italian	$$$–$$$$	186
Adrienne's Pizza Bar	Financial District	Italian	$–$$	163
Aldea	Flatiron District	Mediterranean	$$$–$$$$	171
Alias	Lower East Side	American	$$	170
Amy Ruth's Home Style Southern Soul Food	Harlem	Southern cuisine	$$	168
Angelica Kitchen	East Village	Vegetarian–vegan	$$	162
Antique Garage Restaurant	SoHo	Mediterranean	$$–$$$	183
Aquavit	Midtown	Scandinavian	$$$$	173
Arriba Arriba!	Hell's Kitchen	Mexican	$$	169
Asiate	Upper West Side	French Japanese Fusion	$$$–$$$$	191
Atlantic Grill	Upper East Side	Seafood	$$–$$$	189
Aureole	Midtown	American	$$$$	173
Aurora	SoHo	Modern Italian	$$–$$$	183
Babbo	Greenwich Village	Italian	$$$$	166
Balthazar	SoHo	Bistro	$$	183
Bamiyan	Gramercy	Afghan	$$	164
Barbetta	Midtown West	Italian	$$$	180
Battery Gardens	Battery Park	American Fusion	$$$$	158
Benoit	Upper West Side	French Bistro	$$	191
Benny's Burritos	East Village	Mexican	$$	162
Bereket	Lower East Side	Turkish	$	170
Better Burger NYC	Chelsea	Burgers	$–$$	160
BG	Midtown	American nouveau	$$$–$$$$	173
Big Wong King	Chinatown	Cantonese	$	161
Blue Fin	Theater District	Seafood	$$	185
Blue Ribbon Brasserie	SoHo	American	$$$	184
Blue Water Grill	Union Square	Seafood	$$$$	188
Boat Basin	Upper West Side	American	$–$$	191
Bobo	West Village	French	$$–$$$	192
Bocca di Bacco	Hell's Kitchen	Italian	$$–$$$	179
Boathouse at Central Park, The	Central Park	American–seafood	$$–$$$	159
Bombay Palace	Midtown West	Indian	$$	180
Bongo West Village	West Village	Seafood	$$$–$$$$	193
Bosie Tea Parlour	West Village	French	$–$$	166
Bottino	Chelsea	Italian	$$	160
Bouley	TriBeCa	New French	$$$–$$$$	186
Bread	Little Italy	Italian	$$	169
Brooklyn Star	Brooklyn	American comfort/Soul Food	$$–$$$	158
Brushstroke	TriBeCa	Japanese	$$$–$$$$	187
Buddakan	Chelsea	Pan–Asian	$$$–$$$$	160
Bull & Bear	Midtown East	Steakhouse	$$$–$$$$	176
Burger Joint at Le Parker Meridien	Midtown	American	$–$$	173
Café Gitane	Little Italy	French–North African	$$	169
Café Habana	NoLiTa	Cuban	$	182
Café Sabarsky	Upper East Side	Bistro	$$	189
Cafeteria	Chelsea	American diner	$$	160
Café Un-Deux-Trois	Theater District	French	$$	185
Calvisius Caviar Lounge	Midtown	Caviar	$$$–$$$$	174
Candle 79	Upper East Side	Vegetarian	$–$$	189
Carlyle	Upper East Side	French	$$$	190
Catch	Meatpacking District	Seafood	$$$	171
Caviar Russe	Midtown East	Caviar	$$$$	177
Charlemagne	West Village	American	$$–$$$	193
Chat 'n' Chew	Union Square	American diner	$	188
Chin Chin	Midtown East	Chinese	$$	177
China Grill	Midtown	Chinese	$$$	174
Commerce	Greenwich	New American	$$–$$$	166
Coppelia	Chelsea	Cuban	$$	160
Cornelia Street Café	Greenwich Village	Eclectic	$$	166
Cowgirl	West Village	American	$$	193
Daniel	Upper East Side	French	$$$$	190
db Bistro Moderne	Midtown	French–American	$$$–$$$$	174
Del Posto	Meatpacking District	Italian	$$$	171
Di Fara	Brooklyn	Pizza	$–$$	159
Diablo Royale	West Village	Mexican	$$	193

Name	Area	Style	Price range	Page
Dim Sum Go Go	Chinatown	Chinese–vegetarian	$$	161
Dock's Oyster Bar	Midtown East	Seafood	$$$	177
Dos Caminos Soho	SoHo	Mexican	$$–$$$	184
Eight Mile Creek	NoLiTa	Australian	$$$	182
El Malecon II	Upper West Side	Dominican Caribbean	$	191
Elephant & Castle	Greenwich & West Village	American	$–$$$	167
Eleven Madison Park	Gramercy Park	French–American	$$$$	164
Europa Café	Midtown East	Mediterranean	$	177
Fanelli's Café	SoHo	American	$	184
Fatty Crab	Upper West Side	Malaysian	$$	191
Ferrara	Little Italy	Italian café	$	170
Fiddlesticks Pub & Grill	Greenwich & West Village	American, Irish	$–$$	167
Firebird	Theater District	Caviar–Russian	$$–$$$	185
Five Points	NoHo	American	$$	182
Forty Four	Midtown	American	$$$	174
Four Seasons	Midtown East	Continental	$$$$	177
Frank	East Village	Italian	$	162
Frankie & Johnnie's	Theater District	Steakhouse	$$	186
Freeman's	Lower East Side	American	$$–$$$	190
Gabriel's	Upper West Side	North Italian	$$$	191
Garage Restaurant	West Village	American	$$–$$$	167
Gigino at Wagner Park	Battery Park	Italian	$$	158
Gnocco Cucina & Tradizione	East Village	Italian	$$	162
Gotham Bar and Grill	Greenwich Village	Gourmet American	$$$	167
Gordon Ramsay at the London	Midtown	British Fusion	$$$$	174
Gramercy Tavern	Gramercy Park	Gourmet American	$$$	164
Grand Central Oyster Bar	Midtown East	Seafood	$$–$$$	178
Grimaldi's	Brooklyn	Italian	$	159
Hard Rock Café	Midtown	American	$	174
Harrison, The	TriBeCa	Continental	$$–$$$	187
Hoomoos Asli	NoLiTa	Middle Eastern	$–$$	182
Hudson Place	Murray Hill	American Italian	$$–$$$	182
Inakaya	Midtown	Japanese	$$–$$$	174
Indochine	NoHo	Vietnamese–French	$$$	182
Ithaka	Upper East Side	Greek	$$	190
Jean Georges	Midtown West	French	$$$$	180
Joe's Shanghai	Chinatown	Chinese–Shanghai	$$	162
Katz's Delicatessen	Lower East Side	American–Jewish	$	170
Kittichai	SoHo	Thai	$$	184
Koodo Sushi	Financial District	Japanese	$–$$	164
La Grenouille	Midtown East	French	$$$	178
La Palapa	East Village	Mexican	$$	162
La Promenade des Anglais	Chelsea	French, Italian	$$$–$$$$	161
La Ripaille	West Village	French	$$	193
Le Bernardin	Midtown West	Seafood	$$$$	181
L'Ecole	SoHo	French	$$	184
Le Cirque	Midtown East	French–American	$$$–$$$$	178
Lips	Midtown East	Italian	$$	179
Locanda Verde	TriBeCa	Italian	$$–$$$	187
Lucky Strike	SoHo	French	$$	185
Maialino	Gramercy Park	Italian	$$–$$$	165
Manon	Meatpacking District	Contemporary American	$$$	171
MarkJoseph Steakhouse	South Street Seaport	Steakhouse	$$	164
Markt	Chelsea	Belgian	$$	161
Melibea	West Village	Contemporary Mediterranean	$$–$$$	193
Mercer Kitchen	SoHo	French–eclectic	$$$	185
Mesa Grill	Union Square	South-western	$$	188
Momofuku Noodle Bar	East Village	Noodles	$$	163
Nice Green Bo	Chinatown	Chinese–Shanghai	$–$$	162
Nobu	TriBeCa	Japanese–Peruvian	$$$$	187
Nobu Fifty Seven	Midtown	Japanese–Peruvian	$$$$	175
Noodle Pudding	Brooklyn	Italian	$$	159
Norma's	Midtown	American	$–$$	175
North End Grill	Battery Park	American Seafood	$$–$$$	158
Odeon	TriBeCa	American–French	$$	187
Old Homestead Steakhouse	Meatpacking District	American	$$	171
Opia	Midtown	French	$$–$$$$	175
Ouest	Upper West Side	French–American	$$–$$$	191
Palm	Midtown East	Seafood–steakhouse	$$	179
Palm New York West Side	Theater District	Seafood–steakhouse	$$–$$$	186
Pangea	East Village	Mediterranean	$$	163

Name	Area	Style	Price range	Page
Papillon	Midtown	French	$$$	179
Park, The	Chelsea	Mediterranean	$$$	161
Pasha	Upper West Side	Turkish	$$	192
Pastis	Meatpacking District	French	$$$	171
Per Se	Upper West Side	American Nouveau/French	$$$$	192
Peter Luger Steakhouse	Brooklyn	American	$$-$$$	159
Petrossian	Theater District	Caviar-Russian	$$$	186
Philip Marie	West Village	American	$$-$$$	167
Picholine	Upper West Side	Mediterranean	$$$	192
Pier 72	Upper West Side	American	$-$$	192
Pizzeria Uno	Upper West Side	Italian	$	192
Planet Hollywood	Theater District	American	$	186
Rao's	Harlem	Italian	$	168
Red Cat, The	Chelsea	Mediterranean–American	$$	161
Remi	Midtown	Italian	$$$	175
Republic	Union Square	Asian	$	189
River Café	Brooklyn	Gourmet American	$$$	159
Rock Center Café	Midtown	American	$$	175
Rosa Mexicano	Upper East Side	Mexican	$$	190
Rouge Tomate	Upper East Side	Belgian/Asia	$$$	167
Ruby Foo's	Theater District	Asian	$$	186
Russian Tea Room	Midtown	Russian	$$$$	175
Sacred Chow	West Village	Vegan	$-$$	193
Sal Anthony's SPQR	Little Italy	Italian	$$-$$$	170
Seagrill	Midtown	Seafood	$$$$	175
Serafina Always	Upper East Side	Italian	$$$	190
Smith & Wollensky	Midtown East	American	$$	179
Soto	Greenwich & West Village	Japanese	$$$-$$$$	167
Sprig	Midtown East	American, Italian	$$-$$$	179
Standard Grill, The	Meatpacking District	American, Mediterranean	$$$	172
Strip House	Union Square	American	$$	189
Super Linda	TriBeCa	South American	$$	187
Superfine	Brooklyn	Mediterranean	$$-$$$	159
Sylvia's	Harlem	Southern Soul Food	$	168
Tamarind	Gramercy Park	Indian	$$	165
Tao New York	Midtown	Asian	$$$-$$$$	176
Terroir Tribeca	TriBeCa	American	$$	188
Tomoe Sushi	Greenwich Village	Japanese	$$	168
Totonno's Pizzeria Napolitano	Brooklyn	Pizza	$-$$	159
Trattoria Malatesta	West Village	Italian	$$	179
TriBeCa Grill	TriBeCa	American	$$$	188
Union Square Cafe	Midtown East	American–Italian	$$-$$$	165
Upstairs at 21	Midtown	Gourmet American	$$	176
Veritas	Gramercy Park	Gourmet American	$$$$	166
View, The	Theater District	Continental	$$$-$$$$	186
Water Club	Midtown East	Seafood	$$-$$$	180
World Yacht Dinner Cruises	Midtown West	Gourmet American	$$$	181
Yaffa Café	East Village	American Diner	$	163
Zengo	NoLiTa	Mexican–Asian	$$-$$$	182

RESTAURANTS

Café Sabarsky

CHAPTER 8
Nightlife

New York is known for its shopping and exciting nightlife. After a hard day hitting the shops and sightseeing, it's time to take to the streets at night to discover exactly what makes the Big Apple one of the top cities in the world for evening entertainment.

A glance at any of the listings pages in the press or online will confirm that there is an amazing amount of evening entertainment to choose from. Any night of the week you'll find comedy shows with stand-up routines from some of the best in the business and live music from the hottest bands. The bar scene in NYC is particularly exciting: whether it's soaking up some cool jazz in the West Village or sipping apple martinis in a sophisticated Upper East Side joint, there's a bar or lounge to suit every type of person. And when it comes to theatre, you can take your choice from massive, long-running Broadway shows or edgy one-off productions.

BARS, LOUNGES & PUBS

Here's a selection of bars to drop into while you are out and about in the city, including some that are super swish, some more grungy and some lounges that stay open into the early hours. Lounges are very much an integral part of the New York nightlife scene. Placed somewhere between a plush bar and a club, they're somewhere for you to stay late, listen to DJs and sip cocktails, but most don't have dance floors. Pubs may not be quite the same as the Brit equivalent, but there are some great neighbourhood joints where you can get a pint of Guinness or beer.

CHELSEA
Bathtub Gin Bar: 132 9th Avenue between 18th and 19th Streets, 646-559 1671, www.bathtubginnyc.com.
This little joint has the vibe of a 1920s prohibition-era hideaway, as you enter it through the back wall of the Stone Street

197
NIGHTLIFE

The Rockefeller Center at night

TOP 5 BARS FOR ALFRESCO DRINKING

Brooklyn

Gowanus Yacht Club: 323 Smith Street, 718-246 1321. You'll feel you've really got off the tourist trail at this small outdoor beer garden close to the lovely Carroll Gardens. It attracts a chilled crowd of locals who sip beer and wine beneath the fairylight-bedecked trees before and after sunset. Bar food is also available.

Lower East Side

Barramundi: 67 Clinton Street between Rivington and Stanton Streets, 212-529 6999, www.barramundiny.com. A gorgeous walled garden covered with twinkling fairylights is romantic or cool depending on whom you are with. Attracts a mixed crowd of internationals.

Midtown

The Gansevoort Park Avenue Rooftop Bar: 420 Park Avenue South at 29th Street, 212-317 2900, www.gansevoorthotelgroup.com. Latest venture from the super cool hotel group, which has another property in the Meatpacking district. The rooftop bar is exclusive, with a pool that features a mosaic of a pin-up girl, wrap-around terraces, transparent floors and a sun deck.

Upper East Side

Terrace 5: 1000 5th Avenue at 82nd Street, 212-879 5500, www.moma.org. The terrace café (open in the summer) at the Metropolitan Museum of Art (p114) offers stunning views of the city, particularly at sunset.

West Village

B-Bar & Grill: 40 East 4th Street, 212-475 2220, www.bbarandgrill.com. The large outside patio, with bar, chic furniture and trees, is a magnet for fashionable West and East Villagers and is enclosed and fully heated in winter.

overlooking the river. Outside a rowdy crowd gathers post-work. From all angles, the view of New Jersey at sunset makes it worth a visit. The fact that you can also eat here – the menu features light bites like salads and pizzas – means it is even more appealing. It also has a cigar lounge.

EAST VILLAGE

2A: 25 Avenue A. 212-505 2466, www.2anyc.com/
A real musos hangout – 'grungily fab'. New Wave and punk 1970s music resonate in this cool bar and lounge.

11th Street Bar: 510 East 11th Street between Avenue A and B. 212-982 3929, www.11thstbar.com.
Marked only by an illuminated Guinness sign, this Irish pub is the place to enjoy a decent pint without having to look like you walked out of the pages of a lifestyle magazine. Sometimes has live music entertainment and is open until 4am.

NYINTHEKNOW

Nikki Ridgway, a Brit living in NYC and associate editor at travel website www.Jetsetter.com, reveals the hottest bars in town: 'Elsa (217 East 3rd Street, 917-882 7395, www.elsabar.com) for great cocktails. Bowery Hotel (335 Bowery, 212-505 9100, http://theboweryhotel.com), a chic hotel bar in the East Village. Joseph Leonard (170 Waverly Place, 646-429 8383, http://josephleonard.com), a bar and restaurant in West Village with a late-night menu offering things like east coast oysters and a great wine list. In Tribeca, try Tiny's & The Bar Upstairs (135 west Broadway between Thomas and Duane Streets, 212-374 1135, http://tinysnyc.com) set over 2 storeys of a historic townhouse, or try your chances at getting in to hip cocktail bar Weather Up (159 Duane Street, 212-766 3202, http://weatherupnyc.com).

Angel's Share: 8 Stuyvesant Street between East 9th Street and 3rd Avenue. 212-777 5415.
Dedicated to the art of mixology, this little gem of a bar will rustle up any cocktail you desire. Part of its charm is the fact that it's so hard to find, you'll feel as if you've stumbled across a city secret. Take the stairs to the second floor and veer left past the restaurant to the door at the rear. Inside you'll find a

Coffee Company. Inside, there's a copper bathtub in the middle of the room and visitors have been known to hop in if they've had one too many gin-based cocktails! Open until 4am Thurs–Sat.

Chelsea Brewing Company: Chelsea Pier, Pier 59, West Side Highway at 20th Street. 212-336 6440, www.chelseabrewingco.com. A venue that caters for all types of night-time needs, it's Manhattan's largest micro-brewery, with more than 20 brews on tap. Downstairs there's a sports bar atmosphere, while upstairs in the mezzanine lounge it's more romantic, with a fireplace and 2-storey glass windows

dark, intimate bar where classy city dwellers take their first dates.

Bar on A: 170 Avenue A near 11th Street. 212-353 8231, baronanewyork.com
This bar's been popular with villagers for more than a decade and it's easy to understand why. It's got a lovely laid-back vibe with exposed brick walls, blackboards, snakeskin bar stools, lots of cooling ceiling fans and an excellent selection of beers.

Beauty Bar: 231 East 14th Street between 2nd and 3rd Avenues. 212-539 1389, www.thebeautybar.com.
Deb Parker's theme bar is equipped with 1960s-style hairdryers and chairs, real manicurists, great drinks and a heavy dose of the hip and beautiful.

KGB: 85 East 4th Street between 2nd and 3rd Avenues. 212-505 3360, www.kgbbar.com.
Decorated with deep-red walls, portraits of Lenin and Brezhnev, propaganda posters and an oak bar from when it was a front for the Communist party. The crowd is a mix of actors, writers and drunks who love the private-parlour feel. Up-and-coming writers and successful authors often do free readings, so call to see who's on.

Sutra: 16 1st Avenue between 1st and 2nd Street. 212-677 9477, www.sutranyc.com.
Red velvet and lots of low lit lamps and candles create an intimate atmosphere in this sumptuous lounge bar serving exotic cocktails and known for its cool music. The underground chakra lounge is particularly dark and sexy.

GARMENT DISTRICT
Stitch: 247 West 37th Street between 7th and 8th Avenues. 212-852 4826, www.stitchnyc.com.
A good name for this bar in the heart of the clothing district. Cocktails, such as the Stiletto, are just as well named. Voted best after work bar in New York by www.citysearch.com, it's a place to meet the locals.

GREENWICH VILLAGE
Fat Black Pussycat: 130 West 3rd Street near 6th Avenue, 212-533 4790, www.thefatblackpussycat.com.
A casual crowd hangs out in the front room, where you'll find wooden booths and quirky wall art. We say don't stay around in there, but instead head through a side curtain to discover a lavish bohemian lounge with velvet couches and Moroccan lanterns. Lots of extras here, too, from a pool table to jukebox and web access terminals. Happy hour Sun–Thurs 4–10pm, the entire bar is half price.

Madame X: 94 West Houston Street between

Thompson Street and La Guardia Place. 212-539 0808, www.madamexnyc.com.
There's a real London Soho den-of iniquity feel to this joint, bathed as it is in red and lit by the glow of lanterns. Known for serving pretty potent cocktails and rare imported beers. In summer, head for the black door at the rear and you'll find the outdoor alcove, where red lights above the benches bring the boudoir theme outside. Best of all, you'll probably be able to find a free corner.

NYINTHEKNOW

Mike Ricci, director of communications Hilton Hotels Corporation, north-east US and Canada, says, 'Any bar on 9th Avenue in Hell's Kitchen will make a good night out, particularly Rudy's Bar and Grill (www.rudysbarnyc.com), a real dive with a real Hell's Kitchen atmosphere. It features circular booths with electrical and duct tape holding the ripped vinyl upholstery together. It offers patrons free hot dogs all year round (given the current economy, this is a great value-add!) and there are big burly bouncers outside the door.'

HELL'S KITCHEN
Rudy's Bar and Grill: 627 9th Avenue near 44th, 646-707 0898, www.rudysbarnyc.com. Opened in 1933 and still has the same front door. When you walk through it, the feel of the old neighbourhood saloon is still there,

GoldBar

with cheap beer, free hot dogs and great people!

LITTLE ITALY

GoldBar: 389 Broome Street at Mulberry Street. 212-274 1568, www.goldbarnewyork. com.

This bar from the owners of Cain and former GM of Lotus is lavished in gold, from the skulls in the wall to the chains separating the rooms. The drinks tables are golden love bracelets engraved with Latin sayings and the theme of the cocktails is golden honey.

Boss Tweed's: 115 Essex Street between Rivington and Delancey Streets. 212-475 9997, www.bosstweeds.com.

This is the closest you'll get to a local in Manhattan. The glass-bricked bar offers everything from pints of Guinness to vodka shots, each served up with a great story by bartender and co-owner Stuart Delves. Very entertaining. Has an outdoor beer garden.

Inoteca: 98 Rivington Street at Ludlow Street. 212 614-0473, www.inotecanyc.com. The staff at this wine bar and restaurant are ingratiating and knowledgeable. The crowd is a mixture of neighbourhood denizens and drop-ins from uptown, creating a good atmosphere. Serves food, too.

LOWER EAST SIDE

Attaboy: 134 Eldridge Steet between Broome and Delancey Streets.

Taking over the space formerly occupied by hip New York favourite Milk and Honey bar, this little den is a delight, with less of the intimidating hip of M&H. There's no website, no phone number and no menu but do make the effort to track this place down as the bartender asks about your favourite drinks and whips up a bespoke cocktail to suit your tastes and your mood. Plus this tiny place feels a little bit in-the-know, prohibition-esque, which is never a bad thing.

> ◄ **BRITTIP**
>
> If you're after a quality cigar bar, take a trip to Florio's Grill & Cigar Bar, 192 Grand Street between Mott and Mulberry Streets in Little Italy (212-226 7610), where the large humidor is filled with cigars from around the world.

MEATPACKING DISTRICT

Biergarten: The Standard Hotel, 848 Washington at 13th Street, 212-645 4646, standardhotels.com. Subway A, C, E to 14th Street.

Next to the Standard Hotel's Standard Grill is the outdoor Biergarten, situated under the High Line. It's very popular and you can sit at long tables and choose from the German menu, including sausages and pretzels, and sip draught beers 7 days a week until 2am.

Hogs & Heifers: 859 Washington Street at West 13th Street. 212-929 0655, www.hogsandheifers.com.
It has been around for years and is still going strong. The hogs are the motorcyclists and the heifers are the dames, who are known for hanging their bras on the ceiling.

MIDTOWN

Campbell Apartment Bar: Gallery Level, Grand Central Station, 15 Vanderbilt Avenue between 42nd and 43rd Streets. 212-953 0409, www.hospitalityholdings.com.
This apartment used to be the office/salon of the 1920s tycoon John W. Campbell. The beamed ceiling, huge leaded-glass window and the massive stone fireplace make a unique, almost castle-like space. But the dark wood couches and club armchairs create an intimate place for a drink.

NYINTHEKNOW

Patrick Hickey, Concierge, 70 Park Avenue Hotel, says, 'I really love The Campbell Apartment Bar, which is a bar and cocktail lounge located in a corner of Grand Central Terminal, facing Vanderbilt Avenue. The space was never actually an apartment. It used to be the office of John W. Campbell, an American financier who served on the New York Central's Board of Directors. Or, for unique, vintage cocktails, I head to Flatiron Lounge (www.flatironlounge.com). They have everything from fresh fruit-infused cocktails to martini flights – 3 mini martinis each with a common flavour theme.'

Langans: 150 West 47th Street near 7th Avenue. 212-869 5482, www.langans.com.
This Irish bar and restaurant is a hangout for journalists from the newspaper world, in particular the New York Post. Good place to pick up some brunch or an early-evening pint and listen to the gossip. Rupert Murdoch has been known to pop in from time to time.

Russian Vodka Room: 265 West 52nd Street between Broadway and 8th Avenue. 212-307 5835, www.russianvodkaroom.com.
A brilliant vodka bar that doesn't require you to take out a second mortgage. There are 53 different vodkas, plus cheap smoked fish platters, delicious cocktails and marvellous vodka infusions. It tends to attract the publishing crowd. Happy hour runs 4–7pm every day.

MIDTOWN EAST

PJ Clarkes: 915 3rd Avenue at East 55th Street, 212-317 1616, http://pjclarkes.com. Subway E, M to East 53rd Street.
I came across this old-school bar, established in 1884, during my last visit to the city and felt compelled to put it in the *Brit Guide* as it will appeal to anyone who loves the idea of sitting at a beautiful long wooden bar sipping a cool beer, *Cheers*-style. Treat yourself to a better-than-average bar dish while you're there, such as shepherd's pie.

MURRAY HILL

Tonic East: 411 3rd Avenue at 29th Street. 212-683 7090, www.toniceast.com. Subway 6 to 28th Street
A restaurant downstairs, but it's the rooftop bar that's the fun bit. You'll spot if from the black and red exterior and probably hear it too. Fun, rather than sophisticated.

Campbell Apartment Bar

COOL SCREENINGS

Cool screenings in New York City can be found at the **American Museum of the Moving Image Astoria**, Queens (p278) and where early each year the Annual New York Film Critics: Great Documentaries series featuring more than 20 of the nation's top film critics introduce their favourite documentaries. Also check out the **BAMcinématek** programme at the Brooklyn Academy of Music (718-636 4100, www.bam.org), which holds **The African Diaspora Film Festival** in Feb. Perhaps 1 of the coolest film festivals of them all is **The Tribeca Film Festival** (www.tribecafilmfestival.org) in different locations around the city in spring, which has a great line-up of actors and filmmakers for Q&A sessions with the audiences.

NOHO

Joe's Pub: 425 Lafayette Street between 4th Street and Astor Place. 212-539 8778, www.joespub.com.
This cabaret continues to be a real hot spot. An extension of the Public Theater, Joe's brings you live music, spoken-word performances and a crowd jam-packed with trendy types.

NYIN**THE**KNOW
Diana Biederman who works at the famous restaurant 21 Club (www.21club.com) winds down after a hectic day at the Pier I Café (www.piericafe.com) at 70th Street and the Hudson River, soaking up the open air, scenic river views and dramatic sunsets: 'Perfect for sunset cocktails – the rum smoothies are a must, hanging out with the locals and pet watching. A bit of St Bart's in Manhattan.'

SOHO

The Anchor: 310 Spring Street. 212-463 7406, www.theanchornyc.com.
Top DJs play live to a cool crowd, which sometimes contains the odd celeb. Kanye West, Eve, John Mayer and Jack and Kelly Osbourne, have all been snapped here.

Antarctica: 287 Hudson Street at Spring Street. 212-352 1666, www.antarcticabar.com.
This is one of the best places in the city to enjoy a beer and a game of pool, as it's rarely packed so you can actually get a table. There's also a good jukebox and a friendly crowd once you've finished your game. Also

runs Name Night. Check the website to see a calendar listing male or female names below each day of the week, such as Roger on Tues. If you spot your name, get down there on the right night (with some ID) as the drinks will be free!

Blind Tiger: 281 Bleecker Street at Jones Street. 212-462 4682, www.blindtigeralehouse.com.
Micro-brewery offering more than 30 beers, with great names like Sly Fox Irish stout. It's got a garden for summer, a fireplace for winter and is popular with the locals. Open 7 days a week.

Botanica: 47 East Houston Street between Mott and Mulberry Streets. 212-343 7251.
Serving drinks at decent prices in très chic SoHo, this dark and rather grungy basement bar is a watering hole for artists and college students.

NYIN**THE**KNOW
Head concierge Josephine Danielson at the Four Seasons Hotel says of the Brandy Library bar (www.brandylibrary.com) on 25 North Moore Street in TriBeCa, 'Old-world charm meets downtown chic at this fabulous New York bar. It's one of those places that leaves you saying "only in New York". The people you'll find include a wonderful mix of throwbacks to a bygone era and trendy Manhattanites. And they are known for offering tastings of any spirit imaginable, which is great fun and very sophisticated.'

Brandy Library: 25 North Moore Street at Varwick Street. 212-226 5545, www.brandylibrary.com.
As its name suggests, this bar is dedicated to the finest brandies, plus there are more than 100 cocktails on the menu. Waitresses climb ladders to pick out your chosen tipple from the brandy-lined shelves. A lovely place to end a sophisticated evening, as it stays open until 4am. (See New Yorker in the Know, above).

Café Noir: 32 Grand Street at Thompson Street. 212-431 7910, www.cafenoirny.com.
An extensive wine list at this cute urban oasis that also serves Moroccan comfort food meets Spanish tapas. Think tagines, stews and pitchers of sangria. There's also the occasional live jazz session.

Merc Bar: 151 Mercer Street between Prince and Houston Streets. 212-966 2727, www.mercbar.com.

NIGHTLIFE

5 HOT HOTEL BARS

Chelsea

The Cabanas at the Maritime Hotel: 88 9th Avenue between 16th and 17th Streets. 212-242 4300, www.themaritimehotel.com. Subway A, C, E to 14th Street.
This plant-filled rooftop retreat is the perfect place to sip a martini in winter as it has patio heaters. A prime spot for a celeb spot too.

Plunge at Hotel Gansevoort: 18 9th Avenue at 13th Street. 877-426 7386/212-206 6700, www.hotelgansevoort.com. Subway A, C, E to 14th Street.
Take the lift to the penthouse on the 15th floor and you'll arrive at 1 of NYC's most happening bars. On a dry day it's open-air: if it's rainy or cold there's a glass cover, so you still get the views. The only downside of Plunge is that, despite its name, you're not allowed in the rooftop swimming pool unless you're a guest and it's absolutely packed for most of the week.

Financial District

Bar Seven Five at Andaz Wall Street Hotel: 75 Wall Street at Water Street, 212-590 1234, www.andaz.com. Subway F, Z to Broad Street.
David Rockwell-designed space, with black lacquered tables with gold bulbs hanging above them. Drinks are brought to your table and shaken and poured from a server's cart. There are lots of speciality cocktails on offer such as the 75 Smash – applejack, mint, lemon juice and maple syrup.

Lower East Side

The Lounge at Hotel On Rivington: 107 Rivington Street. 212-475 2600, www.hotelonrivington.com. Subway F to Delancey Street.
One of New York's trendiest hotels has an equally hip bar. A place to see and be seen, there's a master mixologist who orders in fresh fruit, herbs and vegetables to make super fresh cocktails. Live DJs Fri and Sat.

Midtown

Thom Bar at the 60 Thompson Hotel: 60 Thompson Street between Broome and Spring Streets. 212-431 0400, www.thompsonhotels.com. Subway 6, C, E to Spring Street.
A sophisticated decor of dark wood, soft violet seats, brown leather club chairs and polished wood floor make for pleasant surroundings. The entertainment is provided by the chic crowd who know that this boutique hotel is the only place to be seen in midweek. Drinks are surprisingly cheap, such as flavoured vodka for $7.50.

A long-time fixture on the SoHo scene, this cool bar draws an attractive crowd to its luxuriously deep sofas. It's at its best in summer when worn leather chairs get an airing on the sidewalk a great place to sit and people-watch. Be warned: the drinks are pricey at $10-plus.

Milady's: 160 Prince Street at Thompson Street. 212-226 9340.
If you want a beer and not a ridiculously priced cocktail, and a down-to-earth atmosphere then pop in here. It's tiny, plays rock music during later hours and the people-watching is great, from pensioners who have lived in SoHo for decades to young city slickers.

TRIBECA

Bubble Lounge: 228 West Broadway at White Street, 212-431 3433, www.bubblelounge.com.
Champagne lounge since 1996 serving more than 300 types of bubbly and sparkling wines. Live DJs nightly and great food too.

UPPER WEST SIDE

Ding Dong Lounge: 929 Columbus Avenue at 106th Street. 212-663 2600, www.dingdonglounge.com.
Feel like a local at this hip, laid back hangout; think battered old chairs, large wooden tables lit by chandeliers, pool table, live music, daily happy hour 4–7pm. Open every day until 4am.

Shalel Lounge: 65 West 70th Street between Central Park West and Columbus Avenues. 212-799 9030. Subway B, C to 72nd Street.
Dark and dangerous, in a sexy kind of way. The exotic North African atmosphere transports aficionados directly to Morocco or a similar locale and is perfect for late-night drinks with a loved one. Rose petals are strewn on tables, candles flicker and cushions are strewn around.

WEST VILLAGE

Peculier Pub: 145 Bleecker Street between La Guardia Place and Thompson Street. 212-353 1327, www.peculierpub.com.

A truly impressive selection of 350 varieties of bottled beer, with 2 separate menus – 1 listing domestic brews, the other international. It's a bit like a museum to beer once you're inside, from the art of brewing to the evolution of the aluminium can on the walls. It gets packed with students during peak times, so it's best to visit early on weeknights if you want to chat to the bartender about the various brews.

 BRITTIP

If you want a big night out in more than one bar but don't want to travel around, then head to Bleecker Street in the West Village between La Guardia Place and Thompson Street. On this drag you'll find the Peculier Pub (see above), the Red Lion, which has live music and a happy hour from 3–8pm, The Bitter End, GMT Tavern and the Village Lantern, which has comedy, music and food, all within staggering distance.

NIGHTLIFE

CINEMA

AMC Empire 25: 234 West 42nd Street between 7th and 8th Avenues, 212-398 3939. This has 25 screens on 5 levels and has devoted 7 screens on the top floor, known as the Top of the Empire, to repertory classics and independent films. You can catch a pre-show snack – pizza to ribs – in the 42nd Street Food Court.

Film Forum: 209 West Houston Street between 6th and 7th Avenues, 212-727 8110, www.filmforum.org.
A 3-theatre venue showing independent and vintage films. There are seasons, such as a run of films dedicated to Audrey Hepburn, and talks given by directors plus film merchandise on sale.

The Paris Cinema: 4 West 58th Street at 5th Avenue, 212-688 3800, www.theparistheatre.com
This has to be one of the most desirable cinemas in the US. It's a stone's throw from the super swish The Plaza Hotel and Central Park, shows only 1 film at a time and has fabulously comfy seats. However, it's not mega pricey, charging just $14 for adults and $11 for kids, so see what's playing when you're in town.

Quad: 34 West 13th Street; www.quadcinema.com.
A New York institution for 25 years, showing the best of foreign and independent films. It's family owned and in the heart of Greenwich Village, so near to lots of greats shops and restaurants if you're making a night of it.
Regal E-Walk Stadium 13: 247 West 42nd Street between 7th and 8th Avenues, 212-840 7761, www.regmovies.com.

Peculier Pub

Quad Cinema

This mega-plex cinema with 13 screens and all-stadium seating is a modern-day movie palace. A single-storey, hand-painted mural honours the local landmarks of Broadway and Times Square.

The Angelika Film Center: 18 West Houston Street, 212-995 2000, http://angelikafilmcenter.com.
A good selection of the latest art films is shown here, as well as at the Lincoln Plaza Cinemas, 1886 Broadway at 62nd Street, 212-757 2280, http://lincolnplaza.moviefone.com. The Angelika has a café and the Lincoln Plaza Cinemas sell sandwiches and pastries.

BRITTIP

If you're mad about movies and movie stars, head to New York at the beginning of April when the TriBeCa Film Festival takes place. More than 100 films are featured from 31 countries around the world, including world premieres. Tickets for the festival are from $16 for evening and weekend screenings and $8 for daytime and late screenings (www.tribecafilmfestival.org).

Sunshine Cinema: 143 East Houston Street on the Lower East Side, 212-330 8182, www.landmarktheatres.com.
This cinema has 5 comfortable screening rooms, state-of-the-art sound systems and plays excellent art house movies. It has been voted New York's hippest cinema in days gone by.

COMEDY CLUBS

While comedy clubs have started to spring up in cities all over the UK, they've been firmly cemented in New York nightlife since the 1970s. It's a real experience and always worth the money to visit one of these Manhattan institutions, which have produced some of the world's top comedians. These are my selection of the best in the business.

CHELSEA
Upright Citizens Brigade: 307 West 26th Street between 8th and 9th Avenues, 212-366 9176, http://newyork.ucbtheatre.com. UCB (as New Yorkers call it) is held at a 150-seater theatre, meaning you get really close to the stage and performers (which can be a good or bad thing, depending on whether there's audience participation!). Some big names have played here, such as Tina Fey, and celebs have been known to pop in. Tickets start from a bargain $5 and there's something on every night of the week.

FLATIRON DISTRICT
Gotham Comedy Club: 208 West 23rd Street between 7th and 8th Avenues, 212-367 9000, http://gothamcomedyclub.com. This club opened in 1996 and was an instant success. It's elegant and sophisticated, with a solid oak bar and a chandelier. The line-ups are equally dazzling, from surprise guests to comedians who have appeared on Saturday

Night Live and The Tonight Show. Hearty food served too, plus a pleasing cocktail menu – have a chocolate martini for dessert.

MIDTOWN

Caroline's On Broadway: 1626 Broadway between 49th and 50th Streets. 212-757 4100, www.carolines.com.
It opened in 1981 as a small club in Chelsea, but proved such a hit it moved uptown, where it offers live comedy every night of the year, including big names such as Jerry Seinfeld and Rosie O'Donnell.

UPPER EAST SIDE

Comic Strip Live: 1568 Second Avenue at 81st Street. 212-861 9386, www.comicstriplive.com.
Founded in 1975, this is still 1 of the best comedy clubs in the city with some of the biggest names in the business appearing, such as Chris Rock and Adam Sandler. They even hold comedy classes if you fancy taking to the stage yourself – check the website for dates.

Dangerfield's: 118 First Avenue at 61st Street. 212-593 1650, www.dangerfields.com.
Allegedly the oldest comedy club in the country, it was established in 1969 by actor and comedian Roger Dangerfield. It's a magnet for tourists because of its reputation, but locals still frequent it too, drawn by the decent line-ups both newcomers and regulars.

UPPER WEST SIDE

Stand-Up NYC: 236 West 78th Street near Broadway. 212-595 0850, www.standupny.com.
This club has been hosting huge names in comedy – Robin Williams, Roseanne Barr, Jerry Seinfeld – since it opened in 1986. It's not a flashy venue and there's seating for just 175 punters, but it really pulls in the best on the circuit. From $15 cover charge.

WEST VILLAGE

The Comedy Cellar: 117 MacDougal Street between West 3rd Street and Minetta Lane. 212-254 3480, www.comedycellar.com.
This club has been a starting ground for many famous faces for more than 20 years. It's basic, with brick walls and cramped seating, and in a basement so it's not a glam night out in New York, but it will certainly be a funny one. The cover charge is $12 Mon–Tues, $14 Wed–Thurs and $20 Fri and Sat.

GAY BARS & CLUBS

BROOKLYN

Ginger's Bar: 363 5th Avenue between 6th and 7th Streets, Park Slope. 718-788 0924, http://gingersbarbklyn.com. Subway M, R to Union Street.
The drinks are generous at this lesbian hang out, where the pool table at the back is always the most popular spot. The dark wooden bar is also a friendly, neighbourhood place to hang out. Open Mon–Fri 6pm–4am, Sat and Sun 2pm–4am.

CHELSEA

Barracuda: 275 West 22nd Street between 7th and 8th Avenues. 212-645 8613. Subway C, E to 23rd Street.
This club attracts a mellow mix of people. Head to the rear lounge, which has a better atmosphere than the dingy front bar and a decent pool table, and wait for drinks to be brought in by gorgeous young cocktail waiters.

XES Lounge: 157 West 24th Street between 6th and 7th Avenues. 212-604 0212, www.xesnyc.com. Subway F, V, 1 to 23rd Street.
It promises no attitude, sexy bartenders and strong drinks. Love the Starck furniture in here, which goes with the exposed brick walls and patio sporting Japanese maple trees. Drag shows and parties every weekend, very funny week nights, such as karaoke with Hedda Lettuce, smoking allowed on the patio. Open daily 4pm–4am most days (until 2am Mon–Tues) and happy hour 2-for-1 drinks every weeknight 4–9pm.

Eagle: 554 West 28th Street between 10th and 11th Avenues. 646-473 1866, www.eaglenyc.com. Subway C, E to 23rd Street.
A spacious 2-storey watering hole filled with congenial leather-clad S&M New Yorkers. No surprise then that it was voted Best Leather Bar by *New York Magazine*. Open Mon–Sat 10pm–4am, Sun 5pm–4am.

Gym Sports Bar: 167 8th Avenue between 18th and 19th Avenues. 212-337 2439, www.gymsportsbar.com. Subway 1, 9 to 18th Street.
A gay sports bar that serves big drinks at low prices and offers after-work billiards, as well as parties around gay sports leagues and nightly sports events shown on big screens. 2-for-1 Happy Hour Mon–Fri 4pm–9pm and all night Mon.

g Lounge: 225 West 19th Street between 7th and 8th Avenues. 212-929 1085, http://glounge.com. Subway C, E to 23rd Street; 1 to 18th Street.
A super-popular, sophisticated nightspot for gorgeous hunks to see and be seen. Its centrepiece is its oval bar, which the sexy clientele prop up when they're not shimmying to house music. It gets packed later on when the queues build up outside. Open nightly

NIGHTLIFE

4pm–4am; DJ 6pm–1am, G-licious Happy Hour nightly from 4–9pm.

Kurfew: 212-533 1222, www.kurfew.com. Subway A, C, E, F to 34th Street.
America's youngest all-gay party, with big nights out at different gay clubs around town. Sunday night is college fest at the Avalon. Also holds events at SBNY (below). Eight beers for $10, anyone?

SBNY Splash: 50 West 17th Street between 5th and 6th Avenues. 212-691 0073, www.splashbar.com. Subway L, N, R, W, 4, 5, 6 to 14th Street/Union Square.
This is a popular place to hang out on any night of the week, and not just because the handsome bartenders are shirtless. It's done out South Beach style, with a huge dance floor emporium, a downstairs bar for cruising and an adult store in the basement. It's popular with preppy men and those who enjoy attention. Open daily 4pm–4am and there's a smoking area outside. Happy Hour 2-4-1 until 9pm daily.

FAST VILLAGE

B Bar & Grill: 40 East 4th Street between Lafayette Street and the Bowery. 212-475 2220, www.bbarandgrill.com. Subway B, D, F, V to Broadway/Lafayette Street; 6 to Bleecker Street.
Not strictly a gay bar, but very stylish. Previously super-trendy lounge filled with models and gorgeous people (Madonna had been known to drop in). Now it's filled with a more 'bridge and tunnel' after-work crowd. However, the outside space, where you can also smoke, is still a lively place to enjoy drinks on a Fri night.

Boiler Room: 86 East 4th Street at 2nd Avenue, 212-254 7536, www.boilerroomnyc.com.
A great place to start your evening. Guest DJs, but the pièce de résistance is the internet jukebox with hundreds of thousands of tunes, from the Pointer Sisters to Pantera, boys from all neighbourhoods and down-to-earth ambience.

Eastern Bloc: 505 East 6th Street. 212-777 2555, www.easternblocnyc.com.
Walls are painted a tongue-in-cheek red and black and there's something fun on every night of the week here, from Sunday Social with $2 glasses of champagne to drag hosts on a weekday. There's also a daily happy hour with $4 drinks from 7–10pm.

GREENWICH VILLAGE

The Stonewall Inn: 53 Christopher Street between 6th and 7th Avenues, 212-488 2705, www.thestonewallinnnyc.com. Subway 1 at Christopher Street/Sheridan Square.
Restored and reopened, Stonewall is the historic spot where gay activism began and therefore a centre point for the gay community, with multicoloured lights, disco balls and cheesy tunes. Mostly male, there are nightly drag impresarios upstairs. Open daily 2pm–4am; Happy Hour 2-4-1, 2–8pm.

Manhattan Monster, Inc: 80 Grove Street at Sheridan Square. 212-924 3558, http://manhattan-monster.com. Subway 1 to Christopher Street/Sheridan Square.
Probably the most popular bar in Greenwich Village, now in its 29th year. Right on Sheridan Square across from the infamous Stonewall. Happy piano bar draws older crowd; downstairs dance floor draws younger hotties; Mon night has a drag show. Mon, there's a cover charge of $6, Fri & Sat, $8 after 10pm and after 8pm Sun, probably the only club with a cover charge in the Village but you always get a show too. Happy Hour weekdays 4–9pm and Sat 2–9pm, draws the crowds for its free hors d'oeuvres. Open 4pm–4am, party starts at 10pm.

HELL'S KITCHEN

Posh: 405 West 51st Street. 212 957 222, www.poshbarnyc.com. Subway C, E to 23rd Street.
A laid-back lounge bathed in beauty-enhancing low lights. Exposed brick walls, a sound system blaring dance remixes of staples like the Bee Gees and Abba. The back room has a more intimate feel than the packed front bar. Check the website for daily events, which have included fun things like Hot Bingo in the past.

BRITTIP

Head to Posh Bar if it's your birthday, as they promise to give you three drinks for free (take your passport as proof!).

Therapy: 348 West 52nd Street between 8th and 9th Avenues. 212-397 1700, www.therapy-nyc.com. Subway C, E at 50th Street.
A chic, scene lounge with stylish wood-panelled walls under a vaulted skylight in the heart of 'New Chelsea' district Hell's Kitchen. Try one of the appropriately named house cocktails such as Gender Bender or The Freudian Sip. Nightly entertainment, from comedy to drag acts, open Sun–Wed 5pm–2am, Thurs–Sat 5pm–4am. Happy Hour 5pm–9pm daily and there's food, too.

Vlada Lounge: 331 West 51st Street. 212-974 8030, www.vladabar.com. Subway C, E to 50th Street.

Ginger's Bar

NIGHTLIFE

It's worth checking out this sleek Hell's Kitchen bar where the vodka flows, drag queens drift about and there's a 30ft ice bar. There's no cover charge for the nightly shows. Open Tues–Sun 4pm–4am. Happy hour from 4pm, including bites like mini burgers, after 11pm the place erupts into a full-blown nightclub.

LOWER EAST SIDE

Bluestockings: 172 Allen Street between Rivington and Stanton Streets. 212-777 6028, www.bluestockings.com. Subway F, V to Lower East Side/2nd Avenue.
Not strictly a lesbian club or lounge, more

Townhouse

a bookstore and café, but it's a great neighbourhood joint that gives women the opportunity to showcase their talents at open-mike sessions. Open daily 11am–11pm

MIDTOWN EAST

Evolve: 221 East 58th Street at 2nd Avenue. 212-355 3395, www.evolvebarandloungenyc. com. Subway 4, 5, 6 at 59th Street, N, R, W at Lexington Avenue/59th Street.
Boasts 1 of the longest bars in the city, billiard room and outdoor garden patio. Gorgeous bar men and attracts some of the city's smartest gays. Open 7 days a week, 4pm–4am, happy hour 4–8pm.

 BRITTIP

For the lowdown on what's happening on the jazz scene, from shopping to tours to clubs, go to www.bigapplejazz.com – New York City's Jazz Clubs Bible.

MIDTOWN WEST

Escuelita: 301 West 39th Street at 8th Avenue. 212-631 0588, www.escuelita.com. Subway A, C east to 42nd Street.
A fantastic Latino club famed for its fabulous shows and nights of salsa, merengue and Latin-style drag shows. Lots of different shows every night of the week.

UPPER EAST SIDE

Townhouse: 236 East 58th Street. 212-754 4649, www.townhouseny.com. Subway E, V to 53rd Street.
An East Side institution that locals describe as more like an upscale gentleman's club than a bar. Music is more in the background than at some of the larger, louder venues and there are areas for intimate conversations. A classy joint if you're looking for something more relaxed. Note, the dress code here is quite smart, so no ripped jeans or Lycra. Open 365 days of the year.

Lips: 227 East 56th Street. 212-675 7710, www.lipsnyc.com. Subway E, V, 6 to East 51st Street.
Drag dining is the best way to describe this loud and proud restaurant and club. Open nightly Tues–Sun, plus a Broadway brunch on Sun. Lots of seating times, from 5–11.30pm on weekends, and a show with each sitting. The menu has dishes named after drag queens, like Ginger Snapts Caesar salad.

WEST VILLAGE

Cubby Hole: 281 West 12th Street between West 4th and West 12th Streets. 212-243 9041, www.cubbyholebar.com. Subway 1, 2, 3 to 14th Street.

It looks as though the owners of this lesbian bar have raided a New Orleans thrift store a few days after Mardi Gras: hundreds of illuminated plastic blowfish, goldfish and Chinese lanterns dangle from the ceiling. After 9pm, younger gals (and a fair number of guys) take centre stage. There's no karaoke here anymore, but it almost doesn't matter. Like a pianoless piano bar, Cubby Hole is packed full of regulars who like to belt out tunes along with the jukebox. Open Mon–Fri 4pm–4am, Sat and Sun 2pm–4am. Happy hour Mon–Sat until 7pm, half off all wine and beer.

◀▶ BRITTIP

For a Sunday brunch with a twist, head to Smoke (2751 Broadway, 212-864 6662, www. smokejazz.com) where a Jazz Brunch is available from 11am–3.30pm.

Henrietta Hudson's: 438 Hudson Street at Morton Street. 212-924 3347, www.henriettahudson.com. Subway 1, 9 to Christopher Street.
This is probably the most popular lesbian lounge in the city, which has been going for years. Even when there's no specific party, women come from far and wide to hang out at this great watering hole. Every night offers something different – check the website for details of what's on while you're there – with DJs playing everything from hip hop and reggae to house and 80s pop. Great atmosphere and worth staying until the 4am finish. Usually a cover charge after 9pm, from $5–10 depending on the night.

HOTEL BARS

Hotel bars have always been a popular place to meet for New Yorkers. From sinking into leather sofas in legendary hangouts, to propping up the bars in some of Midtown's trendy hotels where the fashionable crowds gather, they make an ideal place to start or end a big night out.

GREENWICH VILLAGE

North Square Lounge at the Washington Square Hotel: 103 Waverly Place at MacDougal Street. 212-254 1200, www. northsquareny.com. Subway A, B, C, D, E, F, V to West 4th Street/Washington Square.
The small, cosy basement space's classic bar and leather banquettes are a reminder of another era, while beautifully stencilled windows offer a glimpse of the current street scene. It attracts a large European crowd, who find it the perfect spot to pore over a

map and a martini, but locals – as well as the occasional celeb – can also be found enjoying the laid-back atmosphere. There is a jazz brunch every Sun afternoon.

MIDTOWN

Cellar Bar at the Bryant Park Hotel: 40 West 40th Street between 5th and 6th Avenues. 212-869 0100, www.bryantparkhotel.com. Subway B, D, F, V, 7 to 42nd Street/Bryant Park.
Models, designers and magazine editors, along with out of towners, prop up the bar beneath the vaulted ceiling, but don't even think about dropping in during Fashion Week – you won't be able to move for the wafer-thin clientele.

The Bar at the Four Seasons Hotel: 57 East 57th Street between 5th and Park Avenues. 212-758 5700, www.fourseasons.com/newyork. Subway N, R, Q, W to 5th Avenue.
The Four Seasons is dynamic in early evening when celebs rub shoulders with power-broking businessmen and hip hotel guests, while a pianist provides the background music. Be sure to sample some of the 15 types of martini on offer and American tapas.

VU Bar at La Quinta Manhattan: 17 West 32nd Street between Broadway and 5th Avenue. 212-736 1600, www.applecorehotels.com. Subway N, R, W to 28th Street.
A cross between a backyard deck and a funky beach bar, this partially enclosed rooftop watering hole is packed year-round with international visitors who appreciate the casual atmosphere and towering views of the Empire State Building.

The Bar at the Four Seasons Hotel

209

NIGHTLIFE

JAZZ

The live music for which New York is most famous is, of course, jazz. A visit to New York City wouldn't be complete without an evening at 1 of the various jazz venues, but it can get very expensive, so it's good to know your way around. At all the main venues it'll cost you from around $25 to hear 1 set, which lasts only 1–1½ hours. It's worth it if you're happy with the music, but the idea of having to move on after only 1 set is a bit strange to us Brits, so be warned!

The most important relatively new venue is **Jazz at Lincoln Center**'s $128-million home at the AOL Time Warner Center at Columbus Circle, with 3 performance spaces – 2 large and 1 intimate. Visit www.jalc.org to find out about events or call the JazzTix hotline, 212-258 9800.

THE MAIN CLUBS

One of the best jazz clubs is the **Iridium** (1650 Broadway at 51st Street, 212-582 2121, www.iridiumjazzclub.com). It's not too touristy, is smaller than many clubs and has a nice intimate feel. Try it for Sunday brunch! The Les Paul trio play every Mon night and the entrance fee to see acts, which are usually on at 8pm and 10pm, varies, but starts at around $30. The **Village Vanguard** (178 7th Avenue South at Perry Street, 212-255 4037, www.villagevanguard.com), probably the most famous club of all, always hosts great talent and sets last the full 1½ hours. Another famous Greenwich Village venue is the **Blue Note** (131 West 3rd Street between MacDougal and 6th Avenue, 212-475 8592, www.bluenote.net), but this is slicker, costs from around $30 upwards and has a glitzy interior. **Swing 46 Jazz & Supper Club** (349 West 46th Street between 8th and 9th Avenues, 212-262 9554, www.swing46.com) offers big bands and small combos to suit hip downtown loungers and traditional uptown swingers who want supper and a show – it's rapidly becoming an institution.

Other good venues include **Birdland** (315 West 44th Street between 8th and 9th Avenues, 212-581 3080, www.birdlandjazz.com) in Midtown West; the **Jazz Standard** (116 East 27th Street between Park and Lexington Avenues, 212-576 2232, www.jazzstandard.com) near Madison Square; **55 Bar** (55 Christopher Street, 212-929 9883, www.55bar.com) has been a West Village institution since 1919 and has shows all week from 6/7pm and late shows 9.30/10pm; open until 4am. **Smoke** (2751 Broadway, 212-864 6662, www.smokejazz.com) on the edge of Harlem is an intimate club with low-hanging chandeliers, red velvet curtains and seating for 70. Open until 3am. Finally, book early for Mon nights at **Café Carlyle** (p213) where Woody Allen and friends play a set.

CHEAP AND CHEERFUL

One of the best off-the-beaten-track jazz venues is in the heart of Greenwich Village at the **Cornelia Street Café** (29 Cornelia Street, 212-989 9319, www.corneliastreetcafe.com). You'll get to see some great musicians play and feel like you're part of the village scene, ditto the Zinc Bar (82 West 3rd Street between Thompson and Sullivan Streets, 212-477 8337, www.zincbar.com), which is one of the most intimate places in town to enjoy live jazz (and other types of music), open until 3am weekends. Arthur's Tavern (57 Grove Street near 7th Avenue, 212-675 6879, www.arthurstavernnyc.com) is a West Village jazz and blues joint that's been going since the 1930s. Some say it's lost its sparkle, but most still love it's scruffy, old-world charm and enjoy a night free of pricey cover charges listening to great jazz. **Fat Cat** (75 Christopher Street at 7th Avenue, 212-675 6065, www.fatcatmusic.org) is a novelty as it features jazz and a games hall with pool, table tennis and shuffleboards.

The cheapest jazz clubs tend to be in Harlem, Queens and Brooklyn, but because they can't afford to advertise you really don't hear about them. Furthermore, most don't even have names on the door. A good place to look for venues and information on who's performing when is www.gothamjazz.com.

MIDTOWN EAST

Oasis at W New York: 541 Lexington Avenue at 49th Street. 212-755 1200, www.wnewyork.com. Subway 6 to 51st Street.
An oasis of tranquillity, the bar heats up when the fashion, art and music crowd descends for cocktails (sip a Flirtini). The ambience is casual cool.

Upstairs at the Kimberly: 145 East 60th Street, 212-702 1600, www.kimberlyhotel.com. Subway 4, 5, 6 to 59th Street.
This hot new bar is on the rooftop of the deluxe Kimberly Hotel and offers 360-degree views of the city. It is open all year round thanks to a retractable glass ceiling and heated floor. You can access the bar from a lift in the street. There are living green walls to marvel at and the iconic Chrysler Building is in full view. Simply stunning.

MIDTOWN WEST

Forty Four at the New York Royalton:
44 West 44th Street between 5th and 6th
Avenues. 212-869 4400, www.royaltonhotel.
com. Subway B, D, F, V to 42nd Street; 7 to
5th Avenue.
The first of the Philippe Starck-designed
hotels is still holding its own against all
newcomers. Forty Four is a beautiful and
stylish little bar with curved booths, low-
lighting and excellent bar staff who can whip
up a decent cocktail or 2. Daily happy hour
and bar menu, too.

BRITTIP

Don't feel that you have to be
staying at a hotel to visit its
bar. Most hotels in the city welcome
passing trade, so do try them out.

Metro Grill at Hotel Metro: 45 West 35th
Street between 5th and 6th Avenues. 212-
279 3535, www.hotelmetronyc.com. Subway
B, D, F, N, Q, R, V, W to 34th Street.
The views of the Empire State Building from
this compact rooftop retreat is one reason
why this is well worth a visit. The cheap beer
and laid-back vibe created by the DJ are two
others.

King Cole Bar at the St Regis Hotel:
2 East 55th Street. 212-339 6721, www.
stregisnewyork.com. Subway E, V to 5th
Avenue at 53rd Street.
The specialities of the (very upscale) house are
the Bloody Mary and the mural behind the
bar, by noted American illustrator Maxfield
Parrish.

Living Room at the W Hotel Times Square:
1567 Broadway at 47th Street. 212-930 7444,
www.wnewyorktimessquare.com. Subway 4,
5, 6, L, N, Q, R, W to 14th Street.
Another of the cool W Bars, this 1 is located
in the lobby and comes with white leather
seating and glowing resin alcoves and bar.
Open until 3am.

MObar at the Mandarin Oriental: 80
Columbus Circle at 60th Street. 212-805
8800, www.mandarinoriental.com/newyork.
Subway A, B, C, D, 1, 9 to Columbus Circle.
In the dazzling Time Warner Center, the sleek
lobby lounge draws the crowds. The cocktails
are $15 but the spectacular view of Central
Park from the 35th floor (not to mention
celebrity sightings) is free.

Salon de Ning at the Peninsula Hotel:
700 5th Avenue, 23rd Floor. 212-956
2888, www.peninsula.com. Subway E, V
to 5th Avenue/53rd Street; N, R, W to 5th
Avenue/59th Street.

TOP 5 CLUBBING TIPS

▶ On Fri and Sat nights, the clubs are
packed with crowds from boroughs
outside Manhattan. For a quieter night,
go on Thurs. Sun is the big night for
Manhattanites, so you'll get the real vibe
then, along with the crowds.

▶ Call ahead early in the evening to find
out if there's a cover charge, when to arrive
and how to dress. Also find out if there's a
party theme on the night that you plan to
go. Clubs can change nightly – for example,
catering for straight people one night, gay
people the next.

▶ The real nightlife doesn't get going until
after midnight, so get some zeds in before
you go out.

▶ Carry some ID with you just in case – it
would be very annoying if you couldn't get
a drink when you're over 21.

▶ Large groups of men don't stand much
hope of getting into straight clubs – they'll
have more chance if they are with a
woman.

NYINTHEKNOW

Jocelyn Ojeda, Eventi hotel's
concierge, says, 'I really like The
Lion (62 West 9th Street, 212-353
8400, www.thelionnyc.com). It
has great signature cocktails – I
especially love the Samo! There's a
fantastic ambience with a classic yet
modern feel. I also like Press Lounge
(653 11th Avenue, 212-757 2224,
www.ink48.com) for its great roof
terrace. When spring is around the
corner and summer close behind,
the open space and incredible
views from Press are like a great
awakening from our snowy winter.
Just west enough to be out of the
limelight yet still a short cab ride to
favourites, Press offers a comfortable
atmosphere to enjoy our NYC skyline
in style. Finally, I recommend the
Pegu Club (77 West Houston Street,
212-473 7348, www.peguclub.com).
It's a little hidden and out of the
way, a little more fun to find and
have incredible drink concoctions.
They take cocktails to an art form
and show you the enjoyment of
spirits to truly appreciate.'

This rooftop terrace is a fusion of east meets
west; think 1930s Shanghai, says the blurb.

Salon de Ning

Whatever the decor, the views of Manhattan's glittering skyline are breathtaking and the prices can be, too, but in beautiful weather you'll feel you're at the centre of the universe – like the power brokers who surround you.

Sky Terrace at the Hudson Hotel: 356 West 58th Street between 8th and 9th Avenues. 212-554 6000, www.hudsonhotel.com. Subway A, B, C, D, 1, 9 to 59th Street/Columbus Circle.
An outdoor rooftop oasis on the 15th floor of this cool hotel. There are sunloungers (which get taken early!) and 10 speciality sangrias, including pear and limoncello. Great views of the Statue of Liberty and Hudson River and open until 10pm, with cocktails served from 3pm–10pm.

The Blue Bar at the Algonquin: 59 West

Rado City Music Hall

44th Street between 5th and 6th Avenues. 212-840 6800, www.algonquinhotel.com. Subway B, D, F, V to 42nd Street; 7 to 5th Avenue.
Once world-famous as the New York literary set's salon of choice, this handsome room provides an intimate and civilised setting for some of the country's leading jazz and cabaret artists to take time out. The clientele is clubby and patrician, but anyone can buy drinks here or dinner in the Oak Room.

TRIBECA
Church Bar at TriBeCa Grand Hotel: 2 6th Avenue at White Street. 212-519 6600, www.tribecagrand.com. Subway A, C, E to Canal Street.
A glossy bar with weekly DJs and all-day and late-night menu. The adjacent The Lounge has low-lying seating in velvet and leather and floor-to-ceiling windows.

LIVE MUSIC
There are some fantastic live music venues in the city, from dingy rock clubs to vast stadiums where legends have played. As many of the venues get booked up quickly, do check websites for listings well before you visit the city so that you'll be able to book tickets in advance.

34TH STREET
Madison Square Garden: 4 Pennsylvania Plaza at 33rd Street and 7th Avenue. 212-465 MSG1 info, www.thegarden.com. Subway A, C, E, 1, 2, 3, 9, B, D, F, N, Q, R, V, W to 34th Street/Penn Street Station.
New York's biggest and most famous big-name pop and rock venue, which doubles up as a sports stadium. Also the Theater at Madison Square Garden, which is underneath, plays host to big-name stars who want to share some intimacy with their audience.

BROOKLYN
barbés: 376 9th Street at the corner of 6th Avenue, Park Slope. 347-422 0248, www.barbesbrooklyn.com. Subway F to 7th Avenue, Brooklyn
Cool bar and performance space owned by two French musicians and long-time Brooklyn residents. Expect to see all manner of live acts here, from Mexican bandas to book readings. The bar has a big selection of single malt scotch and lots of bottled beers and topnotch tequilas.

Knitting Factory: 361 Metropolitan Avenue, 347-529 6696, http://bk.knittingfactory.com. Subway L to Bedford Avenue.
A funky performance venue run by the

Knitting Factory record label, which is well known for avant-garde live bands spanning all types of music, from heavy rock to choral music. There are sometimes poetry readings and film screenings as well as music. Check out the website to see who'll be playing when you're in town. Open until 4am.

GARMENT DISTRICT
Hammerstein Ballroom: 311 West 34th Street between 8th and 9th Avenues. 212-279 7740, www.mcstudios.com.
Elegant pre-war ballroom that holds up to 2,500 people for rock music gigs from the likes of Jay-Z and Alicia Keys to top DJs.

> **◀▦▶ BRITTIP**
>
> For old-school, glamorous cabaret, try the Metropolitan Room at Gotham, 34 West 22nd Street between 5th and 6th Avenues, 212-206 044, www.metropolitanroom.com. It's only been open a few of years, but it was a hit from the start, with fabulous acts.

GREENWICH
Cafe Wha?: 115 MacDougal Street between West 3rd and Bleecker Streets. 212-254 3706, www.cafewha.com.
Village hangout since the beginning of time. There is something fun and exciting on every night of the week here, from Brazilian dance parties to the Cafe Wha? disFUNKtion band playing live funk on Tues night, from the likes of Inaya Day and Mike Davis.

HARLEM
Apollo Theater: 253 West 125th Street between Adam Clayton Powell Jr and Frederick Douglas Boulevards. 212-531 5300 info; 212-531 5301 events hotline, www.apollotheater.org. Subway A, B, C, D, 2, 3 to 125th Street.
This venue started life as a burlesque house for whites only when Harlem was actually a white neighbourhood, but it very quickly changed and became a theatre for blacks with live entertainment. The Amateur Night has been a launch pad for Stevie Wonder and James Brown. When Ella Fitzgerald came here she planned to dance, but at the last moment decided to sing and, as the saying goes, a star was born. Wed's Amateur Night is still going strong today.

LOWER EAST SIDE
Bowery Ballroom: 6 Delancey Street near Bowery. 212-533 2111, www.boweryballroom.com.
Consistently voted 1 of New York's best live rock venues, it's been packing in the punters

Bo Diddley at B B King Blues Club

since it opened its doors in 1998. Great acoustics, a well-stocked bar and lots of great acts. Log on to the website to see who's playing and for advance tickets.

MIDTOWN
B B King Blues Club & Grill: 237 West 42nd Street near 7th Avenue. 212-997 4144, www.bbkingblues.com. Subway 1, 2, 3, 7, N, Q, R, S Times Square/42nd Street.
An intimate supper club that's played host to some of the greats – James Brown, Peter Frampton and Chic. There's a souvenir stall upstairs so you can wear the T-shirt.

Carnegie Hall: 154 West 57th Street at 7th Avenue. 212-247 7800, www.carnegiehall.org. Subway B, D, E, N, R, Q, W to 57th Street.
Built in the Beaux Arts style under the patronage of Andrew Carnegie, this is perhaps one of the most famous classical concert venues in New York and a real landmark. There's also jazz, pop and world music on the calendar. Check the website for details of visiting artists or take a guided tour $10, Mon and Fri 11.30am, 12.30pm (extra 2pm Fri).

Radio City Music Hall: 1260 6th Avenue at 50th Street. 212-247 4777, www.radiocity.com. Subway B, D, F, V to 47th–50th Street/ Rockefeller Centre.
Recently renovated, this splendid Art Deco home to the Rockettes is slap bang in the centre of the city and plays host to some big-name stars.

UPPER EAST SIDE
Café Carlyle at The Carlyle Hotel: 35 East 76th Street at Madison and Park Avenues. 212-744 1600, www.thecarlyle.com. Subway 6 to 77th Street.
A highly glamorous bar and restaurant that specialises in cabaret. Woody Allen occasionally drops by to play clarinet with

The Eddie Davis New Orleans Jazz Band on Monday nights, which you can watch and hear from $145 a head and Bobby Short, a New York favourite, plays piano during spring and autumn.

> **⚑ BRITTIP**
> If want to go to a cabaret club, visit Don't Tell Mama (343 West 46th Street near 9th Avenue, Hell's Kitchen, 212-757 0788, www.donttellmamanyc.com). There's a piano bar and 2 side rooms for excellent shows, with up to 3 performances nightly.

UPPER WEST SIDE

Lincoln Center: 65th Street at Columbus Avenue. 212-875 5400, www.lincolncenter. org. Subway 1, 9 to 66th Street/Lincoln Center.

The major venue for classical music in New York, the Lincoln Center is a collection of buildings that includes the home of the Metropolitan Opera, built on slums that were featured in the film *West Side Story*. The Alice Tully Hall (212-875 5050) houses the Chamber Music Society of Lincoln Center; the Avery Fisher Hall (212-875 5030) is home to the New York Philharmonic; the Metropolitan Opera House (212-362 6000); the New York State Theater (212-870 5570) is the base of New York City Opera; and the Walter Reade Theater (212-875 5600) is home to the Film Society of Lincoln Center. Jazz at Lincoln Center is at the Fredrick P Rose Hall inside the Time Warner Center at Colombus Circle.

You can take a behind-the-scenes tour of the Lincoln Center, which is really the only way to see beyond the ornate lobbies of the buildings, unless you're paying big bucks for a performance. The daily tours cost $17 and are fantastic; each is unique, as you never know what's going to happen, from seeing a rehearsal to bumping into a star in a corridor. They're very popular, so it's best to book in advance on 212-875 5350.

> **⚑ BRITTIP**
> In addition to the tours, you can enjoy the Lincoln Center environment with a series of jazz and folk bands that entertain the crowds for free during the summer. The Autumn Crafts Fair is held in the 1st week of Sept.

Sugar Bar: 254 West 72nd Street between Broadway and West End Avenue. 212-579 0222, http://sugarbarnyc.com. Subway to

72nd Street.

I came across this cool little place in a converted brownstone by accident while researching restaurants on the Upper East Side. Despite its low-key exterior, it turns out this place has been a secret haunt of celebrities over the years, from Whoopi Goldberg to Don King. Tues–Sat you can catch live performances from local and international talent, covering R&B, soul, jazz, Caribbean and African. The food is pretty good, too, with dishes such as red snapper and rib eye steak.

WEST VILLAGE

Le Poisson Rouge: 158 Bleecker Street. 212-505 3474, www.lepoissonrouge.com. Subway A, C, E to West 4th Street.

A great spot for all kinds of interesting nights out. Founded by musicians, it calls itself a 'multimedia art cabaret', which means you can expect live bands, art, film, theatre and dance, all backed by state-of-the-art performance space, including great acoustics. Standing room and seating available.

> **⚑ BRITTIP**
> If you're on a budget, get down to the new Crocodile Lounge (325 East 14th Street between 2nd and 3rd Avenues, 212-477 7747, www.crocodileloungenyc.com), a funky, slightly divy bar with, you've guessed it, crocodiles – look up on the ceiling and you'll spot one – that gives out free pizza from its ovens for every beer you buy.

NIGHTCLUBS & CABARET

The club scene in New York literally changes by the week. Venues are constantly opening, closing and relaunching so we've picked out the best of the well-established clubs, plus a scattering of new or smaller places that are currently creating a stir. By the way, while many of the clubs stay open until 4am, hours do vary so check out the listings in the *Village Voice, Paper, New York Press* and *New Yorker* and on websites such as www.nymag.com and www.nyclubs.com.

CHELSEA

Marquee: 289 10th Avenue at 26th Street. 645-473 0202, www.marqueeny.com. Subway C, E to 23rd Street.

One of the coolest clubs in the city, or so the hype would have you believe, so there's always a massive queue. Once inside it's worth the wait; intimate banquettes around the edge of the room with chandeliers overhead and ice buckets on tables.

CHINATOWN

Happy Endings: 302 Broome Street at Forsyth Street. 212-334 9676, www.happyendinglounge.com, Subway B, D train to Grand Street.

A brothel-turned-bar with a DJ in the basement dance room, where sauna rooms have been converted into private party coves, and a lounge on the 1st floor with red velvet booths filled with hip young things.

BRITTIP

Need to cure a Sunday hangover on the cheap? Head to Crocodile Lounge for a free omelette with every $5 Bloody Mary between 12pm–3pm.

EAST VILLAGE

Lit: 93 2nd Avenue between 5th and 6th Streets. 212-777 7987, www.litloungenyc.com. Subway 6 to Astor Place; F, V to Lower East Side/2nd Avenue.

This art-meets-celebs counterculture joint is the place to come. A haven for indie filmsters, it has an art gallery – The Fuse – a cellar-like dance room downstairs plus live music too.

Webster Hall: 125 East 11th Street between 3rd and 4th Avenues. 212-353 1600, http://websterhall.com. Subway L, N,Q, R, W, 4, 5, 6 to 14th Street/Union Square.

Probably the biggest club in the city, with lots of different rooms with different sounds, so you're bound to find something you enjoy. The best area is the main dance floor in the huge, ornate ballroom. It attracts a fairly straight crowd from the suburbs, but is a fun night out.

BRITTIP

As clubs and club nights change so frequently, log on to www.clubplanet.com to find out what's on where.

FLATIRON

40/40 Club: 6 West 25th Street between Broadway and 6th Avenue. 212-832 4040, www.the4040club.com.

If you want some serious bling, and a possible celebrity sighting, then look no further than rapper Jay-Z's lavish 2-level sports bar and club. It's like being on an MTV set; 18ft tall Champagne tower, video walls showing sports and marble stepped arena. After you've watched the game on the screens, the DJ blasts R&B and hip-hop until 4am. There are 5 VIP lounges tucked away on the 2nd level, including the Jay-Z Lounge that can hold up to 100 guests and has a pool table, oak panelling and collection of pricey sports memorabilia.

GREENWICH VILLAGE

SOB's: 204 Varick Street at Houston Street. 212-243 4940, www.sobs.com. Subway 1, 9 to Houston Street.

The name stands for Sounds Of Brazil, so it's the place to come for the last word in Latin music from salsa to samba and even reggae. It celebrates 30 years in business in 2014.

Greenhouse: 150 Varick Street, 215-807 7000, www.greenhouseusa.com.

Proving nightlife can be green, this hip club is made from recycled and eco-friendly materials. It's a huge glittering space, particularly the transparent ceiling fixture of 5,000 individually hung crystals, with a great atmosphere – the place to be.

HELL'S KITCHEN

PACHA: 618 West 46th Street. 212-209 7500, www.pachanyc.com. Subway C, E to 50th Street.

The Mediterranean–style club that's massive in Europe has hit New York and it's attracting a massive crowd. It's a 2,787m^2/30,000ft^2 building split into 4 levels, each with its own vibe and top-flight DJ.

NYINTHEKNOW

Mike Ricci, director of communications Hilton Hotels Corporation, north-east US and Canada, says, 'For clubbing, I'd recommend Greenhouse (www.greenhouseusa.com) on Varick Street. It claims to be the first eco-friendly club, is made from recycled or recyclable materials and it's a very cool space featuring garden and flower-style lighting on the ceiling. There are also great DJs.'

LOWER EAST SIDE

Libation: 137 Ludlow Street between Stanton and Rivington Streets. 212-529 2153, www.libationnyc.com. Subway F to Delancey Street. DJs play a mix of hip hop, reggae, soul, punk and '80s, Wed–Sat at this sleek club that attracts a good mix of people. It also boasts a seasonal cocktail and tapas menu to help keep you going through the night.

Pianos: 158 Ludlow Street between Rivington and Stanton Streets. 212-505 3733, www.pianosnyc.com. Subway F, J, M, Z to Delancey Street/Essex Street.

A former piano shop turned whitewashed bar space that attracts a cool crowd plus the NYU students from the area. Local and national up-and-coming rock bands play in the somewhat dingy back room, while there's also a more intimate lounge upstairs where DJs play.

Sapphire Lounge: 249 Eldridge Street between Houston and Stanton Streets. 212-777 5153, www.sapphirenyc.com. Subway F to 2nd Avenue.
Pretension and attitude are left at the door in this tiny dance club that plays a great mix of hip-hop, reggae, acid jazz, R&B and disco classics. Opens at 7pm.

Slipper Room: 167 Orchard Street between Rivington and Stanton Streets. 212-253 7246, www.slipperroom.com. Subway F, M, J, Z to Delancey Street/Essex Street.
Adding some real showbiz panache to the Lower East Side, this glitzy retro lounge is the venue for genuinely good cabaret as well as some far out, gender-bending burlesque. A great evening out.

MEATPACKING DISTRICT
Cielo: 18 Little West 12th Street between 9th Avenue and Washington Street. 212-645 5700, www.cieloclub.com. Subway A, C, E to 14th Street; L to 8th Avenue.
The dance floor is sunken but the fabulous sound system hits the heights. Deep Space on a Mon is award-winning. This is one of the hottest spots in the city, and the good news (and bad news) is that it draws the big crowds.

SOHO
Club Room: 310 West Broadway near Grand Street, 212-965 3000, www.sohogrand.com. Not really a nightclub, more a den, with fake palm trees and a Terry O'Neill print of Sean Connery in a hot tub. One of SoHo's coolest hotels also has one of the coolest little lounges, too. It's great for people watching, if you can get in, for this is rather exclusive on a Fri night.

40/40 Club

Naked Lunch: 17 Thompson Street at Grand Street. 212-343 0828, www.nakedlunchnyc.com. Subway 1, 9, A, C, E to Canal Street.
A smart-looking bar playing a mix of hip hop, R&B and '80s. After work hours, you may see a few business types here, but in general it's a more easy-going crowd who just want to shake their booty.

◀▓ BRITTIP
If you go to see a Broadway musical and come out singing, you're in the right frame of mind to visit nearby Pulse Karaoke (135 West 41st Street between 6th Street and Broadway. 212-278 0988, www.pulsekaraoke.com, Subway N, Q, R, S, 1, 2, 3 to 42nd Street/Times Square). It's open until 2am, serves food and the private suites are state-of-the-art so you really can pretend you're Beyoncé (or Jay-Z!).

TRIBECA
Santos Party House: 96 Lafayette Street. 212-714 4646, www.santospartyhouse.com. Subway J, M, Z, N, Q, R, W, 6 to Canal Street. Hosts clubland legends and innovators on a regular basis – definitely one to check out if you're really into your clubbing. There are 2 levels, and the main floor has a live music system so check the website to see what's on when you're in town.

◀▓ BRITTIP
Get dressed up if you are going clubbing. Check the website. If there's an entrance fee, don't wear trainers or jeans – you probably won't get in.

UNION SQUARE
Lilium at the W Hotel Union Square: 201 Park Avenue South at 17th Street. 212-253 9119, www.starwoodhotels.com/whotels. Subway 4, 5, 6, L, N, Q, R, W to 14th Street/ Union Square.
A showy hotel bar-cum-club with trendy interior of wrought-iron black lily sculptures weaving down the walls and a twisted metal ceiling. Up-and-coming DJs play until 4am to a mixed crowd of guests and Manhattanites.

WEST VILLAGE
Sullivan Room: 218 Sullivan Street between Bleecker and West 3rd Streets. 212-252 2151, www.sullivanroom.com. Subway A, B, C, D, E, F, V to West 4th Street.
A great, intimate club with no attitude, which is rare in New York. You can dance to

soulful house with other friendly types, or just lounge around, chat and sip relatively cheap drinks. Has served as a launch pad for young local DJs.

THEATRE

Think about theatre in New York and just one word comes to mind: Broadway, and all the glamour and clamour that goes with it. One of the first things you discover about Broadway, as we Brits think of it, is that it is just a tiny stretch of almost the longest thoroughfare on Manhattan. The Theater District, as it is known, is a congregation of theatres between Broadway and 8th Avenue from about 44th to 52nd Streets (take the N, R, Q, W, 1, 2, 3, 7, 9, S lines to 42nd Street/ Times Square). This is Broadway.

You'll also see and hear the terms 'Off Broadway' and 'Off-Off-Broadway' (yes, really), which refer to uptown and downtown theatres, particularly in Greenwich Village, East Village and SoHo. These theatres are well worth a visit, as they may be offering rarely seen revivals, the innovative work of new playwrights, or productions featuring hilarious, off-the-wall humour. But they do change frequently, so it's best to check out the websites below for details.

BRITTIP

Locate the theatre of the show you really want to see and visit the theatre's box office for same-day or advance ticket sales – you may be able to get reduced rates or discounts.

Of course, Broadway productions are changing all the time, too, but many of the big shows – those that many Brits want to see – do stay around for longer. We have included reviews of those shows we believe will be available for the next couple of years, but for a completely up-to-date guide to what's on at the theatre, look in The New York Times, which has comprehensive listings of dance, classical music, opera, Broadway, Off-Broadway and Off-Off-Broadway every day. Other papers and websites that you can check out include the New Yorker, Village Voice, New York Metro and New York Press. If you want to find out what's on before you go, visit the Keith Prowse or Theatre Direct websites given below.

BOOKING YOUR TICKETS

You can often book tickets in advance in the UK through either your travel agent or Keith Prowse (UK 0870 840 1111 or US 800-669 8687 toll free, www.keithprowse.com). An

Times Square

alternative is to use TicketMaster (212-307 7171, www.ticketmaster.com) or www.lastminute.com.

If booking in New York, try Theater Mania (212-352 3101, or 866-811 4111 toll free, www.theatermania.com); Prime Tickets and Tours (800-480 8499, www.primetickets.com); Telecharge.com (212-239 6200, www.telecharge.com) and All Tickets Inc. (800-922 0716, www.allticketsinc.com).

BRITTIP

Discount coupons for Broadway shows are found at neighbourhood information stands and barrows throughout Manhattan. Also pick them up from NYC's Visitor Information Centre at 810 Seventh Avenue at 53rd Street (212-484 1222, www.nycvisit.com).

Ambassador Theater

For cheaper tickets, go to one of the Theater Development Fund's TKTS 3 booths (212-221 0013, www.tdf.org). The less crowded (but less convenient) downtown booth is in South Street Seaport at 199 Water Street at the corner of Front Street, and John Street, subway J, M, Z, 2, 3, 4, 5 to Fulton Street. For same-day evening performances open Mon-Sat 11am-6pm, Sun 11am-4pm; matinee tickets bought here are for the following day's performance. A booth is also located under the red steps in Father Duffy Square on Broadway at 47th Street, subway 1, 2, 3, 4, 5, 6, N, R, W, A, C to Times Square. It's open Mon, Wed-Sun 3-8pm for evening performance tickets, Tues 2-8pm. For matinees, Wed & Sat 10am-2pm, Sun 11am-3pm. It gets very busy so arrive early for the best selection, then spend the day in Midtown (Chapter 2 New York Neighbourhoods, p50).

BRITTIP

To get fast, accurate, real-time information about available Broadway and off-Broadway tickets at the TKTS Discount Booths, you can now get a TKTS app for your iPhone, Android and Windows phone. Available from itunes, it's free and can save you a lot of hassle and unnecessary journeys.

The third booth is in downtown Brooklyn and 1 MetroTech Center at the corner of Jay Street and Myrtle Avenue Promenade, subway A, C, F to Jay Street. Open Tues-Sat 11am-6pm, closed for lunch 3-3.30pm. Discounts range from 25-50% for same-day tickets to Broadway, Off-Broadway shows and other arts events, and there's a $4 per ticket fee that helps fund the TDF. They accept credit cards, cash, travellers' cheques and gift certificates. If you are flexible about what you would like to see, you can decide to go to a show at the very last minute, since TKTS Midtown is open right until show time.

BRITTIP

Watch out for ticket touts close to the ticket booths. The tickets they are offering might seem like a bargain but an increasing number of the tickets they sell are fakes.

For Off-Broadway shows, the Alliance of Resident Theaters (http://offbroadwayonline. com) has dozens of performances for all budgets daily across New York. Bookings for all the shows and performances below can be made with Theater Direct International

(800-BROADWAY, www.broadway.com) or for the best seats in the house, via the official information and ticket resource, the Broadway Ticket Center, in the Times Square Visitor Center (1560 Broadway between 46th and 47th Streets, open Mon-Sat 9am-7pm, Sun 10am-6pm).

The Hit Show Club (630 9th Avenue at 45th Street, 8th Floor, 212-581 4211, www. hitshowclub.com) and Broadway Bucks (226 West 47th Street between Broadway and 8th Avenue, 10th floor, 212-398 8383, 800-233 7565 toll free, www.bestofbroadway.com) distribute coupons that can be redeemed at the box office for one-third or more off regular ticket prices. If you don't see them in your hotel, pick them up from the offices.

BRITTIP

All the Broadway shows listed here have one interval (unless stated).

LONG-RUNNING & HIT NEW SHOWS

ALADDIN
- ✉ New Amsterdam Theater, 214 West 42nd Street
- 🖰 http://disney.go.com/theatre/
- 🕐 To be confirmed

As of going to press, Disney's sparkling revamped musical Aladdin is due to open at the New Amsterdam Theater in spring 2014. Insiders working on the production say all five hits from the movie will be included, such as 'A Brave New World'. Aladdin as a musical opened more than 20 years ago and has grossed more than $500 million worldwide; this promises to be the most lavish of the lot.

ANNIE
- ✉ Palace Theater, 1564 Broadway
- 🖰 http://www.palacetheatreonbroadway. com
- 🕐 Tues and Thurs 7pm, Weds 2pm, Fri and Sat 2pm and 8pm, Sun 3pm.

A new production of this favourite musical about an orphan who manages to escape to a mansion but can't escape the evil orphanage owner, Miss Hannigan. Anyone who has seen the movie and loves the songs will adore this stage production, and if you're new to Annie, expect to have your spirits lifted.

AVENUE Q
- ✉ New World Stages, 340 West 50th Street between 8th and 9th Avenues
- 🖰 www.avenueq.com
- 🕐 Mon, Wed, Thur, Fri 8pm; Sat 2.30pm and 8pm; Sun 3pm and 7.30pm

NIGHTLIFE

Multi award-winning musical about recent college grad Princeton who moves into a New York apartment way out in Avenue Q. He meets Kate, the girl next door; Rod, a republican; Trekkie, the internet nerd; and Lucy, the sexpot. What makes it more special than most? It's a laugh-out-loud adult musical acted out with puppets.

CHICAGO

✉ Ambassador Theater, 219 West 49th Street between Broadway and 8th Avenue
✆ www.chicagothemusical.com
🕐 Mon, Thurs, Fri, Sat 8pm; Tues, Sun 7pm; matinees Sat 2.30pm; Sun 2.30pm and 7pm

This great musical with wonderful dancing is the winner of 6 Tony Awards and has other productions throughout the world, but many still consider this one to be the best. In fact, it's celebrated its 16th Anniversary. Chicago tells the story of a chorus girl who kills her lover and then escapes the noose and prison with the help of a conniving lawyer. If greed, corruption, murder and treachery are your bag, then this is the musical for you.

BRITTIP

Many theatres have started scheduling Tues performances at 7pm, an hour earlier than customary, to accommodate those who have to travel far or want to dine afterwards.

JERSEY BOYS

✉ August Wilson Theater, 245 West 52nd Street
✆ www.jerseyboysbroadway.com
🕐 Wed Sat 8pm, Tues 7pm; matinees Wed, Sat 2pm, Sun 3pm

This musical chronicles the rags-to-riches story of the group Frankie Valli and The Four Seasons, four blue-collar boys who became one of the biggest American pop music sensations of all time. Sing along to classics such as 'Sherry', 'Big Girls Don't Cry' and 'Can't Take My Eyes off You'.

LET IT BE

✉ St James Theatre, 246 West 44th Street
✆ www.stjames-theater.com
🕐 Mon–Fri 8pm, Sat 2pm and 8pm, Sun 2pm and 7pm

It started as a West End concert to celebrate the Beatles' 50th Anniversary and became a hit musical that debuted at the St James in July 2013. The hit-song journey chronicles the band's rise from Liverpool's Cavern Club to the height of their fame - you'll be able to sing along to every tune, from 'Twist & Shout',

'Hey Jude' to 'Let It Be' and 'Come Together'.

THE LION KING

✉ Minskoff Theater, 200 West 45th Street between Broadway and 8th Avenue
✆ www.disneyonbroadway.com
🕐 Tues 7pm; Sat 8pm, Sun 6.30pm; matinees Wed, Sat 2pm, Sun 1pm

With the original music from Elton John and Tim Rice (which won them Oscar and Grammy awards) combined with new music from Hans Zimmer and Lebo M. Disney tells the story of Simba, a lion cub who struggles to accept the responsibilities of adulthood and his destined role as king. 15 years on Broadway in 2013.

MAMMA MIA!

✉ Winter Garden Theater, 1634 Broadway at 50th Street
✆ www.Mamma-Mia.com
🕐 Mon 8pm; Wed–Sat 8pm; 2pm matinee Sat, Sun; Sun 7pm

If you haven't had a chance to see this fabulously uplifting musical in London, then why not try it in New York? Set on a mythical Greek island, it tells the story of a single mum and her daughter on the eve of her daughter's wedding and comes with 22 cracking ABBA songs.

MATILDA

✉ Shubert Theater, 225 West 44th Street between Broadway and 8th Avenue
✆ us.matildathemusical.com
🕐 Tues 7pm; Wed 2pm and 8pm, Fri and Sat 2pm and 8pm

Based on the Roald Dahl novel, Matilda is a big Broadway hit about an extraordinary little girl who dreams of a better life.

BRITTIP

Queues for the Times Square TKTS booth start long before it opens, so arrive early to get a good choice. But even if you arrive at the last minute, you may catch a show, because the booth stays open right until show time.

THE PHANTOM OF THE OPERA

✉ Majestic Theater, 247 West 44th Street between Broadway and 8th Avenue
✆ www.phantomoftheopera.com/newyork
🕐 Tues 7pm, Mon, Wed–Sat 8pm; matinees Wed, Sat 2pm

The longest-running show in Broadway history, Andrew Lloyd Webber's famous musical of Gaston Leroux's novel set in 19th-century Paris tells the timeless story of a mysterious spectre who haunts the Paris opera house, spooking the owners and falling in love with a beautiful singer. It's won multiple awards and it's so popular for a reason – it's fabulous!

ROCK OF AGES
✉ Helen Hayes Theater, 240 West 44th Street
⌁ www.rockofagesmusical.com
🕐 Mon, Thurs, Fri 8pm; Tues 7pm; Sat 2pm, 8pm; Sun 3pm, 7.30pm

Set in LA's Sunset Strip in the 1980s, you follow the story of Drew from South Detroit and Sherrie, a small town girl, both chasing their dreams of making it big in the City of Angels and falling in love. Songs include 'We Built This City', 'The Final Countdown', 'Wanted Dead or Alive' and 'Can't Fight This Feeling'. Rock on!

BRITTIP
Entertainment Link has detailed info on Broadway and other theatre, as well as sports and family events, the performing arts and music, plus discounts, www.entertainment-link.com.

NIGHTLIFE

SPIDER-MAN: TURN OFF THE DARK
✉ Foxwoods Theater 213 West 42nd Street
⌁ www.spidermanonbroadway.marvel.com
🕐 Tues 7.30pm, Wed 1.30pm and 7.30pm, Fri–Sat 2pm and 8pm, Sun 3pm

Loosely following the comic books and film, it's an eventful show complete with actors flying over the audience and amazing sets of the city skyline. From nerdy Peter Parker being bitten by a spider and becoming super-human to battling against the Green Goblin and scaling skyscrapers, you'll be hooked.

Scheduled to continue its run, but check on the website for 2014 details.

STOMP
✉ Orpheum Theater, 126 2nd Avenue at 8th Street
⌁ www.stomponline.com
🕐 Tues–Fri 8pm, Sat 3pm, 8pm; Sun 2pm, 5.30pm

A very unusual show now in its 15th year. Dancers make their own music by using everyday objects such as dustbin lids, brooms and sticks. The rhythmic beats are infectious and the performers' stamina amazing.

BRITTIP
For fantastic views of Times Square, treat yourself to a drink at the Broadway Lounge on the 8th floor lobby level of the Marriott Marquis Hotel at 1535 Broadway (www.nymarriottmarquis.com).

WICKED
✉ Gershwin Theater, 222 West 51st Street
⌁ www.wickedthemusical.com
🕐 Tues 7pm, Wed 2pm & 8pm, Thurs & Fri 8pm, Sat 2pm & 8pm, Sun 3pm

Long before Dorothy drops in, 2 other girls meet in the Land of Oz. One, born with emerald-green skin, is smart, fiery and misunderstood. The other is beautiful, ambitious and very popular. Based on the 1995 novel by Gregory Maguire, this musical tells the story of their remarkable odyssey, and how these unlikely friends grow to become the Wicked Witch of the West and Glinda the Good Witch.
Awards: 3 Tonys

Wicked

CHAPTER 9
Where to Stay

The beauty of a city as diverse and cosmopolitan as New York is that you can find pretty much any kind of accommodation you desire. From über-romantic suites in super swish hotels to quirky little downtown boutique retreats, you're guaranteed to find something that meets your taste and budget.

By 2016, the city is set to have added another 16,000 hotel rooms, bringing its total to 110,000 rooms in five boroughs. There are some exciting new hotels in the pipeline. Richard Branson, for example, has announced plans for a Virgin hotel in Midtown, for visitors who want a stylish crash pad. Fewer than half of these hotels belong to national or international chains and some of them are also springing up in outer boroughs like Brooklyn and Queens, so the Big Apple is bursting with hotels of character and charm that you're unlikely to find anywhere else.

You may be surprised at the size of some of the rooms in the city, which are on the small side, but remember that Manhattan is a small island where space is at a premium. What rooms lack in size they usually make up for in decor and views, as architects had to design vertically rather than horizontally; many of the high-rise hotels, such as the Four Seasons, offer breathtaking panoramic vistas.

If you're visiting the city for the first time, be sure to do some research before you book so that you can decide which area you would like to be based in. This will save you much time and money on getting around. For example, if your prime reason for visiting the city is for theatres and shopping, you're going to want to be staying in Midtown where everything is on your doorstep. It may be that if you intend to stay for a week it would work out best to stay at two hotels – one in Lower Manhattan and one in Midtown, helping you save on travelling time and expensive cab fares.

The most upmarket hotels have always been clustered on the east side of Manhattan

Conrad New York

BOOKING IT YOURSELF

Unless you're taking a tour operator package, where flight and accommodation are included, you'll want to book accommodation yourself. You can do this directly with the hotel by phone or internet, or through companies that specialise in offering excellent rates at off-peak and low-peak times or can even just guarantee finding you a discounted room in the city during busy periods. These include:

Hotel America Ltd: 08700 464010, www.hotelanywhere.co.uk/america. A British company providing hotel discounts anywhere in the world.

Hotel Conxions: 212-840 8686, www.hotelconxions.com. You can find out about availability and price and book a room on their website.

Last Minute: www.lastminute.com. A great website for booking cheap through to more expensive hotels in New York, complete with description. Also has lots of hotel deals.

Quikbook: 212-779 7666, www.quikbook.com. A service providing discounts on hotels all over America. They promise there are no hidden cancellation or change penalties, and pre-payment is not required.

A great internet discount reservation service can be found at www.hoteldiscount.com, or you can look for cheaper rates through the hotel discount service on www.usacitylink.com.

When discussing room rates with any of these organisations, always check that the prices you are quoted include the New York City hotel tax of 13.25% and the $2 per night occupancy tax or 4% for a 1-bedroom suite.

Also take a look at flash sale sites like www.jetsetter.com which have exclusive daily deals, sometimes as much as 50% off the usual hotel price but usually for a week or two only. Another trusted website for exclusive half-price hotels is www.booking.com which has an app you can download, so you can book your hotel on the move.

from Midtown up to 96th Street. However, in recent years first class hotels have been popping up all over the place and there are now several in SoHo, Greenwich Village and the Financial District. The best deals tend to be around Herald Square and on the Upper West Side, but if you go for these options check you won't be spending more than you need to on transport. The average rate for a room that can accommodate 2 people is around $208 a night – so if you get something for less (and there are plenty of ways to do this), you will be doing well.

◀◳▶ BRITTIP

If you are planning to take in the sights of Lower Manhattan, Chinatown, Lower East Side, SoHo and the Village, choose a downtown hotel. It'll save you loads of time on travel and money on cab fares.

HOTEL TIPS

▶ Demand for hotel rooms at peak times of the year is high, so your best bet for both ensuring a bed and getting the best price is to go in the off-peak times of Jan–Mar and July–Aug.

▶ Most hotels reduce their rates at weekends – including some of the poshest. If you're staying for more than a weekend, negotiate the best rate you can for the rest of your time or switch to a cheaper hotel.

▶ If noise is a particular problem for you, bear in mind that hotels downtown and uptown tend to be quieter than those in Midtown. Also, hotels on streets tend to be quieter than those on avenues, except those nearer the river.

▶ For longer stays, try to choose a hotel room or apartment with a kitchenette, then you won't have to eat out all the time.

▶ Smaller hotels tend not to book large groups, so they often have rooms available even during peak periods.

▶ Ask for a corner room – they are usually bigger and have more windows and, therefore, more light than other rooms and don't always cost more.

▶ Renovation work is often going on in New York hotels so, when making a reservation, ask if any is being done there and, if it is, ask for a room as far away as possible from the work.

Below is the *Brit Guide* pick of the best hotels in Manhattan, priced by room per night, covering all price brackets. They range from romantic hideaways to the latest hip openings to grand hotels that have been on the map for nearly a century.

$	Less than $100
$$	$100–200
$$$	$200–300
$$$$	$300–400
$$$$$	$400 and over

BATTERY PARK CITY

CONRAD NEW YORK $$$–$$$$
✉ 102 North End Avenue
☎ 212-943 0100
⌂ www.conradnewyork.com
🚇 Subway World Trade Center
Opened April 2012 and cemented lower Manhattan's renaissance. There are 463 all-suite rooms, with calming wood and beige interiors; ask for one with a view of the Hudson River for dazzling views day and night. This is a great place to stay for visiting Wall Street, the 9/11 Memorial and Statue of Liberty. Even if you're not staying, pop into the lobby to see the soaring glass atrium and massive swirled blue and purple Loopy Doopy painting by Sol LeWitt, then head to the rooftop bar Loopy Doopy for drinks with a view.

RITZ-CARLTON NEW YORK, BATTERY PARK $$$$$
✉ 2 West Street between Battery Place and West End
☎ 212-344 0800
⌂ www.ritzcarlton.com
🚇 Subway 4, 5 to Bowling Green
A world-class, award-winning hotel with Art Deco-inspired interiors, incredible views of the Hudson River and Statue of Liberty, state-of-the-art business support services and unparalleled service. A 39-storey glass-and-brick edifice in Lower Manhattan, it has 298 sumptuous guest rooms, an outdoor waterfront deck and even the Skyscraper Museum next door (p122).
　　The rooms come with the very finest Frette linens, feather beds and goose-down pillows, cotton bathrobes, Ritz-Carlton pyjamas, marble bathtubs and separate marble shower stalls, silk curtains, in-room safe, working desk with 2 chairs, dual-line cordless phones with voicemail and high-speed internet access. The extensive guest services include a fully equipped health club and spa, massage treatments, limo, complimentary shuttle service in Lower Manhattan and a bath butler. Sheer luxury!

BROOKLYN

ALOFT NEW YORK BROOKLYN $$
✉ 216 Duffield Street
☎ 718-256 3833
⌂ www.starwoodhotels.com
🚇 Subway A, C, F, R to Jay St/Metro Tech
Moderately priced, contemporary hotel that I'd thoroughly recommend. Rooms are small, bright and clean and each has a shower and TV the public spaces are cool too, particularly the small rooftop bar. No restaurant, however there is a 24/7 pantry and with so many good restaurants within strolling distance, you won't miss one.

GLENWOOD HOSTEL $
✉ 339 Broadway between Rodney and Keap Streets
☎ 718-387 7858
🚇 Subway J, M, Z to Marcy Avenue
The choice of backpackers on a very tight budget. The rooms are tiny, there's space for a bed and little else, and the walls are paper-thin so you can hear every move your neighbour makes. It's not popular on web forums, but on the plus side, it's VERY cheap, rates are from $30 for a single. Rentals are available on a nightly, weekly or monthly basis.

KING & GROVE $$$–$$$$
✉ 160 North 12th Street
☎ 718-218 7500
⌂ www.kingandgrove.com
🚇 Subway L to Bedford Avenue
The hip, if more expensive, choice in Brooklyn. K&G has magazine interior-style rooms, pool, Elm restaurant, rooftop lounge with jaw-dropping views of Manhattan, free wi-fi and complimentary bike rental.

🇬🇧 BRITTIP
Brooklyn is without doubt the current New York hot spot, with more hipsters than you can shake a Converse trainer at. If you want an authentic experience in a Brooklynite's home, try www.airbnb.com/brooklyn where you can stay in a shared apartment for as little as $30 a night.

NEW YORK MARRIOTT AT THE BROOKLYN BRIDGE $$–$$$
✉ 333 Adams Street at Tillary Street
☎ 718-246 7000
⌂ www.brooklynmarriott.com
🚇 Subway A, C, F to Jay Street/Borough Hall; N, R to Court Street; 2, 3, 4, 5 to Borough Hall just 5 minutes' walk away

Trump International Hotel & Tower

Although over the water from Manhattan, you gain by getting excellent city views and great facilities, such as a large swimming pool, at competitive prices.

CENTRAL PARK

TRUMP INTERNATIONAL
HOTEL & TOWER $$$$–$$$$$
✉ 1 Central Park West between 60th and 61st Streets
☎ 212-299 1000
🖰 www.trumphotelcollection.com
🚗 Subway N, R to 5th Avenue
Billionaire Donald Trump's first foray into hotels is a shimmering tower that houses 167 rooms and suites, as well as various shops and restaurants. The best thing about the hotel is the views of Central Park and 5th Avenue through floor-to-ceiling windows – simply

Eventi

spectacular. The spa is a must-visit for those in need of pampering. The staff are charming and helpful, from booking theatre tickets to handing you an umbrella if it's raining. Check out the company's other hotel in SoHo, too (p246).

CHELSEA

EVENTI $$$–$$$$
✉ 851 Avenue of the Americas at 30th Street
☎ 212-564 4567
🖰 www.eventihotel.com
🚗 Subway 1 to 28th Street; D, F, N, G to Herald Square
Part of the swish Kimpton group, this lovely little hotel has a large terrace, spa and sexy rooms with huge mirror facing the bed, Frette robes trimmed with zebra print and a mini bar with an intimacy kit! A wraparound terrace on the 5th floor has oversize wicker love seats and views of the Empire State Building.

HOTEL INDIGO CHELSEA-
NEW YORK $$$
✉ 127 West 28th Street between 6th and 7th Avenues
☎ 212-973 9000
🖰 www.indigochelsea.com
🚗 Subway 1 to 28th Street Station
Intercontinental's latest brand, which lies between its budget Holiday Inns and swish Intercontinental properties. It's urban modern; think 24-hour fitness centre, duvets rather than sheets, complimentary wi-fi and a Starbucks.

MARITIME HOTEL $$$-$$$$

✉ 363 West 16th Street at 9th Avenue
☎ 212-242 4300
🖱 www.themaritimehotel.com
🚇 Subway 1, 9 to 14th Street

A fun, stylish hotel where all rooms have a maritime theme; think porthole windows overlooking the Hudson river, teak panelling and blue and white nautical stripes. The 24-hour room service can be enjoyed with the latest on-demand movies plus computer games. There's a sizeable roof terrace and it's in a great location for exploring Chelsea and the Meatpacking District.

FINANCIAL DISTRICT

GILD HALL $$$$

✉ 15 Gold Street, Financial District
☎ 212-232 7700
🖱 www.60thompson.com
🚇 Subway 2, 3 to Fulton Street

Just minutes from Wall Street, this gorgeous boutique retreat is not just for city slickers, it's for anyone who loves their hotels to be stylish and laid-back. Attractions include rooftop bar A60, Thom lounge bar with a menu by Kittichai, its extremely popular Thai restaurant and 126 rooms, 24-hour concierge, Frette robes and mini-bars stocked by Dean & Deluca.

◀▶ BRITTIP

There aren't many hotels with car parks. If you're driving in New York, our tip is the Ramada Eastside (212-545 1800, www.theramada.com), which is a clean, pleasant hotel Lexington Avenue at 30th street where rates start from around $180.

Holiday Inn Wall Street

HOLIDAY INN WALL STREET $$-$$$

✉ 51 Nassau Street
☎ 212-232 7700
🖱 www.ihg.com
🚇 Subway J, M, Z, 2, 3, 4, 5 to Fulton Street

It's not bursting with character, but I think it's a great-value place to stay if you're not on expenses, and the Federal Café serves up quality New York strip steak.

HYATT ANDAZ WALL STREET $$$$

✉ 75 Wall Street
☎ 212-590 1234
🖱 www.andaz.com
🚇 Subway 2, 3 to Wall Street

Andaz is the latest boutique brand from international chain Hyatt, and it's been a hit in London. The Wall Street hotel is the only hotel actually on Wall Street and has

Millenium Hilton

TOP 5 HOTEL POOLS WITH VIEWS

If you like a swim while you're away, check into one of these establishments whose penthouse pools offer some of the best views in Manhattan.

Le Parker Meridien: The penthouse pool provides a perfect retreat for relaxation and a sun deck offers scenic views of Central Park. It's available to hotel guests for free, or you can pay $50 for a day-pass to use it as well as the gym (p234).

Mandarin Oriental: Floor-to-ceiling windows light up an inviting 23m/75ft indoor lap pool on the 35th floor, with amazing views of the New York skyline (p243).

Hotel Gansevoort: This trendy hotel has a suitably cool pool. Take the elevator straight to the top floor and you'll be rewarded with a 14m/45ft heated outdoor pool that also has underwater music. There are plenty of people to watch while you have your dip (p231).

Millennium UN Plaza Hotel New York: 1 United Nations Plaza, 44th Street and 1st Avenue, 212-758 1234, www.millenniumhotels.com. Take a trip up to the 27th floor and you'll be wowed by the wonderful panoramic views through the floor-to-ceiling windows of this 13m/44ft city oasis.

The James Hotel: Okay, it's only a rooftop plunge pool, but that's good enough for me when the heat's rising and you want a cocktail with a view (and potential dip). Open to the public as well as guests at weekends (p245).

250 suites and 350 residential units. Expect chic, masculine interiors perfect for upscale businessmen. The Biergarten in the outside courtyard is popular in the summer. There's also another Andaz further uptown on 5th Avenue, see website for details.

MILLENIUM HILTON $$-$$$$$
✉ 55 Church Street between Fulton and Dey Streets
☎ 212-693 2001
🖰 www.newyorkmillenium.hilton.com
A black skyscraper geared to business, with 471 rooms and 98 suites, a fitness centre and pool. For a stunning view of the harbour, ask for a high-floor room.

BRITTIP
Hotels in the Financial District can be especially good value at weekends when many business people leave the city.

W NEW YORK DOWNTOWN $$$$
✉ 123 Washington Street at Albany Street
☎ 646-826 8600
🖰 www.wnewyorkdowntown.com
🚇 Subway 4, 5 to Wall Street
This hip hotel has everything you'd expect from a cool W; modern, compact, luxury rooms and hangouts for Manhattan's scenesters, including the BLT Bar & Grill and cocktails in the W Living Room Bar & Terrace.

WALL STREET INN $$$
✉ 9 South William Street opposite 85 Broad Street
☎ 212-747 1500
🖰 www.thewallstreetinn.com

🚇 Subway 2, 3 to Wall Street; J, M, Z to Broad Street
An elegant boutique hotel in an old office building in the heart of the financial and historic district. Original features include mahogany wall panels and granite floors and rooms have a home-from-home vibe with thick curtains, large wood-framed bed and luxury linen.

BRITTIP
Confusingly, American hotel lifts use 'L' for lobby or '1' to indicate the ground floor.

FLATIRON DISTRICT

CARLTON $$$-$$$$$
✉ 88 Madison Avenue between East 28th and 29th Streets
☎ 212-532 4100
🖰 www.carltonhotelny.com
🚇 Subway 4, 5, 6 to 28th Street
Revamped rooms by renowned architect David Rockwell have seen this hotel go from standard tourist class to 4-star. There are tall leather headboards, walnut trimmings and plush duvets. The view of the Empire State Building and its excellent location for 5th Avenue and Garment District shopping also make it a great place to check-in.

GERSHWIN $$$-$$$$
✉ 7 East 27th Street between 5th and Madison Avenues
☎ 212-545 8000
🖰 www.gershwinhotel.com
🚇 Subway 6 to 28th Street
Until recently a mega budget hotel, but it's

under new management and the dorms have gone and prices gone up! It's still a character-crammed budget boutique hotel though.

GAY-FRIENDLY HOTELS

CHELSEA PINES INN $$
Chelsea
- ⊠ 317 West 14th Street between 8th and 9th Avenues
- ☎ 212-929 1023
- ⌂ www.chelseapinesinn.com
- 🚖 Subway A, C East to 14th Street; L to 8th Avenue

In an excellent location in Chelsea on the border with the Village, this hotel is one of the best gay hotels in the city. Furnishings are homely (if your home is quite chic) and in the morning, guests wake to the aroma of homemade bread and doughnuts. Open to both men and women. You need to book at least 6–8 weeks in advance.

🇬🇧 **BRITTIP**

Chelsea is the top 'gaybourhood' in New York City, although Hell's Kitchen is creeping into style. The headquarters for HX, Chelsea is one of the best places for gay people to base themselves.

CHELSEA SAVOY HOTEL $$–$$$
Chelsea
- ⊠ 204 West 23rd Street
- ☎ 212 929 9353/866-929 9353 toll free
- ⌂ www.chelseasavoynyc.com
- 🚖 Subway 1, 9, 3 to 23rd Street

This great-value hotel is in a superb location, being close to the Theater District, Financial District, great restaurants, museums and galleries, and SoHo just down the road. The rooms are a good size for NY, with all essential amenities such as bathroom and TV.

COLONIAL HOUSE INN $$–$$$
Chelsea
- ⊠ 318 West 22nd Street between 8th and 9th Avenues
- ☎ 212-243 9669
- ⌂ www.colonialhouseinn.com
- 🚖 Subway C east to 23rd Street

A beautiful place to stay and spotlessly clean. The economy rooms are tiny, but all have cable TV, air con, phone and daily maid service, smoking is allowed in rooms and the price includes breakfast. The hotel was set up by Mel Cheren, the 'Godfather of Disco' and head of production at Paramount, who campaigned about AIDS prevention until he sadly died from the disease himself. The main lobby has been turned into The 24 Hours For Life gallery, featuring some of Mel's original pictures.

Book as early as you can because this place gets packed with groups coming into town for drag conventions and so on. It's especially popular in the summer months because of its roof deck with a clothing-optional area. The hotel has a 24-hour doorman.

🇬🇧 **BRITTIP**

The main event of the gay year is the Heritage of Pride Parade (formerly Gay Pride) in June (p256), where half a million people turn up to parade the streets and party all week. If you're coming then, also catch the NewFest gay film festival in mid-June.

HERALD SQUARE HOTEL $$
Flatiron
- ⊠ 19 West 31st Street between 5th Avenue and Broadway
- ☎ 212-279 4017
- ⌂ www.heraldsquarehotel.com
- 🚖 Subway N, R to 28th Street

Once the headquarters of *Life* magazine, now a small, quirky extremely well-priced hotel (rooms start from $159) near the Empire State Building and Macy's. Every room is different, from chandeliers to iron bed frames and all-white bathrooms. Very original and at a good price, which includes free wi-fi complimentary tea, coffee and hot chocolate in the lobby.

HOTEL 17 $$
Flatiron
- ⊠ 45 225 East 17th Street at Union Square
- ☎ 212-475 2845
- ⌂ www.hotel17ny.com
- 🚖 Subway 6, A, C, E to 14th Street

A hideaway well off the tourist radar. It's where Woody Allen filmed *Manhattan Murder Mystery* and Madonna used to stay and did many photo shoots. Rooms aren't exactly design-led (you're not going to be getting into a Philippe Starck egg bath here) but they do have lots of amenities, including hairdryer, free wi-fi, TV and toiletries. This is a place to lay your head rather than snuggle up for a romantic anniversary, but a total bargain in New York with rooms starting from around $125.

Incentra Village House

KING & GROVE $$$
Gramercy Park
- ✉ 29 East 29th Street between Park and Madison Avenues
- ☎ 212-689 1900
- ⌂ www.kingandgrove.com
- 🚇 Subway 6 to 29th Street

Formerly the Hotel Lola, this is now part of the King & Grove group which includes hip King & Grove Brooklyn (p223). Expect small but tasteful rooms with Frette linen on the bed, cocktail lounge in the lobby and all the added extras you'd expect from an upmarket boutique escape: free wi-fi, 24-hour business centre, complimentary newspaper oh, and there's parking, $45 for 24 hours.

INCENTRA VILLAGE HOUSE $$–$$$
West Village
- ✉ 32 8th Avenue between West 12th and Jane Streets
- ☎ 212-206 0007
- ⌂ www.incentravillage.com
- 🚇 Subway A, C east to 14th Street; L to 8th Avenue

If you're looking for somewhere a bit different to stay, I'd recommend this charming guesthouse. Moderately priced and spread over 2 redbrick townhouses dating back to the 1840s (that's old by American standards!), the 12 suites all have kitchens, phones and private bathrooms and some can even accommodate groups of 4 or 5. All the rooms are decorated with different themes. The Bishop Suite is a split-level apartment, the Garden Room has a private garden filled with flowers and the Maine Room has a 4-poster bed. A 1939 Steinway piano stands in the parlour and anyone is allowed to play.

THE OUT $$
Hell's Kitchen
- ✉ 510 West 42nd Street
- ☎ 212-947 2999
- ⌂ http://theoutnyc.com
- 🚇 Subway

New, extremely stylish hotel that's straight-friendly in the heart of all the action. It boasts a lounge, cabaret, late-night restaurant and even a nightclub. The Spa at The Out, its wellness centre, looks set to be the place to recover from the excesses of the night before.

King & Grove

Gramercy Park Hotel

GRAMERCY PARK

GRAMERCY PARK HOTEL $$$–$$$$
- ✉ 2 Lexington Avenue at Gramercy Park North
- ☎ 212-920 3300
- 🖰 www.gramercyparkhotel.com
- 🚇 Subway L, N, R, 4, 5, 6 to 14th Street/ Union Square

Once a famous hotel where the likes of JFK and Humphrey Bogart liked to spend time, now it's back on the style radar once again, thanks to a multi-million dollar refurbishment. Each room is luxuriously and individually furnished and the attention to detail is pretty impressive, from leather-topped desks to mahogany drinks cabinets and marble bathrooms. It has a much coveted roof club and garden, and the penthouse is incredible, too, with wonderful views of Gramercy Park and a massive bedroom, dining room, multi-media centre and kitchen. Restaurant supremo Danny Meyer runs its hugely popular Italian restaurant, Maialino.

INN AT IRVING PLACE $$$$–$$$$$
- ✉ 56 Irving Place between East 17th and East 18th Streets
- ☎ 212-533 4600
- 🖰 www.innatirving.com
- 🚇 Subway L, N, R, 4, 5, 6 to 14th Street/ Union Square

Delightful, tiny Victorian boutique hotel (there's no sign outside). Each of the 12 rooms has a romantic fireplace, Frette linen, Penhaligon's toiletries, desk and most have a 4-poster bed. There is also Lady Mendl's Tea Salon, and Cibar Lounge. Exquisite.

 BRITTIP

If you hire a car, bear in mind that most hotels charge a parking fee of around $40 a night.

THE MARCEL AT GRAMERCY $$$
- ✉ 201 East 24th Street at 3rd Avenue
- ☎ 212-696 3800
- 🖰 www.themarcelatgramercy.com
- 🚇 Subway 6 to 23rd Street

Catering to a clientele of international crowds from the arts, film and fashion worlds, you'd expect this hotel to be pricier than it is. You can get a standard room from around $229 upwards, which are average size for New York and pleasantly decorated – animal print cushions, cool artwork. Its great location for Midtown and Downtown makes it a winner.

The Marcel at Gramercy

LARCHMONT $–$$

- ✉ 27 West 11th Street between 5th and 6th Avenues
- ☎ 212-989 9333
- 🖱 www.larchmonthotel.com
- 🚇 Subway F to 14th Street

Clean, basic, well-sought-after Village boutique hotel. Wash basin in-room, shared bathrooms. Rates from $90, which includes a continental breakfast.

WASHINGTON SQUARE HOTEL $$

- ✉ 103 Waverly Place between 5th and 6th Avenues
- ☎ 212-777 9515
- 🖱 www.washingtonsquarehotel.com
- 🚇 Subway A, B, C, D, E, F, Q to West 4th Street/Washington Square

Over a century old, this hotel is clearly doing something right. It has a bohemian air and overlooks Washington Square. Bedrooms are quite small but comfortable, with duvets and black and white prints of movie stars on the wall, but the highlight here is the dark 1930s-esque bar – a fab place to end a night and the rates very reasonable and include breakfast. Bob Dylan was known to stay in the 1960s, though he may not approve of the smoke-free rule introduced.

🇬🇧 BRITTIP

If you want to rub shoulders with the stars where you're staying, check in to the Bowery. On her website, www.goop.com, film star Gwyneth Paltrow says, 'The Bowery has been one of my homes-away-from-home. It is a very cool spot, with the people to match. As it is located on Bowery I wouldn't recommend it to the Park Avenue set, but my English rock star friends can't get enough of it.'

LOWER EAST SIDE

BLUE MOON $$$

- ✉ 100 Orchard Street, Lower East Side
- ☎ 212-533 9080
- 🖱 www.bluemoon-nyc.com
- 🚇 Subway F to East Broadway

This 22-room boutique retreat in the trendy Lower East Side has kept lots of character features, such as original walnut window shutters, built-in window seats and original ceiling mouldings, and rooms are quirkily named after celebrities from the 1930s. Situated down a quaint cobbled street, it's a little gem if you don't want to break the bank.

The complimentary continental breakfast served in the lobby includes delicious bagels. Other freebies include wi-fi, gym pass and welcome glass of wine.

BOWERY $$$$–$$$$$

- ✉ 335 Bowery at 3rd Street
- ☎ 212-505 9100
- 🖱 www.theboweryhotel.com
- 🚇 Subway F to Delancey Street

Super cool and discreet. Celebs love it and so do we thanks to its 400-thread count cotton, valet parking, complimentary DVD library and New York Times, iPod docking stations, marble bathrooms and Gemma Restaurant.

HOTEL ON RIVINGTON $$$$–$$$$$

- ✉ 107 Rivington Street between Ludlow and Essex Streets
- ☎ 212-475 2600
- 🖱 www.hotelonrivington.com
- 🚇 Subway F to Delancey Street

Another hip hotel to open up in the Lower East Side, this glass and aluminium 20-storey building is very sleek. The entrance of deep red carpet and velvet curtains isn't the same tone as the rest of the hotel. Low-lying sofas and tables with arty books and very minimalist and tasteful rooms with cloud-like duvets, boxy armchairs in slate grey and flat-screen TVs. If you can afford it, go for 1 of the upper level rooms with great views of the East River from floor-to-ceiling windows. It's also home to popular restaurant Viktor & Spoils, a very cool Mexican taqueria plus tequila bar (the chorizo tacos are addictive).

HOWARD JOHNSON EXPRESS INN $–$$

- ✉ 135 Houston Street between Forsyth and Eldridge Streets
- ☎ 212-358 8444
- 🖱 www.hojo.com
- 🚇 Subway F, V to 2nd Avenue

The Lower East Side celebrated the arrival of its first hotel, a modern, without frills but incredibly well-priced getaway. Right next door is the renovated landmark Sunshine Cinema, which was once a showplace for Yiddish vaudeville and films and is now a multiplex for art films.

OFF SOHO SUITES $$–$$$

- ✉ 11 Rivington Street between Chrystie Street and The Bowery
- ☎ 212-979 9808
- 🖱 www.offsoho.com
- 🚇 Subway F to Delancey Street

Well-positioned apartment alternative to New York's inflated hotel rates, with good-sized, clean suites that can sleep 4 with fully equipped kitchens.

THE STANDARD
COOPER SQUARE HOTEL $$$$

- ✉ 25 Cooper Square, between East 5th and 6th Streets, Bowery
- ☎ 212-475 5700
- ⌂ www.thecoopersquarehotel.com
- 🚖 Subway F to Delancey Street

A 21-storey hotel definitely worth checking out from the developers of the fashionable Standard Hotels and restaurants in LA and Miami. In the heart of the Bowery area, which is fast becoming one of NY's hotspots, it's close to SoHo for shopping and nightlife. It's innovative in a good way; there's no check-in desk (guests are greeted by a host informed electronically of their arrival at the front door), complimentary bikes and breakfast, a tree-canopied back garden, signature scent and a range of indie films in the minibar. If you've money to burn, the penthouse has incredible views.

MADISON SQUARE GARDEN

CHELSEA STAR HOTEL $–$$

- ✉ 300 West 30th Street at 8th Avenue
- ☎ 212-244 7827
- ⌂ www.starhotelny.com
- 🚖 Subway 1, 2, 3, 9 to 28th Street

Cool little, low-budget hotel, which has been imaginatively decorated, particularly the speciality rooms; think Salvador Dali melting clocks and dark blue walls with stars! There are dormitories or private rooms, some of which can sleep up to 4.

MEATPACKING DISTRICT

HOTEL GANSEVOORT $$$–$$$$$

- ✉ 18 9th Avenue at 13th Street
- ☎ 212-206 6700
- ⌂ www.hotelgansevoort.com
- 🚖 Subway N, R to 5th Avenue

The original and still the best, much-fêted 187-room, 23-suite hang-out that was the first boutique hotel to open up in the formerly no-go area of the Meatpacking District. The feature that really makes it a place to head for is the 14m/45ft long rooftop pool with underwater music. The spa, with salon and infinity-edge hydro pools, is great, too, and the TOY New York Asian restaurant and Oyster and Sushi bar in the lobby are worth a visit, but there are lots of other great restaurants within walking distance

MIDTOWN

ALGONQUIN $$–$$$

- ✉ 59 West 44th Street between 5th and 6th Avenues

- ☎ 212-840 6800
- ⌂ www.algonquinhotel.com
- 🚖 Subway B, D, F, Q to 47th–50th Streets/ Rockefeller Center

Famous for the literary meetings held here by Dorothy Parker and her cohorts, the Algonquin underwent a $45m refurbishment some years ago in its 174 rooms and 24 suites. The Round Table Room is a favourite spot for a pre-theatre dinner, while Blue Bar is good for a cocktail or two.

◀▊▶ BRITTIP

If you're travelling with your children (or you're just an animal-lover), consider a stay at The Algonquin to meet its famous cat. Ever since a stray cat wandered into the hotel in the 1930s and was given food and shelter, the hotel's had a resident cat, the latest of whom is the friendly and fluffy Matilda. Kids can even email her at matildaalgonquincat@ algonquinhotel.com before they arrive.

BRYANT PARK $$$$–$$$$$

- ✉ 40 West 40th Street
- ☎ 212-869 0100
- ⌂ www.bryantparkhotel.com
- 🚖 Subway D, B, V, F to 42nd Street

This hide-out for the fashion pack overlooks the park that gives the hotel its name. It's just off 5th Avenue, so ideal if you are on a shopping trip and convenient for visiting all of the major sights. Inside, the rooms resemble (very tiny) New York lofts; think white walls, sleek Italian furniture and cool bathrooms with giant porcelain sinks and stainless steel shelves.

CASABLANCA $$$–$$$$

- ✉ 147 West 43rd Street off Times Square
- ☎ 212-869 1212,
- ⌂ www.casablancahotel.com
- 🚖 Subway 1, 2, 3, 7, 9, N, R, S to Times Square/42nd Street

Calling itself 'an oasis in the heart of Times Square', its elegant Moroccan theme, inspired by the film *Casablanca*, includes ceiling fans, palm trees and mosaic tiles. Small, with just 48 newly renovated luxury rooms, the service is good and it also offers complimentary use

Hotel Gansevoort

of the New York Sports Club, with pool, just steps away.

CHAMBERS $$$–$$$$$
✉ 15 West 56th Street between 5th and 6th Avenues
☎ 212-974 5656
🖰 www.chambershotel.com
🚗 Subway B, Q to 57th Street

Owned by the same team behind the Mercer Hotel in SoHo, it attracts the likes of Jennifer Love Hewitt and Kid Rock to its gorgeous rooms. The ultra-modern decor is comfortable and luxurious and the hotel displays over 500 pieces of original art. The bath tubs are deep, cashmere throws adorn the beds and flat-screen TVs with DVD players grace every

City Club Hotel

room. Its restaurant Mä Pêche (p174) is a great spot for lunch.

THE CHATWAL NEW YORK $$$$$
✉ 130 West 44th Street
☎ 212-764 6200
🖰 www.thechatwalny.com
🚗 Subway N, Q, R, W to Times Square/42nd Street

This polished Art Deco-inspired modern gem restored by architect Thierry Despont evokes the glamour of the '30s and opened spring 2010 in the former home of the Lambs Club in the Theater District. Its 88 bedrooms incorporate retro touches, hi-tech sound systems and big TVs and there's a Red Door Spa.

BRITTIP
Take a look at The Chatwal's Exclusive Offers section on its website before you book. There are a fantastic variety of packages and deals, from 40% off an extra night to fashion trips including a chauffeur-driven car and styling service.

CITY CLUB HOTEL $$$–$$$$
✉ 55 West 44th Street between 5th and 6th Avenues
☎ 212-921 5500
🖰 www.cityclubhotel.com
🚗 Subway 7 to 5th Avenue; B, D, F, V to 42nd Street

The owner-manager Jeffrey Klein is one of the most socially visible hoteliers in the city and some of his very famous friends cocoon themselves in his hotel. Based in an old gentlemen's club building, it is one of the smartest but least showy boutique hotels in New York. There's no queuing in the lobby as check-in happens in your room, which has a big TV hidden in the wall, high-thread linen and vintage books. The three grand duplex suites have private terraces. These rooms are designed to spend time in!

DISTRIKT HOTEL $$$-$$$$

✉ 342 West 40th Street between 8th and 9th Avenues

☎ 212-706 6100

🖰 www.distrikthotel.com

🚇 Subway A, C, E to 42nd Street

Steps away from the New York Times Building and Times Square, Distrikt Hotel New York offers a dedication to detail with impeccable service, cutting-edge technology and comfortable, functional guestrooms. Each of the 155 rooms has Simmons Beauty Rest pillow-top mattresses, Frette bed and bath linen, a 37-in LG flatscreen television, business desk with ergonomic chair, Ecru New York soaps and wi-fi.

EDISON HOTEL $$-$$$

✉ 228 West 47th Street between Broadway and 8th Avenue

☎ 212-840 5000

🖰 www.edisonhotelnyc.com

🚇 Subway N, R to 49th Street

One of New York's great hotel bargains. The Art Deco hotel has 700 rooms, while the coffee shop, the Café Edison, is considered

Edison Hotel

to be the best place to spot lunching theatre luminaries. Book well in advance.

GIRAFFE $$-$$$

✉ 365 Park Avenue South between 26th and 27th Streets

☎ 212-685 7700

🖰 www.hotelgiraffe.com

🚇 Subway 6 to 23rd Street

Small, chic boutique hotel. Each floor has 7 rooms, many with their own balconies adorned with fresh flowers and there's also a roof garden for drinks, complimentary cheese and wine in reception, Bread & Tulips Italian restaurant and access to a nearby health club for guests.

The Hotel @ Times Square

THE PERFECT APPLE

A major hotel chain, Apple Core, runs 5 hotels in excellent Midtown locations with extremely reasonable rates of $139–300 a night. They are: **Red Roof Inn Manhattan** on 32nd Street, west of 5th Avenue; the smoke-free **Comfort Inn Midtown** on 46th Street west of 6th Avenue; **Hotel Times Square** on 46th Street between 5th and 6th Avenues near the Rockefeller Center; **La Quinta Manhattan** on 32nd Street between Broadway and 5th Avenue; and **Ramada Inn Eastside** at 30th Street and Lexington Avenue.

All the hotels offer complimentary continental breakfast, well-equipped fitness centres and business centres. In-room facilities include cable television and pay-per-view movies, free wi-fi, telephones with data port and voicemail, coffee makers, irons and ironing boards. The modern bathrooms all come with marble units and hairdryers.

Occupancy rates are above 90% – so book early through Apple Core's central reservations: 212-790 2710, www.applecorehotels.com.

THE HOTEL@ TIMES SQUARE $$–$$$

✉ 59 West 46th Street between 5th and 6th Avenues
☎ 212-719 2300
🖰 www.applecorehotels.com
🚇 Subway B, D, F, Q to 47th–50th Streets/ Rockefeller Center

A well-priced hotel with excellent amenities that include a fitness centre, coffee makers and irons in the rooms, free local phone calls, wi-fi and continental breakfast (see The Perfect Apple for more bargain hotels, above).

HOTEL WOLCOTT $$$

✉ 4 West 31st Street between 5th Avenue and Broadway
☎ 212-268 2900
🖰 www.wolcott.com
🚇 Subway N, R to 28th Street

It's all about location, location, location at this 200-room hotel. Just 3 blocks down from 5th Avenue and the Empire State Building, this is a favourite with the serious tourist and budget-minded business traveller. Call in advance to find out the bargain seasonal, weekend and holiday rates on offer.

JW MARRIOTT ESSEX HOUSE $$$$–$$$$$

✉ 160 Central Park South at 7th Avenue
☎ 212-247 0300
🖰 www.marriott.com
🚇 Subway 1, A, B, C, D at 59th Street/ Columbus Circle

The position of this upmarket hotel, opposite southern Central Park and a few strides from 5th Avenue, is knock-out. An Art Deco past, but now it's very much a contemporary hotel with the usual upmarket touches, such as leather chairs, heated towel rails and cosy white fluffy robes, plus some cool extras, such as tub phones in the bathroom and an on-site health spa. The rooms are also fabulously quiet, so make a welcome retreat from the noisy city.

LE PARKER MERIDIEN $$$$–$$$$$

✉ 119 West 57th Street between 6th and 7th Avenues
☎ 212-245 5000
🖰 www.parkermeridien.com
🚇 Subway B, D, E to 7th Avenue

A classic New York hotel in the design sense, yet with a traditional French feel, this hotel is not only in an excellent location just minutes from Central Park and Carnegie Hall, but also offers great service and amenities. The recently refurbished rooms have a Zen-like calmness, thanks to the minimalist and cherrywood decor. Great touches include a revolving unit that allows you to watch the massive TV screen either in the sitting area or in the bedroom.

Even if you don't plan to use the swimming pool, you must visit its penthouse location to see the fab views of Central Park. Down in the basement is the massive Gravity gymnasium, which covers everything from Cybex training to aerobics, sauna, massage rooms, spa services and squash courts.

Other facilities include the much-raved-about Norma's restaurant in the lobby, which serves creative breakfast dishes throughout the day (p175).

◀✚▶ **BRIT**TIP
Le Parker Meridien has a complimentary shoeshine service, so don't forget to take your pair for a quick polish while you're there.

THE LIBRARY $$$$–$$$$$

✉ 299 Madison Avenue at 41st Street
☎ 212-983 4500
🖰 www.libraryhotel.com
🚇 Subway 4, 5, 6, 7, S to 41st Street/Grand Central

A fabulous hotel that, you've guessed it, has the theme of a city library. It has the feel of a cosy gentlemen's club when you first walk in, all mahogany panelling, fancy artwork and bookcases. The Love Room has an outside terrace (rare in Manhattan) overlooking Madison Avenue. The rooms are a revelation. Each of the 10 floors is dedicated to a category that you'd find in a real library, such as philosophy or art and literature, and there are books and artworks in rooms to match the theme of each level. Original and luxurious, but pricey.

THE LONDON NYC $$$–$$$$$
- ✉ 151 West 54th Street
- ☎ 212-307 5000
- ⌂ www.thelondonnyc.com

The former Rihga Royal New York Hotel has been transformed into an über-hip destination: out with the tired furnishings and in with deluxe rooms with high-speed internet access. London chef Gordon Ramsey's first restaurant in the city is here and there are lots of offers, such as a London Suite from $299 per night, so check the website.

MANSFIELD $$$–$$$$$
- ✉ 12 West 44th Street between 5th and 6th Avenues
- ☎ 212-944 6050
- ⌂ www.mansfieldhotel.com
- 🚇 Subway B, D, F, Q to 47th–50th Street/ Rockefeller Center

A beautiful lobby with vaulted ceiling and white marble marks the Mansfield out as an elegant hotel for those also wanting the charm of a boutique establishment. The rooms have plush robes and Aveda toiletries and its M Bar, with its domed skylight and mahogany bookshelves, has been described by Zagat as 'an off the beaten path, classy, romantic sweet spot'.

METRO $$–$$$
- ✉ 45 West 35th Street between 5th and 6th Avenues
- ☎ 212-947 2500
- ⌂ www.hotelmetronyc.com
- 🚇 Subway B, D, F, N, Q, R to 34th Street

Well located near the Empire State Building, which can be seen from its rooftop garden terrace, this hotel is great value for money, offering plenty of Art Deco inspired style and loads of amenities, like a big gym, beauty salon and rooftop garden terrace.

THE MODERNE $$$–$$$$
- ✉ 243 West 55th Street between Broadway and 8th Avenue
- ☎ 212-397 6767
- ⌂ www.modernehotelnyc.com
- 🚇 Subway C, E, 1, 9 to 50th Street

There are only 34 rooms, 5 on each floor, in this smart boutique getaway that lies close

TOP 5 CELEBRITY HOTELS
Check out where the stars check in

Gramercy Park Hotel: Janet Jackson, Chace Crawford, Kid Rock (p229)

The Bowery: Ashley Olsen, Blake Lively, Gwyneth Paltrow, Rachel Bilson (p230)

60 Thompson: Kirsten Dunst, Jessica Simpson, Christina Aguilera, Matt Damon (p244)

The Greenwich Hotel: Robert De Niro, Mel Gibson, Spike Lee, Uma Thurman (p248)

The Carlyle: Tom Cruise and Katie Holmes hosted a tea party for daughter Suri here (p249)

to Carnegie Hall and The Museum of Modern Art. You can lie in soft Belgian linen beneath a Warhol print of Marilyn Monroe or pamper yourself with the Gilchrist & Soames goodies in the very plush bathrooms.

MORGANS $$$–$$$$
- ✉ 237 Madison Avenue
- ☎ 212-686 0300
- ⌂ www.morganshotel.com
- 🚇 Subway 4, 5, 6 to 6th Avenue and 34th Street

This is considered the hotel that fired up the design-led boutique phenomenon and it's still going strong today, thanks to its unique sense of style and effortless cool. The bedrooms are apartment-style havens, all ivory, camel and taupe soft furnishings.

THE PENINSULA $$$$$
- ✉ 700 5th Avenue at 55th Street
- ☎ 212-956 2888
- ⌂ www.peninsula.com
- 🚇 Subway F to 53rd Street; 6 to 51st Street

A beautiful hotel that has undergone a massive $45m renovation in the public areas, restaurants and 239 guestrooms and suites. These are of classic contemporary style with touches of Art Nouveau, and oversized marble bathrooms where you can watch TV from the bath. The state-of-the-art technology allows you touch-button control of your environment, and a water bar is on hand for hangover recovery. The views from rooftop bar Salon de Ning are fabulous and afternoon tea in the Gotham Lounge is ideal if you need a break from shopping.

THE PLAZA $$$$$
- ✉ 768 5th Avenue at 59th Street
- ☎ 212-759 3000
- ⌂ www.fairmont.com/theplaza
- 🚇 Subway 6 to 51st Street

A true New York landmark built in the style of a French Renaissance chateau. Built by Henry

The Plaza

Janeway Hardenbergh and opened to the public on 1 October 1907, its position next to Central Park and 5th Avenue is unbeatable as a base in NYC. After renovations, it now offers 282 guest rooms, including 102 suites, which the hotel claims boast the largest square footage of any luxury hotel in NY. Proving that it really is firmly in the 21st century, it also offers all guests an iPad during their stay. Other developments include exclusive boutiques that sell food as well as clothing and accessories, a Caudalie Spa, Warren Tricomi Salon and fitness centre.

While those who adored The Plaza may be sceptical of the changes, enough has been preserved of its glamorous traditions to keep even the most die-hard patron happy. The Palm Court has been fully resorted and once again offers afternoon tea, for which it was famous. Likewise, the opulent Grand Ballroom (where Catherine Zeta Jones and Michael Douglas had their wedding celebrations) and Terrace Room have been restored to their former glory. The legendary Oak Room and Oak Bar are still intact, but there's also a new Champagne Bar and stylish Rose Club, both located in the 5th Avenue lobby and bound to be an instant hit with New York's stylish crowd. You're likely to recognise the building from the string of films and TV shows that have been shot in and around it, such as *North by Northwest, Funny Girl, The Way We Were, Cotton Club, Crocodile Dundee, Home Alone 2* and *The Sopranos*, as well pictures from celebrity events.

ROYALTON $$$–$$$$

✉ 44 West 44th Street between 5th and 6th Avenues
☎ 212-869 4400
🖰 www.royaltonhotel.com
🚗 Subway B, D, F, Q to 42nd Street

Still an in place with the magazine and showbiz crowd, despite the fact that this hotel, originally designed by Philippe Starck, first opened in the 1980s. Its theatre-style lobby, recently re-created by New York design firm Roman and Willian, runs the length of an entire block and is worth a visit alone. The 168 rooms have been refurnished by Charlotte Macaux and include neutral shades,

Royalton

Warwick

built-in banquettes running the entire width of the room, mahogany furniture and crisp white linens. Starck's sumptuous bathrooms now have slate and mirrored tiles and 1.5m/5ft Roman soaking tubs. The Forty Four bar is a stylish place for a cocktail (p211). Check out the special offers section on the website before you book.

⚑ BRITTIP

For a cheaper way to see the city in style, check out the ACE Hotel (20 West 29th Street, 212-679 222, www.acehotel.com). Just 3 blocks from the Empire State Building, it's a 12-storey, 260-room gem of a Midtown hotel. It's edgy without being intimidating – DJs play in the lobby bar, the Breslin dining room serves up organic and seasonal English-style grub and No 7 Sub Shop is a great place to pick up a sarnie for a picnic in Central Park. There are funky bedrooms with murals on the walls, with words like 'Play Safe'.

SHOREHAM $$$–$$$$$
✉ 33 West 55th Street at 5th Avenue
☎ 212-247 6700
🖰 www.shorehamhotel.com
🚗 Subway F to 5th Avenue
This hotel won awards for its ultra-modern decor following its renovation. It now has a

new bar, restaurant, fitness centre and some more good-sized rooms. Added extras include some interesting art works in the lobby and public areas and in-room complimentary cappuccino and espresso machines.

WARWICK $$$–$$$$
✉ 65 West 54th Street at 6th Avenue
☎ 212-247 2700
🖰 www.warwickhotelny.com
🚗 Subway B, D, F, Q to 47th-50th Streets/ Rockefeller Center
A medium-sized hotel built in 1927 with good-quality rooms and excellent service in an excellent location. In its heyday many a Hollywood celeb stayed here, including Cary Grant. Randolph's Bar remains a favoured meeting place and a great spot for lunch or a light dinner in its recently opened restaurant, Murals on 54, which offers innovative Continental cuisine.

Shoreham

DIAMOND DISCOUNTS

If you've got your flights and are hunting out a hotel, you can cut room rates significantly by taking advantage of the Secret Sale section on discount website www.quikbook.com. Rooms drop to up to 40% of their usual price, I've seen some 4-stars drop as low $130 per night. The catch? You don't find out the name until you book. However, you do get a good description and there have been some excellent places up for grabs recently.

MIDTOWN EAST

70 PARK AVENUE $$$–$$$$

✉ 70 Park Avenue at 38th Street
☎ 212-973 2400
🖱 www.70parkave.com
🚇 Subway 4, 5, 6 to 42nd Street

A lovely boutique hotel with a home-from-home atmosphere whose motto is 'Live Life Well'. It has the Silver Leaf Tavern, a bar-restaurant popular with locals as well as guests, and excellent room facilities, as well as services like a hosted evening wine tasting, morning newspaper, valet parking for $52 a day, 'Forgot it? We've Got It' essential travel items you may have forgotten (I'd forgotten toothpaste, so this was great!), and access to the nearby spa and fitness centre.

BRITTIP

If you're planning a romantic jaunt to the Big Apple, 70 Park Avenue has a Romance Sommelier, who can arrange all manner of dreamy things, from rose petals on your bed to a private helicopter tour of Manhattan and in-room massage.

DYLAN $$$–$$$$

✉ 52 East 41st Street between Madison and Park Avenues
☎ 212-338 0500
🖱 www.dylanhotel.com
🚇 Subway S, 4, 5, 6, 7 to Grand Central/42nd Street

Located in the former Chemist's Club building, this small hotel was developed to preserve the 1903 Beaux Arts structure. A mezzanine lounge and bar overlooks the dramatic, high-ceilinged restaurant, Benjamin Steakhouse. The 107 suites are elegant rather than overtly fashionable and amenities include a state-of-the-art digital entertainment system.

ELYSÉE $$$$–$$$$$

✉ 60 East 54th Street between Park and Madison Avenues
☎ 212-753 1066
🖱 www.elyseehotel.com
🚇 Subway 6 to 51st Street

A small hotel dating from the 1920s whose decor includes antique furnishings and Italian marble bathrooms (hint: this isn't the place to stay if you love minimalism). Once a home-from-home to movie stars, it's still filled with discerning guests, who have use of a nearby sports club as the hotel has no gym.

FITZPATRICK GRAND CENTRAL $$$

✉ 141 East 44th Street between Lexington and 3rd Avenues
☎ 212-351 6800
🖱 www.fitzpatrickhotels.com/grandcentral
🚇 Subway S, 4, 5, 6, 7 to Grand Central/42nd Street

The Fitzpatrick Family Group of hotels continues its Irish theme at this hotel just across from Grand Central station. It includes an Irish pub and you can order a traditional Irish breakfast here. Check out the shopper's package, to help you get the best of shopping in New York.

BRITTIP

For sleek New York style without too hefty a price tag, check into one of the W New York hotels, a small chain that continues to spring up around the city. W New York The Court (212-685 1100), W New York The Tuscany (212-686 1600), W New York Union Square (212-253 9119), W New York Times Square (212-930 7400) and W New York on Lexington Avenue (212-755 1200) each offer exceptional standards of minimalist-style accommodation and their bars are often the hotspot of the district. View them all at www.whotels.com.

FITZPATRICK MANHATTAN $$$–$$$$

✉ 687 Lexington Avenue between East 56th and East 57th Streets
☎ 212-355 0100
🖱 www.fitzpatrickhotels.com/manhattan
🚇 Subway 4, 5, 6 to 59th Street

The 91 rooms and suites are equipped with everything from trouser presses to towelling robes, useful after indulging in the whirlpool bath you'll find in many of the rooms. Irish celebs and dignitaries often make this their home when in town and The Fitz is a friendly bar and restaurant that locals use too.

FOUR SEASONS $$$$–$$$$$
- ✉ 57 East 57th Street between Madison and Park Avenues
- ☎ 212-758 5700
- ⌂ www.fourseasons.com
- 🚇 Subway 4, 5, 6 to 59th Street

This soaring hotel has access to some of the best views of the city. It's expensive and the rooms are a touch on the small side, but you get electronically controlled curtains, marble-clad bathrooms and the best service in the world.

GANSEVOORT PARK AVENUE $$$$
- ✉ Corner of Park Avenue and 29th Street
- ☎ 212-317 2900
- ⌂ www.gansevoorthotelgroup.com
- 🚇 Subway 6 to 28th Street

A 249-room hotel that promises an uptown experience with a downtown vibe. The dramatic 3-storey lobby and rooms are designed by Manhattan-based architect Stephen B. Jacobs and interior designer Andi Pepper, as is the chic Infusion bar. Unusually for NYC, some of the rooms have balconies and floor-to-ceiling windows. There's also an amazing heated indoor-outdoor rooftop pool, unobstructed views of the Empire State Building, Exhale spa, including a yoga and core studio, Cutler Salon, fitness room, sauna and an Italian trattoria. The rooftop bar is exclusive, with a pool that features a mosaic of a pin-up girl, wrap-around terraces, transparent floors and a sun deck.

KIMBERLY $$$
- ✉ 145 East 60th Street
- ☎ 212-702 1600
- ⌂ www.kimberlyhotel.com
- 🚇 Subway 4, 5, 6 to 59th Street

Nestled in the fashionable East Side and a short walk from Times Square, Rockefeller Center and the Theater District, this is a very comfortable and convenient place to base yourself while in town. The rooms are sumptuous with fluffy white pillows and lots of polished wood and the service is excellent, including helpful extras such as travel confirmations, reservations at restaurants and tickets to Broadway shows. There isn't a fitness centre, but you get complimentary access to the New York Health and Racquet Club. However, the best thing about the

TOP 5 HOTEL SPAS
The Cowshed Spa at SoHo House (p246)

The Peninsula Spa at The Peninsula New York (p235)

Plus One Spa at Trump International Hotel & Tower (p224)

Spa at Four Seasons Hotel (left)

Spa at Mandarin Oriental (p243)

hotel we've discovered is the rooftop lounge, Upstairs, which is $372m^2/4,000ft^2$ of fabulousness; the views at night are truly spectacular.

✚ BRITTIP

There's the chance to go for a trip along the scenic East River on a sunset cruise or take Sun brunch on the New York Health & Racquet Club's yacht for just $25 if you're a guest at The Kimberly.

KITANO HOTEL $$$–$$$$$
- ✉ 66 Park Avenue at East 38th Street
- ☎ 212-885 7000
- ⌂ www.kitano.com
- 🚇 Subway S, 4, 5, 6, 7 to Grand Central/42nd Street

A first-class, Japanese-run hotel with top-notch service and a deliciously decadent, deep-soaking tub in each room. In the Murray Hill area, it has Manhattan's only authentic Japanese tatami suite. From Wed–Sat there's live jazz in the Bar Lounge and the odd celeb stays over, including tennis ace Maria Sharapova.

NEW YORK PALACE $$$$–$$$$$
- ✉ 455 Madison Avenue between 50th and 51st Streets
- ☎ 212-888 7000
- ⌂ www.newyorkpalace.com
- 🚇 Subway 6 to 51st Street

Built in 1882, the opulent Palace rises 55 floors from its prime spot in Midtown and is made famous for a whole new generation as a regular setting in hit TV show Gossip Girl. The main hotel is in the atmospheric Villard Houses, but the adjacent Towers, which has just had a multi-million dollar revamp, has the advantage of more luxurious, larger rooms. Its new American restaurant, Maloney & Porcelli, is a hit and the outdoor lounge situated inside the courtyard of the palace's Villard Mansion, serves great cocktails.

Pod Hotel

POD HOTEL $-$$$

✉ 230 East 51st Street between 2nd and 3rd Avenues

☎ 212-355 0300

🖱 www.thepodhotel.com

🚇 Subway 6 to 51st Street

A massive hit in Japan, the pod-style hotel has now hit Manhattan. Your pod is a tiny space, just big enough to fit a bed and not much else, and consequently prices are lower. It's ideal if you've got a small budget but don't want to end up in an old-fashioned B&B or hostel. Choices vary from a Bunk Pod, which is perfect if you're travelling with a friend as you get 2 bunked twin beds with a reading

light, 25cm/10in LCD TV with headphones, iPod docking station, free wi-fi. There's even just enough room for a closet and safe. The shared bathrooms, of which there are many, have rain-head showers, designer sinks and marble and granite interiors. Queen Pods are the most spacious rooms and most expensive and have a workspace, 50cm/20in TV and tiny private bathroom.

THE ROOSEVELT $$-$$$$

✉ East 45th Street at Madison Avenue

☎ 212-661 9600

🖱 www.theroosevelthotel.com

🚇 Subway S, 4, 5, 6, 7 to Grand Central/42nd Street

Built in 1924, this classy hotel was named after President Theodore Roosevelt and has thankfully been restored to its original grandeur with crystal chandeliers, soaring columns, red, gold and wood rooms and lots of marble. The opening of its beautiful Rooftop Lounge, Mad 46, with cool day beds, has proved a hit.

THE TOWERS OF
THE WALDORF-ASTORIA $$$$$

✉ 100 East 50th Street at Park Avenue

☎ 212-355 3100

🖱 www.waldorfastoria.hilton.com

🚇 Subway 6 to 51st Street

A boutique hotel occupying the 28th to the 42nd floors of the Waldorf-Astoria (p241), this is one of the most exclusive addresses

Gansevoort Park Avenue

in New York, filled as it is with presidents of countries and global corporations. Thanks to the hotel's security arrangements (it has its own private car parking facilities underground), this is the place where treaties and mergers have been negotiated and signed, momentous peace initiatives have begun and unforgettable music has been made.

The hotel has its own dedicated entrance, lobby, concierge desk, reception and private lifts operated by white-gloved attendants. Guests have included the Duke and Duchess of Windsor, who maintained their New York residence here, Jack and Jackie Kennedy, Frank Sinatra and Cole Porter, who wrote many of his most famous compositions in a room here.

The rooms are not so much rooms or suites, but rather more like apartments. Many come with dining rooms, full kitchens and maids' quarters. Four-footed guests are greeted with a biscuit!

VANDERBILT YMCA $–$$
📧 224 East 47th Street at 2nd Avenue
☎ 212-912 2500
🏠 www.ymcanyc.org
🚗 Subway 6 to 51st Street

One of the oldest buildings in Manhattan, though not the plushest, is named after its benefactor Cornelius Vanderbilt. The rooms are tiny and will set you back around $105 for a single; if you want a double with a private bathroom it rises to around $160 per night.

Waldorf-Astoria

It's part of a community centre, so you get access to 2 swimming pools and a gym. Free wi-fi in the lobby and 24-hour security, too.

WALDORF–ASTORIA $$$–$$$$$
📧 301 Park Avenue at 50th Street
☎ 212-355 3000
🏠 www.waldorfastoria.com
🚗 Subway 6 to 51st Street

A colossus of a hotel in more than one sense, it's an Art Deco marvel with a wonderful history and has been designated a New York City landmark since 1993. It had a $50m makeover a few years ago, which includes a $5.5m revamp of Peacock Alley, the hotel's top restaurant headed by chef Cedric Tovar, and a Guerlain Spa.

Vanderbilt YMCA

It all started in 1893 when millionaire William Waldorf Astor opened the 13-storey Waldorf Hotel at 33rd Street. It was the embodiment of Astor's vision of a grand hotel and came with 2 innovations – electricity throughout and private bathrooms in every guest chamber – and immediately became the place to go for the upper classes. Four years later, the Waldorf was joined by the 17-storey Astoria Hotel, built next door by Waldorf Astor's cousin, John Jacob Astor IV. The corridor between the 2 became an enduring symbol of the combined Waldorf and Astoria Hotels.

In 1929 it closed, and on its original site now stands another icon of the New York skyline, the Empire State Building. In the meantime, the Waldorf-Astoria was rebuilt in Midtown, opening its doors in 1931 and immediately dubbed New York's first skyscraper hotel. It rose 42 storeys high, stretched from Park Avenue to Lexington and contained an astonishing 2,200 rooms. It was such an amazing event, opening as it did in the middle of the Depression, that President Herbert Hoover broadcast a message of congratulations. Ever since, the Waldorf-Astoria has had a long association with presidents of countries and corporations.

◀━▶ BRITTIP ─────
If you're not happy with the quality of your room, change it. Americans wouldn't tolerate anything but the best, so why should you?

The Art Deco aspects of the hotel were brought back into view during a restoration in the 1980s when architects found a huge cache of long-lost treasures, including a magnificent 148,000-piece mosaic depicting the Wheel of Life, by French artist Louis Regal, in the Park Avenue lobby, 13 allegorical murals by the same artist and ornate mouldings on the ceilings. The legendary Starlight Roof nightclub with its retractable roof, which had epitomised glamour and sophistication in the 1930s and 1940s, was restored during the same period.

Another $60m upgrade in 1998 saw the Park Avenue Cocktail Terrace and Sir Harry's Bar being restored to their full Art Deco glory. Oscar's, named after the Waldorf-Astoria's famous style-setting maître d' Oscar Tschirky, was redesigned by Adam Tihany, the hottest restaurant designer in town.

Of course, you'll want to know about the service – excellent – and the standard of the rooms – large, for New York, beautifully decorated and with marble-encased en-suite bathrooms. What more could you ask for?

MIDTOWN WEST

AMERITANIA $$
✉ 230 Broadway at West 54th Street
☎ 212-247 5000
🖰 www.ameritaniahotelnewyork.com
🚗 Subway 1, 9 to 50th Street; B, D east to 7th Avenue

Located just outside the Theater District and near Restaurant Row, so very convenient if you want to be at the heart of things. Well appointed with simple, modern, comfortable rooms.

DREAM $$–$$$
✉ 210 West 55th Street
☎ 212-247 2000
🖰 www.dreamny.com
🚗 Subway N, R to 5th Avenue

If you're seeking peace and tranquillity, then Vikram Chatwal's beautiful hotel promises to deliver, though you needn't forego the hi-tech: its modern, eclectic-style rooms have plasma TVs and iPod players. Highlights include original art, rooftop lounge with sensational views and Serafina, a popular Italian restaurant.

EMPIRE $$$
✉ 44 West 63rd Street
☎ 212-265 7400
🖰 www.empirehotelnyc.com
🚗 Subway 1, 2, A, C, D trains to Colombus Circle/59th Street

I discovered this hotel while researching the Columbus Circle area and thought it was a great base from which to explore the Lincoln Center, Columbus Circle shops and Central Park. The 422 rooms are very tasteful and decorated in earthy tones, but the pièce de rèsistance here, I felt, was the pool deck. The rooftop area, with floaty white awnings above the swimming pool, drinks service and private cabanas, which you can rent, with iPod docking stations and even mini refrigerators and TVs, is jaw-dropping stuff.

HILTON NEW YORK $$$$$
✉ 1335 6th Avenue at 53rd Street
☎ 212-586 7000
🖰 www.hilton.com
🚗 Subway B, D, F, Q to 47th–50th Streets/Rockefeller Center

After a $100m renovation, one of the city's largest hotels now has a beautiful new façade and entrance lobby, plus two new restaurants and lounges.

HUDSON $$–$$$$$

✉ 356 West 58th Street between 8th and
   9th Avenues
☎ 212-554 6000
🖰 www.hudsonhotel.com
🚇 Subway A, B, C, D, 1, 9 to 59th Street/
   Columbus Circle

Built on the site of the former Sesame Street
studios, this Ian Schrager and Philippe Starck
collaboration is heaving with chic guests. It's
loud and proud, so don't check in if you are
looking for peace and quiet in the city. There's
a buzzy outdoor patio area and Tequila Park,
serving 40 varieties of the spirit. Rooms are
stylish but very small. In a great location for
Central Park, the Lincoln Center and Theater
District, but definitely on the west side of
town so keep this in mind when considering
your sightseeing plans.

LANGHAM PLACE
5TH AVENUE $$$$–$$$$$

✉ 400 5th Avenue at West 37th Street
☎ 212-695 4005
🖰 www.langhamhotels.com
🚇 Subway 34 Street/Herald Square

It's 5-star all the way at this just-opened
outpost of London's famous Langham hotel,
which dates back to 1865. There's a lounge
with British and American comfort food
on the menu, an extensive cocktail list and
nightly jazz at 8pm. Opening in 2014 is the
Chuan Spa, focusing on traditional Chinese
medicine.

MANDARIN ORIENTAL $$$$–$$$$$

✉ 80 Columbus Circle at 60th Street
☎ 212-805 8800
🖰 www.mandarinoriental.com
🚇 Subway A, B, C, D, 9 to 59th Street/
   Columbus Circle

An exquisite hotel on the top floors of the
AOL Time Warner Center on the north-west
arc of Columbus Circle, the 248 rooms and
suites are steps away from Central Park and
just a stroll from 5th Avenue. Inside, the
luxurious rooms are simply breathtaking, with
floor-to-ceiling windows offering spectacular
views of the Manhattan skyline. Hang out at
the trendy MO bar, or enjoy dinner in Asiate
on the 35th floor, which offers a fusion of
French and Japanese cuisine. If you're tired
after your journey, try a massage at the
excellent spa.

THE NIGHT HOTEL $$$–$$$$$

✉ 132 West 45th Street between 6th and
   7th Avenues
☎ 212-835 9600
🖰 www.nighthotelny.com
🚇 Subway B, D, F, V to 47th Street/
   Rockefeller Center

This stylish, petite 72-room hotel's black and
white, modern Gothic decor is refreshingly
cool in a city full of beige neutral hotel
rooms. It's sexy and stylish Nightlife bar and
restaurant is a great place to unwind after a
day's sightseeing or work.

SOFITEL $$$–$$$$

✉ 45 West 44th Street at 5th Avenue
☎ 212-354 8844
🖰 www.sofitel.com
🚇 Subway 7 to 5th Avenue/Bryant Park

French-run outfit that soars 30 storeys in a
curved limestone tower. The 398 rooms are
tightly packed and on the small side, but the
decor is tasteful. The top floors have private
balconies and wonderful views and Gaby, the
hotel's Art Deco French restaurant, is a great
place to dine.

WELLINGTON $$$–$$$$

✉ 871 7th Avenue at 55th Street
☎ 212-247 3900
🖰 www.wellingtonhotel.com
🚇 Subway N, R to 57th Street

Renovations, which include a swish marquee,
have moved the Wellington up from bargain
stay category. The 600 rooms and suites are
comfortably furnished (think homey, rather
than funky), with a mix of king, twin and
double rooms plus a scattering of 1-bedroom
suites. All have high-speed wi-fi access. The
best thing about this hotel is still its location
– deep in the heart of Midtown within
striking distance of Carnegie Hall, 5th Avenue,
the Rockefeller Center and Times Square. If
you can get a corner room with a view of 7th
Avenue, you'll understand the big deal about
the bright lights associated with the Theater
District – they're absolutely stunning viewed
from this position.

MURRAY HILL

HOTEL 31 $–$$$

✉ 120 East 31st Street at Lexington Avenue
☎ 212-685 3060
🖰 www.hotel31.com
🚇 Subway 6 to 33rd Street

The 72 rooms are a mix of shared and private,
packed with young Europeans. Essentials such
as air con and cable TV and even a 24-hour
concierge service. If you can get past the
flowery bedspreads and striped wallpaper, it's
fantastic value for the location.

SOHO

6 COLUMBUS CIRCLE $$$

✉ 6 Columbus Circle between West 58th
   and 60th Streets
☎ 212-204 3000
🖰 www.thompsonhotels.com

60 Thompson

🚗 Subway 1, B, C, D to 59th Street/
Columbus Circle
Overlooking Columbus Circle and Central
Park, this 88-room and suite inspired urban

retreat has a 1960s modernist feel. Standard
rooms (small, posh linen, cool artwork, iPod
dock, mini bar stocked by Dean & Deluca)
start from around $233, which isn't bad for a
slice of what is still one of the chicest hotels
around.

60 THOMPSON $$$–$$$$$
✉ 60 Thompson Street between Broome
and Spring Streets
☎ 877-431 0400
🖰 www.60thompson.com
🚗 Subway C, E to Spring Street
A sleek, 14-storey, 100-bedroom hotel that
is a great retreat from the bustling streets
of SoHo. Rooms are designed for relaxing
in – the best are on the top floor and have
breathtaking panoramic views of landmarks
such as the Empire State Building. The front
patio, sheltered by stands of black bamboo,
is a wonderful place to just sit and people-
watch and Thai restaurant Kittichai is a
favourite of New Yorkers (p184). Outstanding!

CROSBY STREET HOTEL $$$–$$$$
✉ 79 Crosby Street between Prince and
Spring Streets
☎ 212-226 6400
🖰 www.crosbystreethotel.com
🚗 Subway N, R to Prince Street
A gorgeous 86-room escape, tucked away on
a quiet cobbled street in the heart of SoHo

Columbus Circle

Penthouse Terrace at the SoHo Grand

and very popular with visiting Brits. All the rooms have high ceilings, floor-to-ceiling windows and interior design by Kit Kemp. The Crosby Bar pulls in Manhattanites, there's also a leafy garden and 99-seat screening room.

HOLIDAY INN SOHO $$
✉ 138 Lafayette Street at Canal Street
☎ 212-966 8898
🖱 www.hidowntown-nyc.com
🚇 Subway N, R to Canal Street
Well-equipped, spotless rooms available at excellent prices.

THE JAMES $$–$$$
✉ 27 Grand Street at Thompson Street
☎ 212-465 2000
🖱 www.jameshotels.com
🚇 Subway 2, 3 to Wall Street
A newly built property with wonderful outdoor spaces throughout, including an urban garden and rooftop pool deck and bar. A 2-storey glass wall in the sky lobby offers views of the garden plus a glimpse of the neighbouring sculpture garden, city and river views. In a nod to the creative neighbourhood in which it's located, there's lots of work by local artists on the wall, too.

MERCER $$$–$$$$
✉ 147 Mercer Street at Prince Street
☎ 212-966 6060
🖱 www.mercerhotel.com
🚇 Subway N, R to Prince Street
A bijou 75-room boutique hotel in a Romanesque revival building slap-bang in

the middle of SoHo. Offering a taste of New York loft living, it quickly gets packed with the fashionable and young corporate sets. Rooms even provide condoms in the bathroom and video games to play on the TV, and The Kitchen is a very popular 200-seat eatery with super chef Jean-Georges Vongerichten at the helm.

MONDRIAN SOHO $$$–$$$$
✉ 9 Crosby Street
☎ 212-389 1000
🖱 www.mondriansoho.com
🚇 Subway N, Q, R, W, 6, J, M, Z to Canal Street
This super sleek hotel is part of the über-hip Mondrian hotels, the others being in Los Angeles and South Beach. It's very calming and chic: think blue and white fabrics, large

Mondrian SoHo

mirrors and blue floors. In the lobby, custom-
designed furniture steals the show. Even if
you're not staying, it's worth a visit for the
Isola Tratorria & Crudo Bar, a spectacular
space with trees and chandeliers and seriously
tasty food.

SOHO GRAND $$$$
✉ 310 West Broadway between Grand and
Canal Streets
☎ 212-965 3000
🖰 www.sohogrand.com
🚇 Subway C east to Canal Street
Famous for its style, this was the first real
top-notch hotel to open in the SoHo area in
1996. Cocktails and light meals are served in
the Grand Bar, an intimate, wood-panelled
club room, as well as the fashionable Salon,
a lively lounge that is excellent for people-
watching and pet-friendly, so perhaps dog-
watching, too.

SOHO HOUSE
NEW YORK $$$$–$$$$$
✉ 29-35 9th Avenue between West 13th
and 14th Streets
☎ 212-627 9800
🖰 www.sohohouseny.com
🚇 Subway 1, 9 to 14th Street
SoHo House is the baby sister of London's
Soho House and has already proved a similar
magnet for celebrities and media bigwigs
with its chandeliers-meets-Corbusier decor,
24 bedrooms, Cowshed Spa and cinema. It's
actually a private members' club, but if you're
lucky enough to book one of the rooms
you can use the members' facilities, which
includes the fabulous rooftop pool that has
already gained iconic status as the set for one
of the classic *Sex And The City* episodes.

SOHOTEL $–$$$
✉ 341 Broome Street
☎ 212-226 1482
🖰 www.thesohotel.com
🚇 Subway J to Bowery Station
Travel off-season (Jan, Feb and Aug) and rates
here can drop to below the magic $200 mark.
It's no dive either, despite the price drop, with
a prime location in SoHo and great decor;
exposed brick walls, Louise XIV-style chairs
and glass chandeliers.

TRUMP SOHO NEW YORK $$$$
✉ 246 Spring Street
☎ 212-842 5500
🖰 www.trumpsohohotel.com
🚇 Subway C, E to Spring Street
This 46-storey silver and glass tower opened
in spring 2010 and boasts spectacular views
of the city's skyline, Hudson river, Statue of
Liberty and Empire State Building, so ideal
for those who want to feel in the heart of
the city. There are 391 rooms and suites with
floor-to-ceiling windows, furnishings by
Fendi Casa and custom bedding by Bellino.
With just 12 rooms per floor, they're actually
a decent size, which is unusual for NYC. Its
aim is high-end luxury, and with amenities
like The Spa at Trump (with New York's only
authentic luxury hammam), new Japanese Koi
Restaurant, seasonal Bar d'Eau on the stylish
pool deck and The Library, outfitted with
Taschen books, it certainly achieves it.

THEATER DISTRICT

COURTYARD BY MARRIOTT
TIMES SQUARE SOUTH $$–$$$
✉ 114 West 40th Street between 6th
Avenue and Broadway
☎ 212-391 0088
🖰 www.marriott.com/new-york
🚇 Subway B, D, F, Q to 42nd Street
Functional hotel with spacious rooms all have
a sitting area, large work desk, 2 phones and
in-room coffee facilities.

NEW YORK MARRIOTT
MARQUIS $$–$$$$
✉ 1535 Broadway at 45th Street
☎ 212-398 1900
🖰 www.marriott.com/new-york
🚇 Subway N, R, S, 1, 2, 3, 7, 9 to Times
Square/42nd Street
Its location in the heart of Times Square and
Broadway make this a popular tourist spot.
Rooms are comfortable. Book a Times Square
view room for one of the best light shows
on earth. Attractions include Crossroads
American Kitchen & Bar with a mirrored
spiral bar, big fitness centre and it's also
home of The View, New York's only revolving
restaurant.

BRITTIP
Got some free time and want
to get lots off your hotel rate?
Log on to www.priceline.com and
bid for your room! Now a big craze
in the US, you make a bid and then
wait to see.

FOR SOMETHING DIFFERENT

HouseTrip: (www.housetrip.com). Great website that allows native New Yorkers to rent their flat out, meaning you get to live like a local if only for a few days. Renters are rated (like eBay) to make sure standards stay high. There's lots of choice on the website, from compact 1-bedroom apartments in the Upper East Side through to palatial pads in Midtown. You get what you pay for, but in general renting an apartment works out cheaper than a hotel, plus it can be more fun, particularly if there's a group of you. I tried it out and was impressed. My only complaint would be that HouseTrip's New York office, where you have to collect your key from, is up 4 flights of stairs (there's no lift), which is tough work to climb with a suitcase!

Inn New York City: 266 West 71st Street between Broadway and West End Avenue, 212-580 1900, www.innnewyorkcity.com. $$$–$$$$. This romantic boutique retreat has just 4 suites, each with a kitchen, and is fantastically placed for shopping, theatres and restaurants.

Jazz on the Park Hostel: 36 West 106th Street at Central Park West, 212-932 1600, www.jazzhostels.com. $–$$ Clean, comfortable rooms for the budget traveller. Double and 'dormitory' rooms, laundry room, rooftop terrace and garden. Price includes breakfast. Sister hostels include Jazz on the Town (307 East 14th Street in the midst of the bars, restaurants and clubs of East Village, 212-228 2780) and a new hostel, Jazz on Harlem (104 West 128th Street, 212-222 5773).

OneFineStay: (www.onefinestay.com). Similar to HouseTrip, though slightly higher end, this site sells itself as the unhotel, allowing you to rent a place from a local.

PARAMOUNT HOTEL
TIMES SQUARE $$–$$$$$
✉ 235 West 46th Street between Broadway and 8th Avenue
☎ 212-764 5500
🖰 www.nycparamount.com
🚗 Subway C, E, 1, 9 to 50th Street

Dating back to 1928, this hotel is an NYC institution, largely due to its amazing location slap bang in the middle of Times Square. There's a glorious sweeping staircase in the lobby and 597 small but well equipped rooms. The mezzanine restaurant is good for people-watching; ditto the Paramount and Library bars.

PREMIER HOTEL
TIMES SQUARE $$$–$$$$
✉ 133 West 44th Street between 6th Avenue and Broadway
☎ 212-789 7670
🖰 www.milleniumhotels.com
🚗 Subway N, R, S, 1, 2, 3, 7, 9 to Times Square/42nd Street

A 4-star getaway with great location in Times Square, steps away from 5th Avenue and Broadway. Lovely city skyline views from the 125 rooms, which are elegant and a good size, particularly the bathrooms, which have actual baths (or European soaking tubs as the Americans call them!). The Lounge on the mezzanine is open 24 hours a day.

RADISSON MARTINIQUE
ON BROADWAY $$–$$$$
✉ 49 West 32nd Street at Broadway
☎ 212-736 3800

🖰 www.radisson.com
🚗 Subway B, D, F, N, Q, R to 34th Street

Set in a beautiful French Renaissance style building, this hotel is good value for money with the average rate nightly $157. There are 533 clean, tasteful rooms, a cocktail lounge and KumGangSan, an excellent Korean and Japanese restaurant with 2-storey waterfall and eat-in cave!

ROOM MATE GRACE HOTEL $$–$$$
✉ 125 West 45th Street
☎ 212-354 2323
🖰 www.room-matehotels.com
🚗 Subway V, F, B, D to Grand Central

Fairly cheap, chic boutique hotel inches from Times Square right in the middle of Manhattan. The bedrooms aren't huge, but they're still plush, and there's free wifi, a pool with underwater sound system plus bar with DJs every Fri and Sat.

TIME $$–$$$
✉ 224 West 49th Street between Broadway and 8th Avenue
☎ 212-246 5252
🖰 www.thetimeny.com
🚗 Subway C, E, 1, 9 to 50th Street

Themed around Alexander Theroux's book *The Primary Colours* (not Times Square, as you might think), this brightly coloured bolthole is the perfect place if you want to stay in a touristy area in style. Primary colours are used throughout, of course: red rooms are for lovers, blue if you're feeling sad and yellow if you're a bit lacklustre. The colours continue through to the finishing touches, such as

Paramount Hotel

bowls of jellybeans in matching shades. There's a buzzing Inc bar downstairs, where guests have included the likes of Liza Minnelli. Also home to the highly rated Serafina restaurant.

WESTIN NEW YORK AT TIMES SQUARE $$$$
- ✉ 270 West 43rd Street at 8th Avenue
- ☎ 212-201 2700
- ⌂ www.westinny.com
- 🚇 Subway A, C, E, N, R, S, 1, 2, 3, 7, 9 to 42nd Street/Times Square

A large, 863-room hotel, that's got something to suit all types. It is particularly family-friendly; families will love Feel Good Family Time, which includes upgrade, complimentary children's meals when you purchase an adults meal, cinema tickets and popcorn and minibar credit. There's a kids menu for breakfast, lunch and dinner and there's also Nintendo Wii systems to keep older kids happy!

TRIBECA

COSMOPOLITAN HOTEL $$$-$$$$
- ✉ 95 West Broadway at Chambers Street
- ☎ 212-566 1900
- ⌂ www.cosmohotel.com
- 🚇 Subway 1, 2, 3 to Chambers Street

Finding a pleasant, comfortable Downtown hotel that's not going to cost you megabucks a night can be tricky. That's where this hotel steps in. It's not exactly the TriBeCa Grand, but most of the 20 and 30-somethings who pay from $350 here are happy with the neutral decor and grateful for added extras like Frette linen, Gilchrist & Soames toiletries, iPod docking stations and complimentary wi-fi.

THE GREENWICH HOTEL $$$$-$$$$$
- ✉ 377–383 Greenwich Street at Northmoore Street, TriBeCa
- ☎ 212-941 8900
- ⌂ www.thegreenwichhotel.com
- 🚇 Subway 1 to Franklin Street Station

This fabulous hotel has made lots of headlines because it's been developed by actor Robert DeNiro, with his partner Ira Drukier. They allegedly poured $43m into the 6-storey getaway that sits nicely alongside his existing portfolio, which includes the TriBeCa Film Institute. It's instantly recognisable as the terracotta brick building at the corner of Northmoore and Greenwich Streets. There are 88 rooms, all of which are individually furnished, from Tibetan silk rugs to oak floors and small libraries. It's very luxurious, with toiletries developed specially for the hotel, iPod docking stations, mini-bars stocked in advance with guests' preferences and you can even have a newspaper from your home town delivered (though that's within the US, rather than the UK!). There's also an inner courtyard that is incredibly serene, and Shibui Spa. The outside tables at Locanda Verde, the hotel's Italian taverna, are a lovely spot for lunch or dinner.

SMYTH TRIBECA $$$-$$$$
- ✉ 85 West Broadway, TriBeCa
- ☎ 212-587 7000
- ⌂ www.smythhotel.com
- 🚇 Subway A, C, 1, 2, 3 to Chambers Street

Part of the chic Thompson hotels portfolio, it might not be as edgy as some of the others in the group, but you can't fail to feel content with this retreat's simple, modern interior, 24-hour concierge, Kiehls toiletries, Plein Sud restaurant, serving delicious dishes like poisson cru and flatbreads cooked in the restaurant's brick oven, bar and lounge.

TRIBECA GRAND $$$$-$$$$$
- ✉ 2 Avenue of the Americas (6th Avenue) at Church Street
- ☎ 212-519 6600, UK freephone 0800-028 9874
- ⌂ www.tribecagrand.com
- 🚇 Subway 1, 9 to Franklin Street

Sister property to the extremely stylish Soho Grand, this was the first major hotel to open in the TriBeCa area. It's popular with the film crowd, thanks to its 98-seat private screening room (there are weekly screenings that guests can go to) and the annual TriBeCa Film Festival that it hosts. Amenities in the 201 rooms, including studio 'digital lifestyle' rooms and a Grand Suite with rooftop terrace, include access to Apple iPods and iPads, gourmet mini bar, Frette bathrobes, oh, and a pet goldfish on demand.

UPPER EAST SIDE

BENTLEY $$–$$$
✉ 500 East 62nd Street at York Avenue
☎ 212-644 6000
🖥 www.hotelbentleynewyork.com
🚇 Subway 1, 5, 6, N, R to Lexington Avenue/59th Street

Within walking distance of Bloomingdale's, many of this great-value hotel's 197 good-size rooms overlook Upper East Side Manhattan, with fab river and skyline views. The rooftop restaurant and bar has a 360-degree view of the city. Rates include breakfast and start at $143 online.

THE CARLYLE $$$$–$$$$$
✉ 35 East 76th Street between Madison and Park Avenues
☎ 212-744 1600
🖥 www.thecarlyle.com
🚇 Subway 6 to 77th Street

Established in the 1930s, The Carlyle is a timeless classic, patronised by a wide range of people from world leaders and top businessmen to It girls and leading lights in entertainment and the arts. Brilliantly positioned on Madison Avenue, it is a true New York landmark. The 180 apartment-style rooms and suites are elegant and very plush – some even have grand pianos and all have whirlpools in the bathrooms. In fact, it feels as though you're staying in your elegant Upper East Side pied-à-terre rather than renting a hotel room. If you really want to push the boat out, there's a breathtaking Royal Suite on the 22nd floor. It's famous for its impeccable and discreet service but also for its live music in Café Carlyle where Woody Allen regularly plays jazz on Mon nights (p210).

FRANKLIN $$$
✉ 164 East 87th Street between 3rd and Lexington Avenues
☎ 212-369 1000
🖥 www.franklinhotel.com
🚇 Subway 4, 5, 6 to 86th Street

Known for its good service, this pleasant Art Deco boutique hotel has some nice touches in its rooms, such as original photography, Bulgari goodies, very comfortable beds with plush linen and flatscreen TV.

HOTEL PLAZA-ATHENEE $$$$–$$$$$
✉ 37 East 64th Street between Madison and Park Avenues
☎ 212-606 4600
🖥 www.plaza-athenee.com

🚇 Subway 6 to 68th Street

Upmarket, uptown discreet getaway loved by in-the-know tourists and locals alike. What the 114 rooms lack in size they make up for in elegant antique French furnishings; the 35 suites are bigger. The hotel has introduced a great range of packages for tourists, such as the Romance Package that includes roses and champagne on arrival. The Arabelle Restaurant is also the place to brunch.

THE LOWELL $$$$$
✉ 28 East 63rd Street at Madison Avenue
☎ 212-838 1400
🖥 www.lowellhotel.com
🚇 Subway N, R, W to Lexington Avenue/59th Street

Classic Upper East Side retreat, far from the hustle and bustle of Midtown. Everything here looks and feels very expensive, from the marble floors to the mahogany desk lobby. The 47 suites and 23 deluxe rooms are decorated like the interiors of a Park Lane princess's home; think rich fabrics and plush sofas. Some even have a working fireplace, although there are hi-tech touches, such as a flat-screen TV at the foot of the bath, Bulgari toiletries and posh water at turndown.

BRITTIP

Staying on the Upper East Side can be pretty expensive in a hotel, so consider an apartment instead. New website www.housetrip.com (p247) has some quality affordable flats to rent. I tried it out and the place I stayed in was clean and comfortable and I loved feeling like a real New Yorker. Be warned: as space is such a premium, many apartments are on the cosy side and have tiny kitchens (New Yorkers eat out a lot!). The website also has other apartments for rent around the city.

Tribeca Grand

THE MARK $$$$-$$$$$
- ✉ 25 East 77th Street between 5th and Madison Avenues
- ☎ 212-744 4300
- 🖱 www.themarkhotel.com
- 🚇 Subway 6 to 77th Street

A recent refurbishment has breathed new life into this super-smart hotel, where the likes of Kate Moss and Johnny Depp used to hang out in the '90s. It was 1 of the city's first really beautiful upmarket boutique hotel and the mix of swanky rooms and suites full of the latest Bang & Olufsen equipment and marble bathrooms combined with the most discreet service in town will ensure it stays at the top.

✪ BRITTIP
When making a booking directly with a hotel, make sure they send you confirmation of your reservation (by email is simplest).

SHERRY-NETHERLAND $$$$-$$$$$
- ✉ 781 5th Avenue at East 59th Street
- ☎ 212-355 2800
- 🖱 www.sherrynetherland.com
- 🚇 Subway 4, 5, 6 to 59th Street

A true New York institution, this is 1 of the grand hotels with real charm and is also the permanent home of many a celebrity. The city view suites are the rooms to bag and it also boasts the Harry Cipriani Restaurant, popular with ladies who like to lunch.

UPPER WEST SIDE

DAYS HOTEL BROADWAY $$-$$$
- ✉ 215 West 94th Street at Broadway
- ☎ 212-866 6400
- 🖱 www.dayshotelnyc.com
- 🚇 Subway 4, 5, 6, N, R to Lexington Avenue/59th Street

A 349-room hotel which isn't going to win any awards for design or innovation, but it's a clean and inexpensive place close to Broadway, and you get free wi-fi, free coffee in-room, hair dryer and fitness room.

NYLO NYC $$-$$$$
- ✉ 2178 77th Street at Broadway
- ☎ 212-362 1100
- 🖱 www.nylohotels.com
- 🚇 Subway 1, 9 to 79th Avenue

Taking over the space formerly occupied by On The Ave hotel, Nylo opened late 2013 and has cool, comfortable rooms, a Chinese cuisine Red Farm restaurant and the ever-popular Serafina, an Italian eatery, continues to operate at the hotel. New bar LOCL opens soon.

HOTEL BEACON $$-$$$
- ✉ 2130 Broadway at 75th Street
- ☎ 212-787 1100
- 🖱 www.beaconhotel.com
- 🚇 Subway 1, 2, 3, 9 to 72nd Street

Good-sized rooms and suites, some with a third bed and all with kitchenettes, so ideal if you're travelling in a group. Plus the 25-storey hotel is well located for the American Museum of Natural History, the Lincoln Center and Central Park.

WEST VILLAGE

THE JANE $$
- ✉ 113 Jane St
- ☎ 212-924 6700
- 🖱 www.thejanenyc.com
- 🚇 Subway A, C, E, L to 8th Avenue/14th Street Station

Landmark waterfront property in the Far West Village, originally the American Seaman's Friend Society Sailors' Home and Institute built in 1908, has been reborn as an excellent 200-room micro hotel for young travellers 'with more style than money'. Rates start at around $110.

FURTHER AFIELD

If you're planning on going on a huge shopping spree at the 200-plus discount stores at Woodbury Common Premium Outlets (p156), you might want to stay overnight to make the most of opening hours.

✪ BRITTIP
If you're travelling in a group of 10 or more, the Days Hotel Broadway offers discounts on rooms.

THE THAYER HOTEL $$-$$$
- ✉ 674 Thayer Road, West Point, New York
- ☎ 845-446 4731 or freephone 800-247 5047
- 🖱 www.thethayerhotel.com

A 3-star hotel at West Point – the scene of a decisive battle in the War of Independence and now home to one of the most famous officer training camps in America, with fabulous views of the Hudson River. The hotel has comfortable en-suite rooms and there's a restaurant open for breakfast, lunch and dinner and the lounge, which overlooks the river, is open until 1am Fri–Sat. Shop-and-stay packages are available.

ACCOMMODATION REFERENCE GUIDE

Hotel	Area	Style	Price range	page
6 Columbus Circle	SoHo	Boutique chic	$$$	243
60 Thompson	SoHo	Boutique chic	$$$-$$$$$	244
70 Park Avenue	Midtown East	Medium-priced gem	$$$-$$$$	238
ACE Hotel	Midtown	Excellent value	$$$	237
Algonquin	Midtown	Excellent value	$$-$$$	231
Aloft New York Brooklyn	Brooklyn	Excellent value	$$	223
Ameritania	Midtown West	Excellent value	$$	242
Bentley	Upper East Side	Excellent value	$$-$$$	249
Blue Moon	Lower East Side	Boutique chic	$$$	230
Bowery	Lower East Side	Boutique chic	$$$$-$$$$$	230
Bryant Park	Midtown	Boutique chic	$$$$-$$$$$	231
Carlton	Flatiron District	Medium-priced gem	$$-$$$	226
Carlyle, The	Upper East Side	Landmark	$$$$-$$$$$	249
Casablanca	Midtown	Medium-priced gem	$$$-$$$$	231
Chambers	Midtown	Boutique chic	$$$-$$$$$	232
Chatwal New York, The	Midtown	Traditional luxury	$$$$$	232
Chelsea Pines Inn	Chelsea	Gay-friendly	$$	227
Chelsea Savoy Hotel	Chelsea	Gay-friendly	$$-$$$	227
Chelsea Star Hotel	Madison Square Garden	Total bargain	$-$$	231
City Club Hotel	Midtown	Boutique chic	$$$-$$$$	232
Colonial House Inn	Chelsea	Gay-friendly	$$-$$$	227
Conrad New York	Battery Park City	Modern luxury	$$$-$$$$	223
Cosmopolitan Hotel	TriBeCa	Excellent value	$$-$$$	248
Courtyard by Marriott Times Square South	Theater District	Excellent value	$$-$$$	246
Crosby Street Hotel	SoHo	Modern luxury	$$$-$$$$	244
Days Hotel Broadway	Upper West Side	Excellent value	$$-$$$	250
Distrikt Hotel	Midtown	Modern luxury	$$$-$$$$	233
Dream	Midtown West	Theme	$$-$$$	242
Dylan	Midtown East	Boutique chic	$$$-$$$$	238
Edison Hotel	Theater District	Excellent value	$$-$$$	233
Elysée	Midtown East	Traditional luxury	$$$$-$$$$$	238
Empire	Midtown West	Medium-priced gem	$$$	242
Eventi	Chelsea	Medium-priced gem	$$$	224
Fitzpatrick Manhattan	Midtown East	Medium-priced gem	$$$-$$$$	238
Fitzpatrick Grand Central	Midtown East	Medium-priced gem	$$$	238
Four Seasons	Midtown East	Modern luxury	$$$$-$$$$$	239
Franklin	Upper East Side	Medium-priced gem	$$$	249
Gansevoort Park Avenue	Midtown East	Modern luxury	$$$$	239
Gershwin	Flatiron District	Total bargain	$-$$	226
Gild Hall	Financial District	Boutique chic	$$$$	225
Giraffe	Flatiron District	Excellent value	$$-$$$	233
Glenwood Hostel	Brooklyn	Total bargain	$	223
Gramercy Park Hotel	Gramercy Park	Modern luxury	$$$-$$$$	229
Greenwich Hotel, The	TriBeCa	Traditional luxury	$$$$-$$$$$	248
Herald Square Hotel	Flatiron District	Gay-friendly	$$	227
Hilton New York	Midtown West	Upmarket	$$$$$	242
Holiday Inn Soho	SoHo	Total bargain	$$	245
Holiday Inn Wall Street	Financial District	Excellent value	$$-$$$$	225
Hotel 17	Flatiron District	Gay-friendly	$$	227
Hotel 31	Murray Hill	Total bargain	$-$$$	243
Hotel Beacon	Upper West Side	Excellent value	$$-$$$	250
Hotel Gansevoort	Meatpacking District	Boutique chic	$$$-$$$$$	231
Hotel Indigo Chelsea-New York	Chelsea	Medium-priced gem	$$$-$$$$	224
Hotel Plaza-Athenee	Upper East Side	Traditional luxury	$$$$-$$$$$	249
Hotel on Rivington	Lower East Side	Boutique chic	$$$$-$$$$$	230
Hotel @ Times Square	Midtown	Excellent value	$$-$$$	234
Hotel Wolcott	Midtown	Excellent value	$$$	234
Howard Johnson Express Inn	Lower East Side	Total bargain	$-$$	230
Hudson	Midtown West	Medium-priced gem	$$-$$$$$	243
Hyatt Andaz Wall Street	Financial District	Boutique chic	$$$$	225
Incentra Village House	West Village	Gay-friendly	$$-$$$	228
Inn at Irving Place	Gramercy Park	Traditional luxury	$$$$-$$$$$	229
James, The	SoHo	Modern luxury	$$-$$$$	245
Jane, The	West Village	Excellent value	$-$$	250
JW Marriott Essex House	Midtown	Upmarket	$$$$-$$$$$	234
Kimberly	Midtown East	Medium-priced gem	$$$	239
King & Grove	Brooklyn	Modern luxury	$$$-$$$$	223
King & Grove Gramercy Park	Gramercy Park	Medium-priced gem	$$$	228
Kitano	Midtown East	Upmarket	$$$-$$$$$	239

Hotel	Area	Style	Price range	page
Langham Place 5th Avenue	Midtown West	Upmarket	$$$$–$$$$$	243
Larchmont	Greenwich Village	Total bargain	$–$$	230
Le Parker Meridien	Midtown	Upmarket	$$$$–$$$$$	234
Library, The	Midtown	Theme	$$$$–$$$$$	234
London NYC, The	Midtown	Modern luxury	$$$–$$$$$	235
Lowell, The	Upper East Side	Traditional luxury	$$$$$	249
Mandarin Oriental	Midtown West	Modern luxury	$$$$–$$$$$	243
Mansfield	Midtown	Medium-priced gem	$$$–$$$$$	235
Marcel at Gramercy, The	Gramercy Park	Medium-priced gem	$$$	229
Maritime Hotel	Chelsea	Theme	$$$–$$$$	225
Mark, The	Upper East Side	Traditional luxury	$$$$–$$$$$	250
Mercer	SoHo	Boutique chic	$$$–$$$$$	245
Metro	Midtown	Excellent value	$$–$$$	235
Millenium Hilton	Financial District	Medium-priced gem	$$–$$$$$	226
Moderne, The	Midtown West	Boutique chic	$$$–$$$$	235
Mondrian Soho	SoHo	Modern luxury	$$$–$$$$	245
Morgans	Midtown	Boutique chic	$$$–$$$$	235
New York Marriott at the Brooklyn Bridge	Brooklyn	Excellent value	$$–$$$	223
New York Marriott Marquis	Theater District	Medium-priced gem	$$–$$$$	246
New York Palace	Midtown East	Traditional luxury	$$$$–$$$$$	239
Night Hotel, The	Midtown West	Theme	$$$–$$$$$	243
Nylo NYC	Upper West Side	Medium-priced gem	$$–$$$$	250
Off Soho Suites	Lower East Side	Total bargain	$$	230
Out, The	Hells Kitchen	Gay-friendly	$$	228
Paramount Hotel, Times Square	Theater District	Medium-priced gem	$$–$$$$$	247
Peninsula, The	Midtown	Upmarket	$$$$$	235
Plaza, The	Midtown	Landmark	$$$$$	235
Pod Hotel	Midtown East	Total bargain	$–$$$	240
Premier Hotel Times Square	Theater District	Medium-priced gem	$$$–$$$$	247
Radisson Martinique on Broadway	Theater District	Excellent value	$$–$$$$$	247
Ritz-Carlton New York	Battery Park City	Modern luxury	$$$$$	223
Room Mate Grace Hotel	Theatre district	Boutique chic	$$–$$$	247
Roosevelt, The	Midtown East	Medium-priced gem	$$–$$$$	240
Royalton	Midtown	Modern luxury	$$$–$$$$	236
Sherry-Netherland	Upper East Side	Traditional luxury	$$$$–$$$$$	250
Smyth Tribeca	TriBeCa	Modern luxury	$$$–$$$$	248
Sofitel	Midtown West	Upmarket	$$$–$$$$	243
Soho Grand	SoHo	Modern luxury	$$$$	246
Soho House New York	SoHo	Boutique chic	$$$$–$$$$$	246
Sohotel	SoHo	Excellent value	$–$$$	246
Standard Cooper Square Hotel, The	Lower East Side	Modern luxury	$$$$	231
Thayer Hotel, The	West Point	Further afield	$$–$$$	250
Time	Theater District	Theme	$$–$$$	247
Towers of the Waldorf-Astoria, The	Midtown East	Landmark	$$$$$	240
TriBeCa Grand	TriBeCa	Modern luxury	$$$$–$$$$$	248
Trump International Hotel & Tower	Central Park	Upmarket	$$$$–$$$$$	224
Trump SoHo New York	SoHo	Modern luxury	$$$$	246
Vanderbilt YMCA	Midtown East	Total bargain	$–$$	241
W New York Downtown	Financial District	Modern luxury	$$$$$	226
Waldorf–Astoria	Midtown East	Landmark	$$$–$$$$$	241
Wall Street Inn	Financial District	Medium-priced gem	$$$	226
Washington Square	Greenwich Village	Excellent value	$$	230
Wellington	Midtown West	Medium-priced gem	$$$–$$$$	243
Westin New York at Times Square	Theater District	Medium-priced gem	$$$$	248

Carlton Hotel

CHAPTER 10

What's On When

New Yorkers love an excuse to party, from celebrating the changing of the seasons to championing their cultural roots. In fact, judging by the number of parades, open-air concerts and festivals taking place every month, it's a wonder anyone gets any work done. The good news is that you can be sure that whatever time of year you decide to visit the Big Apple, there will be some truly spectacular entertainment going on, and what's more, most of it is free!

ANNUAL AND BIENNIAL EVENTS

JANUARY AND FEBRUARY
Winter Restaurant Week
Citywide. Last two weeks in Jan. 212-484 1222, www.nycgo.com/restaurantweek. Amazing offers at dozens of restaurants, including some *Zagat* highly-rated joints. For daily offers check out www.twitter.com/nycgo.

Winter Antiques Show
24 Jan–2 Feb 2014. 7th Regiment Armory, Park Avenue at 67th Street, 718-292 7392 or 718-665 5250, www.winterantiquesshow. com.

Admission $20 with catalogue. Open daily noon–8pm; Sun and Thurs noon–6pm. The Winter Antiques Show kicks off New York's winter season with a glitzy Opening Night Party on 24 Jan, but as tickets for that event start at $500 each your best bet is to wait until the next day to see the treasures within. From the simplicity of arts and crafts to ornate baroque clocks, you can be sure there will be fine antiques to suit everyone's taste. Private collections from all over America are also on show.

> **BRITTIP**
>
> A central number for New York events is 212-484 1222; and a website that reports many free events is www.newyorkled.com. A good events site for planning ahead is www.new.york.eventguide.com.

Chinese New Year Parade/Lunar New York
Chinese New Year begins on 31 Jan 2014 (it's the Year of the Horse). Chinatown around Mott Street, 212-484 1216, www. explorechinatown.com.
New York City is known for having some of the most authentic celebrations of

Central Park

the Chinese New Year in the US, and the festivities range from a firecracker ceremony to the magnificent dragon parade in Chinatown to various other performances around the city. The party continues for 10 days.

Black History Month

Throughout Feb. A series of shows is put on to celebrate the African-American experience in New York. See the newspapers and guides for cultural events, concerts and lectures scheduled around the city, or visit http://nymag.com for detailed listings of events.

Grammy Awards

Late Feb. Madison Square Garden, 212-465 6741, www.grammy.com.
The Grammy Awards are to music what the Oscars are to the movies. Over the years, Los Angeles and New York have played tug-of-war with the Grammy Awards show and New York has won. You may not get to attend the Awards, but you can go stargazing by the red carpet as celebs arrive in their limos.

MARCH AND APRIL

St Patrick's Day Parade

17 Mar. 5th Avenue between 44th and 86th Streets. www.saintpatricksdayparade.com.
One of the bigger parades the city has to offer. If you're in town, you won't be able to miss the sea of green that goes with this annual Irish-American day. The parade starts at 11am up 5th Avenue from 44th to 86th Streets and the festivities go on late into the night.

◀▚▶ BRITTIP

A good vantage point to watch the St Patrick's Day parade is the steps of St Patrick's Cathedral (p79), where the Bishop of New York greets the marching bands.

Greek Independence Day Parade

Sun closest to 25 Mar (when Greek Independence Day falls in the Orthodox Lent, the parade is shifted to Apr or even May). Along 5th Avenue to 49th Street, 718-204 6500.

This one's a Zorba-style parade with lots of flag waving and national dress, as well as plenty of Greek food, music and dancing.

Easter Parade

Easter Sun. 5th Avenue between 49th and 57th Streets.
This is not an official parade, just a chance to watch strollers flaunting Easter bonnets from gorgeous to outrageous. The steps of St Patrick's Cathedral (p79) are an advantageous viewing spot. Kick-off is at 10am, so arrive early to bag a space.

New York City Ballet Spring Gala

8 May 2014, David H Koch Theater, 20 Lincoln Center Plaza, 65th Street at Columbus Avenue, 212-870 5570, www.nycballet.com. Student rush tickets (available on day of performance) cost $20 (212-870-7766). The box office is open 10am to 7.30pm Mon and 10 am to 8.30pm Tues–Sat. The New York City Ballet performs its spring season in New York before touring. Go to see the world-famous dancers, who this year will be performing choreography by Justin Peck to a commissioned score by Sufjan Stevens.

MAY AND JUNE

See also New York City Ballet (above).

American Ballet Theater

May–July. Metropolitan Opera House at the Lincoln Center, 212-362 6000, www.abt.org. Going to see the ABT at the Met is exhilarating. The majesty of the Metropolitan Opera House combines with the passion, power and movement of 1 of the world's most innovative dance companies to create a magical experience. The Theater also runs an ABTKids programme.

Cuban Day Parade

Usually the first Sun in May. Free.
Lively day-long Cuban carnival with salsa bands and partying into the night along 6th Avenue that ends at the Cuban Independence statue of José Marti on Central Park South.

TriBeCa Film Festival

Late Apr–early May. TriBeCa area, 212-941 2400, tribecafilmfestival.org.
The 12-day TriBeCa Film Festival was founded in 2002 by Robert DeNiro, Jane Rosenthal and Craig Hatkoff as a response to the attacks on the World Trade Center. The now prestigious festival showcases independent movies, runs workshops and has a children's film programme, as well as Q&A sessions with actors and filmmakers. During the week, local restaurants offer cut-price meals. You can buy tickets for the various events online or from the main box office at 15 Laight Street.

SUMMER IN THE CITY FOR FAMILIES

Puppet shows, free story-telling, films and workshops in libraries – these form just a part of what's on offer in the city throughout the summer, so you'll be hard pressed to find a moment's peace! To find out what's going on where and when, pick up a copy of *Events For Children* from any branch of the New York Public Library. Most are free or very good value for money.

Here is an outline of some of the many activities available for children in summer. More details can be found by month in this chapter or in Chapter 11 Getting Active.

Central Park
The park is a year-round winner, but summer time is when it really comes into its own. Specific children's events abound, from canoeing to field days, all listed under the Kids to Do section on www.centralparknyc.org, while the whole family can enjoy offerings put on by the **Central Park SummerStage** (212-360 2756, www.summerstage.org) at Rumsey Playfield at the 5th Avenue 69th Street entrance which has around 30-35 performances throughout June, July and August.

New York Philharmonic Young People's Concerts: Avery Fisher Hall, 10 Lincoln Center Plaza, 212-875 5656, www.nyphil.org.
A series of summer Sat concerts where children aged 6–12 get to meet the musicians and try out their instruments for an hour before the concert. Book early, however, as they're very popular. You'll also be in the right spot for the Lincoln Center's free Out-of-Doors Festival, with events throughout Aug (p259). The Lincoln Center also offers a family programme of music and dance afternoons for children.

Puppet Theater: 212-680 1400, www.hensonfoundation.org.
Sign up on the website for puppet happenings that may time with your visit.

Lincoln Center Out-of-Doors: Lincoln Center plazas and Damrosch Park, 212-LIN COLN, www.lincolncenter.org.
A free festival for all ages running throughout Aug with specific events for families and children.

9th Avenue International Food Festival
Mid-May (18th-19th in 2013, check website for dates). 9th Avenue between 42nd and 57th Streets, 212 581 7029, http://ninthavenuefoodfestival.com. Noon-5pm both days.
This two-day festival, which has been running for 40 years, is a gourmet's delight. Hell's Kitchen cooks up a feast of foods from around the world and hundreds of stalls line the streets selling every type of food imaginable. Go for lunch and then walk it all off by strolling on down to Chelsea's fabulous art galleries nearby.

Fleet Week
Last week in May.
New York City Fleet Week brings thousands of sailors and marines from US naval vessels to the Big Apple and includes dozens of military demonstrations. Unless you're a boat nut, it's normally not worth visiting the huge armada of US Navy – free tours are offered daily – and other ships that visit New York, but this week they'll be very hard to miss.

Lower East Side Festival of the Arts
Last weekend in May. Along East 10th Street. Theater for the New City, 212-254 1109, www.theaterforthenewcity.net.
Running since 1996, deep in the heart of the neighbourhood that helped create the East Coast Beat Movement, method acting and pop art. It's a free, 3-day indoor and outdoor annual arts festival and carnival for everyone, with more than 250 performers and 70 groups, offering everything from drama to dance, music and poetry, art to food.

Washington Square Outdoor Art Exhibition
Memorial Day weekend in May, the weekend that follows it and every Labor Day Weekend in Sept. Washington Square, 212-982 6255, www.washingtonsquareoutdoorartexhibit.org.
An old and revered tradition of arty Greenwich Village (it's been going since 1933), this is a huge outdoor art show with easels and food trolleys set up in the streets all around the park.

Puerto Rican Day Parade
Second Sun in June from 11am. 5th Avenue between 44th and 85th Streets, 718-401 0404, www.nationalpuertoricandayparade.org.
This is a New York parade on a grand scale – expect more than 100,000 marchers and 3 million spectators. The largest of several Puerto Rican celebrations in the city, with 3 hours of colourful floats, music and dancing, from 2pm at St Patrick's Cathedral on 5th Avenue.

St Patrick's Day Parade

WHAT'S ON WHEN

Museum Mile Festival

Second Tues in June. 5th Avenue between 82nd and 104th Streets, 212-606 2296, www.museummilefestival.org.

Museum Mile is neither a museum nor a mile, but nine museums stretching along 5th Avenue and Central Park on the Upper East Side. All are worth a visit. During the festival you can get into all of them, including the fabulous Metropolitan, for free from 6–9pm. An added perk is the fascinating outside entertainment, including live bands and street art. The festival has been going since 1978 and now attracts more than 50,000 visitors each year. The fun starts on the steps of the National Academy Museum on 88th Street at 6pm.

Theater Under the Stars

The Great Lawn, mid-park, from 79th to 85th Street, Central Park, 212-768 4242, www.centralpark.com or www.nycvisit.com.

Broadway kicks off New York's summer outdoor concert season in Central Park with a free showcase of its hottest talent performing major show songs at 8.30pm. Award-winning celebs and hot new talent sing and dance for 90 minutes backed by a 35-piece orchestra.

> **BRITTIP**
>
> Check out the many street fairs from spring to autumn throughout the city with food, craft and other stalls. Visit www.nycstreetfairs.com and www.nyctourist.com.

Mermaid Parade

Sat 21 June, 2014. 8th Street between Steeplechase Park and Broadway, Coney Island, Brooklyn, 718-372 5159, www.coneyisland.com/programs/mermaid-parade.

The Mermaid Parade celebrates the beginning of summer. Catch the B, D or F trains to Stillwell Avenue on the Sat following the 1st official day of summer to sample a wild and boisterous scene of carnival floats and costumes. The parade is followed by the Mermaid Parade Ball.

Heritage of Pride March and PrideFest

Last Sun in June. Rally: Hudson River Park Pier 26. Parade: 5th Avenue, 212-807 7433, www.nycpride.org.

Kicks off with a Friday rally, which in 2013 was held at Hudson River Park's Pier 26, with various bands and performers. On Sunday there's a traffic-stopping parade along 5th Avenue, with more than 50 floats, the fun continues with various parties, the hottest being the new pool party with Hed Kandi on the sundeck of Hotel Americano.

Central Park SummerStage

June–Aug. Rumsey Playfield, Central Park at 72nd Street and Central Park West, 212-307 7171 for tickets to benefit concerts or 212-360 2756 for information, www.summerstage.org. Subway 1, 2, 3, 9, B, C to 72nd Street.

You can experience many kinds of entertainment for free in New York and some of the best are the free weekend afternoon concerts put on by the SummerStage, which celebrated its 25th anniversary in 2011. Featuring over 30 performances from top international artists, on weeknights, dance and spoken-word events are also put on in Central Park. Last year pop star Ben Howard took to the stage.

◀▶ BRITTIP

To find out which free concerts will be on while you're in New York, join Facebook group www.facebook.com/SummerStageNYC

New York Philharmonic/Metropolitan Opera Parks Concerts

Various sites in summer, www.nycgovparks.org, 212-875 5656, www.nyphil.org, 212-362 6000, metopera.org (Met).
These free, open-air events in parks around the city are wildly popular so arrive early to stake out a site.

Shakespeare in the Park

Late June–late Aug. Delacorte Theater, Central Park at 81st Street, 212-539 8500 info, 212-967 7555 to order tickets, www.publictheater.org.
Plays held in Central Park's open-air theatre every summer are free. There are two each year – one Shakespeare and one American – with performances almost nightly. Although free, you still have to get tickets to see them, which are available from 1pm on the day of the performance, and the queues are long.

Bryant Park Summer

Every Mon June–Aug. 6th Avenue at 42nd Street, 212-768 4242, www.bryantpark.org. Bryant Park is 1 of the few green spaces available in the Midtown area, and this is a summer-long series of events, from Tai Chi to piano, where top pianists from around the world come to play the park's resident piano. See website for details.

Midsummer Night Swing

Mid-June to mid-July. Damrosch Park, Lincoln Center for Performing Arts, Josie Robertson Plaza, Columbus Avenue at 62nd Street, 212-875 5766, http://www.midsummernightswing.org Single tickets from $17.
Considered the city's hottest outdoor dance party, with dance-filled nights when energetic bands play everything from swing to salsa. Lots of dance instructors are on hand to give lessons in every type of dance, or you can just listen to the live music.

Celebrate Brooklyn! Performing Arts Festival

All summer. Prospect Park Bandshell, 9th Street at Prospect Park West, Park Slope, Brooklyn, 718-855 7882, www.bricartsmedia.org.
Here's a very good reason to break out of Manhattan and visit one of the outer boroughs – for New York's longest running festival of free music, dance, theatre and film events lasting 9 weeks. In 2012, Hot Chip and Sigor Rós performed.

JULY AND AUGUST

See also American Ballet Theater at the Met, Thursday Night Concert Series, Central Park SummerStage, New York Philharmonic/

Shakespeare in the Park

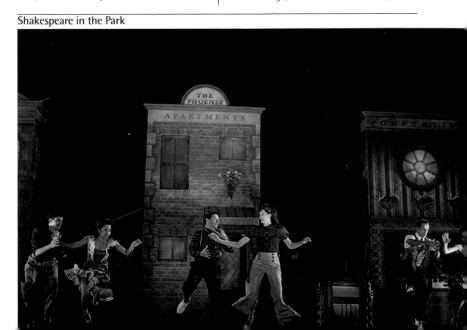

OTHER MEMORABLE DAYS IN NYC

Super Bowl Sunday (day of National Football League's championship): Usually first Sun in February

Groundhog Day (day on which behaviour of groundhog coming out of its burrow predicts spring): 2 February

Valentine's Day: 14 February

St Patrick's Day (celebration of Irish heritage, lots of New Yorkers wear green, drink and parade!): 17 March

April Fools Day: 1 April

Good Friday/Spring Holiday (holiday to commemorate crucifixion of Jesus or 'Spring Holiday' in schools and universities that want to avoid direct reference): Late March/ early April

Earth Day: 22 April

Arbor Day (day for planting trees): Last Friday in April

Cinco de Mayo (celebration of Mexican culture): 5 May

Mother's Day: Second Sunday in May

Flag Day (commemorates the adoption of the US flag): 14 June

Father's Day: Third Sunday in June

Women's Equality Day: 26 August

Patriot Day (in remembrance of victims of 11 September 2001 attacks): 11 September

Citizenship Day (to commemorate the adoption of the constitution): 17 September

Rosh Hashanah (beginning of Jewish high holidays and new year on Hebrew calendar): September or October

Halloween (bigger deal in NY than in the UK): 31 October

Pearl Harbor Remembrance Day: 7 December

Winter solstice: 21 December

Christmas Eve: 24 December

Kwanzaa (African–American holiday celebration created in 1966): 26 December– 1 January

Met Opera Concerts, New York Shakespeare Festival, Bryant Park Free Summer Season, Midsummer Night Swing and Celebrate Brooklyn! Performing Arts Festival (p257).

Concerts in the Abby Aldrich Rockefeller Sculpture Garden

July. Museum of Modern Art, 11 West 53rd Street between 5th and 6th Avenues, 212-708 9400, www.moma.org. Subway E, V to 5th Avenue/53rd Street.

An added bonus to visiting the little gem that is MoMA is the series of free classical and jazz concerts that are presented in the museum's sculpture garden every summer.

Fourth of July

The Americans still celebrate achieving independence from their colonial masters – and they do it in style! Throughout New York there are various celebrations going on, but by far the biggest and most spectacular is Macy's Fireworks Spectacular, which is held on the East River between 14th and 51st

Streets, 212-494 4495, www.macys.com. A good spot to see the $1 million, 30-minute firework extravaganza is from FDR Drive (Franklin D Roosevelt Drive) or from Pier 17 at South Street Seaport. Another popular event is the Travis Fourth of July Parade (718-494 0378) where the town of Travis is decorated in red, white and blue and marching bands and costumed characters take to the streets.

Summer Restaurant Week

Mid-July. 212-484 1222, www.nycgo.com/ restaurantweek.

Since 1992, more than 150 of the city's finest restaurants have been offering bargain 3-course fixed-price lunches and dinners for 2 weeks in July.

Summer Garden Concerts

July-Aug. Flushing Town Hall, 137-35 Northern Boulevard, Queens, 718-463 7700, www.flushingtownhall.com.

A diverse line-up with many musical styles including country, jazz, soul and oldies.

Lincoln Center Festival
Mid–late July. Lincoln Center for the Performing Arts, 140 West 65th Street, although venues vary. 212-875 5766, www.lincolncenter.org.
A veritable feast of dance, drama, ballet, children's shows and multimedia and performance art, involving both repertory companies and special guests, at venues inside and outside at the Lincoln Center.

Harlem Week
Late July/Aug. Various venues, 212-862 7200, www.harlemweek.com.
Not strictly a week, more a month-long programme of parties, performances and activities. The largest black and Hispanic festival in the world, its highlight is the street party with R&B, gospel and All That Jazz. In addition to the music, there are films, dance, fashion, sports and exhibitions. What a great way to experience Harlem!

Lincoln Center Out of Doors
Aug. Lincoln Center plazas and Damrosch Park, 212-LIN COLN, www.lincolncenter.org.
Over 100 free outdoor performances including music and dance events, storytelling, puppetry and other family events.

SEPTEMBER AND OCTOBER
See also Washington Square Outdoor Art Exhibition (May and June); Concert Series in the Rockefeller Sculpture Garden (p258).

West Indian-American Day Parade
First Mon of Sept (Labor Day). 5th Avenue to Christopher Street in Brooklyn, 718-467 1797, www.wiadca.com.
Fabulous festival celebrating Caribbean culture with food (all along Eastern Parkway) and entertainment from top Caribbean artists. It's attended by more than 3 million people, including brightly costumed marchers put on a special children's parade on the Sat, with an even bigger event on Labor Day (first Mon in Sept).

Feast of San Gennaro
Mid-Sept for 11 days. Mulberry Street to Worth Street in Little Italy, 212-768 9320, www.sangennaro.org.
Held in honour of the Neapolitan saint, this festival, which has been held since 1926, is the best time to see what is left of the once-bustling Little Italy that is now reduced to just Mulberry Street. There are lots of fairground booths, plenty of food – look out for the cannoli-eating contest – and even more vino.

Broadway on Broadway
Sept (varies, last year 9 Sept) at Times Square, 212-768 1560,
www.broadwayonbroadway.com.

Quintessentially New York – a free annual concert when numbers from Broadway shows are performed live on a giant outdoor stage by a galaxy of celebrities surrounded by TV cameras. It all ends in a big finale with loads of confetti.

DUMBO Art Under the Bridge Festival
Late Sept. Brooklyn, between Manhattan and Brooklyn bridges. 718-624 3772, http://dumboartsfestival.org.
The single largest urban forum for experimental art in the USA, where more than 1,500 emerging and professional artists show their work in 250 open galleries. The parade of concepts (robots, remote-controlled vehicles and floats) kicks of the show in the neighbourhood, Down Under the Manhattan Bridge Overpass.

New York Philharmonic Young People's Concerts
Avery Fisher Hall, 10 Lincoln Center Plaza, 212-875 5656, www.nyphil.org.
A series of Sat concerts (1 Oct 2013; 1 Feb, 2014; 12 April 2014) where children aged 6–12 get to meet the musicians and try out their instruments for an hour before the concert. Book early, however, as they're very popular.

◀◆▶ **BRITTIP**
Parades are great fun, but they also provide perfect opportunities for pickpockets, so keep your bags and wallets close to you – and never put your wallet in your back pocket.

Columbus Day Parade
Second Mon in Oct at 11.30am–3pm, 5th Avenue between 44th and 79th Streets, 212-249 9923, www.columbuscitizensfd.org
The traditional celebration of the first recorded sighting of America by Europeans is now somewhat controversial in some quarters, but despite its lack of political correctness, Columbus Day still gets the big 5th Avenue parade treatment, which is well worth a view. The parade has nearly 1 million participants plus celebrities – the likes of Frank Sinatra, Sophia Loren and Luciano Pavarotti have all paraded in the past.

New York City Marathon
Last Sun in Oct/first Sun in Nov. Staten Island to Central Park, 212-423 2249, www.ingnycmarathon.org/
Starts at the Staten Island side of the Verrazano Narrows Bridge as a mad pack of 35,000 men and women run 42km/26.2mls around all five boroughs, to finish at the Tavern on the Green in Central Park at West 67th Street. If you would like to enter the marathon you need to fill out an application form and then wait to see if you get picked. You can do this through the website. It's a pricey $347 to enter, which should inspire you to train!

Halloween Parade
31 Oct at 7pm. 6th Avenue from Spring Street, Greenwich Village to 16th Street, 212-475 3333, www.halloween-nyc.com.
A uniquely Village event, with the outlandishly over-the-top costumes (or lack of them!) on (or off!) many of its participants.

Macy's Thanksgiving Day Parade

The organisers decree a different theme each year and a lot of work goes into the amazing outfits that range from the exotic to the nearly non-existent. It attracts between 50,000 ghouls, ghosts and onlookers. So get creative and dress up to join in – only those in fancy dress can march.

NOVEMBER AND DECEMBER
See also New York City Marathon (see left).

Macy's Thanksgiving Day Parade
Thanksgiving Day, 9am. From Central Park West at 77th Street to Macy's (p141) on Broadway at 34th Street, 212-494 4495, www.macys.com/parade
Definitely one for the family, this is the Big Mama of all New York's parades, with enormous inflated cartoon characters, fabulous floats and the gift-giving Santa Claus himself. New Yorkers in the know like to come by and watch it being set up the night before between 77th and 81st Streets off Central Park West. The parade is even televised for the rest of America. If you miss it, you can go to see Santa in Santaland in Macy's until Christmas.

Christmas Tree Lighting Ceremony
Late Nov/early Dec 7–9pm. The Rockefeller Center, from 5th–7th Avenue between 48th and 51st Streets, 212-632 3975, www.rockefellercenter.com.
The Rockefeller Center (p78) in front of the towering RCA building provides the magical setting for the annual switching on of nearly 8km/5mls of dazzling lights on a huge Christmas tree topped by a Swarovski crystal star. The plaza leading up to the tree is decked with lights, too!

New Year's Eve Ball Drop
31 Dec, midnight, Times Square, 212-768 1560, www.timessquarenyc.org.
This event is a real New York classic, though you may prefer to watch safely on TV rather than be packed in with the freezing masses. Remember, Times Square is a misnomer – it's a junction, so there isn't really that much room and all the side streets get packed too. If you do manage to get a good spot, though, you'll see the giant glitterball of 180 bulbs and 12,000 rhinestones being dropped along with 1 tonne (yes, really) of confetti, to bring in the New Year. The revellers kick off at 5pm, so get there early.

New Year's Eve Fireworks in Central Park
31 Dec, midnight, 5th Avenue and 90th Street or Bethsheda Fountain (Central Park at 72nd Street) are the best viewing spots, 212-360 3456, www.nycgovparks.org. The hot apple cider and spirit of camaraderie begin at 11.30pm.

CHAPTER 11

Getting
Active

N ew York is as famous for its parks as it is for the Statue of Liberty – and there's not *only* Central Park. The parks are very busy and remarkably safe, but be prudent about going into the less populated areas and especially cautious about visiting them at night. Visit www.nycgovparks.org for loads of information about every park in New York.

CENTRAL PARK

✉ From Central Park South at 59th Street to 110th Street in Harlem
☎ 212-310 6600
🖑 www.centralparknyc.org
🚌 Subway A, B, C, D run along the Upper West Side to 59th, 72nd, 81st, 86th, 96th and 103rd Streets; 1, 9 to 59th Street/Columbus Circle; 2, 3 to 110th Street in the North; N, R, W to 57th Street or 5th Avenue on the South side
🕐 Daily 6am–1am; visit the website for weekly scheduled events and tours around the park
$ Free

This is the New Yorkers' playground and meeting place and attracts 25 million visitors every year. Covering 6 per cent of Manhattan, its 341ha/843 acres stretch 96km/6ml from Central Park South at 59th Street to Central Park North at 110th Street, with 5th Avenue and Central Park West forming its eastern and western boundaries. It was created over

a 20-year period by architect Calvert Vaux and landscaper Frederick Law Olmsted, was completed in the 1860s and had its 150th Anniversary in 2003.

✠ BRITTIP

Central Park has featured in countless movies and TV shows, from *Sex And The City* to *Spiderman*, *Friends* and *Maid in Manhattan*. If you want to visit some of the famous spots, take a guided Central Park movie sites tour (the expert will also point out which celebs live around the park). A one-hour tour is offered hourly from 9am to 6pm and costs $50 for 2 people. To book go to www.centralpark.com/guide/tours/walking/movie-tv-sites-tours.html or call 347-871 4499.

To enter from the south, cross the street from **Grand Army Plaza** at 5th Avenue and 59th Street. Immediately in front of you is the Pond, and then the **Wollman Memorial Rink** (62nd Street), which hosts a Victorian amusement park in the summer and ice-skating in the winter. Close by is the **Visitor Information Center**, where you can pick up free maps and schedules of events, including the series of free concerts and dramas performed at the **SummerStage** (p256). Here also are the **Gotham Miniature**

Central Park

Golf Course (a gift from Donald Trump), The Dairy, a 19th century-style building with an interactive touchscreen information kiosk and an exhibition on the park's history and design and the antique carousel (65th Street). To the east is the Central Park Wildlife Center (63rd–66th Streets) and the Central Park Zoo and Tisch Children's Zoo (p263).

BRITTIP
Wear good shoes as this park is big – to walk all the paths would add up to 93km/58ml!

The Sheep Meadow (66th–69th Streets) to the north of the carousel is much used by New Yorkers for picnics and sunbathing. To its left is the Tavern on the Green restaurant and to the right is the Mall (69th–72nd Streets), a tree-lined walkway where locals skate and run in summer. Follow the Mall to the top and you will find the Central Park Bandshell (70th Street), one of the park's concert venues. Further north is the Loeb Boathouse (74th and 75th Streets), which is home to The Boathouse at Central Park restaurant (p159) and where you can hire bikes and boats (p267). One of the Parks' most visited spots is Strawberry Fields (72nd Street). With a mosaic of the word 'Imagine' in the centre, it is a memorial to John Lennon who lived in the Dakota Building nearby.

Continuing north, you will come to the Ramble (71st Street), a heavily wooded area scattered with paths and streams and a great place for bird-watching, which leads to the Gothic revival Belvedere Castle (74th Street) housing another information centre. Also here are the Delacorte Theater, where summer productions are presented by Shakespeare in the Park (p257) and the Great Lawn (79th–86th Streets) where the Philharmonic and Metropolitan Opera concerts are held – the only time you can witness tens of thousands of New Yorkers all being quiet at the same time (p257).

BRITTIP
The Philharmonic/Met Concerts are thrilling and surprisingly tranquil. Join tens of thousands of New Yorkers with your picnic on the Great Lawn 2 or 3 hours ahead of concert time. The first concert of the season ends with fireworks.

Further north again is the huge Jacqueline Kennedy Onassis Reservoir (86th–96th Streets). A well-kept secret is the formal 2.4-ha/6-acre, 3-part Conservatory Garden

(104th–106th Streets), where dozens of wedding parties come for photographs on summer weekends. It was bequeathed by the Vanderbilt family, and there are free tours and concerts in the summer.

BRITTIP
Join some of the great volunteer-led tours in Central Park, such as Conservatory Gardens Tour (Sat, April–Oct, 11am and monthly Wed at noon, lasts 75 min) or Amble Through The Ramble, a stroll through the 38-acre woodland at Belvedere Castle (times and dates vary). More info at www.centralparknyc.org.

CENTRAL PARK FOR FAMILIES

Top of the pile for all-round entertainment, Central Park has 21 playgrounds among its many attractions. For the schedule of current events, exhibits and workshops visit www.centralparknyc.org and click: Bring the kids.

Enter through the Grand Army Plaza at the southern end of the park at 59th Street to find these family-friendly places.

BELVEDERE CASTLE DISCOVERY CENTER
✉ Mid-park at 97th Street
☎ 212-722 0210
🚇 Subway B, C to 79th Street
🕐 Tues–Sun 10am–5pm
$ Free
Sitting on Vista Rock, this is the highest point in the park and gives great views in all directions. The Henry Luce Nature Observatory includes exhibits on flowers, trees and birds in the park. The kids can borrow Discovery Kits, a backpack with binoculars, guidebook, maps and sketching materials for bird-watching in the Ramble and other locations. For children aged 6 and up; those under 12 must be with an adult.

CAROUSEL
✉ Mid-park at 64th Street and 5th Avenue
☎ 212-439 6900
🖱 www.centralpark.com/pages/attractions/carousel.html
🚇 Subway N, R to 5th Avenue; 6 to 68th Street
🕐 Apr–Nov daily 10am–6pm; Nov–Apr weekends and holidays 10am–4.30pm, weather permitting
$ $3 a ride
A carousel has been on this site since 1871 when the original was powered by a blind mule and a horse that walked a treadmill in

GETTING ACTIVE

an underground pit. The current electrical ride was donated by the Michael Friedsam Foundation in 1951. It features some of the largest hand-carved horses in the US.

CHARLES A DANA DISCOVERY CENTER

✉ North East Corner at the Harlem Meer/110th Street between 5th and Lenox Avenues

☎ 212-860 1370

🚊 Subway 2, 3, 6 to 110th Street

🕐 Tues–Sun 10am–5pm, 4pm in winter

$ Free

This is the park's only environmental educational centre with children's workshops year-round. Free, the centre sponsors workshops, musical performances and park tours and also loans fishing poles for fishing in the well-stocked Meer. Its catch-and-release fishing programme is open to all ages and you can fish for large-mouth bass, catfish, golden shiners and bluegills. Open April–Oct.

🇬🇧 BRITTIP

Pick up a pony carriage for a 45-minute ride around Central Park at Central Park South (59th Street between 7th and 8th Avenue) or make a reservation online at www.centralpark.com, in which case you can personalise your tour. Rates vary, but a pre-arranged booking for a 45-minute ride is around $165.

CENTRAL PARK ZOO AND TISCH CHILDREN'S ZOO

✉ Mid-park at 5th Avenue between 63rd Street and 66th Streets

☎ 212-439 6500

🖱 www.centralparkzoo.com

🚊 Subway N, R to 5th Avenue; 6 to 68th St

🕐 Nov–Mar daily 10am–4.30pm; Mar–Oct Mon–Fri 10am–5pm, weekends and holidays 10am–5.30pm

$ $18 adults, $15 seniors, $13 3–12, under 3s free

A small but attractive zoo and conservation centre. Exhibits include a polar bear, tamarin monkeys and red pandas, plus other endangered species. Watch the sea lions being fed at 11.30am, 2pm and 4pm. Tisch Children's Zoo is available for toddlers and there is a rainforest journey for older children. Call to register for programmes. The Dancing Crane Cafe is kid-friendly and healthy, there's a picnic spot and the Zootique is a shop full of exciting toys, games and souvenirs.

TOP 5 PARKS AND GARDENS
Battery Park: p264; Brooklyn Botanic Garden (p264) in spring or New York Botanical Garden (p265) for the rest of the year; Central Park: p261; Luna Park, Union Square: p265; Riverside Park: p265.

NORTH MEADOW RECREATION CENTER

✉ Mid-park at 97th Street

☎ 212-348 4867

🚊 Subway B, C, 6 to 96th Street

🕐 Sept–Jun Tues–Fri 10am–6pm, Sat–Sun 10am–5pm, closed Mon; July–Aug Mon–Thurs 10am–8pm, Fri 10am–6pm, Sat–Sun 10am–5pm

$ Free

Open to all ages, the park's largest open space at 9.3ha/23 acres provides free Field Day Kits that include everything you need to equip a family for a day of fun and games in the park, including a basketball, football, Frisbee, skipping rope and hula-hoops. Call in advance to register. The Center also has a 6m/20ft climbing wall with adventure programmes for children and lends equipment for the basketball and handball courts.

SWEDISH COTTAGE MARIONETTE THEATER

✉ Mid-park West at 79th Street

☎ 212-988 9093

🚊 Subway B, C to 79th Street

🕐 Oct–Jun Tues–Fri 10.30am and noon, Sat, Sun 1pm

$ $10 adults, $7 children

Formerly a 19th-century Swedish schoolhouse, this cottage was moved to Central Park in 1876 and now holds various marionette plays for children throughout the year. Book in advance; no credit cards.

THE WOLLMAN RINK

✉ Mid-park East between 62nd and 63rd Streets

☎ 212-439 6900

🖱 www.wollmanskatingrink.com

🚊 Subway N, R W to 5th Avenue/59th Street

🕐 Nov–Mar Mon and Tues 10am–2.30pm, Wed and Thurs 10am–10pm, Fri and Sat 10am–11pm, Sun 10am–9pm

$ $11 adults, $6 children, $9 seniors (Mon–Thurs); $17, $6, $9 (Fri–Sun); skate rental $7 extra, spectators $5

You feel like you're in a movie when you skate (or try to) here, what with the skyscrapers all around and the romance – it's on my must-do-in-New-York-at-least-once list. Skating for

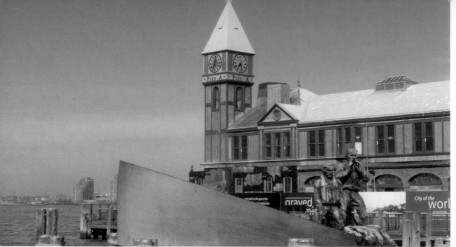

The Pier at Battery Park

beginners and ice dancing are offered on this popular rink. An ideal and scenic place to take children and join in the traditional activity of a New York winter.

GETTING ACTIVE

BRITTIP

Fancy a lifeguard's job earning a minimum $13.57 ph at the city's pools and beaches? British students are encouraged to apply by April (www.nycgovparks.org).

THE MAIN PARKS

Battery Park: With a decent yet distant view of the Statue of Liberty, this park is situated at the southern tip of Manhattan; it is a beautiful space overlooking New York Harbor and the Hudson River. Here's where you can see Andy Goldsworthy's Garden of Stones (p117) and The Solaire, the city's first 100% green building (212-417 2000, www. batteryparkcity.org).

Brooklyn Botanic Garden: This botanic garden is famous for its cherry trees that bloom from mid-Mar to late May – you can watch their progress on the garden's website. More details on (p270) (718-623 7200, www.bbg.org).

BRITTIP

Go Fish! in the 800km/500ml of shoreline, inland lakes and rivers around New York City. Get the low-down from www.nycgovparks.org.

Bryant Park: This small park is a great spot for a picnic lunch or you could dine at the fancy restaurant here. It even puts on free films and concerts on Mon nights during the summer (p257) and there are lots of free activities too, from early morning Tai Chi to juggling lessons and knitting, check the website for details as they change frequently. The Beaux Arts-style Le Carrousel – specially created to complement the park's French classical style – costs $2 a ride and is open 11am–7pm daily. Park open 7am–11pm May– Sept, 7am–7pm winter (212-768 4242, www. bryantpark.org).

Carl Schurz Park: In the family-friendly Upper East Side, this is next to Gracie Mansion (p75), once the official residence of the mayor of New York, and has an esplanade along the river. It is a popular destination for families and fitness fanatics, especially at weekends. There are lots of events in the park, including the annual Gracie Square Art Show in the first weekend of Oct where around 100 artists exhibit their work, 10am–5pm, rain or shine (212-459 4455, www.carlschurzparknyc. org).

City Hall Park: This space near the Woolworth Building and civic buildings (p82) is charming. Given a major facelift in 1999, parts of the park have been restored to the way they were in the 18th and 19th centuries, in particular the beautiful lanterns surrounding the Jacob Wrey Mould Fountain.

Gramercy Park: East 20th and 21st at Irving Place. One of the prettiest squares in the city, and New York's last private park: visitors can only peek through the railings. The townhouses were designed by some of the city's best architects – think Stanford White and Calvert Vaux – and lived in by some distinguished residents. The brasserie in the Gramercy Park Hotel (p229) is great for lunch.

Luna Park, Union Square: This park is the gateway to Downtown, a stone's throw from the East Village, SoHo and Greenwich Village, and as close as New York gets to a European piazza. It has an open-air restaurant and is right by the Union Square green market (www.grownyc.org/greenmarket), open year round on Mon, Wed, Fri and Sat.

New York Botanical Garden: From antique treasures to family adventures, this extensive, wonderful garden in the Bronx is a must-see. In 2006, it launched the Nolen Greenhouses for Living Collections, considered the most sophisticated behind-the-scenes greenhouses in botanic gardens in America. Get there by train from Grand Central station. More details on p277 (718 817 8700, www.nybg.org).

Prospect Park: A 213-ha/526-acre urban oasis in the heart of Brooklyn, this is an incredible park that was landscaped by the

New York Botanical Garden

same designers as Central Park. It has a wealth of open spaces, activities, events and museums. More details are given in Chapter 12 Taste of the Outer Boroughs (p273) (718-965 8951, www.prospectpark.org).

Riverside Park: Stretching over 6.5km/4ml along the Hudson River from 68th to 155th Streets, this is New York's narrowest park. It is also one of only 5 official scenic landmarks in the city, designed by Frederick Olmstead of Central Park fame. A combination of winding paths and rock outcrops and English country garden, it also has a buzzing marina at 79th Street where you can have a light meal. Make sure you get a glimpse of Riverside Drive, which winds along it as its one of the most attractive streets in the city, with a canopy of American Elms hanging over late 19th-century townhouses. Open 6am–1am daily (212-870 3070, www.riversideparknyc.org).

Riverside Park

Washington Square Park: In the heart of Greenwich Village, this popular park is best known for its bohemian character. It is not so much a park as an area covered in tarmac and filled with a hotchpotch of individuals who flock here to snack and people-watch. The main attraction is the marble Washington arch designed by Stanford White and built in honour of George Washington's inauguration as the first US president. More details on p000 (212-NEW YORK, www. washingtonsquarepark.org).

◀▣▶ BRITTIP

New York is one of the safest cities in the US, so do get off the pavements and wander into the parks. They're easy to navigate and offer a refreshing break.

SPECTATOR SPORTS

Any New Yorker will tell you that they read their newspapers from back to front. That's just how important sports are to them, and they have plenty to choose from: 2 football teams and 2 baseball teams to support, plus basketball, hockey, tennis and racing. But it can be really tough to get in to watch some of the games, especially to see football's New York Giants and the Mets baseball team in action. Still, it's worth making the effort just to see another side of New York life. If you can't get tickets directly through the box offices listed below, then try Ticketmaster on 212-307 7171, www.ticketmaster.com.

An expensive alternative is to try one of the companies that specialises in selling tickets at exorbitant prices – anything from $100 for a football game to $1,000 for a baseball game. They include Prestige Entertainment on 800-243 8849 or 800-2 GET TIX, www.prestigeentertainment.com; Ticket City on 1-800-SOLD-OUT or 800-765 3688, www.ticketcity.com.

A third alternative is to try a ticket tout – known as 'scalpers' – outside Madison Square Garden. However, your best bet is to ask the concierge at your hotel.

MADISON SQUARE GARDEN

This venue on 7th Avenue at 32nd Street (subway A, C, E, 1, 2, 3, 9 to 34th Street/Penn Street) is home to all the following teams. Buy tickets from the Garden Box Office in person at 4 Pennsylvania Plaza, call Ticketmaster on 212-307 7171 or visit www.thegarden.com.

NBA's New York Knicks basketball team: Nov–June

NHL's New York Rangers ice-hockey team: Oct–April

WNBA New York Liberty women's pro basketball team: May–Aug

Madison Square Garden is also famous for its boxing Fight Nights, and it hosts college/high school basketball matches. Since January 2007, the New York Titans of the National Lacrosse Team have also been playing here.

FOOTBALL

The two teams are the **New York Giants** (201-935 8111, www.giants.com) and the **New York Jets** (516-560 8200, www. newyorkjets.com). Both teams play at the new MetLife Stadium in New Jersey and tickets are notoriously hard to come by (for Giants tickets call 201-935 8222, or go to the ticket office based at the West Gate of MetLife Stadium between the Pepsi and Verizon gates, open Mon–Fri 9am–5pm. You'll have just as hard a time getting tickets for the Jets as for the Giants (see website for ticket details). The season runs Sept–Jan.

BASEBALL

The new Yankees Stadium, between 161st and 164th Streets and River Avenue, cost $800m and has a 53,000 capacity and the smoothest grass surface you're likely to see. (Subway 4 (weekdays only), D to 161st Street/Yankee Stadium). Box office 718-293 4300 or www. yankees.com.

The **New York Mets** play at Citi Field in Flushing Meadows in Queens (Subway 7 to Mets/ Willets Point Station), 718-507 8499/ TI000, www.mets.com. The season is April–Sept and post-season games are played in Oct/Nov by the best teams for a gargantuan amount of money. It costs a fortune to get into one of these games, which is why the stands are usually filled with season ticket holders and a scattering of celebs.

HORSE RACING

One of the four local tracks is **Aqueduct Stadium** in Queens (110-00 Rockaway Blvd, Jamaica) (subway A to Aqueduct Racetrack) Oct–May every Wed–Sun. Free admission 2 Jan–early March, 718-641 4700, www.nyra. com.

The $1m **Belmont Stakes** race, on a Sat in early June, is the major event at the **Belmont Park Racetrack** (2150 Hempstead Turnpike, Elmont, Long Island) (take the Long Island Rail Road's 'Belmont Special' from Penn Station at 7th Avenue and 34th Street) May–July, 516-488 6000, www.nyra.com/belmont. Tickets from $20 including $5 admission to the clubhouse, gates open 11am.

GETTING ACTIVE

TENNIS

The US Open is held every year at the US Tennis Center in Flushing Meadows, Queens (subway 7 to Willetts Point/Shea Stadium), from late Aug–early Sept. For tickets call TicketMaster on 1-866-OPEN-TIX or the USTA Billie Jean King Tennis Center Ticket office on 718-760 6200 or visit www.usopen.org. Like Wimbledon, tickets for the finals are impossible to get, but it's worth seeing some of the earlier rounds to watch how it's done American style (p281 in Chapter 12 Taste of the Outer Boroughs for details on Shea Stadium and Queens).

GET STUCK IN

To take part in sports in New York, go to Central Park.

BIKING

You can rent bikes from the Loeb Boathouse, Central Park, East 72nd Street and Park Drive North (212-517 2233, www.thecentralparkboathouse.com) for $9 per hour for a cruiser, $15/$6 (kids) per hour, for a 21-speed bike including helmet, leaving a credit card deposit or ID and $200 cash or credit card; 10am–6pm Apr–Nov. Get to the boathouse with the free trolley shuttle service every 15 minutes from 5th Avenue. For other bike rental information, see p83.

BRITTIP
Skate on the drives circling Central Park when they are closed to traffic, Mon–Fri 10am–3pm and 7–10pm and all weekend.

BOATING

Also from the Loeb Boathouse (212-517 2233, www.thecentralparkboathouse.com), you can rent a rowing boat for $12 per hour and $2.50 each additional 15 minutes with a $20 deposit, cash only. Open 10am–dusk. Four people are allowed in each boat. There are also three kayaks now for hire.

HORSE RIDING

Riding in Central Park is no longer an option since the Claremont Academy closed, but pretty riding trails wind through The Ravine, in Prospect Park, which gives you a good excuse to head out to Brooklyn. Take a guided trail ride for $37 (book in advance) from Kensington Stables (718-972 4588, www.kensingtonstables.com).

ICE-SKATING

The Wollman Memorial Rink, mid-Park between 62nd and 63rd Streets (212-439 6900, www.wollmanskatingrink.com) is open Nov–Mar Mon and Tues 10am–2.30pm, Wed and Thurs 10am–10pm, Fri and Sat 10am–11pm, Sun 10am–9pm. $11 (Mon–Thurs) $17 (Fri–Sun) adults, $6 (Mon–Thurs) $6 (Fri–Sun) children, $5 (Mon–Thurs) $9 (Fri–Sun) seniors; skate rental $7 extra, spectators $5.

The Trump Lasker Rink, north-Park at 106th Street, is a bit rougher but less crowded at $6.75 for adults, $2.25 seniors and $3.75 students and $6.50 for skate rental. Call 914-492 3857 or visit www.wollmanskatingrink.com for information on lessons.

ROLLER SKATING

On a hot summer's day, Central Park is filled with thousands of in-line skaters. The most popular places to skate are:

The Bandshell: for skate dancers and those who like to watch them.

The Mall: between 69th and 72nd Streets, a tree-lined walkway where locals skate in summer.

West Drive at 67th Street: a slalom course has been set up here for all to try.

Wollman and Lasker Rinks: in summer these rinks are set up for the hot-shot in-line skater; fascinating to watch, too.

BRITTIP
May is Bike Month in the parks and over 150 bike-related events from rides, races and art shows to a film festival can be found on www.transalt.org. Keen cyclists may be interested in the Five Boro Bike Tour, a great way to 'do' New York.

RUNNING

Every day, hundreds of runners encircle Central Park. If you want to run here, it helps to know the distance. The outer loop of the Park is approximately 10km/6ml. The middle loop is about 6km/4ml and the Reservoir loop is about 2km/1¼ml. The Road Runners Club (212-860 4455, www.nyrr.org) can provide information on running in New York. Or, for a fun run and a chance to meet some locals join the New York branch of the Hash House Harriers (212-427 4692, www.hashnyc.com), the 'drinking club with a running problem'.

SWIMMING

Cool off for free in the Lasker Pool (Mid-Central Park from 108th to 109th Streets) – by far one of the favourite kids' activities in Central Park. It is open every day during summer 11am–3pm and 4–7pm. Click on activities on www.centralparknyc.org or call 212-534 7639. Another free outdoor pool can

Strolling in Central Park

GETTING ACTIVE

be found at the Asser Levy Recreation Center, 392 Asser Levy Place, East 23rd street at FDR Drive (Subway 6 to 23rd Street). Open from 6.30am–9.30pm Mon–Fri and 8am–4.45pm Sat–Sun from July through to Labor Day and is clean and not too packed. (212-447 2020).

TENNIS

There are more tennis courts in Central Park than anywhere else in Manhattan. The Tennis Center can be found between West 94th Street and West 96th Street, near the West Drive (Subway 1, 6, 9, B, C to 96th Street). Courts are open April–Nov, from 6.30am until dusk and a single play costs around $15 per person per hour (for reservations and information on lessons call 212-280 0205, www.centralpark.com/guide/sports/tennis. html). For tennis courts all around the city, visit www.nycgovparks.org.

YOGA

Here are some of the best teachers in town. Laughing Lotus Yoga Centre, 59 West 19th Street at 6th Avenue (212-414 2903, www. laughinglotus.com) teaches a vinyasa (flow) style of yoga at all levels. Check the website for details including a groovy Friday Midnight Yoga with live music! Kula Yoga, 28 Warren Street between Church and Broadway (Subway 1, 2, 3, A, C to Chambers Street), also teaches a vinyasa style of yoga, with day and evening classes (212-945 4460, www. kulayoga.com). If you're staying around SoHo, pop into the SoHo Sanctuary (119 Mercer Street between Prince and Spring streets) for a 1-hour yoga session of SoHo Yoga, $110 (212-334 5550, www.sohosanctuary.com). Sal Anthony's Movement Salon, 190 3rd Avenue (212-420 7242, www.movementsalon.com) offers daily 1-hour yoga sessions for $15, plus Pilates and Gyrotonic classes (no, we don't know what that is either!) in a pretty building in the Gramercy area.

Boating in Central Park

CHAPTER 12

Taste of the Outer Boroughs

You may be surprised that it's just a 10-minute taxi drive across the Brooklyn Bridge to Brooklyn, a fascinating borough that houses many interesting sights if you have time. Head north-east and you'll hit Queens, 15 minutes from Manhattan, the largest New York borough and one of its most cosmopolitan, with attractions including the stadium that's home to the Met baseball team. A trip across the East River from Harlem takes you to the Bronx, once one of New York's dodgiest areas but now home to some surprisingly good tourist attractions, such as the Bronx Zoo. Of the many islands around Manhattan, Staten Island, south of Lower Manhattan is worth a visit for the ferry ride alone, which passes the Statue of Liberty.

A TASTE OF BROOKLYN

Named after the Dutch city Breukelen, Brooklyn, in the very north of Long Island, was once a city in its own right, until it became part of New York City in 1898. Some still refer to the event as its annexation and the borough certainly has its own unique style and language, Brooklynese, which is most obvious in the pronunciation of words such as absoid (absurd), doity (dirty), noive (nerve) and toin (turn). One of the most populous of the city's five boroughs with about 2.5 million residents and accessed by ferries and bridges, Brooklyn houses a melting pot of nationalities that make up its colourful and well-defined neighbourhoods.

Famous Brooklynites include Woody Allen, Barbra Streisand and Mel Brooks, and the John Travolta movie *Saturday Night Fever* was set in Bay Ridge, an Italian neighbourhood in the south. Its architecture has been noticed by celebrities and arty types and a whole host have moved in to enjoy its cool art scene (and lower rents than Manhattan).

The two most important 'sightseeing' areas are Brooklyn Heights and Prospect Park, home to the Brooklyn Botanical Gardens and the cutting edge Brooklyn Museum, but there's also fun to be had and a stunning beach at Coney Island, America's original amusement park now enjoying a renaissance.

BROOKLYN HEIGHTS

Whether you've had lunch or dinner, a walk across the stunning Brooklyn Bridge will certainly help the digestion. It's the most famous bridge in New York and was the world's largest suspension bridge when it was completed in 1883. The views are fantastic and strolling along the wooden walkway gives an insight into why it took 16 years

Brooklyn Children's Museum

KIDS' STUFF IN THE BOROUGHS

These neighbourhoods are a wonderful place to spend time with children. The massive Prospect Park, for example, has its own children's museum, a zoo, a boating lake and wildlife activities, and America's largest amusement park at Coney Island lies to the south. Try these for size:

Bronx Zoo: p276.

Brooklyn Children's Museum: right.

New York Aquarium, Coney Island: p275.

Prospect Park: p273.

Queens County Farm Museum: p280.

WonderWheel, Coney Island: p275.

to build. If you've walked to Brooklyn from Manhattan via the bridge, you'll find yourself in the heart of Brooklyn Heights.

By the water's edge is the River Café (p159), a refined and elegant setting to soak up fantastic views of the Manhattan skyline. Night-time is best, when the twinkling lights in the skyscrapers look just like a picture postcard. Have a drink at the bar to enjoy the best views before tucking into a sumptuous supper. It is expensive and you will have to book well in advance, but it's an experience you are never likely to forget. Jackets are essential after 5pm.

BRITTIP

Born and bred in Brooklyn, Tony Muia works for A Slice of Brooklyn Bus Tours. 'My favourite summer spot in NYC, which most out-of-towners don't know but which is a true NYC summer hidden gem, is L&B Spumoni Gardens (www.spumonigardens.com) a pizza restaurant in the Bensonhurst section of Brooklyn. The place has been around since 1939, is a true Brooklyn landmark, and is where cast members of *The Sopranos* regularly used to swing by when they were in the neighbourhood. It's still run by the Barbati family and I like to grab some slices and sit outside.'

The Heights themselves are home to some of the most beautiful and sought-after brownstone townhouses in New York. These were built in the early 18th century when bankers and financiers chose to escape Manhattan, yet could still be close enough to keep an eye on their money. Once again, Brooklyn Heights is much in demand as an

area of tranquillity close to the mayhem of the city. If you walk along the Esplanade, you will see the docks that were the setting for Marlon Brando's movie *On The Waterfront.*

BRITTIP

Williamsburg is fast becoming the hippest place to hang out in Brooklyn, and New York for that matter. It's an ethnic melting pot with a thriving arts community.

BROOKLYN BOTANIC GARDEN

- ✉ 1000 Washington Avenue between Eastern Parkway and Empire Boulevard
- ☎ 718-623 7200
- ⌖ www.bbg.org
- 🚗 Subway 2, 3 to Eastern Parkway; Q to Prospect Park
- 🕐 Tues–Fri 8am–6pm, Sat, Sun 10am–6pm, closed Mon; Nov–mid-Mar closes 4.30pm daily
- $ $10 adults, $5 students and seniors, under 12s free

Right next door to Prospect Park and the Brooklyn Museum, the Botanic Garden has 10,000 different kinds of plants from around the world. It includes the world-famous Rose Garden, Japanese Garden, a Shakespeare Garden and the Celebrity Path, which commemorates some of Brooklyn's more famous children. It is most famous, though, for its Japanese cherry trees and huge collection of beautiful bonsai. Relax and enjoy the vibe in its Terrace Café.

BRITTIP

Head to Brooklyn Botanical Gardens if you're in town at the end of April for Sakura Matsuri, the spring 2-day Cherry Blossom festival, and sample Japanese art and food.

BROOKLYN CHILDREN'S MUSEUM

- ✉ 145 Brooklyn Avenue at St Mark's Avenue, Crown Heights
- ☎ 718-735 4400
- ⌖ www.brooklynkids.org
- 🚗 Subway 3, C to Kingston Avenue
- 🕐 Spring, Sat–Fri 10am–5pm, Mon closed; rest of year Wed–Fri 1–6pm, Sat, Sun 11am–6pm, closed Mon, Tues
- $ $9, under 1s free

New York's first green museum is a fabulous place for children, this was the first-ever museum for little ones. They can have a ball here in a sensory room, going into greenhouses, playing with synthesisers, operating water wheels to dam a stream, dancing on the keys of a walk-on piano and playing instruments from around the world. There's a Kids' Café, check the website for up-to-date details and information about workshops, performances and events.

BROOKLYN HISTORICAL SOCIETY

- ✉ 128 Pierrepont Street at Clinton Street
- ☎ 718-222 4111
- ⌂ www.brooklynhistory.org
- 🚗 Subway 2, 3, 4, 5 to Borough Hall, A, C, F to Jay Street/Borough Hall, M, R to Court Street
- ◷ Wed-Fri, Sun 12-5pm, Sat 12-5pm, closed Mon, Tues
- $ $6 adults, $4 students and seniors, under 12s free

It's said that 1 in 7 Americans can trace their roots to Brooklyn and, as many US families originally came from the UK, you could find family links here. Plus there are innovative exhibitions, educational programmes and a wonderful library.

BROOKLYN MUSEUM

- ✉ 200 Eastern Parkway at Washington Avenue
- ☎ 718-638 5000, TTY 718-399 8440
- ⌂ www.brooklynmuseum.org
- 🚗 Subway 2, 3 to Eastern Parkway/Brooklyn Museum
- ◷ Wed, Fri-Sun 11am-6pm, Thurs 11am-10pm, first Sat of month 11am-11pm, all other Sat 11am-6pm, closed Mon, Tues
- $ Suggested donation $12 adults; $8 concessions and children; under 12s free

◀️🇬🇧▶️ BRITTIP
To enjoy some of the delicious Middle Eastern cuisine that centres around Brooklyn's Atlantic Avenue, join a tour with Savory Sojourns (p90), whose expert guide Addie Tomei will reveal this treasure trove of sights and smells with stops at delicatessens and markets, where you can try treats such as fresh pitta.

It has a magnificent glass entrance pavilion, complementing the beautiful 19th-century Beaux Arts building that has housed this huge and important art museum since 1897. A new central lobby and public plaza have also been constructed, making the building the most visitor-friendly museum in NYC. With one of the best collections of Egyptian art in the world, housed on the third floor, it also has an extraordinary collection of Auguste Rodin sculptures among the million objects in its permanent collection. Well known for its African art, it was the first-ever museum to display what were once considered to be anthropological objects as fine art. The museum has a long tradition of collecting non-Western art and, since 1934, it has concentrated on fine art. The collections comprise: Egyptian, Classical and Ancient Middle Eastern Art; Painting and Sculpture; Arts of Africa, the Pacific and the Americas; Asian Art; Decorative Arts; and Prints, Drawings and Photography.

◀️🇬🇧▶️ BRITTIP
The Brooklyn Art and Garden ticket gives an 8% saving on separate tickets to the Brooklyn Museum and the Botanic Garden.

The Brooklyn Museum is known for its ground-breaking art exhibitions and has a cinema theatre that screens movies and documentaries coinciding with the exhibitions. In March 2007, it hosted 1 of the biggest arts events of the year in New York, the opening of the Elizabeth A Sackler Centre for Feminist Art on the 4th floor. The Brooklyn Museum also organises gallery talks, films, concerts, tours and performances for children and adults. Check the website for what's on while you're there.

The museum has its own subway stop at Eastern Parkway, 1 stop from Brooklyn's Grand Army Plaza. This stands in a complex of 19th-century parks and gardens that includes Prospect Park, the Brooklyn Botanic Garden and the Wildlife Centre. It takes about 30 minutes to get to the museum from Midtown.

◀️🇬🇧▶️ BRITTIP
The Grand Army Plaza is home to the 2nd largest open-air green market in New York. Held every Sat 8am-4pm, it sells more than 600 varieties of farm-fresh fruits, vegetables, baked goods, dairy products and more.

GRAND ARMY PLAZA AND PROSPECT PARK

- ✉ At the intersection of Flatbush Avenue, Eastern Parkway and Prospect Park West
- ☎ 718-965 8951
- ⌂ www.prospectpark.org
- 🚗 Subway 2, 3 to Grand Army Plaza; B, F, Q, S to Prospect Park
- ◷ Open daily 5am-1am
- $ Free

This urban oasis with 237ha/585 acres of meadows, waterfalls, fields and forest is

Brooklyn Bridge

one of Brooklyn's most beautiful areas. The enormous Prospect Park and Grand Army Plaza were laid out by Olmsted and Vaux after they'd completed Central Park, and many feel that these creations were even better. It contains the following:

The Arch: New York's answer to the Arc de Triomphe, the elaborately carved, 24m/80ft arch provides a grand gateway to Prospect Park, plus a majestic overview of both the park and Manhattan. It was built as a memorial to the defenders of the Union in the Civil War, and is now the base for a series of bronze sculptures grouped around the Plaza, including one of John F Kennedy.

Audubon Center

Long Meadow: At nearly 1.6km/1ml in length, the Long Meadow stretches from the Park's northern end at Grand Army Plaza to its western end at Prospect Park Southwest. Once the home of grazing sheep and lawn tennis and croquet players, it is now frequented by strollers, kite-flyers and the Little League Baseball. At the Picnic House you'll find WCs and picnic tables, while the Metropolitan Opera and the New York Philharmonic Orchestra put on summer events here (p257), 718-965 8951.

The Long Meadow is accessible via the Grand Army Plaza and any entrance along Prospect Park West, such as 3rd or 9th Street. It is free to enter and is only closed 1–5am.

🇬🇧 **BRITTIP**

Walking tours to Brooklyn's 'Gold Coast', the celebrity-packed Park Slope and its masterpiece of design, Prospect Park, are offered by Big Onion (212-439 1090, www.bigonion.com).

The Bandshell: Close to Long Meadow, this is one of the park's main attractions for live outdoor entertainment. With its 3-storey-high acoustic shell, raised stage and large circular plaza, the Bandshell features food and drinks, WCs and first-come, first-served seating in the 2,000-seat plaza or 5,000-seat lawn. In addition to musical performances, it hosts film events on its 6.5x15m/21x50ft movie screen. But it is best known for the Celebrate Brooklyn! Performing Arts Festival – a series of music, dance, film and spoken word performances each June–Aug at 7.30pm for a $3 donation, which attract nearly 250,000 people per season. For further information, 718-855 7882, www.bricartsmedia.org. The nearest subway is the F train to 15th Street/Prospect Park Station or the 2, 3 to Grand Army Plaza.

The Ravine: One of Prospect Park's most natural features, here you will find a steep narrow gorge lined with the trees and foliage of Brooklyn's only forest. Still recovering from decades of overuse that caused soil erosion, the Ravine and surrounding woodlands have been gradually restored by the Prospect Park Alliance since 1996. You can explore on your own or take one of the weekend guided nature tours.

The Ravine is open daily 5am–1am, with tours by arrangement from the Audubon Center at The Boathouse. For information on tours, 718-287 3400. Best subways are the F to 15th Street/Prospect Park or 7th Avenue or the Q to 7th Avenue.

Lefferts Historic House

PROSPECT PARK FOR FAMILIES

With nature trails, wildlife and activities from boating, skating and baseball to arts and crafts, there is plenty of entertainment for the family in this mini Central Park.

Audubon Center at The Boathouse

- ✉ Lincoln Road/Ocean Avenue entrance to Prospect Park
- ☎ 718-287 3400 Audubon Center; 718-965 8999 events hotline
- 🖰 www.prospectpark.org
- 🚗 Subway Q, S, B to Prospect Park
- 🕐 April–Nov Thurs–Sun and school holidays noon–5pm; Dec–Mar weekends and school holidays noon–4pm
- $ Free admission. Electric boat tour $8 for those aged 13 and over, $4 for 3–12s, children 2 and under free. Pedal boat rental available from the Wollman Rink for $15 per hour.

The design of this beautiful 1905 Beaux Art boathouse, with its elegant arches, decorative tiles and classical balcony, was based on a 16th-century Venetian library. Now an official Historic New York City Landmark, it is home to the state-of-the-art Audubon Center, which is dedicated to preserving wildlife and natural education. Families can take tours along the new Lullwater Nature Trail or on the Lullwater by the electric boat Independence (April–Oct), as well as one of four nature trails or participate in family activities such as craftwork, music and technology sessions. Regular weekly events include afternoon crafts and birdwatching most Sat and Sun (times vary, so check website) and don't miss the annual Macy's Fishing Contest mid-July.

The Carousel

- ✉ Children's Corner, Prospect Park, at intersection of Flatbush and Ocean Avenues and Empire Blvd
- ☎ 718-789 2822
- 🖰 www.prospectpark.org
- 🚗 Subway Q, S, B to Prospect Park
- 🕐 Noon–5pm April–May and Sept–Oct weekends Jun–Aug Thurs–Sun, plus all public holidays
- $ $2 per ride; 5 tickets for $9

Right next door to the zoo and museum is the magnificently carved carousel, which is now 100 years old features 51 horses, a lion, giraffe, a deer and 2 dragon-pulled chariots. It is also one of the few carousels in the world that is wheelchair accessible.

Lefferts Historic House

- ✉ Children's Corner, Prospect Park, at intersection of Flatbush and Ocean Avenues and Empire Blvd
- ☎ 718-789 2822
- 🖰 www.prospectpark.org
- 🚗 Subway Q, S, B to Prospect Park
- 🕐 April–Dec Thurs–Sun 12am–5pm; Dec–March 12am–4pm
- $ Free

Right by the main Grand Army Plaza entrance to Prospect Park stands this restored 18th-century farmhouse, built by Dutch settlers in Brooklyn. Children can play with traditional toys, cooking tools, and take part in craft activities such as candle-making, sewing, butter-churning and making fire with a flint and steel. At weekends throughout the summer, stories are told under a tree, there are hoop games to play and gardening to do including planting potatoes and flax, which are harvested by the kids in the autumn.

Prospect Park Zoo
- ✉ Prospect Park, 450 Flatbush Avenue
- ☎ 718-399 7339
- 🖰 www.prospectparkzoo.com
- 🚍 Subway Q, S or B to Prospect Park
- ◷ Mar–Oct Mon–Fri 10am–5pm; weekends and holidays 10am–5.30pm; Nov–Mar daily 10am–4.30pm
- $ $8 adults, $6 seniors, $5 children 3–12; under 3s free

Again close to the Grand Army Plaza entrance to Prospect Park, this is Brooklyn's only zoo. It features nearly 400 animals and more than 80 species in an environment that gives children close-up views of some of the world's most unusual creatures. They include prairie dogs, wallabies, tamarin monkeys, baboons, a red panda and a vibrant band of birds, reptiles and amphibians. The interactive Discovery Center is open every weekend 11am–3pm. Other fun family activities include Storytelling Tues and Games Thurs in summer 11am–1pm and 2.30pm–4pm, milking cows mid-May to mid-Oct or catching the daily sea lion feeding at 11.30am, 2pm and 4pm.

The Wollman Rink
Like its namesake in Central Park, it usually offers ice-skating in winter, but was closed at the time of going to print due to construction. Check the website www.prospectpark.org/visit/places/wollman_rink_closed for details of the lakeside project, including two fabulous new ice rinks.

NEW YORK TRANSIT MUSEUM
- ✉ Schermerhorn Street at Boerum Place
- ☎ 718-694 1600
- 🖰 www.mta.info/mta/museum/
- 🚍 Subway M, R to Court Street; A, C, G to Hoyt-Schermerhorn Street
- ◷ Tues–Fri 10am–4pm, Sat, Sun 11am–5pm, closed Mon
- $ $7 adults, $5 seniors and children 3–17; Wed seniors free

A great museum for transport buffs in an old subway station in Brooklyn Heights. Steel, Stone and Backbone traces the tale of the city's subway and includes old subway cars

that you can get on, and you can even hang on to one of the original leather straps that created the nickname of 'straphangers' for people who use the subway. The museum also has an art gallery, a classroom for a children's workshop, a computer lab and a reference library. The main interactive exhibit depicts the history of buses and trolleys in the city, with a display of more than 200 trolleys and buses. There is also a film about the building of the subway, old turnstiles, maps and a gift shop.

JEWISH CHILDREN'S MUSEUM
- ✉ 792 Eastern Parkway at corner of Kingston Avenue, Crown Heights
- ☎ 718-907 8833
- 🖰 www.jcmonline.org
- 🚍 Subway 3 to Kingston Avenue
- ◷ Mon–Thurs 10am–4pm, Sun 10am–5.30pm; closed Fri, Sat (apart from select eves)
- $ $13 per person; $10 seniors; children under 2 free

The first of its kind in the world, opened in 2005 at a cost of $35m by Jewish Children International, its interactive multimedia exhibits entertain and educate children of all backgrounds about Jewish heritage.

> ◀🇬🇧 **BRITTIP**
> Visit www.coneyisland.com for the schedule of quirky shows by the seashore, such as the Coney Island Circus Sideshow and the Mermaid Parade.

CONEY ISLAND
At the Southern end of Brooklyn, America's largest amusement park is undoubtedly tacky, and has definitely seen better days, but that doesn't stop children having fun, making it a great family day out.

It has around 35 rides and other attractions along a 6.4km/4mls stretch and the Native American Indians called it 'land without shadows' as its stunning beach was bathed in sunlight all day.

> ◀🇬🇧 **BRITTIP**
> Try one of Nathan's hot dogs (516-338 8500, www.nathansfamous.com) a Coney Island institution and still sold from its original site. Nathan holds an eating contest here every 4 July; the record is 68 hot dogs with buns in 10 minutes!

Gentrification is spilling over from Brooklyn making this an up-and-coming neighbourhood, with a $1.5bn renovation and expansion plan that started in 2007 and continues, adding a water park, a manmade canal for boat rides, 21 rides and shopping, hotels and cinemas. In the meantime, MCU Park (718-499 8497, http://brooklyncyclones. com) has been bringing in the crowds to see the popular baseball league team The Brooklyn Cyclones.

NEW YORK AQUARIUM
- ✉ 610 Surf Avenue at West 8th Street, Brooklyn
- ☎ 718-265-FISH
- ⌁ www.nyaquarium.com
- 🚇 Subway F, Q to West 8th Street, NY Aquarium
- ◷ Winter (to April) 10am–4.30pm; spring (31 Mar–25 May); summer (26 May–3 Sept) 10am–6pm (until 7pm weekends); autumn (4 Sept–4 Nov) Mon–Fri, 10am–5pm, until 5.30pm weekends.
- $ $9.95 (reduced rate while building work is done), under 3 free.

Still recovering from the effects of Hurricane Sandy, the museum is rebuilding but also expanding the exhibition and creating new experiences. In 2014 plans include a new shark tank and by 2016 a new immersive experience. Despite the hurricane disruption, you can still see sea lions perform in the aquatheater and rays and eels glide over coral reefs in the conservation hall.

BRITTIP
Stroll along Coney Island boardwalk to Brighton Beach and Little Odessa, a thriving Russian community with traditional bathhouses, bookshops and restaurants serving borscht, vodka and caviar.

WONDERWHEEL
- ✉ Boardwalk at Denos Vourderis Place (3059 West 12th St), Coney Island
- ☎ 718-372 2592
- ⌁ www.wonderwheel.com
- 🚇 Subway Q to West 8th Street, B, F, Q, N to Stillwell Avenue
- ◷ April, May, Sept, Oct open weekends and holidays only. Open Mon–Sun from noon–late during summer
- $ $7 adults or pack of 54 $25

A New York landmark, the wheel was built in 1920 by the Eccentric Ferris Wheel Company using 100% Bethlehem Steel forged right on the premises. WonderWheel is now part of Coney Island's heritage and there are 5 other big rides to experience as part of the Coney Island Renaissance project.

A TASTE OF THE BRONX

Diversity drives the energy of this vibrant destination in the northernmost tip of the city. Nearly 50% of Bronx residents are Latino, including its most famous former resident Jennifer Lopez, with the highest concentration hailing from 'the islands' – Puerto Rico and the Dominican Republic – and Mexico. However, traditions from Italy and Ireland continue to flourish, and there is a growing number of Asian immigrants.

The Bronx history dates back to 1609 when Henry Hudson took refuge from a storm here. It is the northernmost borough of New York and the only 1 on the mainland. In 1639 Jonas Bronck, a Swedish captain from the Netherlands, settled here with his wife and servants. The story goes that when people left Manhattan to visit them, they'd say they were going to the Broncks' and the name stuck.

BRITTIP
If you want to eat in the Bronx, visit the Neighbourhood section of the Bronx Museum of the Arts website www.bronxmuseum.org for some suggestions.

The Bronx has a mixed reputation, but parts of it are very safe and have attractions that make a visit here well worthwhile. In the north lies the beautiful Botanical Garden that includes a huge chunk of the original forests that once covered New York, and the Bronx Zoo, a leading wildlife conservation park. The part you don't want to visit is the south Bronx, but even here things are improving.

BRONX MUSEUM OF THE ARTS
- ✉ 1040 Grand Concourse at 165th Street
- ☎ 718-681 6000
- ⌁ www.bronxmuseum.org
- 🚇 Subway B, D to 167th Street/Grand Concourse, 4 to 161st Street/Yankee Stadium
- ◷ Mon–Wed closed; Thurs–Sun 11am–6pm
- $ Free

Housed in an attractive glass building, the museum's collection consists of more than 700 contemporary works of art in all media by African, Asian and Latin American artists. The building has been awarded the Art's Commission's Excellence in Design prize, and the gallery, events space and outdoor terrace to sit and absorb the edgy vibe of this vibrant area are certainly impressive.

Bronx Zoo

BRONX ZOO AND WILDLIFE CONSERVATION SOCIETY

✉ Bronx River Parkway at Fordham Road
☎ 718-220 5100
🖰 www.bronxzoo.org
🚇 Subway 2, 5 to East Tremont Avenue/ West Farms Square
🕐 April–Nov Mon–Fri 10am–5pm, Sat, Sun 10am–5.30pm daily; rest of the year 10am–4.30pm
$ $16.95 adults, $14.95 seniors, $12.95 children, under 3s free; suggested donation on Wed; under 17s must be accompanied by an adult; cheaper Nov–Mar; individual attractions/rides $3–5 each, Total Experience ticket that includes admission and all rides $29.95 adult, $24.95 seniors, $19.95 children

The Bronx Zoo is known as New York's 'wild backyard' and respected worldwide for its tradition of conservation and ecological awareness alongside the naturalistic habitats it provides, such as the African Plains where antelope roam. It is the largest urban zoo in America and houses 4,000 animals and 600 species. The Congo Gorilla Forest is a 2.5ha/6-acre rainforest, inhabited by 2 troops of gorillas. Other highlights include the rare snow leopard in the Himalayan Highlands and meeting grizzly bears. Don't miss Tiger Mountain, which takes you within a whisker of the largest cat.

Disney-style rides include a guided monorail tour through Wild Asia, an aerial safari, camel rides and a zoo shuttle; plus there's also a children's zoo. Some exhibits

and all the rides, apart from the bug carousel, are open only April/May–Oct.

LITTLE ITALY

Actually Belmont or simply Arthur Avenue, this area is tagged the Little Italy of the Bronx. Take the D train to Tremont Avenue and walk east to Arthur Avenue. Have a relaxing lunch at one of the many Italian restaurants. The old-world Belmont District is a charming area filled with shops selling every Italian delicacy. To catch a movie stop by the Enrico Fermi Cultural Centre in the Belmont Library (610 East 186th Street at Hughes Avenue, 718-933 6410, www.nypl.org/locations/belmont).

✠ BRITTIP

If you want to discover more of Little Italy and the Irish neighbourhood of Woodlawn, contact Susan Birnbaum, who runs SusanSez NYC Walkabouts (917-509 3111, www.susansez.com). She leads tours around Arthur Avenue and beyond on her Bronx Walkabout.

Now go north on Arthur, east on Fordham Road past Fordham University to the Bronx Park.

✠ BRITTIP

For a taste of real Italy, pop into Mike's Deli in the Arthur Avenue Retail Market (718-562 0129, www. arthuravenue.com).

NEW YORK BOTANICAL GARDEN

- ✉ Bronx River Parkway and Fordham Road
- ☎ 718-817 8700
- 🖰 www.nybg.org
- 🚌 B, D or 4 to Bedford Park and then BX26 bus or Metro-North from Grand Central.
- 🕐 Year-round 10am–6pm, closed Mon
- $ Grounds only ticket $10 adults, $5 seniors/students, $2 children 2–12, under 2s free. Free to all Wed and Sat 10–11am.

⚓ BRITTIP

The Botanical Garden is just a road away from the Bronx Zoo – sadly, that is an 8-lane highway and the entrances are 1.6km/1ml apart. In the absence of a pedestrian link, take a short taxi ride. Call Miles Car Service on 718-884 8888.

A New York masterpiece according to the *New York Times*. The garden originally supported by magnates Cornelius Vanderbilt, Andrew Carnegie and J. P. Morgan, society folk still support these gardens. Check out the Peggy Rockefeller Rose Garden, with over 2,700 bushes. This is one of the oldest and largest botanic gardens in the world, and the magnificent Victorian iron and glass conservatory near the main entrance is modelled on the one at Kew Gardens in London. It has been refurbished to perfection and is home to the gardens' highlight, A World of Plants, a trip through the world's ecosystems. In the grounds, you can see the stunning Bronx River Gorge where the meandering waterway tumbles over a rocky outcrop formed by the retreat of the Wisconsin Ice Sheet. For thousands of years, New York was covered by a hemlock forest and a 16ha/40-acre fragment remains. Look out for the old rock carving of a turtle drawn by the Weckquasgeek Indians. The 50 gardens and 100ha/250 acres include The Everett Children's Adventure Garden, a great outdoor science experience for kids, and the Family Garden, created by children. There are also puppet shows, dance and music concerts, and other events throughout the year.

VAN CORTLANDT HOUSE MUSEUM

- ✉ Van Cortlandt Park, Broadway at West 246th Street
- ☎ 718-543 3344
- 🖰 www.nscdny.org
- 🚌 Subway 1 to 242nd Street/Van Cortlandt Park
- 🕐 Tues–Fri 10am–3pm, Sat, Sun 11am–4pm, closed Mon
- $ $4

Once an 18th-century family-run plantation and the oldest house in the Bronx, Van Cortlandt House was turned into a museum at the end of the 19th century by the National Society of Colonial Dames. Now you can walk through the family's public and private rooms, including a slave bedchamber, and see the fascinating decorative art collections from the colonial and federal periods.

WAVE HILL

- ✉ West 249th Street at Independence Ave
- ☎ 718-549 3200
- 🖰 www.wavehill.org
- 🚌 Subway A to 207th Street or and then the Bx7/Bx10 bus on Broadway northbound to West 252nd Street or take 1 train to West 242nd Street where a free shuttle runs at 10mins past the hour from 9.10am–3.10pm
- 🕐 15 March–31 October 9am–5.30pm; 1 Nov–14 March 9am–4.30pm, closed Mon. Greenhouses open 10–noon and 1–4pm daily
- $ $8 adults, $4 seniors/students, $2 children over 6; free Tues and Sat 9am–noon year-round

A scenic public garden and cultural centre, Wave Hill holds international events throughout the year. The pergolas on the Grand Lawn are particularly worth the visit, where you can sit beneath them surrounded by a rainbow of beautiful plants and gaze across the Hudson. Carry on with a stroll through the elliptical Garden and Wild Garden for more spectacular vistas. Check the website for details, but there are lots of events and activities during the week, from Tai Chi Chuan on Sat to family gallery tours and free garden walk.

Bronx Zoo

YANKEE STADIUM

- ✉ River Avenue at 161st Street
- ☎ 718-293 4300
- 🖱 www.yankees.com
- 🚇 Subway 4 (east side), (weekdays only), B and D (west side) to 161st Street/Yankee Stadium

After the original Yankees Stadium was demolished in 2009, a new Yankee Stadium, which cost a cool $1.3bn, became the legendary New York Yankees new home in Queens. As for the old Yankee home, it's to become a green space for the South Bronx featuring soccer and football fields, tennis and basketball courts and even a waterfront esplanade with play and picnic areas.

BRITTIP

Sports fans can enjoy a hot dog and a drink at the Sidewalk Café on the Plaza next to Gates 4 and 6 at the Yankee Stadium.

Yankee tickets are notoriously hard to come by, but if you really want to see a game while you're in the Big Apple, try online at www.yankees.com/ticketspecials, email tickets@yankees.com or go to the ticket office at the stadium and ask about the availability of single-game tickets, which they do issue every season.

A TASTE OF QUEENS

The largest of all the New York boroughs at $290km^2/112ml^2$, Queens has the highest percentage of first-generation immigrants. Given the borough's suburban look, it is hard to imagine it as the densely forested area it was 4 centuries ago. Then it was inhabited by the Algonquin Indian tribes, who fished in its freshwater streams and creeks, hunted game and gathered shellfish from its bays. It is also difficult to picture 17th-century Queens and the borough's early Dutch and English farmers, along with Quakers fighting for religious freedom.

Yet there remain places where such scenes can easily be reconstructed, such as at the Jamaica Bay Wildlife Refuge (www.nyharborparks.org/visit/jaba.html) on open marshland, once the territory of Jameco Indians and now home to many species of birds spotted along the nature walkways, and the Queens County Farm Museum (p280). This has the largest tract of farmland left in New York and its colonial farmhouse is thought to date back to 1772.

Today, Queens is as much about the ethnic diversity of the borough and in each of the places mentioned in this section you will find many examples of the cultures of people from Asia, the West Indies, Latin America and Greece. In fact, Queens is home to the largest Greek population outside of Greece; Astoria is the Athens of the United States, with authentic restaurants and markets on the main thoroughfare of Ditmars Boulevard. Jackson Heights is a little India, with colourful sari shops, restaurants and video stores with the latest Bollywood offerings.

In fact, so diverse is this sprawling borough that the local subway line number 7 has been jokingly renamed the International Express. It's also home to JFK and LaGuardia airports, so Queens is often the first entry point for millions of people to New York and the US.

BRITTIP

For shopping, attractions, events, tours and restaurants in Queens, click on to www.itsinqueens.com or call 718-592 2082.

AMERICAN MUSEUM OF THE MOVING IMAGE

- ✉ 35th Avenue at 36th Street, Astoria
- ☎ 718-7777 6888
- 🖱 www.movingimage.us
- 🚇 Subway G, R, V to Steinway Street
- ⏰ Weds–Thurs 10.30am–5pm, Fri 10.30am–8pm (free admission 4–8pm), Sat–Sun 11.30am–7pm
- $ $12 adults, $9 seniors, $6 children (3–18), under 3 free

The only museum dedicated to the art, history, technique and technology of moving image in the US with more than 130,000 artefacts. It covers a wide subject matter, from 19th-century optical toys to the latest in digital art. You can enjoy watching films from around the world here, from Chinese cinema to the latest underground flicks. You can also view the vast collection, which includes licensed merchandise, technical apparatus, costumes, photography and computer games. A great experience for children and adults alike.

BRITTIP

After you've been to the American Museum of the Moving Image, head to 31st Street and Broadway for a spot of Greek-style lunch.

LITTLE ASIA

- ✉ Roosevelt Avenue and Main Street

The nearby jumble of Chinese, Korean, Thai and Vietnamese markets and restaurants offers everything from soft-shell turtles to bentwood bows. At 45–57 Bowne Street is the beautiful Hindu Temple Society of North America (718-460 8484, www.nyganeshtemple.org), which is adorned with carvings of Hindu gods and is open Mon–Fri 8am–9pm, 7.30am–9pm weekends..

Dinner: Choopan Kabab House, 43–27 Main Street, 718-539 3180. A great place to try out Afghan fare. Alternatively, you could sample Korean food at the 24-hour Kum Gang San, 128–38 Northern Boulevard between Bowne and Union Streets, 718-461 0909, www.kumgangsan.net.

Night spot: There are operettas, flamenco and tango shows at the Thalia Spanish Theatre (41–17 Greenpoint Avenue, Sunnyside, 718-729 3880, www.thaliatheatre.org, subway 7 to 40th Street).

> ◀🇬🇧▶ **BRITTIP**
> For more information on the arts in Queens, contact the Queens Council on the Arts on 718-647 5036 or visit www.queenscouncilarts.org.

LITTLE INDIA
Take the International Express – subway 7 from Times Square to the 74th Street/Broadway station and, at 74th Street between Roosevelt and 37th Avenues at Jackson Heights – to find this Indian haven. Stroll through the cumin-scented streets looking at the intricately embellished gold and silk on display. Two stops you should include are the Menka Beauty Salon (37–56, 74th Street, Jackson Heights, 718-424 6851) where traditional henna designs are drawn on the skin, and the Butala Emporium (37–46 74th Street, Jackson Heights, 718-899 5590), which sells everything from Southern Asian art and children's books in Punjabi to Ayurvedic medicine and religious items.
Lunch: Travel 1 stop to 82nd Street in Elmhurst for a delicious Argentinian lunch – go for the signature mixed grill parrillada – at La Fusta (80–32 Baxter Avenue, 718-429 8222, www.lafustanewyork.com).

NEW YORK HALL OF SCIENCE
- ✉ 47–01 111th Street at 47th Avenue, Flushing Meadows/Corona Park at 48th Avenue
- ☎ 718-699 0005
- 🖱 www.nysci.org
- 🚇 Subway 7 to 111th Street
- 🕐 Mon–Fri 9.30am–5pm, Sat–Sun 10am–6pm (April–Aug). Tues–Fri 9.30am–5pm, Sat–Sun 10am–6pm (Sept–March)

- $ $11 adults, $8 seniors and children 2–17, free Sept–June Fri 2–5pm and Sun 10–11am

The bubble-shaped building features memorable daily science demonstrations and 450 interactive exhibits explaining the mysteries of digital technology, quantum theory, microbes and light and also offers slides, whirligigs, space nets and a giant teeter-totter (seesaw). Rated as the best science museum in the country, all events are free with admission.

THE NOGUCHI MUSEUM
- ✉ 9-01 33rd Road at Vernon Boulevard, Long Island City
- ☎ 718-204 7088
- 🖱 www.noguchi.org
- 🚇 Subway N, W to Broadway stop in Queens, F to Queensbridge/21st Street or 7 to 33rd Street/Vernon Boulevard (Wed–Fri), then Q103 bus or take the Sunday Shuttle from Manhattan
- 🕐 Wed–Fri 10am–5pm; Sat, Sun 11am–6pm; closed Mon, Tues
- $ $10 adults, $5 seniors/students, pay what you wish first Fri of the month

If you love your ballet and Balanchine in particular, you'll enjoy seeing some of the sets created by this Japanese artist, who strove to bring art and nature into the urban environment. These were Noguchi's studios and there are now more than 300 of his works on display.

> ◀🇬🇧▶ **BRITTIP**
> Back to the Old Country – The Ethnic Apple Tour offered by Bike The Big Apple (877 865-0078, www.bikethebigapple.com) is a full day tour that leaves every Fri at 10am year round, weather permitting, and costs $95.

P.S.1 CONTEMPORARY ART CENTER
- ✉ 22–25 Jackson Avenue at 46th Avenue, Long Island City
- ☎ 718-784 2084
- 🖱 http://momaps1.org
- 🚇 Subway E, V to 23rd Street/Ely Avenue; G to 21st Street/Van Alst; 7 to 45th Road/Court House Square
- 🕐 Thurs–Mon noon–6pm
- $ Suggested donation $10 adults, $5 seniors/students

All forms of artistic expression are found in the oldest and second largest non-profit-making arts centre, affiliated to MoMA and known for its cutting edge exhibitions. Check

TASTE OF THE OUTER BOROUGHS

out paintings and videos of performance art that depict elements of American culture and life in the 20th and 21st centuries.

✠ BRITTIP

Why not travel to Queens by Water Taxi (www.nywatertaxi. com)? Cruise up the East River and get off at Hunter's Point near the P.S.1 Contemporary Art Center.

QUEENS BOTANICAL GARDEN

- ✉ 43-50 Main Street, Flushing
- ☎ 718-886 3800
- ⌂ www.queensbotanical.org
- 🚇 Subway 7 to Main St/Flushing then Q44 or Q20 bus or walk 8 blocks
- ⊙ Tues–Sun 8am–6pm (1 April–31 Oct). Tues–Sun 8am–4.30pm (1 Nov–31 March)
- $ $4 adults, $3 seniors and $2 students/children over 3. April – October. Nov-March Free.

A beautiful botanical garden spread over 16ha/39 acres, bursting with plants, shrubs and trees created for the 1939 World Fair. There's also an HSBC children's garden, where the wee ones get to learn about plants, gardens and nature while playing in a fun environment.

QUEENS COUNTY FARM MUSEUM

- ✉ 73-50 Little Neck Parkway at Union Turnpike, Floral Park
- ☎ 718-347 3276
- ⌂ www.queensfarm.org
- 🚇 Subway E, F to Kew Gardens/Union Turnpike, then take the Q46 bus to Little Neck Parkway
- ⊙ Mon–Fri 10am–5pm outdoor visiting only; free tours of the farmhouse are available Sat, Sun only 11am–4pm. Check website for paying special events like wine tasting or dinner on the farm days.
- $ Free, $6 farmyard tour and hayride, $6 apple pressing workshops

This 19-ha/47-acre site is the only working historical farm that still exists in New York and includes the 18th-century Adriance farmhouse, barns, outbuildings, a greenhouse and livestock. Animal feed is on sale to feed the sheep and goats, making it popular with little ones, as are the tractor-drawn hayrides offered on weekends April–Oct.

QUEENS MUSEUM OF ART

- ✉ New York City Building, Flushing Meadows/Corona Park
- ☎ 718-592 9700
- ⌂ www.queensmuseum.org
- 🚇 Subway 7 to Willets Point/Shea Stadium

New York Hall of Science

Staten Island Ferry

🕐 Wed–Sun 12–6pm; closed Mon–Tues
$ Suggested donation $5 adults; $2.50 seniors and children; children under 5 free.

Currently closed due to an expansion project but at the time of going to press, due to open in late 2013. Check the website for news. When it's back in business expect even more interesting and diverse exhibits than previous years, which have included Frank Oscar Larson's 1950s street photography and Three Points Make A Triangle, an exhibition featuring 31 local artists.

◀▮▶ BRITTIP

If you get thirsty, pop into one of the many fun, friendly and lively Irish pubs in Queens. Mary McGuire's (38–04 Broadway, Astoria, 719-728 3434) and the newer, Woodhaven House (63–98 Woodhaven Boulevard, 718-894 5400, www.woodhavenhouse.com) in Rego Park are highly recommended.

SOCRATES SCULPTURE PARK

✉ 32-01 Vernon Boulevard at Broadway, Long Island City
☎ 718-956 1819
🖥 www.socratessculpturepark.org
🚇 Subway N or W (Mon–Fri only) to Broadway/Long Island City
🕐 Daily 10am–sunset
$ Free

A great place to take children as they can climb, romp and run around these massive sculptures laid out in the park. Hard to believe it was once an abandoned riverside landfill and illegal dumpsite! It also has films outdoors in summer.

◀▮▶ BRITTIP

The iconic Shea Stadium was demolished in 2008 and the Mets now play at Citi Fields, 126th Street and Roosevelt Avenue, Flushing, http://newyork.mets. mlb.com. Visit their site for full information on the latest fixtures and prices.

A TASTE OF STATEN ISLAND

With its picturesque scenery, Staten Island deserves its Indian name Monacnong, which means 'enchanted woods'. It's long been a haven for Italian-American and Irish-American populations and hasn't had a vast melting pot of cultures like the other outer boroughs. But in recent years that has slowly begun to change, with the population growing and diversifying. Hispanics now account for around 12% of the population, while 6% is Asian.

Even if you don't have much time you should try to fit in a trip on the free Staten Island Ferry, which leaves Manhattan Island from Battery Park (p80) and offers brilliant views of Downtown and the Statue of Liberty.

◀▮▶ BRITTIP

Staten Island has constructed its own uplifting memorial to the 9/11 attacks that looks like outstretched wings or a flower about to blossom. It is on the adjacent North Shore Waterfront Esplanade.

ALICE AUSTEN HOUSE

A unique museum in the restored Victorian house and garden of Alice Austen, one of America's first female documentary photographers (see p102).

BRITTIP

Head to the South Beach Boardwalk for a free summer concert, or to Midland Beach for sandcastle building and the Sea Turtle Fountain where kids can play under the sprinklers.

HISTORIC RICHMOND TOWN

- ✉ 441 Clarke Ave between St Patrick's Place and Richmond Road
- ☎ 718-351 1611 ext 280
- ⌂ www.historicrichmondtown.org
- 🚌 S74 bus from the ferry to Richmond Road and St Patrick's Place
- ☼ July–Sept Wed–Sun 1–5pm
- $ Adults $8, seniors $6, children 5-17 $5. Free admission Fri 1–5pm

A magnificent 40.5-ha/100-acre village that features buildings from 300 years of life on the island including the oldest schoolhouse still standing, which was built in 1695 (that's really old by American standards!). Guided tours 2.30pm daily. In the summer season, costumed interpreters and craftspeople demonstrate the chores, gardening, crafts and trade of daily life in this rural hamlet.

JACQUES MARCHAIS MUSEUM OF TIBETAN ART

- ✉ 338 Lighthouse Avenue
- ☎ 718-987 3500
- ⌂ www.tibetanmuseum.org
- 🚌 From Staten Island Ferry take bus S74 to Lighthouse Avenue
- ☼ Wed–Sun 1pm–5pm
- $ $6 adults, $5 seniors/students; $3 children under 12 galleries and gardens

One of New York's best-kept secrets, which the Dalai Lama visited in 1991. It has terraced gardens and a fishpond. Inside, there are Tibetan, Nepalese and Mongolian arts from the 17th to the 19th century. There are also Tai Chi and meditation classes, see website for details.

SNUG HARBOR CULTURAL CENTER

- ✉ 1000 Richmond Terrace between Tysen Street and Snug Harbour Road
- ☎ 718-448 2500
- ⌂ www.snug-harbor.org

- 🚌 Bus S40 from the Ferry to Snug Harbor
- ☼ Dawn until dusk
- $ Free

On this plot of land once stood some rundown retirement homes for fishermen, which were going to be demolished. However, the local residents wanted it to be used for the community's benefit, and the result is a fascinating park containing 26 buildings modelled on historical architecture. The various buildings are used for events during the year, like the Harmony Fair in June, a celebration of world music, dance, food and culture, which take place at The Music Hall at Snug Harbour, the second oldest in the city (the oldest being Carnegie Hall).

BRITTIP

Download a Staten Island map and info (or order by mail) from www.statenislandusa.com.

The Staten Island Botanical Park (718-448 2500), open Mon–Sun, dawn to dusk daily (free) houses the internationally renowned Chinese Scholar's Garden, which has courtyards, pools, a Tea House and pure-flow bridge. Open Tues–Sun 10am–4pm. Admission is $5 for adults, $4 students/seniors/children and guided tours for $4 per person.

Also in the grounds is Staten Island Children's Museum (718-273 2060, www. statenislandkids.org), with entertaining interactive exhibitions such as crawling through an ant hill to watch butterflies emerging from the chrysalis. Open Tues–Sun 12–5pm when school is in session, 10am–5pm during school holidays, and costs $6 for the over 1s. Great Explorations takes children from the rainforest canopy to dog-sledding and building an igloo and there's a chance to be a fireman or host a radio show among other options. There's daily Storytime and Feeding the Animals sessions, a range of activities for tots and weekly creative workshops including Up4Art on Sat and Clay Day on Wed.

ST MARK'S PLACE, ST GEORGE

On the hill above the St George Ferry terminal, St Mark's Place is the only landmarked historical district on Staten Island. Here New York's fabulous skyline forms the backdrop to a collection of residential buildings in Queen Ann, Greek revival and Italianate styles. Visit www.preserve.org/ stgeorge for a self-guided walking tour.

CHAPTER 13
Essentials

TRAVEL INSURANCE

Travel insurance is essential. Medical cover in the US is very expensive and if you are involved in an accident you could be sued, which could be very costly indeed. If you do want to make savings in this area, don't buy insurance from tour operators as they are notoriously expensive; go direct to the insurers.

Check first whether you get travel insurance as part of your home insurance (try **Privilege**, 0800 068 7639, www.privilege. com), a premium bank account, or your credit card (such as **Sainsbury's Gold**, www. sainsburysbank.co.uk).

If not, the first thing to consider is whether to go for an annual worldwide policy. If you plan to make more than one trip in any given year, it will almost certainly be better value, and it may even compare favourably if you are only doing the one trip, especially for a family. You will need to choose your destination area (so to include the US will be more than just Europe, for example) and check the maximum number of trips allowed and the maximum number of days per trip. If this is not for you, just look for the best deal on straightforward holiday cover for the length of your stay.

Shop around for the best deals – new customers may well find introductory discounts. You can go to the insurers direct, or there are now a host of price comparison websites to choose from, such as **MoneySupermarket**, which also has lots of advice on choosing the right insurance (www.moneysupermarket.com), **Confused** (www.confused.com) and **GoCompare** (www. gocompare.com).

Companies offering annual worldwide insurance policies include the **AA** (0800 975 5819, www.theaa.com), **Aviva** (0844 891 1104, www.aviva.co.uk), **Barclays** (0800 107 7168, www.barclays.co.uk), Churchill (0800 032 6534, www.churchill.com), **Direct Travel** (0845 605 2700, www.direct-travel.co.uk), **Post Office** (0800 294 2292, www.postoffice. co.uk) and **Travel Insurance Direct** (0844 482 0027, www.oinc.com), although there are many more.

CHECK YOUR COVER

Policies vary not only in price but also in the cover they provide. In all cases, you need to ensure that the one you choose gives you the following:
▶ Medical cover of at least £2 million in America.
▶ Personal liability cover of at least £2 million in America.
▶ Cancellation and curtailment cover of around £3,000 in case you are forced to call off your holiday.
▶ Cover for lost baggage and belongings of around £1,500. Most premiums only offer cover for individual items worth up to around £250, so you will need additional cover for any expensive items.
▶ Cover for cash (usually around £200) and documents, including your air tickets, passport and currency.
▶ A 24-hour helpline to make it easy for you to get advice and instructions on what to do in an emergency.

THINGS TO WATCH OUT FOR

Tick the box: You don't have to buy through your tour operator but you may have to tick a box to opt out – rather than opt in – so be alert. You usually need to give them your policy number.

Read the policy: You should receive the policy document before you go. Check it immediately as you may only have 7 days to cancel and request a refund if you are not happy.

Don't double up on cover: If you have an all-risks house insurance policy on your home contents, this will cover your belongings outside the home and may even cover lost money and credit cards. Check if this covers you abroad, and includes your belongings when in transit, before buying insurance for personal possessions.

Dangerous sports cover: In almost all cases, mountaineering, racing and hazardous pursuits such as bungee jumping, skydiving, horse riding, windsurfing, trekking and even cycling are not included in normal policies.

Make sure you qualify for full cover: If you have been treated in hospital during the 6 months prior to travelling or are waiting for hospital treatment, you may need medical evidence that you are fit to travel. If your doctor gives you the all clear (the report may cost £25) and the insurance company still says your condition is not eligible for the insurance you want, shop around to find the right cover.

HEALTH HINTS

Don't allow your dream trip to New York to be spoilt by not taking the right kind of precautions.

MEDICATION

If you are on regular medication, make sure you take sufficient for the duration of your trip. Always carry it in your hand baggage, in case your luggage goes astray, and make sure it is clearly labelled. If you should need more for any reason, remember that many drugs have a different name in the US, so check with your GP before you go.

> **BRITTIP**
> While we're on the subject of drugs, Class A drugs such as cocaine and heroin are illegal in the state of New York and, despite its liberal tendencies, so is marijuana. If you're caught with 25g/2oz or less of marijuana you can end up in prison for 5 days or be slapped with a large fine.

IN THE SUN

Although the biggest season for New York is winter, many Brits still travel to America at the hottest time of the year, the summer, and most are unprepared for the sheer intensity of the sun. Before you even think about going out for the day, apply a high-factor sun block (at least factor 15) as it is very easy to get sunburnt when you are walking around sightseeing or shopping. It is also a good idea to wear a hat or scarf to protect your head from the sun, especially at the hottest times (11am–3pm), to prevent you from getting sunstroke. If it is windy, you may be lulled into thinking that it's not so hot.

> **BRITTIP**
> Always carry plenty of water, even in winter. Air conditioning and heating are dehydrating and you'll find yourself wanting to keel over without lots of liquid. It is best to avoid drinking alcohol during the day.

SECURITY

AT YOUR HOTEL

In America, your hotel room number is your main source of security. It is often your passport to eating and collecting messages, so keep the number secure. When checking in, make sure none of the hotel staff mentions your room number out loud. If they do, give them back the key and ask them to give you a new room and to write down the new room number instead of announcing it (most hotels follow this practice in any case). When you need to give someone your room number – for instance, when charging a dinner or any other bill to your room – write it down or show them your room card rather than calling it out.

When in your hotel room, put on the deadlocks and security chains and use the door peephole before opening the door. If someone knocks and you don't know who it is, or they don't have any identification, phone the reception desk. When you go out, lock the windows and door properly, even if you are just going to the ice machine.

> **BRITTIP**
> American banknotes are similar in size and colour so familiarise yourself with them in the safety of your room and keep large and small denominations separate.

CASH AND VALUABLES

Most hotels have safe deposit boxes, so use these to store important documents such as airline tickets and passports. Keep a separate record of your travellers' cheque numbers. When you go out, do not take all your cash and credit cards with you. Always leave at least one credit card in the safe as an emergency back-up and only take enough cash with you for the day.

Using a money belt is a good idea and, if your room does not come with its own safe, leave your valuables in the main hotel safe.

SAFETY IN CARS

Unless you have a driver, a car in New York is not a good idea. If you do hire a car, however, be sensible. Never leave your car unlocked or leave any valuable items on the car seats or anywhere else where they can be seen. Always put maps and brochures in the glove compartment as these will be obvious signs that your car belongs to a tourist.

NEW YORK STREET SAVVY

It may surprise you to know that New York City remains the safest big city in the USA,

EMERGENCIES

Police, fire or ambulance: Dial 911 (9-911 from a hotel room) free, even from mobiles.

Medical emergency: Call the hotel front desk as many have arrangements with doctors for house calls. If they don't, they may tell you to go to the nearest A&E (they call it ER), but that's not a good idea (haven't you seen *ER?*). Instead contact **New York Hotel Urgent medical services** (212-369 8688, http://travelmd.com), **Dial-a-Doctor** (516 521 7040), or walk in or make an appointment at a **DOCS Medical Center** at 55 East 34th Street (212-252 6000), 1555 3rd Avenue (212-828 2300) or 202 West 23rd Street (212-352 2600).

Pharmacy: Most 24-hour pharmacies are run by the Duane Reade chain. The most central is at 224 West 57th St at Broadway (212-541 9708, www.duanereade.com), near Columbus Circle.

Dentist: Call First District Dental Society (212-679 3966 or 212-371 0500). After hours, try the 24-hour Emergency Dental Associates (212-972 9299, www.nysdental.org).

British information services: This is the information service of the British embassy in Washington and acts as the political, press and public affairs office of the New York Consulate-General, which covers the states of New York, New Jersey, Connecticut and Pennsylvania (845 3rd Avenue, NY, NY 10022, www.ukinusa.fco.gov.uk).

according to the FBI. Although the city is nowhere near as dangerous as it used to be, it is still a large city and there are always people on the lookout for an easy opportunity, so just use normal caution and common sense.

▶ Always be aware of what is going on around you and keep an arm free – criminals target people who are preoccupied or have both arms laden down with packages or bags.

▶ Stick to well-populated, well-lit areas and, if possible, don't go out alone.

▶ Don't engage any suspicious people, such as street beggars, in conversation, though you can tip buskers if you wish.

BRITTIP

It cannot be stressed enough that you should only ever carry as little cash as possible – and never count your money in public.

▶ Visible jewellery can attract the wrong kind of attention. If you are a woman wearing rings, turn them round so that the stone or setting side is palm-in.

▶ If you're wearing a coat, put it on over the strap of your shoulder bag.

▶ Men should keep wallets in front trouser or inside coat pockets or in a shoulder strap.

▶ Watch out for pickpockets and scam artists, especially in busy areas, as you would in any big city.

▶ Pickpockets work in teams, often involving children to create a diversion.

▶ Do not carry your wallet or valuables in a bumbag. Thieves can easily cut the belt and disappear into the crowds before you've worked out what has happened.

A useful trick is to have 2 wallets – a cheap one carried in your hip pocket or bag containing about $20 in cash and some

out-of-date credit cards, and another hidden somewhere on your body or in a money belt containing the bulk of your cash and credit cards. If you are approached by someone who demands money from you, your best bet is to get away as quickly as possible. Do this by throwing your fake wallet or purse in one direction, while you run, shouting for help, in the other. The chances are that the mugger will just pick up the wallet and run off rather than chase after you. If you hand over your wallet and just stand still, the mugger is more likely to demand your watch and jewellery, too. This advice is even more important for women, who could be vulnerable to personal attack or rape if they hang around.

BRITTIP

The new $100 bill shows an enlarged portrait of Benjamin Franklin. It contains a Crane & Co. security feature that allows an underlying image to shift when moved to prevent counterfeiting.

Of course, remember that this is very much common sense and applies if you are travelling almost anywhere in the world, especially in a major city. New York is a busy, feisty city, but it is a great holiday destination and no doubt you'll have a brilliant time and want to come back soon!

BRITTIP

Keep your passport in the hotel safe and carry a photocopy of the original. If you lose it, fill out a report on www.gov.uk/report-a-lost-or-stolen-passport and check out the information on how to get home.

Index

Major page references are indicated in **bold**

INDEX